Computer Forensics and Digital Investigation with EnCase® Forensic v7

Suzanne Widup

Mc Graw Hill Education

New York   Chicago   San Francisco
Athens   London   Madrid   Mexico City
Milan   New Delhi   Singapore   Sydney   Toronto

Cataloging-in-Publication Data is on file with the Library of Congress

McGraw-Hill Education books are available at special quantity discounts to use as premiums and sales promotions, or for use in corporate training programs. To contact a representative, please visit the Contact Us pages at www.mhprofessional.com.

Computer Forensics and Digital Investigation with EnCase® Forensic v7

Copyright © 2014 by McGraw-Hill Education. All rights reserved. Printed in the United States of America. Except as permitted under the Copyright Act of 1976, no part of this publication may be reproduced or distributed in any form or by any means, or stored in a database or retrieval system, without the prior written permission of publisher, with the exception that the program listings may be entered, stored, and executed in a computer system, but they may not be reproduced for publication.

All trademarks or copyrights mentioned herein are the possession of their respective owners and McGraw-Hill Education makes no claim of ownership by the mention of products that contain these marks.

1234567890   DOC DOC   10987654

ISBN   978-0-07-180791-3
MHID   0-07-180791-8

Sponsoring Editor Meghan Riley Manfre	**Proofreader** Emilia Thiuri
Editorial Supervisor Jody McKenzie	**Indexer** Karin Arrigoni
Project Manager Raghavi Khullar, Cenveo® Publisher Services	**Production Supervisor** George Anderson
Acquisitions Coordinator Mary Demery	**Composition** Cenveo Publisher Services
Technical Editor Joseph Shaw	**Illustration** Cenveo Publisher Services
Copy Editor Lunaea Weatherstone	**Art Director, Cover** Jeff Weeks
	Cover Designer Jeff Weeks

Information has been obtained by McGraw-Hill Education from sources believed to be reliable. However, because of the possibility of human or mechanical error by our sources, McGraw-Hill Education, or others, McGraw-Hill Education does not guarantee the accuracy, adequacy, or completeness of any information and is not responsible for any errors or omissions or the results obtained from the use of such information.

For My Family and Friends

Without your patience, understanding, and unwavering support,
I would never have been able to succeed.

and

For John Hoover, White Knight

About the Author

Suzanne Widup (@SuzanneWidup) has a wealth of experience in security engineering and analysis with a specialty in digital forensics in large enterprise environments. Her current work involves data breach research, including tracking publicly disclosed data breaches in the VERIS Community Database (VCDB).

She is the founder of the Digital Forensics Association and the author of *The Leaking Vault,* a series of papers on publicly disclosed data breaches. Suzanne has served as the technical editor on two books: *The Computer Incident Response Planning Handbook* and *The Computer Forensics InfoSec Pro Guide*. She is a co-author of the widely read Verizon Data Breach Investigations Report and a frequent speaker at conferences on this and other topics.

Suzanne holds a B.S. in Computer Information Systems from Saint Leo University, and an M.S. in Information Assurance from Norwich University.

About the Technical Reviewer

Joseph W. Shaw II has been working in information security for more than 19 years, with experience in various industry verticals. He is currently a manager at global professional services organization Alvarez & Marsal, where he provides expertise in digital forensics with an emphasis on incident response, Windows malware analysis, and reverse engineering. His current duties also include teaching Macintosh forensics, mobile device forensics, and incident response classes domestically through A&M and to foreign law enforcement agencies through the US Department of State's Office of Antiterrorism Assistance. Joseph is a SANS Lethal Forensicator and holds the following certifications: CISM, CISSP, EnCE, and GAWN. His writing works also include being a contributing author to *The Computer Forensics InfoSec Pro Guide* and co-author of *Unified Communications Forensics: Anatomy of Common UC Attacks* with Nicholas Grant. You can find him on Twitter at @josephwshaw.

Contents at a Glance

Contents

Acknowledgments

No book gets to publication in a vacuum—it takes a team of people to make it happen. I would like to thank my first editing team of Amy Jollymore, Ryan Willard, and Amanda Russell, and my final editing team of Meghan Manfre and Mary Demery for all of your help and support in getting this book out into the world. Thank you to Neal McCarthy for introducing me to Amy and giving me this opportunity. Thank you to Joseph Shaw, who has been an excellent technical editor—any mistakes in here are entirely my own.

Thank you to my team of readers who provided invaluable feedback that made this book so much better: William Taroli, Kevin Gibbons, Melissa Tosetti, Lawrence Pingree, Jon Eldridge, "SF Bob" Moseley, Paul Keser, and one reader who must remain in stealth mode.

Finally, thank you to Jeff Hedlesky of Guidance Software, for all your patience and assistance.

Introduction

Are you just starting out with EnCase for the first time and wondering how to get going? Are you familiar with prior versions of EnCase and considering making the move to the new version? Then this book is for you!

Why This Book?

When I set out to write this book, it was basically because the book I wanted when I started out with EnCase didn't exist. I wanted a book that would walk me through use cases with the software, and that is the approach I took. I already had a solid grounding in digital forensic theory and was comfortable with looking for artifacts in the Windows operating system. What I didn't have was the experience with EnCase to know how to accomplish the tasks to complete my investigation.

As you move through the chapters in this book, you will see that I walk you step by step through how to accomplish the most common investigative tasks using EnCase Forensic.

Who Should Read This Book

This is not a book on digital forensic theory. This book assumes familiarity with that body of knowledge and is focused on getting the reader to the point where they can use EnCase Forensic to perform digital investigations.

If you are comfortable with the theory, and want a book that will get you up to speed on EnCase, then this book is for you. The language is clear and straightforward, and geared toward getting you proficient with EnCase as quickly as possible. There are numerous step by step sample procedures provided (called Run Books), which you can customize for your own organization's needs. There is advice on the steps that should first be taken to get your organization to the state of forensic readiness if you are new to performing digital investigations. There is advice on customizing the interface and the output to best suit your needs. All of these things, while not forensic theory, can be quite important to the efficiency of any forensic lab environment using EnCase.

RUN BOOK

The Run Book icon calls your attention to the step-by-step sample procedures included in the chapters. You can also find the Run Books in Appendix C, "Sample Run Books."

This book will be useful for people who have some experience with EnCase versions prior to version 7. With version 7 came a significant redesign of the user interface, and practitioners who have been hesitating to make the move to the newer version should find this book quite helpful. I point out the major differences in the look and feel, as well as how to accomplish those tasks you know how to complete in the old version. We look at some of the features of the new interface that aren't well known that can really make a difference in how you interact with the tool.

This book will be useful for people who have no experience at all with EnCase. It begins with the installation of the product and moves on from there. It doesn't assume any familiarity with EnCase, so you get to start from the beginning. We cover a great many important topics in this book, using a commonly downloadable set of evidence from the National Institute of Standards in Technology (NIST) CFReDS Hacking Case. This allows readers to follow along with the same evidence that I am using and compare their results.

What This Book Covers

This book will walk you through the following:

▶   Forensic readiness—preparation that should be undertaken before investigations are performed by an organization

▶   Installing and customizing EnCase for your environment

▶   Basic EnCase concepts

▶   Adding, processing, and ultimately presenting evidence

▶   The most efficient way to locate the artifacts you are looking for and how to handle them in the EnCase interface

▶   Automation options for EnCase, including EnCase Portable and EnScripts

How This Book Is Organized

This book is designed to be read from start to finish, chapter by chapter. This is particularly true beginning with the case study introduced in Part II. As we progress through the case, we add bookmarks for the artifacts we've identified and perform processes that provide results we use in subsequent chapters. However, if you are looking for a quick procedure for a specific task, Appendix C contains all of the sample Run Books from all of the chapters.

Part I: Preparing for the Forensics Function   Part I is designed to get you started both with performing forensic investigations in your organization and with EnCase. Chapter 1, "The Road to Readiness," provides a good overview of the types of things that should be considered prior to an organization electing to perform investigations. Chapter 2, "Getting Started," walks you through the installation of EnCase, and introduces the interface and customization options. Chapter 3, "EnCase Concepts," introduces the EnCase evidence file formats, how to migrate evidence that is in the legacy formats, and how to use the new encryption features of the product.

Part II: Beginning with EnCase Forensics   Part II introduces the NIST CFReDS Hacking Case study, which is used through the rest of the book. Chapter 4, "Adding Evidence," covers the multiple methods for adding different types of evidence into EnCase. Chapter 5, "Processing Evidence," introduces the EnCase Evidence Processor and some of the modules it contains. Chapter 6, "Documenting Evidence," introduces more EnCase interface features, such as bookmarking, the Set Include (home plate), and the blue check, and how they affect EnCase's behavior.

Part III: Looking for Artifacts   Part III builds on the prior section and introduces more of the EnCase interface. Chapter 7, "Further Inspection," continues with additional Evidence Processor modules. Chapter 8, "Analyzing the Case," introduces the powerful Case Analyzer and walks you through how to create custom modules. Chapter 9, "Keywords and Searching," is an in-depth treatment of using keywords in EnCase. You are provided with an introduction to GREP and examples of how to use this powerful search option to minimize the false positive rate in your search terms.

Part IV: Putting It All Together   Part IV introduces the additional tools to make you more efficient when performing investigations. Chapter 10, "Conditions and Filters," shows you how to build your own powerful criteria to narrow down the results you are getting to those that are most relevant to your case. Chapter 11, "Hash Analysis and Timelines," shows you how to work with hash sets and libraries to include or exclude large numbers of files quickly based on their characteristics. Chapter 12, "Reporting," shows you how to make the most of the EnCase reporting interface and customize the reports to suit your needs. Chapter 13, "Wrapping Up the Case," discusses evidence lifecycle management and the considerations that should be taken when performing investigations over a period of time.

Part V: Automation in EnCase   Part V discusses the options for automating repetitive tasks in EnCase. Chapter 14, "EnCase Portable and App Central," is an introduction to the EnCase Portable tool. App Central is Guidance Software's marketplace for developers and other practitioners to offer EnScripts to others. Chapter 15, "An EnScript Primer," is an introduction to the built-in programming language included with EnCase.

Part VI: Appendixes   Part VI contains appendixes for your reference. Appendix A, "Rosetta Stone for Windows Operating Systems," is an at-a-glance reference to where some of the Windows artifacts are located for the user-level versions of Windows. Appendix B, "EnCase Version 7 Keyboard Shortcuts," is a compilation of some of the keyboard shortcuts found in the product. Knowing the key combinations to perform common tasks can save the examiner time. Appendix C, "Sample Run Books," gives you step-by-step procedures for the various tasks that we have covered in the chapters. They should serve as a good basis for organizations to build their own procedures for their examiners to follow, as well as a training tool for people who are new to forensics, or just new to EnCase. Appendix D, "EnScript Class Hierarchy," is a visual reference to the EnScript language. It shows all of the classes and serves as a visual reference to the inheritance structure of EnScript.

Preparing for the Forensics Function

This first section is devoted to covering the topics that should be addressed to start you off down the path using good forensic practices. Chapter 1 addresses the processes, policies, and procedures that should be in place prior to undertaking forensic examinations on behalf of your organization. If your organization is just beginning to handle cases in-house, these are items of prime importance to consider. Even if your organization has been handling cases for some time, it doesn't hurt to see the topics presented in case there are areas you haven't encountered yet. Many organizations find themselves in a situation where an incident prompts them to spin up a forensic investigation function without the benefit of putting these kinds of measures in place. You may be in that situation—where you've been handed the software and a computer that may have been involved in an event, and told to "do forensics." If that is the case, Chapter 1 should give you an idea of the pitfalls you could face if you don't give sufficient consideration to how you are going to approach the challenge.

Chapter 2 walks you through the installation of EnCase Forensic and gives you the basic introduction to the interface. The various options for customization are covered, and you should be generally comfortable with how the user interface works by the end of the chapter. In this chapter, you are shown how to create a case and add evidence, as well as what some of the options are used for and the considerations for using them.

Chapter 3 covers some of the basic concepts that are used throughout EnCase's suite of products. The EnCase Evidence file types are discussed, as well as the differences between the legacy file formats and the current versions. Encryption is addressed, you are shown how to create your encryption keys, and some considerations for using encryption in a multiuser lab environment are discussed.

These first three chapters set the stage for the rest of the book. Even if you have been using EnCase for some time now, it is worth going through them to see the differences in the interface (particularly if you are used to a version prior to 7). I know when I first switched to the new interface, I was frequently frustrated by knowing how to accomplish a task in the older version but challenged to do the same thing in the new one.

The Road to Readiness

Before embarking on the mission of performing digital investigations in-house (as opposed to having a third party perform them on an ad hoc or contract basis), there are a number of important steps that should be taken. The preparation is as important—if not more important—as the execution of the investigations. Cases handled without adequately defined methodologies, policies, and procedures have a higher risk of their evidence or methodology being challenged by the opposition in court. Digital forensics requires a high level of organization and attention to detail to ensure that mistakes are not made and evidence is not compromised in the course of the investigation. The goals of a forensics readiness effort are to ensure that the digital investigations function is supported by repeatable, defensible, efficient processes and to ensure the integrity of the deliverables. The forensic readiness planning activity should be used to identify gaps in your organization's policies, procedures, equipment, training, and staffing in pursuit of those goals.

Forensic Readiness

What is forensic readiness? How do you know if you have achieved it? The term *forensic readiness* describes the state of an organization that has completed the effort to properly prepare for performing digital forensic investigations. Policies are supported by a foundation of repeatable processes and trained, well-equipped personnel (see Figure 1-1).

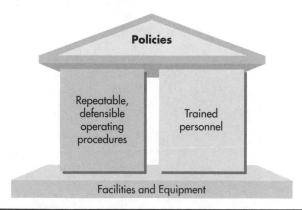

Figure 1-1   *Forensic readiness structure*

Forensic readiness activities include:

1. Adopt or develop policies to support the collection, preservation, and analysis of digital evidence for eventual presentation in court.

2. Acquire the required equipment and facility in support of performing digital forensic investigations.

3. Adopt or develop operating procedures describing how these activities will be performed, which are derived from and support the policies established in step 1.

4. Ensure trained personnel are in place to perform the work.

You know you have reached your goal when digital evidence is consistently collected in a forensically sound manner with no "angles of attack" that can be leveraged by opposing counsel to introduce reasonable doubt. The cost is minimized when the team has the training, equipment, policies, procedures, and management support to perform their duties efficiently. Since most organizations do not have the performance of digital forensics as one of their core business activities, cost containment is an important part of the readiness preparations.

A good place to begin is to determine the primary sources of cases in your organization. Who are your critical customers and what does the workload look like? How is that work currently being handled? Are risks being introduced by the current processes? The need for forensic readiness is driven by a business requirement: to support the groups that are tasked with handling allegations of misconduct in your organization. In a corporate setting, this is frequently human resources (HR), legal, corporate security (by which I mean the team responsible for physical as opposed to data security), and the incident response group within your information security team. An additional requirement that your legal team may have is the support of civil litigation. The handling and production of electronically stored information (ESI) for electronic discovery (e-discovery) and requests from regulatory bodies is a common source of additional work for the forensic team. The requirements for evidence handling remain the same for both types of cases, and the forensic analysts have the tools and training for this work. The greatest cost savings may come from supporting this work internally if your organization has a significant demand. Third-party forensic investigators, typically provided by outside law firms, come at a high cost.

Another consideration is where the forensics team belongs in the organization. In many companies, it resides in information security but can sometimes be found under legal or even in the financial risk organization. The decision is frequently a matter of executive sponsorship, and how the corporation conveys authority and handles the potential for conflicts of interest. The main goal is to allow the team to function with appropriate corporate guidance while maintaining the greatest degree of impartiality and autonomy. If the team is not allowed to function impartially and to follow the case where the evidence leads, the risk is that the organization may be perceived as enforcing their policies in an inconsistent fashion. This opens the door to allegations of favoritism and discrimination that can be devastating in a court case.

Ultimately, forensic analysts function best when they are allowed to be finders of facts. The people who investigate allegations should not be the same people who are in charge of dispensing the penalties—this is an important place to maintain the separation of duties. Findings reports are written up and delivered to the group that requested the investigation (who were charged with vetting the case merits before moving forward with fact finding). This separation in the corporate environment is similar to that found in the judicial system—the police are charged with performing investigations, and they deliver the results of their findings to the prosecutor or other authority to make a determination as to the final disposition of the case. The law enforcement structure has more autonomy (and more rules) than the corporate structure, given their authority from the government, but typically the people who are investigating crimes are not the people sitting in judgment on the consequences.

Policies

There are a number of policies that need to be in place before you have achieved any measure of forensic readiness. One of the most important is to have some form of an acceptable use policy for how computers on the organization's network are allowed to be utilized. The staff must be given guidance as to which activities are permissible, and which are not. Ideally, they should be required to sign an acceptable use policy as a condition of continued employment, which documents that they have read and acknowledged the rules. This will be influenced by the corporate values, local cultural and behavioral norms, and applicable laws and regulations that govern working in the organization. If there is no policy outlining acceptable use (and thus prohibited use), then there is no foundation for enforcement. Additionally, privacy laws must be taken into consideration for the location where the activity is performed. Your legal team should be consulted about the content of this type of policy, as well as the legality of any evidence sources you plan to use. If the source of the evidence is against the law to collect, or the proposed method of collection is in violation of the law, your legal team needs to warn you of this before you're in the middle of a case. They are tasked with making the determination of whether there is case law that indicates the person accused of wrongdoing would have had an expectation of privacy when using the resources of the company unless certain steps are taken to dispel that expectation. The organization must take these steps prior to engaging in investigations or they are taking on risk that may outweigh the behavior they are trying to combat. An example of this is the Hewlett-Packard pretexting case where investigators allegedly used questionable tactics to gain access to information on a case that landed the company in the middle of a media nightmare when their methods came to light (see Kim Zetter, "Phone Scam Charge Rocks HP," *Wired Magazine*, www.wired.com/gadgets/pcs/news/2006/09/71727). The forensics investigator and the person from the firm's legal department should maintain a close working relationship and be in regular contact to ensure that the legal decisions are made by counsel (who is authorized to practice law) and not by the investigator. This will also serve to help shield them from personal liability given that they are working in good faith under the direction of legal counsel.

Another issue that frequently affects the course of an investigation is the data retention policies of the organization. How long critical logs are kept and email is retained, and how difficult it will be to get to the data you require, are all important issues to consider from a policy standpoint. If your logs are not centralized across the organization, and if the system clocks are not synchronized across all systems, your investigator's job is much more difficult. With centralized logs, the data volume can be very high in a large enterprise. It is not uncommon for these systems to have only short duration of data collection before the logs are either compressed to save disk space or moved to secondary storage. Either of these makes the time required to access the data longer, which can be critical, both in investigations and incident response. The investigations team should have input into the decisions made about log retention and management to ensure data that is retained is useful for their purposes.

Determine how backups are handled across the enterprise. Are laptops and desktops automatically backed up, or do they require some voluntary action on the part of the user of the system? How frequent are the server backups? Do your personnel have the ability to pull data from the backup systems directly? Is there an index they can query in advance to determine if the data being requested exists? These questions must be explored and answered so that when the time comes, your team does not waste time pursuing data that is no longer retrievable. If the window of time that you can go back to is shorter than the average time you are being asked to investigate, discussions should be held with the groups that manage the infrastructure to extend the window. As with the retention policy, the investigations team is a stakeholder in the backup systems. The organization's legal department should also be consulted to ensure that their needs are met for both regulatory and civil litigation requirements.

> **TIP**
>
> *One best practice is to have the sanitized findings (take the confidential details out of the data) of the investigations team communicated to the other information security groups so that they will know what is happening on the organization's defensive front line.*

While there are many different organizational structures and potential groups with overlapping responsibilities for handling various areas of risk, engineering, and compliance, I am using a structure to explain generally how this feedback loop would benefit the teams who are responsible for information security (see Figure 1-2). The engineering team in this context is responsible for building the security controls into new and existing infrastructure, and needs to know what is being exploited and where the infrastructure protections need shoring up. The team responsible for risk and compliance in the organization needs to know the events that have occurred to better assess the risk and the potential costs associated using real-world data. The forensics team has a view into the techniques that the company's insiders are using to bypass the existing security controls, as well as how the company's defenses have failed in incidents. This data is extremely valuable since it provides concrete examples of areas where the organization has been susceptible to malicious behavior. Real-world data takes the events that are used in risk assessment equations out of the realm of "this might happen," and into the realm of "this is happening now and should not be ignored." This can be a powerful story to tell when asking for funding for the tools to augment the existing protections.

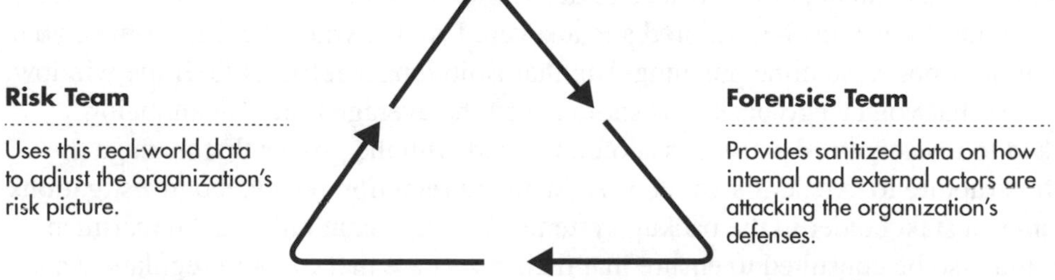

Using Real-World Data to Improve Security
Taking us from the potential attack vectors to those being used against us

Engineering Team
....
Uses real-world data to develop mitigating controls to actual avenues of attack that have been used.

Risk Team
....
Uses this real-world data to adjust the organization's risk picture.

Forensics Team
....
Provides sanitized data on how internal and external actors are attacking the organization's defenses.

Figure 1-2 *Security improvement cycle*

This brings us to another important point—if you aren't measuring what is going on in your organization, you're missing a really important opportunity not only for improvement of the security posture overall, but also to justify the controls you need to protect the data and systems of the company. You need to determine what to measure, and you need a methodology for putting the things you're measuring into a form that supports decision making. I recommend using the VERIS Framework (www.veriscommunity.net/), because it is geared towards recording the data points around security incidents. Measuring and recording data around the types of cases you are handling will help you to determine if there are areas that need to be addressed as far as tools or training. If you begin seeing more of a specific type of case, and it becomes a trend, this lets you identify the need to address your team's ability to handle the caseload.

Having the foundational policies in place, we can now look at conferring authority to perform investigations in a corporate environment. If an employee brings an allegation against another employee, it should first be brought to the appropriate human resources person for verification that it is a legitimate request. The human resources analyst can then start the notification phase of the investigation and engage the forensics team. The other customer groups function the same way—this way they do not need to revamp their processes to accommodate the forensics team. The customer groups notify the investigations team when a newly vetted case has come in, and the forensic analyst delivers their findings back to the customer group (i.e., HR), who are then responsible for determining the appropriate action based on the findings. Why should this process be structured this way? While the forensics team is a fact-finding organization, there exists a potential for misuse. Consider the following scenario: Anna contacts HR with sexual harassment allegations against her manager, Greg Smith, a VP in the company. Greg suspects Anna has told someone that he has been harassing her, and goes directly to the forensics team's manager (whom he outranks in the corporate hierarchy) to put pressure on the team to give him access to all of Anna's email. If the forensics team is not shielded from taking direct requests, then conceivably someone of Greg's managerial level could abuse his power and pressure the team to provide access to the data. As an investigator, I have seen this dynamic in practice. When the requestor is told they must go through HR (or other appropriate group), they frequently rethink the request. If the requestor does not want the scrutiny of the case-vetting process, that is a red flag. The forensics team should keep HR informed of any attempts to circumvent the process.

There needs to be a definition of who can initiate a case, how the cases are handled, how evidence is handled, how investigations are conducted, how cases are turned over (what that handoff looks like) and how cases are closed. Also, define who is allowed to perform investigative functions and run tools that gather the data used in forensic work so that if someone is using those same tools without authority, you have recourse. This is generally the case for certain classes of information security tools such as network port scanners and sniffers.

Finally, there needs to be a discussion of the criteria for bringing in law enforcement to an investigation. This is another discussion to have with legal and senior management. Having such criteria defined ahead of time will eliminate the uncertainty as the case is in progress.

Methodology

Your organization's methodology is a combination of the policies, procedures, and workflow that are established to accommodate requests for investigations and evidence collection. There are many ways to approach an investigation, and a full survey of them is beyond the scope of this book. I recommend you perform your own research and determine which methods best meet your organization's needs. There are some excellent references available, and I recommend you start building your organization's technical forensic library as part of this activity. Certainly, a good place to start is with the "C's" of digital forensics: Carrier, Carvey, Casey, and Cowen. Dr. Brian Carrier's *File System Forensics* (Addison-Wesley Professional, 2005) provides an excellent reference for a solid grounding in the topic. Harlan Carvey has written a number of books on forensics, including the indispensable *Windows Registry Forensics* (Syngress, 2011). Eoghan Casey has published numerous books on forensic topics, including *Digital Evidence and Computer Crime* (Academic Press, 2011). Finally, David Cowen's *Computer Forensics InfoSec Pro Guide* (McGraw-Hill, 2013) is a great place for a beginner to start. These books will provide you with both a strong theoretical grounding and a reference for establishing your methodology and procedures. Having a library of good forensics books will serve you well when something comes up that the team does not handle all of the time. Having a reference available to verify the specifics of an artifact is critical to ensuring the data is interpreted correctly.

In general, investigations can be broken down into several phases (see Table 1-1). These phases are frequently iterative. For example, as the case evolves, the analyst may be required to go back to the collection phase when another relevant data source is identified. Also, in the course of testing hypotheses, new facts may come up that require further analysis or the addition of new subjects to the collection pool.

The first phase begins when the forensics team is notified that a case has been initiated and they are asked to begin an investigation. This will often be from the business customers or from internal information technology (IT)/information security personnel in the event of a potential incident. Consider implementing a group email address directed to all of your investigators for your customers to use to send requests and inquiries. This helps keep the entire team in sync and ensures that someone can fill in during employee absences. Once notification has been received, an analyst should contact the customer and get the details of the case.

Input(s)	Investigation Phase	Output(s)
Investigation request Case details, subject(s), location(s), environment	**Notification**	Created case in case management and forensics tool(s) Case plan
Location(s) of evidence sources Custodian(s) of evidence Circumstances of collection Type(s) of evidence Volume of data anticipated	**Evidence gathering**	Chain of custody documentation Evidence collected/preserved Scene documentation Triage/evidence prioritization Beginning of case log (narrative)
Copies of evidence collected in prior phase Case particulars (i.e., types/format of data sought)	**Evidence processing**	Evidence processed as appropriate, i.e., signature analysis, file carving, expansion of compound files Documentation updated
Evidence processed in prior phase Detailed information on case allegations	**Examination and analysis**	Event reconstruction Hypothesis formulation and testing Case log updated with results
Results of prior phase	**Reporting**	Case findings report Sanitized data to other groups
Notification from customer the case has been resolved and signoff on closure by both customer and legal department	**Case closure**	Evidence disposition according to lifecycle process Original equipment disposition according to policy

Table 1-1   *Phases of an Investigation*

Pay special attention to the data sources, the environment (is this a collection where the person will not know you are gathering evidence?), and the specifics of the case that might lead to further evidence sources. Safety considerations of personnel who will be conducting the collection must always be a priority. Workplace violence is an unfortunate possibility in these situations. The organization may already have policies and procedures established for the corporate security group that addresses personnel safety, and collaboration with this team is advisable.

A case should be created in the case tracking tool that the organization uses. The case tracking tool can be as complex as a software package specifically designed to track cases and maintain a repository of the electronic evidence, or as simple as an Excel spreadsheet, depending on the needs, budget, and case volume of the organization.

In anticipation of receiving evidence, a case should also be created in the forensics tool(s) that will be used for further processing or analysis. Finally, the case log should be started and kept up to date with all of the actions taken, decisions made, and findings in a narrative, date/time stamped format. In particular, make certain that the findings and actions taken are documented well enough to allow another examiner to duplicate the efforts. For a reference with samples of documentation, consult the National Institute of Justice's *Forensic Examination of Digital Evidence: A Guide for Law Enforcement* (www.ncjrs.gov/pdffiles1/nij/199408.pdf).

In the evidence gathering phase, data sources are acquired in a forensically sound manner and working copies made (and their integrity verified) for further analysis and processing. What do I mean by "forensically sound"? Evidence is considered to be collected in a forensically sound manner when the process of collection does not alter the evidence to the extent possible, and where any unavoidable changes are thoroughly documented and justified. The method of collection must also be documented. Chain of custody documentation is initiated upon acquisition, and the scene documented thoroughly. Particularly for large cases, a triage or prioritization of the evidence should be undertaken to ensure that the evidence is processed in a logical manner. A good reference for this work is the National Institute of Justice's *Electronic Crime Scene Investigation: A Guide for First Responders* (www.ncjrs.gov /pdffiles1/nij/219941.pdf).

When the case is under significant time pressure, such as in an incident response scenario where someone is actively attacking an organization's computer systems, investigators may resort to previewing data as a triage measure. This means that, using forensically sound procedures, they will take a quick look at a number of evidence sources to rule in or rule out those affected. Once this type of triage has been completed, they will decide which systems need to be acquired based on their findings. Incident response is a fluid situation, where containment is one of the first priorities, and using this type of technique helps to speed up the process and weed out the volume of suspected systems to just those that are actually affected.

The evidence processing phase is for all of the prework that must be done to prepare evidence for analysis. EnCase uses the Evidence Processor for this, and you have a number of options that we will discuss in Chapter 5. The actions you take for initial processing will be determined by the procedures established for your team, the type of evidence you are processing, and the particulars of the case. The overall goal is to prepare the evidence for the forensic analysis to begin, and the evidence must be in a form that facilitates this activity.

The examination and analysis phase is where the forensic analyst will be looking at the evidence, forming and testing hypotheses, and determining to the extent possible whether there is evidence to support or refute the allegations of the case. They should also be noting any indication that the security controls of the organization need improvement. If they find websites that are not blocked but should be, for instance, they should take note and communicate the information to the appropriate party after the investigation concludes. If they find that the subject of the investigation has found a novel way to exfiltrate data, noting that and providing feedback to the group responsible for remediation will serve to strengthen the organization's security posture.

It is particularly important during the examination and analysis phase to make certain to keep the case log up to date with any findings. If the analyst's findings are challenged later by opposing counsel, for example, a neutral third party can be brought in to verify their work if the log is sufficiently detailed. It is a good practice to have a process defined to handle challenges of this type.

The reporting phase is when the analyst generates their findings report. The report should have sufficient detail to allow the reader to follow the narrative of what was found and why it is important, but be explained in such a way that the layman can understand it. The report should have an executive summary section at the beginning where the findings are outlined in a succinct manner for those who need to just have the results accessible quickly. There are sample reports in the National Institute of Justice's *Forensic Examination of Digital Evidence: A Guide for Law Enforcement*, along with sample forms.

TIP

Since cases may end up being presented in court, writing the findings report is excellent practice for explaining something to a jury. If the average person cannot understand the report, it likely needs to be explained better.

Finally, the case closure phase is when a case is fully resolved and the retained evidence and any equipment can be disposed of or returned according to your organization's policies. Sign-off on case completion should be obtained by the original requesting person or group prior to any evidence disposal. The case files and documentation should be handled in accordance with the policies established for case management. As a final check, sign-off from your legal team should be solicited to ensure there are no legal or regulatory requirements for retention of this data. The case documentation should include sign-off from appropriate stakeholders that the data can be destroyed. The method of destruction should also be documented.

Finally, with the closure of a case, the organization should hold a postmortem review to determine if there were any lessons to be learned from the case. For instance, were there any barriers encountered from a policy or procedure standpoint that could use improvement? Were there any technical challenges that should be addressed? These types of quality assurance activities should be a normal part of the process for closing a case.

Procedures

Once your policies are in place, you can derive your procedures from them. For instance, if you have defined your evidence handling policy, you can use that to build the procedure for end-to-end management of the evidence lifecycle in your organization. Specify on a detailed level the methods that your team will use to collect evidence. If you haven't performed this in the organization, start talking to your customers about where most of the evidence comes from. Is it on laptops? Are they encrypted? Do you need the ability to acquire entire servers? Are there remote locations? Will you need to enable collections over the network or have someone who is on-site able to follow your direction on the collection? Does your team have the ability to capture volatile data before a system is shut down? This is where you start to define your collection plans for the various types of data sources in the organization. Your customers should be able to help point out those data sources—either those that have been involved in the past or that are coming down the road—that contain data that is especially sensitive or at high risk for abuse. These are the data sources to document a collection plan for first, and then prioritize as you go along with the less likely data sources following after.

If you are dealing with encrypted data, you should begin working with the group that supports the encryption tool to determine how you will handle collections from these devices. This is also a good time to get a sample of the data that is available from the logs of systems that have high-risk data to ensure that you are getting the events that will actually be of use in an investigation. If, for instance, the users all share one account, it is better to know and see about addressing the ability to attribute actions or events to a specific user now, rather than during a critical investigation when something has happened and people want to know who the user was.

You will need to get some idea of the scale of the potential evidence, particularly to ensure you have the ability to collect and process the requested volume of data. Determine if you will be doing logical or physical collections. Is the data on an array with hundreds of terabytes of data? Is it in a RAID configuration that makes physical collection problematic? These are the questions you'll need to answer as part of developing the collection plan for each data source. Document contact information for the data owner and the person or group responsible for administering the application. If elevated privileges are required and not granted to the forensic examiner, you'll need a person to call who can facilitate, or even proxy, the access. This is also the time to determine the impact of the acquisition process on the business. If this is a mission-critical order processing system that cannot stand downtime without significant financial cost, that will affect how you go about the collection. You will need to determine whether it is technically feasible given the tools at your disposal to perform the collection, or if it warrants involving an external third party with specialized capabilities. Some of your collection plans will include this type of outside help when the impact on the company or the need to augment your in-house expertise is a component of the case.

Investigations should have some basic steps that are performed based on their case type. This will be part of the methodology you use—for instance, if you have a computer image, your methodology may direct the analyst to run the image through the EnCase Evidence Processor with specific options chosen each time as a preparatory action prior to starting analysis. Options that identify and organize all email, expand specific types of compound files, and recover deleted files are examples of standard processes that you may choose to perform upon evidence intake. These preparatory actions should be documented in a procedure so that every image is handled the same way for a specific class of case. If the case involves only email obtained from the exchange server, and not a full disk image, the process will be handled differently. Regardless, the procedure will be documented, and all examiners are expected to follow the accepted methodology. Identifying the most common data sources for cases will help guide you in prioritizing the procedures that need to be documented. Standardization on a process will also help to identify those areas where EnScript—EnCase's built-in scripting language—would be a good option to automate the evidence processing. We will cover the automation options for EnCase in Part V.

Having these procedures defined and published to the team has a number of benefits. It helps keep everyone on the same page when performing the same type of cases, which allows for those more junior to gain confidence in the methodology by reinforcement and repetition. It keeps busy analysts on track as they work through multiple cases at a time if they have defined steps for the prep work on cases. Finally, it ensures that everyone is handling the cases the same way, so if one person is unavailable for a time, another team member should be able to determine where in the process they are and quickly ramp up with the case processing. All steps in performing investigations cannot be scripted in this manner—there is still a large amount of work that is dictated by the merits of the case and what is found during analysis. However, procedures that are repeatable and show how classes of activities are handled will help the organization both maximize the shared workload and keep the cost of investigations down.

In technology operations, there is a concept of a Run Book—a set of processes to perform given a specific set of circumstances. These procedures we've discussed will serve as the Run Book for your forensics team. In this book, I will be providing sample Run Book procedures as we cover common topics. These can be used and customized to suit your organization, and should assist you in your forensic readiness preparations.

Organizing the Work

Computer forensics is a field where documentation is a critical part of the job requirements. The need for organization and adherence to policies and procedures cannot be stressed enough when performing digital investigations. Evidence handling must be thoroughly documented from collection to analysis to presentation in court to the end of the evidence lifecycle and destruction. All media must be wiped and verified prior to use, and this too must be meticulously documented. All decisions made and actions taken must be documented so that the analyst can be called to testify (sometimes years later) about exactly what they did on this case and why. All tools must also be verified to be performing as expected prior to use, and this must be documented as well. All of this shows the need for organization, or the forensic group will be buried in documentation without a clear way to manage it all. This is where the policies and procedures are most important—adherence to them ensures that all members of the team are performing the tasks in the same defensible manner. Paper documents should not be ignored, and while much can be done to keep the process as paper-free as possible, files need to be created for case documentation and managed just like those in the electronic realm.

A case management tool is vital for keeping track of all the cases and tasks that need to be performed, but care should be given to who will have access to the data within. Ideally, the forensic team will be the only users, and no outside administrative level privileges will be granted to other organizations. This means that the support for the infrastructure will reside within the group, but it maintains the confidentiality of the data, which is a major concern in investigations.

Infrastructure Considerations

There are a number of infrastructure considerations that should be explored in preparation for collecting evidence and performing digital investigations. As mentioned above, are all the systems in your organization synchronizing their clocks? Does your organization allow for shared user accounts? If so, how will your investigators be able to attribute activities using a shared account to a specific person? This is particularly of concern with accounts where there are elevated privileges associated, such as a system administrator account. Does your organization enable logging on all devices? What type of logging and events are recorded? I have seen cases where the organization enabled security logs only on the servers, not on the desktops or laptops. This significantly hindered the investigations where servers were not involved.

Another infrastructure concern is in the deployment of the forensic tools and providing access for the analyst to perform the necessary collection from a variety of data sources. This is a consideration that frequently runs into significant pushback from operational support groups that are concerned with giving the level of access required to an outside group. To collect data from certain sources, administrator level access may be required. This makes those who support the infrastructure understandably nervous to have someone else with this powerful access. The concern is typically that it could be used to make environmental changes that would impact their systems. This is more common with network-based collection (such as EnCase Enterprise Edition or EnCase eDiscovery Edition), but you may run into this in other instances when trying to gain access to a resource for collection.

The Lab

The forensic lab needs to be a secure location with physical access controls that allow the organization to show who has accessed the room and when. This is not a room that the janitorial staff, for instance, should be able to access. Depending on your organization's needs, solutions such as badge-based access or physical keys in combination with video surveillance to record traffic in and out of the lab may be used. However you do it, you must be able to demonstrate that only those with authorized access have been able to enter the lab unescorted. The access control method should be approached with an eye toward negating any challenges raised regarding the physical integrity of the lab. A good resource for building out the forensics lab is Andrew Jones and Craig Valli's *Building a Digital Forensic Laboratory: Establishing and Managing a Successful Facility* (Syngress, 2008). In addition, you may want to look into obtaining accreditation for your lab, or aligning your processes with the accreditation body's requirements if accreditation is not desired. The American Society of Crime Laboratory Directors Laboratory Accreditation Board (ASCLD/LAB) is one such entity providing international accreditation. Their program is based on the ISO 17025 standards and supplemented by additional requirements. They have a section for digital and multimedia evidence accreditation.

A visitor log should be located at the entrance, and visitors must be signed in and out by the members of the team. The log should contain details about the person, their affiliation, and the reason for the access. Visitors should be escorted and supervised during visits, and contact with evidence should be strictly limited to the reason for their visit.

The lab should contain sufficient work surfaces for multiple simultaneous acquisitions as well as analyses to be performed. It will also need a secure storage location for evidence that is further access controlled. A safe large enough to accommodate hard drives and computers is a good example. A locking file cabinet for case files is also recommended. The size of the lab and storage equipment will depend on the anticipated case load, how many people will need to be working in the lab at a time, and the expected method of evidence storage. If physical imaging is performed onto hard drives and many cases are expected, a larger safe will be needed than in the case of an organization that expects only a few cases a year. A storage array is useful for storing working copies of the evidence files for analysis in a central location and also provides a backup to the original collection media.

Tools must be put through a verification process prior to use. The Computer Forensics Tool Testing (CFTT) Project's website (www.cftt.nist.gov/) is a good resource for information on how to test and validate your tools. There are also tool testing images available to test your tools against so you have a known set of evidence to work with. Finally, Marshall University has a site (http://forensics .marshall.edu/Digital/Digital-Publications.html) that publishes the results of their validation testing.

A forensic area network (FAN) is beneficial to allow the analysis machines to communicate with shared storage arrays established within the lab. This network should be separated from the wider corporate network, but if connectivity must be present, then security controls and active monitoring of the traffic between the two networks should be put into place (Figure 1-3).

Consider encrypting the evidence files for additional protection when they are at rest on the storage medium. Any time the evidence is used, copied, moved, etc., a log should be kept as part of the evidence handling documentation. Integrity of evidence should be verified at this time as well to ensure no changes have been introduced (see "Evidence on the Move" in Chapter 2). Audit logs should be enabled on the forensic systems as well as that manage the centralized storage to keep track of any access or changes to the evidence.

Some labs have their evidence arrays set to read-only access for the analysis machines, which will act as a write blocker and provide an additional layer of protection. Virtualization is also common in digital forensics for both analysis and processing systems. A common practice is to use VPN and two-factor authentication to access the forensic lab as a whole, and in some cases, for the analysis machines specifically as well.

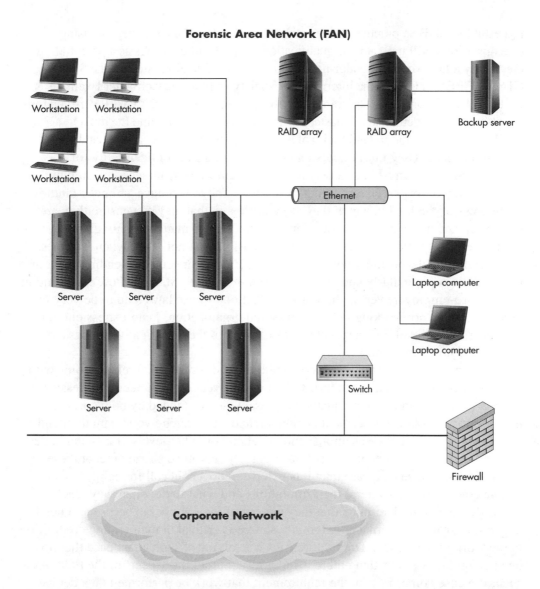

Figure 1-3 *Example forensic area network (FAN)*

Staffing

Your forensic team must be staffed with professionals who have been trained in both forensic theory and the toolset your organization uses. They must be thoroughly familiar with the policies mentioned above to ensure they will recognize a violation when they find one. They must also be trained on the procedures your organization has established. Best practice is to have them certified on the tools they are using (the opposition will look at their qualifications to perform their jobs as a potential credibility attack vector). Vendor-neutral forensics certifications such as the SANS GIAC GCFE and GCFA, the International Society of Forensic Computer Examiner's CCE, and the Information Assurance Certification Review Board's CCFE certifications are also useful to demonstrate mastery of the forensic theory behind the tools.

The team must understand their roles and responsibilities regarding each case you accept. They must understand the need for strict confidentiality for investigations, and must have a way to recuse themselves from a case if they find they have a real *or perceived* conflict of interest. They must have an understanding of the laws of the land in which they are working so that they can ensure they are in compliance in their investigations and particularly in matters of surveillance. There are many actions that are technically feasible, but not legal, when it comes to collecting evidence and monitoring the activities of subjects, depending on your locale. This is particularly noticeable between the United States (whose laws tend to be very pro-employer) versus the European Union (whose laws tend to be very pro-privacy). If you are working in a multinational organization, I can't stress enough the necessity of involving corporate counsel early in the investigative process to ensure you are compliant.

The team members should be encouraged to build professional relationships with law enforcement that may have jurisdiction in the event of an incident. Professional associations frequently offer educational presentations attended by both corporate investigators and law enforcement personnel, and encouraging your team to attend these events can be both educational and beneficial on other levels. It is much better to be able to call someone in law enforcement whom you've already met at these events for assistance on a case than it is to have to do a cold call for help.

The team must be aware of their limitations and what to do when they reach them. Being able to determine that they are out of their area of expertise and need help either from an internal or external resource is critical in maintaining credibility in the work they perform. Digital forensics is evolving at such a fast pace that no one person knows everything there is to know about all the aspects of the field. As such, if a case comes in with the requirement that work be performed on a device or data source that is wholly beyond the expertise of the team, a process must be defined to either bring in outside expertise or communicate the issues to the case stakeholder.

Finally, consider engaging a vendor to provide staff augmentation via forensic or incident response retainers in the event that your caseload suddenly skyrockets. Having that agreement already worked out will help keep your people from burning out if the workload suddenly spikes due to litigation or incidents. If, for example, your organization becomes the target of a hacktivist group such as the Anonymous hacking collective, the resulting response has the potential to overwhelm your staff. Having an existing relationship with a source of experienced examiners will allow for a quick response, particularly if you have already negotiated a contract. Often, the fees involved can be minimized if a contract is negotiated during a less urgent period rather than at the heart of a large investigation or a highly publicized data breach.

Summary

Forensic readiness requires quite a lot of preparation before you can say with any confidence that your organization has done the necessary due diligence preparing for the forensic function. We've discussed the main points that need to be addressed, which can be a time-consuming process. However, when you have all of the policies and procedures in place, the equipment acquired and installed, and the staff trained, you should be in good shape for your charter of performing digital investigations. Having completed all this prep work, it is time to start putting it to good use.

Getting Started

At some point in your readiness process, you will have ordered the computer hardware and software, and are ready to start getting the forensic workstation(s) built. That is where we come to the point of needing to install EnCase Forensic and get it set up for use. We will go over the steps to install the product, and some of the considerations for use in a multi-examiner environment. Then we will discuss the interface and some of the foundational concepts for using EnCase.

Installing the Software

Before you can use EnCase Forensic, you must first obtain all the components to install the application and get it running properly. When you purchased the product, you should have received a package with the following items:

▶ A packing slip

▶ The product DVD case (if not taking electronic delivery of the software)

▶ The EnCase Forensics manual

▶ The security dongle (USB key)

▶ An email with links to download the product and a certificate or license file (usually the option if you don't opt for physical media)

DVD Installation

If the installation screen does not automatically display after you insert the DVD into the computer, you can launch the setup from the DVD in Windows Explorer (Start | Right click | Explore). The setup file should be labeled ef_setup_7xxxx.exe, with the x's representing the specific version number. Double-clicking on that program will launch the installer and display the initial installation screen.

Downloaded Installation

If you obtained your product via an emailed link, download the files from the link provided. If you have a link for a certificate or license file, download those as well—these are options for use without a dongle (physical security USB key)—or if you are upgrading from a version 6 dongle to version 7, these files allow you to continue

Name	Date modified	Type	Size	Tags
release_notes_v70202	12/3/2011 2:38 PM	Compressed (zipp...	139 KB	
ef_setup_70202_english	12/3/2011 2:41 PM	Application	136,980 KB	
ef_user_manual_v7	12/3/2011 2:39 PM	Compressed (zipp...	18,006 KB	

Figure 2-1 *EnCase files downloaded*

to use your existing version 6 dongle. At the bare minimum, download the installer file, the manual, and the release notes from the links provided. Figure 2-1 shows what they look like in Windows Explorer.

You can see by the names that we're going to be installing EnCase version 7.02.02, and the user's manual and release notes are zipped archives. If your file is still zipped up in an archive, be sure to decompress it first before installing. To start the install, double-click on the unzipped setup file (ef_setup_70202_english in this case) and the installer will launch. The rest of the installation is the same regardless of where the install files were obtained.

Figure 2-2 shows the default installation path, which is configurable to where you would like to install the product. It also shows the version of the software you

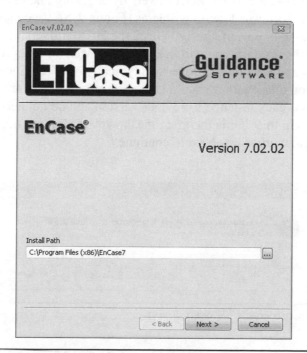

Figure 2-2 *The EnCase install path dialog*

are installing. The three dots (ellipses) button next to the path text box (also known as the browse button) will bring up a window that will allow you to browse to the installation location you prefer, or you can just type the path into the text box by hand and click Next.

If you haven't already created the folder you selected for the installation folder, you will get a dialog asking if you want EnCase to create the folder for you (Figure 2-3). In practice, I make the installation folder EnCase_[version], with the portion in square brackets representing the version I am installing. So for this example, it would be EnCase_7.02.02. It should be noted that EnCase is contained completely within its folder structure to allow multiple versions of the software to exist on the computer together with separate installation locations. This is useful when testing out a new version while keeping your production version intact and usable. I do recommend working each case in only one version of the software—don't migrate mid-case if you can help it because there have been problems with the changes in functionality between the point release versions causing issues with the cases.

You may also want to keep the installation files preserved on separate media in case you ever need to install a specific version again to revisit a case.

You are next shown the EnCase Forensic License Agreement (Figure 2-4). Read through and click the check box next to "I Agree" if you do. Click Next to continue.

If this is the first time this software has been installed on this computer, you will need to install the HASP or CodeMeter drivers by checking one of these two boxes, although checking both won't cause problems (Figure 2-5). If you are using your dongle from a previous version, then you need the HASP drivers. If you received a new dongle with the product, you will need the CodeMeter drivers. The CodeMeter dongles are full-sized USB thumb drives and typically have the CodeMeter logo on them. The path you chose earlier should be grayed out, so you cannot make changes here. If you have already installed a previous version and do not need the dongle drivers, you can skip this. If it is the first time, however, you will need those to make the security dongle work. Click Next to continue.

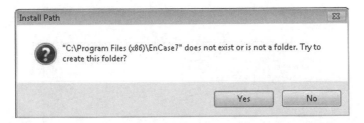

Figure 2-3   *The EnCase create file path dialog*

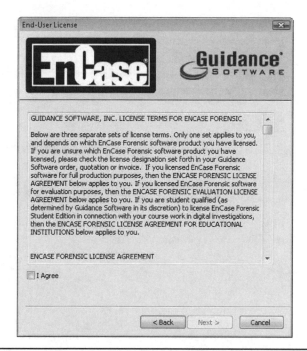

Figure 2-4   *The EnCase end user license agreement dialog*

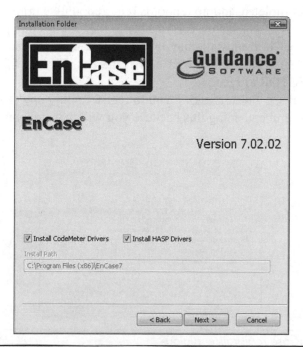

Figure 2-5   *The EnCase CodeMeter and HASP drivers dialog*

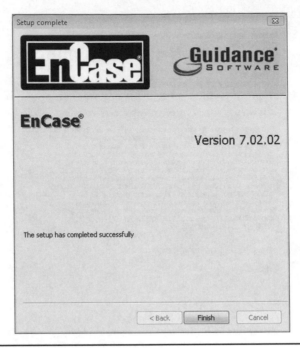

Figure 2-6   *The Install complete screen*

Installation is completed, and no reboot is required, unlike prior versions of the product (Figure 2-6). If you have a cert or license file, you need to put it in the appropriate directory in the installation path. In Windows Vista and later versions, that will be [INSTALL DIRECTORY]\Certs. If there is a license file, place it into [INSTALL DIRECTORY]\License.

Finally, you will see a dialog asking you to register your copy of EnCase Forensic (Figure 2-7). I recommend doing this because you will then get emails with product

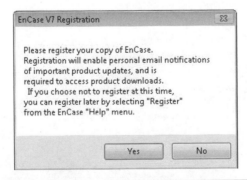

Figure 2-7   *The EnCase registration dialog*

updates, and it will also give you access to the customer support portal. You don't have to register at this time. If you want to register the product later, as the dialog says, you can always do so from the Help menu inside of EnCase.

Creating a New Case in EnCase

You might think that the first step is to create a new case in the tool, but that would be getting ahead of ourselves. There remains some preparation work to be done. The first step is to determine the underlying file structure that you will use when you work with EnCase Forensic on actual cases. Standardizing on a common set of case folders for every case will help keep your (and your fellow analysts') work organized and consistent across all cases. The structure you put in place now will serve you and your organization going forward. This is so important that you should give some thought as to what folder structure you want to use, and where it should be stored, as it can potentially save you many hours when trying to manage multiple cases simultaneously.

If you do not change where the default location will be for your cases, EnCase will create them under the Windows profile of the user account that launched the program. This can be an issue for multiuser environments where more than one analyst may need to work on a given case. By default, I am the only user with access to my files and folders in my Windows profile. This means that if I launch EnCase and create a file under my profile, I am the only one with permission to work with that case or the evidence if I also located it under the same file path. If there are others on the team who need to perform tasks on the case, they will not have access.

Another problem with locating the files under the user profile is that will put the case data on the same volume by default as the operating system. There are multiple problems with keeping your case files located there. First, a potential challenge to your evidence's integrity is that it was cross-contaminated by other case data, or by the operating system itself, if your evidence is not sufficiently segregated. The assertion by opposing counsel in court could be that this cross-contamination is responsible for the artifacts found—not the actions of the accused. This claim is based on the practice of commingling data among the operating system, the application, and the cases if they are all in one shared folder. So if you keep the evidence and all case work separate from the operating system, and indeed separate from each other, this negates the premise for that challenge. The second reason for using a different drive from the operating system is for performance. EnCase operations can be resource intensive, and this is one less point of contention between the application and the operating system if they are not on the same volume. In fact, some examiners will even split their cases up further to have the Index or

Temp folders on additional volumes if their hardware environment is sufficiently robust. So, to follow best practices, you should plan on using a separate wiped and verified volume for your case data.

> ### NOTE
>
> *What is wiped and verified? This refers to using a program or hardware designed to sanitize the hard drive prior to use (usually by writing a specific character to every sector on the drive) and then looking at the drive with a hex editor to verify that no data remains on the drive. Once this is performed, it should also be documented in the log that is kept for this specific media, as I mentioned in Chapter 1.*

A further good practice is to ensure that whenever possible, evidence is kept inside a forensic container, such as the EnCase evidence file (E01, Ex01, L01, or Lx01). This is an additional defense against the argument of cross contamination, with data that must be carved out of the case also being exported into a new evidence file. While this is not always possible, given the need to share files with third parties (not all of whom will have a tool that can read EnCase evidence files), it remains a good practice. With many forensic labs moving to virtualized analysis machines and network attached storage, wiping individual media becomes more problematic. Forensic teams should take particular care that data is not shared between cases. When sharing data outside of the forensic lab, sterilization procedures become especially important on the media being sent to third parties.

When you create a new case, EnCase will create a new folder structure for you under the location you designate. These new folders include the Email, Export, Tags, and Temp folders. Each of the default folders serves a purpose in the EnCase environment. The Email folder is used for processing email evidence. The Export folder is used as a central case-specific location for the analyst to copy files out of the EnCase environment. This is frequently performed to allow the use of a third-party tool for further examination, to view the items in their native application, or even to provide them to an external party for inspection or processing. Files and folder structures with their full contents are also easily copied from the EnCase environment to this folder for further examination. The Tags folder is used for Tags storage, which we will discuss in Chapter 6. The Temp folder is a designated area for EnCase to put all temporary files that are created in the course of the examination. Sometimes analysts find it useful to view a file in the native viewer associated in Windows, and this keeps all the files that are generated in those instances in one segregated location. When EnCase is shut down gracefully (i.e., no crash is involved), it will clean up these files (by deleting them) as it exits. However, in the event of a crash, EnCase will not be able to clean up after itself, and you should go in and delete these temporary files manually. This is a good idea to ensure that you are not using more disk space than you need, and as a step when you close a case or even if a case becomes dormant for a time.

If you follow a common methodology across all your cases, you will be able to ensure that you have not missed an important step. Additionally, developing your methodology for cases helps to ensure that you follow the same defensible procedure each time, regardless of time pressures or externalities that may cause the examiner additional stress. One example of this is during an incident response scenario—for example, you work for a company and find out a system has been hacked. This tends to be a high-stress time, with management demanding frequent progress reports and urgent pressure to provide answers. If you approach this situation with a standard set of steps, you are less likely to skip something major in response to the environment. The time to define these procedures is before an incident occurs, as part of the forensic readiness process.

As a practitioner setting up a new environment for case work, I typically create a template folder that I can easily duplicate when a new case comes along. It includes the folder structure the organization uses, as well as blank copies of any standard documentation files that are used for each case, such as an evidence tracking sheet or the request form used to authorize a case. So in addition to the standard folders created by EnCase, you can include a Documentation folder with those files, and an Evidence folder to store any evidence you obtain. These are all stored under a Cases parent directory and organized by the name of the case (or whatever the organization uses to differentiate one case from another). Figure 2-8 shows an example of a case structure in Windows Explorer using version 6 of EnCase.

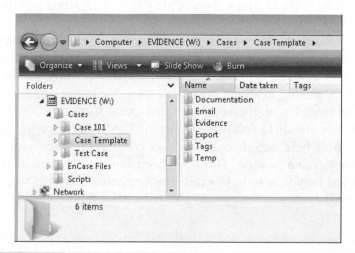

Figure 2-8 *Case template folder structure*

Once this is set up as a template, copy and paste the entire directory structure, and then rename the folder to the new case designation. This provides a fresh set of documentation files, as well as a standard path for keeping all the case-related data in one place, separate from all other cases as well as the operating system. However, with version 7, creating a new case must be done first in EnCase before creating the new directory structure in Windows Explorer. If not, EnCase will delete the file structure first and then create its own—destroying the work you've done to put the template in place. To accommodate this, you can make a few changes to the Case Template folder structure so that you can simply go in and copy the folders under the Case Template directory to the new case structure once it has been created. Basically, you need to remove the folders that EnCase will create by default, so you are left with just the Documentation and Evidence folders under the case template. You may want to add or subtract folders based on the needs of your organization, but the most important point is that the order of operation has changed in version 7 from creating the folder structure first to creating the case within EnCase first.

As a forensic analyst, get into the habit of putting the same types of data into the same locations for each case. This will help to streamline not only the work as you perform the examination but also finding and producing the data at a later date. If your work habits are consistent, this becomes second nature, and several years down the road when a case actually makes it to court, you will not have problems trying to remember where in your case directory structure you put a specific piece of evidence. This is particularly true of the Export folder—this directory is where you should be putting any files you export out of the EnCase environment. Some examiners create additional subfolders under the Export directory to represent the type of file exported—such as text documents, graphic files, or spreadsheets. This additional step can make finding a specific file much easier when it comes time to produce it.

Finally, the Evidence folder is where copies of the acquired evidence should be stored. In this book, I assume we are working on a copy of the evidence, since examiners should never be working on original evidence directly. Further, when making a copy or moving evidence copies from one file location to another, each copy should be treated as original evidence, and chain of custody and integrity management steps should be followed. Under the Evidence folder, you may want subdirectories for where each piece of evidence came from—such as a workstation name or the subject and location. This helps keep you organized on the front end of the case, and you may want to mirror this structure under Export as well to keep the items segregated.

Evidence on the Move

There are tools available to facilitate evidence transfer. Evidence Mover by Microforensics is one such tool, which will create the hash of a file, transfer it, hash the destination file, compare the two hashes, and report on any errors. However, in the absence of automated tools, the basic steps can be accomplished by using open source software:

1. Create a hash of the file(s) you need to transfer.
2. Copy the file(s) to the destination.
3. Create a hash of the same file(s) on the destination location.
4. Compare the hash(es) to make sure nothing has changed.
5. If the hash(es) do not match, go back to step 1 and repeat until they do.
6. Document what you did, including preserving both hashes.

Since we are not going to create the folder in Windows Explorer first, we are ready to create the case within EnCase Forensic. To begin, launch EnCase from either the desktop icon or the Start | All Programs | EnCase 7 menu item. This will bring up the EnCase environment. If you open EnCase without having a security dongle plugged in and recognized by the system (or certificate/license file in place), EnCase will launch in Acquisition mode. Figure 2-9 shows EnCase in Acquisition mode, with the banner across the top of the window.

If the product cannot communicate with the security dongle, you will not be able to use most of the features. You will, as the mode implies, be able to perform an acquisition. This ensures that if there are problems when in the field, the acquisition of data is not halted due to not having a functional dongle. It also allows for unlimited acquisition regardless of how your license is structured with Guidance Software. You can open cases and acquire evidence in Acquisition mode; it is when you want to perform analysis that you require the dongle.

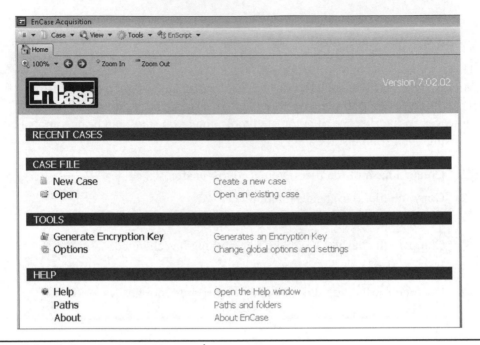

Figure 2-9   *EnCase in Acquisition mode*

The most common mode of operation is to use the program with the dongle installed and recognized. When EnCase is launched in this manner, the title bar on the top of the EnCase environment displays as shown in Figure 2-10.

There are other differences—the EnScript menu item that was grayed out (disabled) in Acquisition mode is active now, and our Recent Cases have been populated (if appropriate).

Alternatively, if you have an EnCase Network Authentication Server (NAS) installed, you can handle the authentication over the network and will not need a security dongle attached to each machine. This is a common setup in a lab environment. For more information on this product (which is outside the scope of this book), see the EnCase User Manual for the version of the software you are using. The NAS product is distributed separately from EnCase Forensic.

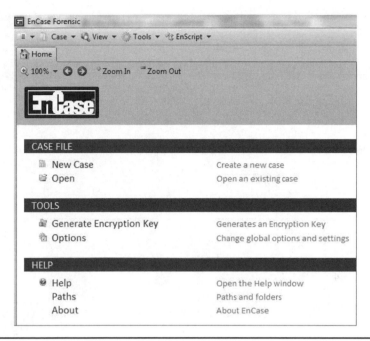

Figure 2-10   *EnCase in Authenticated mode*

The EnCase Home Screen

If you have used prior versions of this product, you will immediately notice that
version 7 has a very different look and feel. The new version of EnCase introduced
significant changes to the way EnCase displays information, and how you interact
with the program. Nowhere is this more apparent than when you first start the
program. Figure 2-11 shows the previous Encase version's opening screen (version 6).

In past versions of EnCase, the layout included the four panes Tree, Table, View,
and Filter. Version 7 of the product introduced the Home screen as the first place you
find yourself when the product launches (Figure 2-12).

There are far fewer options presented to you, and the menus and buttons on the
toolbars have been drastically altered. On the Home screen, there are three sections:
Case File, Tools, and Help. EnCase now uses tabs, much like a web browser, and as
you open new ones they will be displayed across the top, just under the application
menu bar. Rather than enumerate each of the menus and options on the page, let's
start learning the new environment by using it to create our first case.

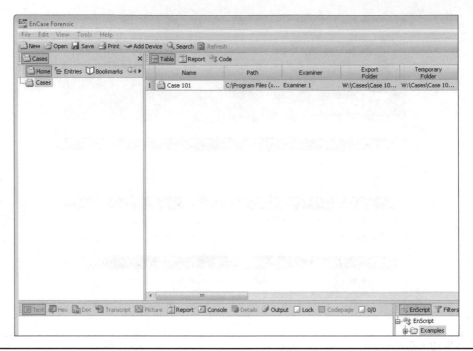

Figure 2-11   *The EnCase 6 opening screen*

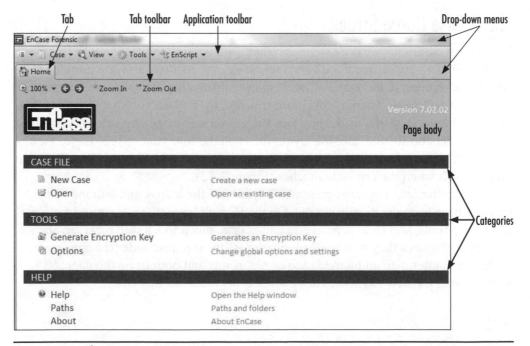

Figure 2-12   *The EnCase 7 Home screen*

Click on New Case on your Home screen. Alternatively, you can choose New Case from the Case menu on the top toolbar. This brings up the Case Options dialog, with the Basic template selected by default (Figure 2-13).

Templates are new to version 7 of EnCase and can be very useful. For example, if you define a custom template with all the data you want to make sure is collected for each case, you can then use it to enforce consistency among multiple analysts. EnCase comes with several templates by default, and we will discuss them further in Chapter 3. For our purposes, choose #2 Forensic from the left pane and look at the options this gives you in the Case Info pane at the bottom right. These match most closely what we would normally see recorded at a bare minimum, so we'll be using this option.

In the Name text box, you'll want to give the case a name that matches the folder structure you created previously. The Full Case Path is grayed out and will automatically fill in based on what you select for the Base Case Folder path and the name of the case. For the Base Case Folder, this should be the top level folder

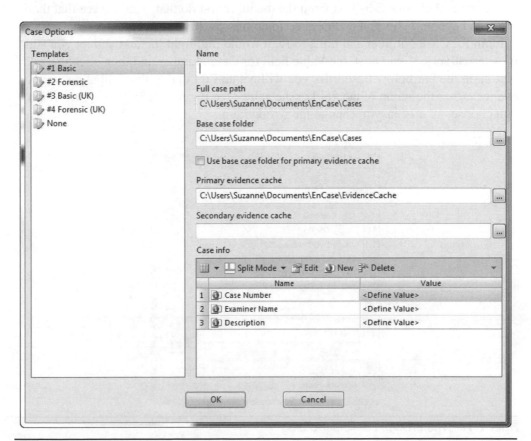

Figure 2-13 *The Case Options dialog with the basic template*

where you store your cases. You can either provide an alternate location for the Primary Evidence Cache folder, or check the box next to "Use base case folder for primary evidence cache". If you leave the default, it is set to a subdirectory under the Documents folder of the profile of the user that ran the program. This is not a desirable location for this data. Starting in Version 7, EnCase no longer performs most functions in memory (RAM), but instead caches the data to the hard drive. This results in a fair amount of disk activity, and for performance reasons the evidence cache should not be on the same volume as the operating system.

These defaults can be changed, and I'll show you how to do that in the case options and global options sections below. For all of these paths, you can either type them in by hand if you remember the appropriate value, or use the browse button to the right of the text box to allow you to find the location.

Figure 2-14 shows the dialog that allows you to set the path for any of these locations. Finally, we want to fill in the values for the fields in the Case Info section. You can do this several ways. You can right-click the Value field of the item you want to change and choose Edit Text from the menu. If you do that, you can see that there is also a keyboard shortcut (F2) defined to do this. So if you clicked on the Value column for Case Number and pressed F2, it would highlight the text and let you edit it. Alternatively, if you click the Value field for Case Number and then click the Edit button on the bar below Case Info, you will get an Edit dialog that will allow you to change either the name of the field or the value (see Figure 2-15). Be careful which you choose, as it is easy to change the wrong item.

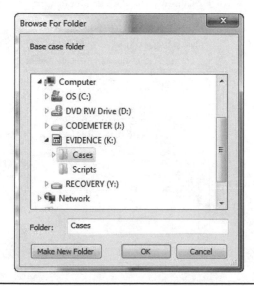

Figure 2-14 *The Browse For Folder dialog*

Figure 2-15   *The Edit "Case Number" dialog*

When you are finished, you should have something like the screen shown in Figure 2-16 (with appropriate changes to suit your environment):

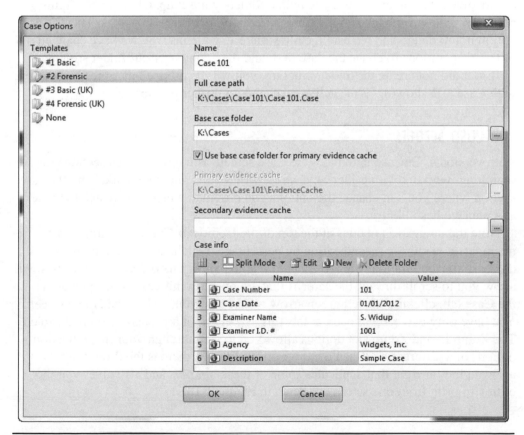

Figure 2-16   *The Case Options dialog showing your selections*

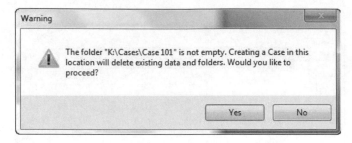

Figure 2-17 *Error on case creation if folders already exists*

Your drive letter may vary with the actual location of your case work drive, and the actual path should reflect the case structure folders you set up earlier. Click OK to create the case. If you created the folders from your template prior to creating your case, you will get the error displayed in Figure 2-17.

If you click Yes, EnCase will delete and recreate the folders, losing the work you did to create the folders from the template folders you set up. Clicking No at this point just drops you back into the Case Info dialog to change the paths. There is no option not to delete and recreate the file structure, which is why we have changed our order of operations to create the case first, and then copy over our folder structure.

If you did not create the folder structure, you will be dropped into the Case screen, with Case 101 showing as the active case, and no further prompting.

The Case Screen

With version 7, EnCase introduces the Case screen. You have various sections for searching, working with evidence, dealing with reports and bookmarks, and the case section where you can change the options you provided when you created the case and manage hash libraries.

Note the navigation options at the top of the Home tab. The 100% drop-down menu lets you choose magnification by percentage, which lets you increase and decrease the amount that you are zoomed into the view. The right and left arrows will allow you to scroll through the screens that are open. In this case, since you are in the Case tab, clicking the left green arrow would take you back to the Home screen. You have only two screens open at this time, so the right arrow is currently disabled. The Zoom In and Zoom Out options allow you to step through your magnification options in a different way than the drop-down. Finally, there is the drop-down menu arrow at the far right that duplicates some of these options, and also gives you the option to print from this screen as shown in Figure 2-18.

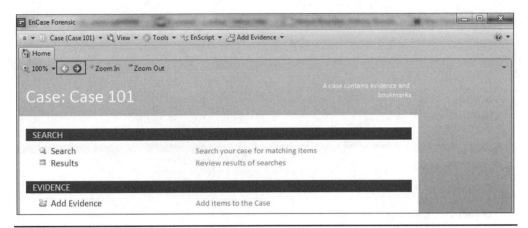

Figure 2-18   *The EnCase Case screen navigation*

Now that you have created the new case, you should save it. There are two types of saves in EnCase—the case save and the global save. They are similar, in that they will both save all of the case-specific data for that particular case. But they differ in one important aspect—only a global save will save configuration changes to the EnCase environment that affect all cases. An example of this would be if you created a new global keyword—one that you want to use against multiple cases. You would not preserve this new keyword unless you performed a global save.

There are several methods to perform a case save. They include:

► Choosing Save from the Case screen

► Clicking the Save Case menu on the top application bar

► Using the keyboard shortcut of CTRL-S (holding down the CTRL key while pressing the S key)

Methods to perform a global save include:

► Choosing Save All from the top-left drop-down menu on the application menu bar

► Using the keyboard shortcut of CTRL-SHIFT-S (holding down both the CTRL and SHIFT keys while pressing the S key)

Any of these options will bring up the Save As dialog the first time you save a case. Note that when you make changes that are only saved when performing a global save, EnCase will not warn you upon exit that the changes will be lost. Further, the AutoSave global option only affects the .Case file, not the environment.

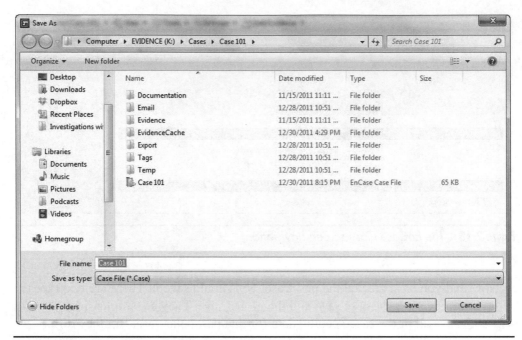

Figure 2-19   *The case Save As dialog*

Browse to the location you specified as your top level Case folder (in our example this would be the K:\Cases\Case 101 folder) and save the case there. Note that some examinations require multiple case files, and some analysts prefer to create a Case Files folder under this top level location to store them separately. It is all about personal preference and your organization's standards, but consistency is critical to helping you manage your cases, particularly in a multi-analyst environment. However, it is a recommended practice to make your changes now when you are just setting up the environment and before you have worked on any cases. Once you have everything set up, you can then do a global save and use them going forward.

Customizing the Interface

There are two places to customize the interface—the case options and the global options. First, let's go over the case-specific options.

The Case Options

The case options are accessible by clicking Options in the Case section of the Home screen where you can see the information you provided about this case when you created it including:

▶ The case name you assigned

▶ The analyst's name and ID#

▶ The folder paths that you defined

How a case is named will depend on your organization's policies. Some examples are the name of the primary subject of the investigation, or if it is a lawsuit, the name of the litigation matter as filed in court. The analyst's name and ID will also be dependent on policy: Do you use full names? First initial, last name? Employee ID? If this is law enforcement, do you have some other designation such as officer's badge number? These should be established in the preparation work we discussed in Chapter 1.

You can change these if you need to, but you don't at this point. It is good to know where to go to reassign the values in a case, however, should the need arise.

The Global Options

There are a number of global customizations that can be performed on the EnCase interface to suit the individual analyst's preference for a working environment. These are accessed through the Options dialog (Figure 2-20). This dialog is accessed by selecting Options from the Tools menu. The Options dialog opens and we are presented with quite a few tabs. Not all of these tabs are important to go over just now, but we will look at a few that make a difference in how your environment works.

The Global Tab

This tab is arguably one of the most important in the Options window. In this tab, you can change the defaults for:

▶ How conditions are displayed (true/false)

▶ How lost files are displayed

▶ How pictures are displayed

▶ How dates and times are displayed

▶ Which code page is used

Figure 2-20   *Options dialog, Global tab*

Conditions are displayed by default in the Table pane as having a bullet point (solid circle) if the condition resolves to true and nothing displayed if the condition resolves to false. You can change this to any character you want—and a "T" for true and "F" for false is a common change to make here. The symbol is used for compatibility with non-English versions of the product, but you can change this to suit your preference.

Lost files can be flagged if you choose this option. By default they are not flagged. The picture formatting is discussed below. Date and time formats can be configured several ways to reflect the examiner's preference as well.

New to version 7, in the Pictures Options area, note the Force Ordered Rendering In Gallery check box. This is off by default, and EnCase will render the pictures in order of size—smallest to largest—so that the pictures will come up quickly in the

Gallery view. When this option is checked, however, it forces EnCase to render the pictures in the order you have them sorted, which may not be as fast. This is something to keep in mind when setting this option.

> ### TIP
> *I recommend that you change the Invalid Picture Timeout value to a lower number — the default of 12 seconds can be a very long time for each picture if there is a problem rendering.*

The choices made in this tab become the new default for the EnCase environment, so choose carefully. Also note, for the choices you make on this and other tabs, there is no "return to default" button. If you are going to change the values of anything in this area, my advice is to record the previous value before you make any changes. That way you know what it should be set back to if you don't like the results. The choices you make are saved once you click OK. It does not require additional case or global saves to make these changes persistent.

The Date Tab

Another new addition with version 7 of EnCase is the option to Display time zone on dates. This can be useful if you are using evidence files from multiple time zones.

The Data Paths Tab

This is new to version 7 as well, and allows you to share evidence files and other EnCase files such as EnScripts, search criteria, and conditions with fellow analysts. This is typically pointed to a mapped shared drive to allow everyone to use a central location.

As you can see, there are a large number of options that you can customize in this dialog with its many tabs. We'll discuss them further as features come up, but in the meantime, you should take some time to familiarize yourself with the various options they present.

Adding Your First Evidence

Much of the interface is not viewable until you add an item of evidence. If you look at the options for adding evidence, you will notice that there is no option for just adding a single file that is in its native format. Why would you want to do this? Well, for instance, say you have a case where you've been asked to look at someone's Exchange email from the server. The Exchange administrator provides you with

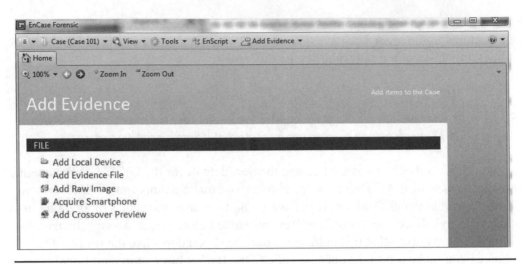

Figure 2-21   *Options for adding evidence*

a single file with a PST extension. How do you get this into EnCase? It's actually very simple, although if you hadn't seen someone do it, it might not occur to you that it is supported. Looking under the Add Evidence screen or the Add Evidence pull-down menu from the Case screen, you will not find any mention of adding single files.

There is an Add Evidence File option in the screen shown in Figure 2-21, but that is only to add files that are in the EnCase evidence file format—not single files you have acquired in their native format.

To add a single file, simply drag and drop a file from Windows Explorer (or your desktop, etc.) into EnCase. However, you will need to be in the Evidence Browser to do this. You can see this on the Case screen under the Browse section (Figure 2-22). Clicking the Evidence link opens the Evidence Browser.

EVIDENCE	
🗃 Add Evidence	Add items to the Case
BROWSE	
⌺ Evidence	Evidence in the case
🖾 Records	Processed data, such as email and internet artifacts
REPORT	
🖾 Reports	Reports created from report templates

Figure 2-22   *The EnCase Evidence Browser*

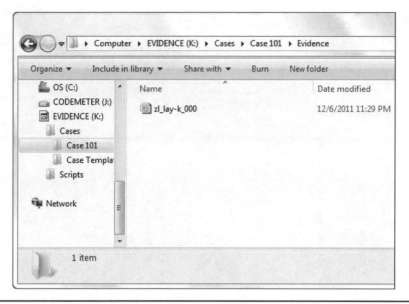

Figure 2-23 *Windows Explorer with Ken Lay's PST file*

Once there, you will be dropped into the Evidence Browser screen. We will discuss how navigation works in this part of EnCase in just a second, but first, we need to pull in our evidence. For demonstration purposes, I am using one of the Enron email archives (in Outlook PST format) that is hosted by the EDRM.net site. This is an excellent site for information on eDiscovery and the surrounding processes and requirements, but they also host the entire set of PST files collected in the Enron litigation case. For this example, I chose a small but pivotal file—Ken Lay's PST, which you can see in Figure 2-23, as shown in Windows Explorer.

Now I can drag and drop this PST file from the Windows Explorer window onto the Tree pane (the left-most pane that says "Evidence"), and you should see something like the screen shown in Figure 2-24.

This shows that the PST file is brought in as a single piece of evidence. The View pane at the bottom shows some details about the file, and in the Table pane on the top right, "Single Files" is a hyperlink. If you click on that link, Single Files now shows up in the Tree pane under Entries. If you then highlight Single Files in the Tree pane, you will see the individual file we added in the Table pane (Figure 2-25).

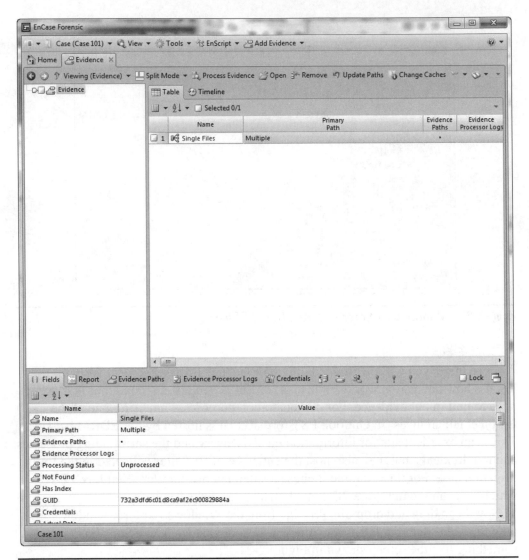

Figure 2-24 *The Evidence Browser with single files activated*

You have a number of choices as to what you can do from here; most will be covered in a later lesson in depth (see Chapter 8 for dealing with PST files). But this gets us to a point where we can see our evidence in the Evidence Browser, and we can now explore navigation and how the tabular view screen works. Since we have added evidence to this case, we should perform another case-level save to ensure it will be in our case and ready for use the next time we open this case.

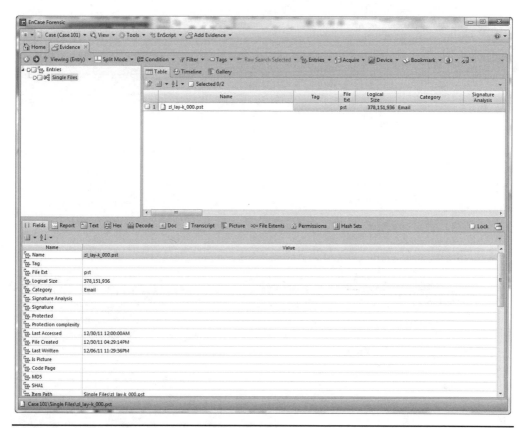

Figure 2-25 *The EnCase Evidence Browser showing our PST*

Navigating EnCase

Now that we have our first case opened and saved, and we are working with EnCase in authenticated mode, we can talk a bit about navigation. For those of you who have used prior versions of EnCase, the Evidence Browser will be the most familiar to you in terms of the visual interface. Where before we had the Tree, Table, View, and Filter panes, we now have only the Tree, Table, and View panes in the Evidence Browser. Figure 2-26 shows each of the panes.

Each of these panes serves a specific purpose, and what happens in one pane causes more detail to appear in the subsequent pane. Each of the panes can be resized, and they can be moved around as well. Resizing is accomplished by positioning your

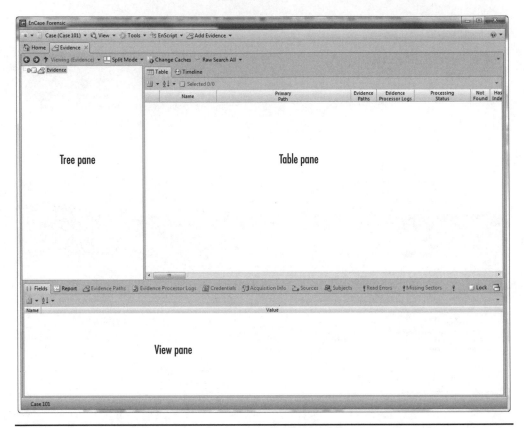

Figure 2-26   *Navigation panes in the EnCase Evidence Browser*

mouse over the double vertical or horizontal sizing lines. Your cursor will change to a double arrow, and you can click and drag the boundary to where you want it. You can also undock some tabs. Using the drop-down arrow menu at the far right of the View pane, there is an option to undock from the Tab menu. Once undocked, if you want it to return to the previous docked state, click the close button (the X at the far top right of that window) to close the tab.

The Tree Pane

The Tree pane shows all the evidence that has been added to the case in a hierarchical tree structure, much like the Windows Explorer file manager does. As with Windows Explorer, when you click on a directory in the Tree pane, more detail is shown in the

Table pane next to it. The tree structure operates just like Windows Explorer using plus and minus signs to expand and contract the directory tree structure and provide more detail. Additionally, if you right-click on items in the Tree pane, you will see a context menu that pertains to the item you have selected. When you select a folder in the Tree pane, you can see the details of its contents in the Table pane. In this manner, the level detail becomes more granular as it flows from one pane to another providing drill-down views into our case.

The Table Pane

The Table pane's contents are controlled by your actions in the Tree pane. The Table pane shows the detail of whatever item is selected in the Tree pane, and there are numerous ways to either include or exclude items from displaying based on how they are selected. The columns in the Table pane are also dynamic and depend on the properties of the items being displayed. This is configurable by the user to a certain extent, and the columns can be dragged to reorder them. Sorts, filters, and conditions can be applied to the data to change how it is viewed. Many of the context menu items that used to be available when you right-clicked on the column contents have been dispersed to other parts of the user interface with version 7. However, subsequent versions have restored much of the right-click functionality.

The View Pane

The same relationship that exists between the Tree and Table panes is in place between the Table and View panes. Again, what is displayed in the View pane is dependent on what is selected in the Table pane. The View pane is where the most detail is provided, and the highest level of granularity is achieved on a specific item. Only one item at a time is displayed in the View pane, but multiple views can be had of the same item by clicking on the tabs across the top. The View pane can display the item in Text, Hex, Doc, Transcript, Picture, and Report formats. Not all of these formats will display for all items—it is dependent on the characteristics of the item being shown. There are also some new options on the View pane's button bar that were added in version 7.

Run Book: Creating a New Case

1. Launch EnCase.

2. Click New Case on the Home screen.

3. Choose a case template type.

4. Fill in information on file paths, examiner, etc.

5. Save the case.

6. Copy additional files/folders from your established template folder in Windows Explorer.

Summary

We have covered quite a bit of information in this chapter—installation of the product, creating a case, adding some initial evidence, learning about basic navigation and how to customize our environment. We've also added our first Run Book process and addressed how evidence should be moved from computer to computer when doing so by hand. In the next chapter, we'll look at some basic EnCase concepts and build on this beginning.

EnCase Concepts

I
n this chapter, you are introduced to some of the fundamental concepts you'll need to be familiar with for using EnCase. They include the case file, which is where EnCase stores the work that you do in your case; the new evidence file format and some of the features that are now available to you; using the encryption options and how to convert legacy evidence files into the new format; and templates, which can be customized to suit the needs of your situation.

The EnCase Case File

When you create a new case and save it for the first time, EnCase creates a case file (with the file extension .Case). This is where the details of the case and the case-specific work you've done in the tool are saved. When you perform a case level save, as we discussed in Chapter 2, this is the file you are changing.

So what does a saved case file contain? Everything you've done in the case. It contains the results of your work on the evidence, including bookmarks, tags, keywords you've created, the results of the searches you have performed, reports you have created, and so on. This file is constantly changing, which is why the automatic backup is so important. If EnCase crashes midway through a case, your actions may be lost if you haven't saved your case in a while. However, if you have configured EnCase to do periodic automatic saves, chances are that you will avoid losing much work. It also helps if the case file becomes corrupted—you can go back to the case backup file. By default, your case is saved every 30 minutes, and you can go to the Case menu and choose Case Backup to determine if you have enabled this feature.

You can see some of what is contained in the case file by opening it in EnCase and looking at the Case Info Items link under the Case section of the Home tab (Figure 3-1). This shows you the basic information you entered when you created the case.

		Name	Value
1		Case Number	101
2		Case Date	01/01/2012
3		Examiner Name	S. Widup
4		Examiner I.D. #	1001
5		Agency	Widgets, Inc.
6		Description	Sample Case

Figure 3-1   *The Case Info Items tab*

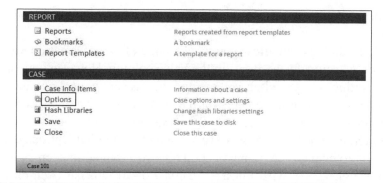

Figure 3-2   *Case options from the Home tab*

There are some case-specific options that are configurable. These are accessible from the Options dialog in the Home tab once you have an open case (Figure 3-2).

Clicking on the Options link brings up the Options dialog—which contain options specific to this case, and should not be confused with the Global Options dialog that makes changes to the way the EnCase environment is configured regardless of the open case.

As you can see in Figure 3-3, this dialog contains some of the same information as the Case Info Items tab, but here you can also see the settings for the case backup

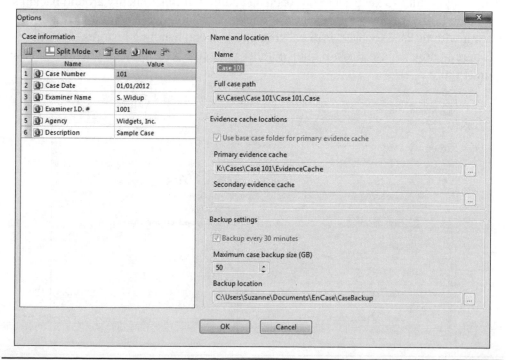

Figure 3-3   *The Case Options dialog*

and the evidence cache(s). You set these parameters when you created the case for the first time.

Both of these dialogs will allow you to edit some of the information associated with the case—specifically the items in the Value column. However, as you can see, many of the settings chosen when you created the case are grayed out and cannot be changed. You are able to change paths for the evidence cache and backup location, but you can no longer make a change to the check boxes associated with those two settings. In fact, the backup settings were located in the Global Options dialog, with the option to change how many backup files you wanted to keep as well, for versions 7 through 7.3.01. With EnCase version 7.04.01, this has been moved off the Global Options and into the Case Options. When you create a new case now, you no longer have the option to specify how often you want the case backup to run as well. It will prompt you if you deselect the Backup Every 30 Minutes check box, asking if you are sure you want to disable this feature—which makes this a toggle for whether you will be performing auto-save backups of the .Case file.

Case Backups

This brings us to another important point. With the restructure of the Global option that previously allowed you to define how often the case file would be backed up and how many backup files to keep, there has been an addition of functionality around backups. Guidance Software now provides a Case Backup Dashboard as a central location for dealing with tasks associated with backing up cases and handling restores.

There is now a Case Backup choice under your case's menu once you have a case open (Figure 3-4).

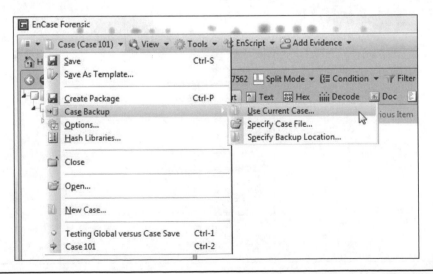

Figure 3-4   *The Case Backup menu*

You have several options for the submenu. I chose Use Current Case, but you can also use this to set up backups for another case file, or to change where you want the backup file to be stored. Having chosen Use Current Case, EnCase brings up the Case Backup dialog, where you can do a number of new things (Figure 3-5).

Clicking the Create Scheduled button on the menu bar will generate an immediate backup of the existing case file. This term is a bit misleading, in that it implies that you can schedule a backup for a future date/time when it actually means "make a backup right now."

The Create Custom option allows you to save the case backup under a new name as well. You can also restore from an existing backup or change your settings in this section.

When you create a backup, it will be placed in the folders as listed. This interface works like the Tree and Table panes, so clicking on a folder in the left pane will display the backups that have been completed as shown in Figure 3-6.

In the Case Options dialog, we saw that the backups were set to every 30 minutes. This Scheduled folder is where those backups will be listed. If you click on the Create Scheduled button, the backup created from that operation (in addition to the regularly scheduled every 30 minute backups) will also be listed here.

The Daily, Weekly, and Monthly folders will contain backups that are arranged by their proximity to the current date—for instance, if the backup was made a week ago, it will appear in the Weekly but not the Monthly folder. The backup file that was generated closest to the current day's local midnight time will be in the Daily folder. There may be others that are on the same date, but they will be in the Scheduled folder.

As I mentioned, you can also create a custom backup. Clicking Create Custom brings up the dialog shown in Figure 3-7.

Provide a name for the file, and it will go into the default location you specified when you created the case. You will see the backups created this way in the Custom folder.

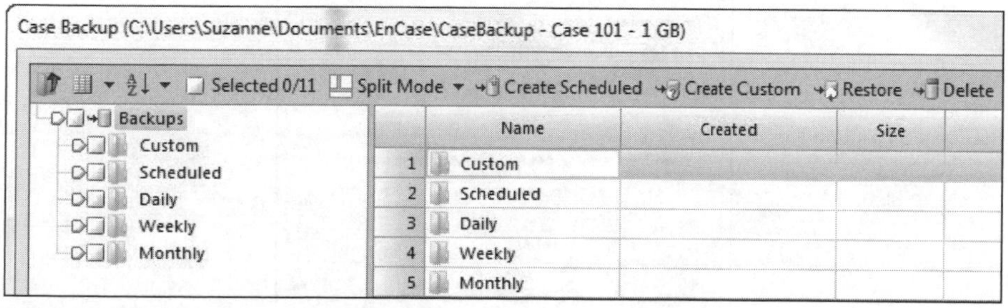

Figure 3-5 *The Case Backup dialog*

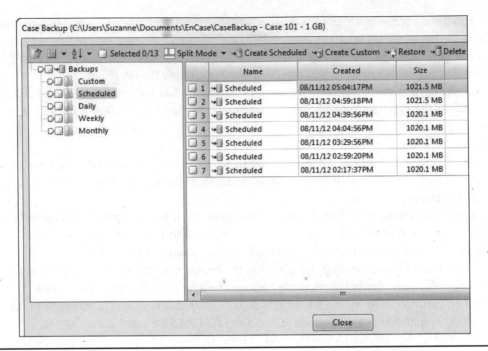

Figure 3-6   *Scheduled backup list*

Your final option is to make changes to the settings. You do this by clicking the Change Case Settings button on the menu bar. This will open the dialog shown in Figure 3-8.

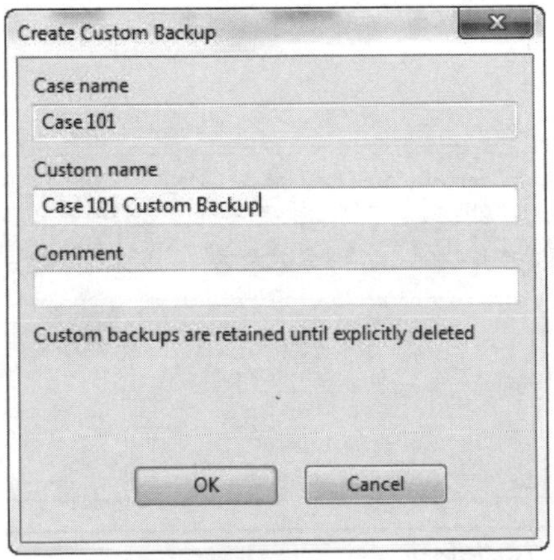

Figure 3-7   *The Create Custom Backup dialog*

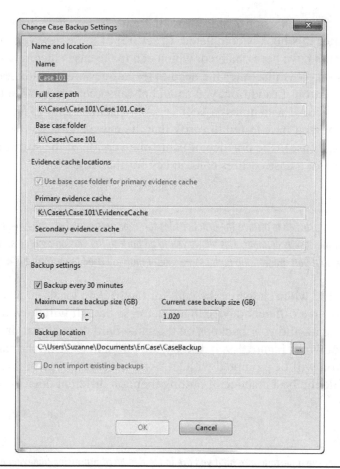

Figure 3-8   *The Change Case Backup Settings dialog*

You can turn backups off by unchecking the Backup Every 30 Minutes check box (you will be prompted for confirmation). You can also change the maximum total case backup size and the folder location where backup files are stored. This dialog also lets you know the current case backup size, which is helpful in determining how large to make that maximum value. By default, EnCase stores a maximum of 48 scheduled backups, 7 daily backups, and 5 weekly backups. The monthly backups are automatically kept until the maximum size is reached, and then the oldest are deleted until the total is again under that maximum.

There are also options to delete backups and to restore from a specific case file. You cannot restore from the case file when you have one open, however. You would be prompted to close the file and then make a selection. When you have no open case, you will find the Case Backups option on the Case menu.

Since the release of version 7 of EnCase, there have been nine point releases, and will be more after this book is completed. In several of these new versions, the case structure elements have been changed, which can make cases incompatible from version to version. This illustrates the need to test all new versions before migrating to them in production. In addition, you should always keep the version that you worked a specific case with unless a later version was necessary to fix a problem you encountered (and you have tested to verify that the new version will not undo your prior work on the case). The practice of using one version of the software from the start to the finish of a case ensures consistency for that case.

TIP

Make it a practice to archive the installer files for prior versions when you have cases in them, even if the case is dormant. This allows you to go back to the version associated with a specific case so that you are working in the same toolset that you used to perform the original analysis.

One final point: when choosing the path for the backup location, a best practice is to store those on a different device than your case data. It will do you no good to store your case data and your backups on the same hard drive if that drive fails.

In fact, as shown in Figure 3-9, if you try to put the backup on the same device as your case, you will be prompted with an "Are you sure?" type of message. While you can override the best practice of putting them on different devices, it is not recommended.

NOTE

You may see a performance hit if you are in the middle of processing/indexing a case and also have a backup running on the same drive.

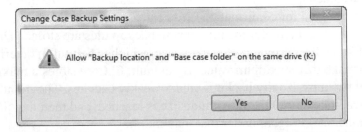

Figure 3-9 *Backup warning*

The EnCase Evidence File

When you acquire evidence in EnCase, it is saved in the EnCase Evidence File Format. This format is a bit-by-bit copy of the data (copied in blocks) along with a cyclic redundancy check (CRC) verification value. The CRC values are calculated on each block of data, and if a change is made to that data, the CRC result will not match—indicating to EnCase that something has gone wrong in the acquisition process and thus alerting the examiner performing the acquisition that there is a problem. EnCase will specify which block of data has experienced the problem. This specific block(s) can be reacquired separately, instead of requiring the entire evidence file to be reacquired. However, in practical experience, I prefer to perform the entire acquisition again until I get a clean file, time permitting. Keep in mind, if you do decide to go back and reacquire just those specific blocks using this feature, you will need to be comfortable in explaining what you did and why (potentially in court), which is why I recommend reacquiring the entire device for simplicity's sake.

Once the acquisition is completed, EnCase will generate the acquisition hash value on all the data (it does not use the CRC values or the headers to this file when doing the calculation—only the data blocks themselves). When you later add evidence to a case, EnCase will compute a verification hash and compare this to the acquisition hash. If they match, the evidence file is verified and added to the case. If they do not match, EnCase pops up a notification indicating that there was a problem with the evidence verification. If these two hashes do not match, this indicates that something in the evidence file has changed since the acquisition hash was completed.

With the upgrade from EnCase version 6 to version 7, Guidance Software has not only made major changes to the way the product looks and behaves, it has also introduced version 2 of the EnCase Evidence file. For those who are familiar with .E01 and .L01 files, there are a number of similarities. Both formats store data in blocks with their related 32-bit CRC value, and the hash if specified during acquisition. Both support MD5 and/or SHA-1 hashing algorithms. The new Evidence File Format, with the file extensions of .Ex01 and .Lx01, adds a number of new capabilities. One of the most important is support for encryption of the data. If the evidence files are encrypted, and they are subsequently intercepted or lost, the data is still protected from a loss of confidentiality even if the recipient had the ability to open the files in EnCase. Even in a hex editor, the files would be unreadable because the person who intercepts them does not have the encryption key to decrypt them.

The new format also provides support for the bzip2 compression algorithm to make the stored evidence files more compact. Both versions of the EnCase Evidence File Format are documented in the Guidance Software Document Library.

It is important to note that while you can open .E01 and .L01 evidence files in EnCase version 7 and above, the older versions of EnCase cannot open the new .Ex01 and .Lx01 evidence files, with one exception. EnCase 6.19.1 has the ability to open .Ex01/.Lx01 files, but it is not able to generate them. There is no other backwards compatibility in the older versions of EnCase to handle the new file format.

Reacquiring Evidence

There may come a time when you have evidence in the old .E01 or .L01 formats and want to convert it to the new .Ex01 or .Lx01 formats. For instance, if you want to take advantage of the encryption support, or you want to change the compression options, you can reacquire the evidence and make those adjustments. If you need to share the evidence file with another EnCase user, you can choose options that will only allow them to decrypt the evidence file.

You reacquire evidence by opening the evidence file in EnCase, and from within the Evidence Browser, placing a blue check next to the top level entry for that evidence file. Then you can right-click on that hard drive icon in the Tree pane and choose either Acquire (for .E01 to .Ex01 files) or Create Logical Evidence File (for .L01 to .Lx01 files) from the pop-up menu as shown in Figure 3-10.

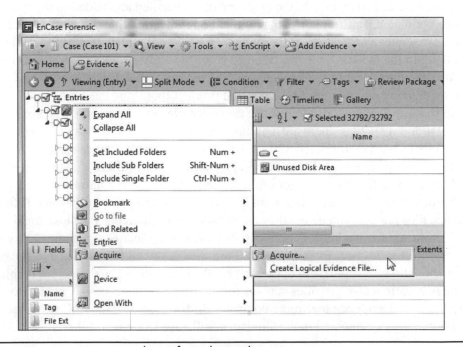

Figure 3-10   *Reacquiring evidence from the Evidence Browser*

When should you choose to acquire versus create a logical evidence file? Generally, Acquire is your best option when you have a device level image to create. If you have an entire drive you want to image, for example, and you want to include all of the drive—both allocated and unallocated—then choose to Acquire and create an .Ex01 file. If, in contrast, you want to acquire files that are already on a file system (such as an Outlook PST file that has been extracted from the Exchange email server), this is a good candidate for a logical evidence file.

E01 to Ex01 Options

Using the Acquire Device dialog (Figure 3-11), you can reacquire your evidence, and by choosing to output it as Ex01, move it from the old format into the new Evidence File Format. The Location tab is asking for the output path for the .Ex01 file you will create with this process. I am using the evidence file associated with the case study we will use in future chapters.

The Format tab gives you options to change the compression and the verification hash algorithm, and for adding encryption. The Advanced tab allows you to adjust the block size, start and stop sector, and the error granularity. The error granularity refers to what portion of the block is zeroed out when errors are encountered—this defaults to Standard, which sets this value equal to the block size value. If you choose the Exhaustive option, the value is set to 1 sector, which will take more time, but should save more data. This tab also allows you to configure the number of reader threads

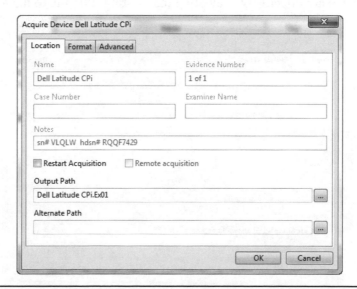

Figure 3-11   *The Acquire Device dialog*

(this is only enabled if you selected .E01 format), which are how many threads are reading from the evidence you are acquiring (range from 1 to 5 with a default of 0); and the number of worker threads (both file formats), which work on the compression of the data (range of 1 to 20, with a default of 5). If you are not sure what value you want here, I recommend you take the defaults. For a system that is dedicated to evidence acquisition, choosing the maximum makes sense, but unless that is the case, you will be competing against any other processes you have functioning on your system, so prioritize accordingly.

TIP

The Advanced tab of the Acquire Device dialog has one option that you may find particularly useful. EnCase will now allow you to keep the Globally Unique Identifier (GUID) associated with the evidence. In prior versions, this GUID would change when you reacquired the evidence, and as forensic examiners, we don't like anything that changes from one copy of an evidence file to another. Changes to evidence is something we have to be prepared to explain in a court of law. The Keep GUID option is now checked by default.

L01 to Lx01 Options

As you can see in Figure 3-12, the options for creating a logical evidence file are similar to the Acquire Options dialog. You have the option of creating a new file or adding the selected files to an existing logical evidence file. Again, by specifying the .Lx01 file extension, we are effectively converting the existing .L01 file to the new format.

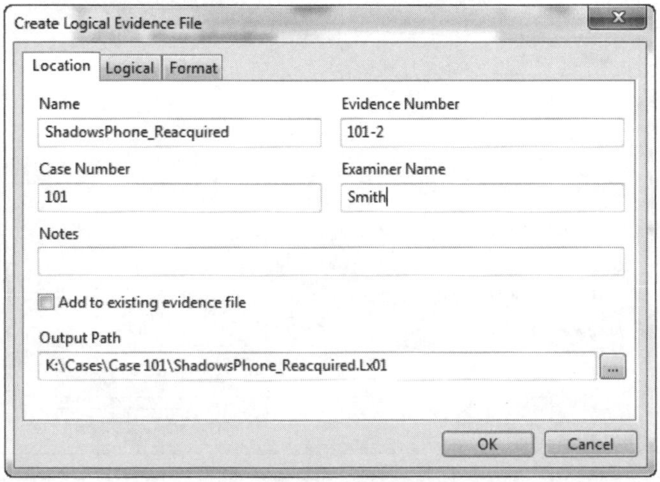

Figure 3-12   *Create Logical Evidence File options dialog*

The main advantage of creating a logical evidence file is to be able to pick and choose what files you want it to contain. It still copies them in a forensically sound manner, preserving all the meta data and the integrity of the files, but you can create subsets of the entire device and share just what you need to. The option to add to an existing evidence file is an example of that type of functionality. If you have already created a .Lx01 file, you can just add more contents using this option. As with the Acquire Device dialog, you need to enter (or browse to) the path where you want EnCase to store the new logical evidence file you are creating.

On the Logical tab, you have more options that are associated just with logical acquisitions. Since you can select which files you want to put in a logical evidence file (you are not restricted to taking the entire set of files unless you want to—it is dependent on which files you have selected with a blue check), it shows you a list of how many files and their size. You can also specify a target folder if you prefer.

The Format tabs of both the Acquire Device and the Create Logical Evidence File dialogs are quite similar. They both contain the option of selecting either the legacy (.E01/.L01) or current (.Ex01/.Lx01) file formats.

NOTE

If you select the legacy version of the file format, the Password option becomes enabled.

The Acquire Device dialog allows for the selection of MD5 and/or SHA-1 as a verification hash (or none), while the only option for the entry hash is MD5 or none. Both allow for compression to be turned on or off. Both allow for the file segment size to be adjusted. The file segment size tells EnCase when to split the evidence file into segments. These will be named in ascending order (for example, .Ex01, .Ex02, .Ex03, etc.) until the evidence acquisition has completed. They will all be placed into the same directory and have the same base name, just the file extension will increment.

TIP

Why split an evidence file up? This is used primarily when burning them onto fixed media such as a DVD. If you can't fit the entire evidence file on one disc, you can split it up and make it small enough.

Using Encryption with Ex01 and Lx01 Files

In the prior section, I discussed the Format tab from the Acquire Device and Create Logical Evidence File dialogs. Figure 3-13 shows the dialog, but the steps are very similar when doing this with logical evidence files.

Figure 3-13   *The Acquire Device dialog Format tab*

To encrypt the evidence file you are creating, click the Encryption button on this tab (or the Create Logical Evidence File dialog—they lead to the same place). The Encryption Details dialog will launch, where you can set up the encryption (Figure 3-14).

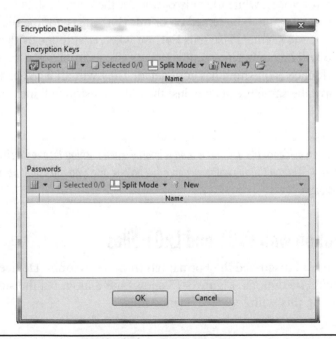

Figure 3-14   *The Encryption Details dialog*

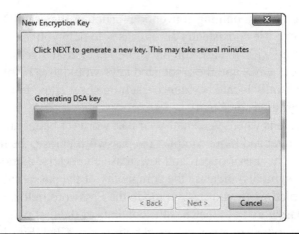

Figure 3-15 *The New Encryption Key dialog*

If you haven't already, you will need to generate your encryption keys. To do this, click the New button at the top right of the dialog's menu. The New Encryption Key dialog will appear (Figure 3-15). Click Next to generate the new key pair (public and private).

A progress bar will appear on this window, and then you will be presented with a Password dialog (Figure 3-16). You can change the name of your key here; for instance, if you use the same key for all your cases, you may want to call it by the analyst's name, or if you generate a new key for each case, that would be another option. You can see the default is Encryption Key1, which is not very descriptive. The name will increment the number at the end if you generate another key, so you can see where it could get confusing quickly if you don't give these keys relevant names.

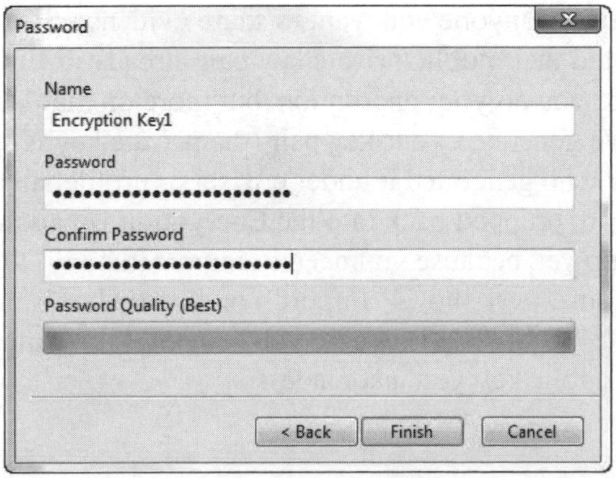

Figure 3-16 *Generating the encryption key pair*

I recommend deciding on a naming convention—such as the case ID, or some other identifier that you can use consistently across cases to help you identify which case each key is associated with, in case you have to go back to it a year later. A tracking method that lists your cases and the associated keys would also be of use (a section in the case file or a centrally located evidence tracking sheet come to mind as potential methods for managing this problem).

The Password field is where you enter your password (or better and more secure—a passphrase). The longer and more complex the password/phrase, the more the quality bar will turn green. The use of upper- and lowercase characters, numbers, and special characters (such as symbols) increase the complexity of the passphrase. The Finish button will be disabled when you start typing in the Password field and will be enabled when the second password field matches the contents of the first one. That is how you can tell that you typed identical values in both boxes. Click Finish when this is completed, and you will see a dialog that asks you where to save the newly generated public key. The default is with the evidence file that you just created. EnCase uses public key cryptography, which encrypts files using a pair of keys—a public key and a private key. Specifically, you encrypt a file you want to share with your private key and their public key. The person you send the file to can then decrypt the file using their private key and your public key.

CAUTION

This brings up an important point—protection of the private keys. A public key is meant to be shared with those whom you want to share encrypted files. The private key, in contrast, needs to be protected from unauthorized access and is not meant to be shared. It is a good practice to keep a copy of this key someplace other than the hard drive where it is typically used, so that in an emergency, you can recover it.

It should be noted that anyone you want to share evidence files with is going to need to have generated their public/private key pair already in EnCase and sent you the public key before you do your encryption, but more on that later.

Now that you have generated your key pair (the private key is stored in the profile directory of the user who generated it under c:\Users\<profilename>\My Documents\ EnCase\Keys), you are dropped back into the Encryption Details screen. Your public key is not showing up yet, because you need to import it. To do this, click on the open folder icon (mouse-over shows "Import") on the top box's menu bar. You will see the Import dialog (Figure 3-17), where you can enter the path to the key you want to import (the public key you just made).

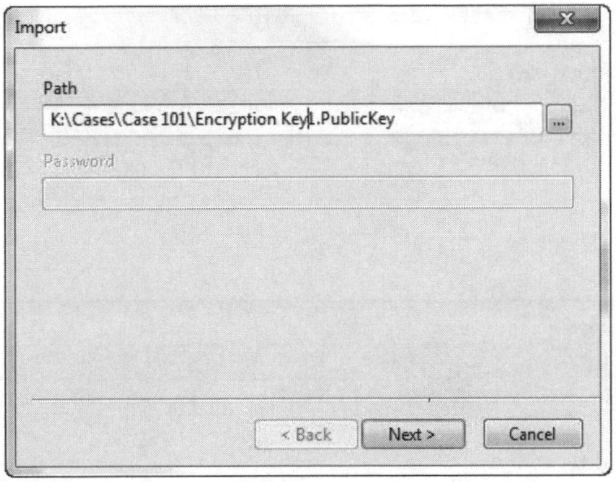

Figure 3-17 *The Import Key dialog*

Verify the path to your new key is correct, or browse to a new location and select it. Click Next. You are then presented with a Password dialog where you can give the key a display name for the Encryption Details dialog to show in the list (Figure 3-18).

Note, this won't change the actual name of the public key you select—this is just for display in the list that the Encryption Details section shows you. However, descriptive names here are just as important to help you remember which key goes with the evidence file(s).

Clicking Finish gets you back to the Encryption Details dialog, and now you can see that you have your key listed (Figure 3-19). Select it with a blue check,

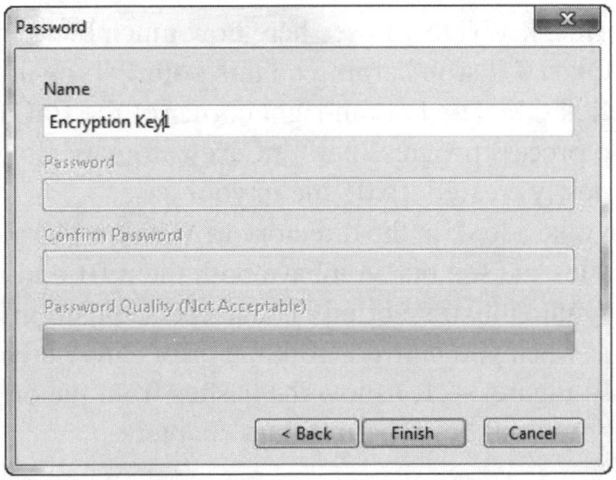

Figure 3-18 *Adding a descriptive name*

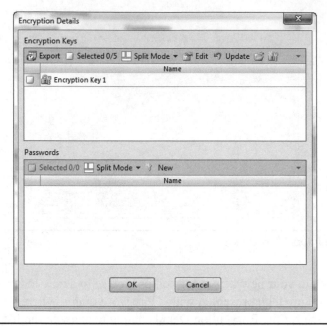

Figure 3-19 *The Encryption Details dialog with your key added*

and click OK. EnCase will then proceed with creating the evidence file with the parameters you specified. You can see the progress bar at the bottom right corner of the interface. When the file creation completes, you are prompted to enter the password and select the key you chose to allow for the verification process to begin (Figure 3-20).

Select the appropriate key. (Do you see here how much better it would be with descriptive names? Okay, I'll stop harping on this point.) Type in the password you assigned to it, and click OK. The bottom-right corner of the EnCase interface will show the verification process progress bar. EnCase automatically replaces the .E01 evidence with your newly created .Ex01 file in your case.

You can now also take a look at the directory in Windows Explorer where you stored the evidence files and see that you have both the .E01 and .Ex01 files there.

Another point I want to illustrate briefly is that the acquisition and verification hashes do not change when you convert from the prior EnCase Evidence File Format to the new version. In Figure 3-21, I show the hashes from the original .E01 evidence file for the case study we will be using in future chapters.

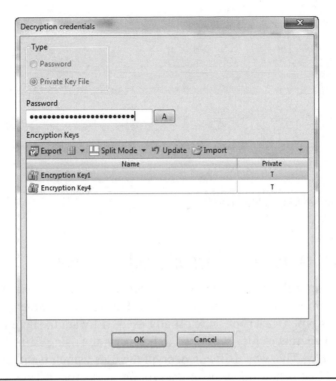

Figure 3-20   *The Decryption Credentials check dialog*

You can see that the MD5 acquisition and verification hashes are identical and that the evidence file is fully verified. Now look at the same data for the .Ex01 evidence file that we created (Figure 3-22).

The MD5 hashes remain identical. You can also see that I generated both MD5 and SHA-1 hashes for this evidence, and that both hash values verify correctly. The fact that the hashes remain identical regardless of the Evidence File Format is due to the fact that the calculations for these hashes are done solely on the data. The data is not changing, only the format it is stored in, so the integrity remains consistent.

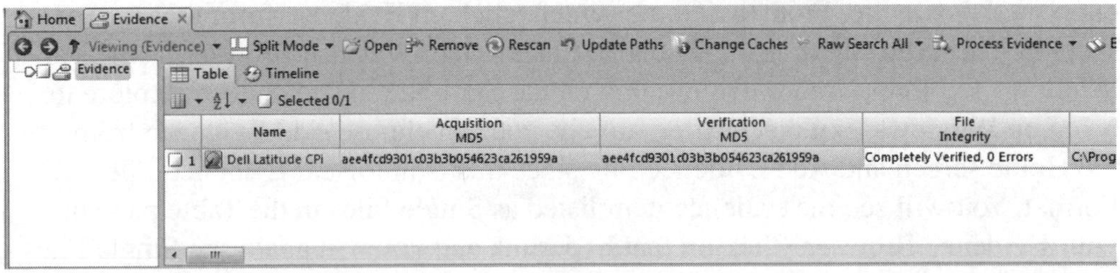

Figure 3-21   *E01 evidence file hashes*

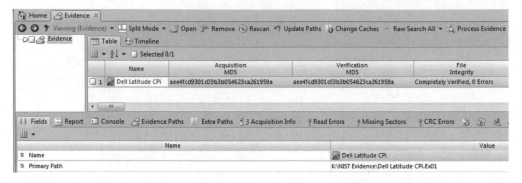

Figure 3-22   *Ex01 evidence file hashes*

Using Encryption to Share Files with Other Parties

The prior exercise will give you encrypted evidence files, but the example used our own public and private keys to encrypt the files. This is for example purposes only, and not how this type of encryption is usually used. If I want to share an evidence file with Bill, the evidence files will need to be encrypted using Bill's public key and my private key. That way, Bill can decrypt the files using his private key and my public key. That is how this type of encryption works for sharing files—the recipient's public key must be used during encryption, so their private key will be able to decrypt the file. We will need to import our colleague's public key into our system so that we can perform this.

The steps are the same—we're just reacquiring evidence to take advantage of the encryption. You can do this with evidence in both the legacy and the current formats. The only change is that when we are in the Encryption Details window, we import Bill's public key for the encryption.

Now let's say that you received a file from Bill that he encrypted with his private key and your public key. How do you work with the evidence file that he encrypted before sending it to you? With your case open, you add the evidence file just how you normally would. For this example, Bill gave you the Ken Lay email file as an encrypted .Lx01 file. From the Home screen, click on Evidence from the Browse section. Then you can drag the evidence file into the Evidence Browser from your Windows Explorer window (right-click on the Start button and choose Explore to bring up Windows Explorer). Alternatively, you can choose Add Evidence from the Home screen and Add Evidence File since this is in logical Evidence File Format. You will see the evidence item listed as Single Files in the Table pane of your Evidence Browser. Click on that hyperlink and you will again see Single Files

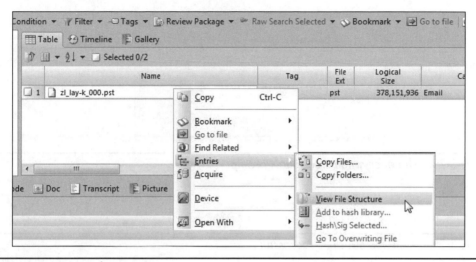

Figure 3-23   *View File Structure*

in the Table pane, with it also listed under Entries in the Tree pane. Double-clicking on Single Files in the Table pane will get you to an entry "zl_lay-k_000.pst" in the Table pane. This is an indication that the file decrypted correctly. If it had not, you would not have been able to see the contents of the file, and would have seen an error instead.

Now if you tried to double-click on this entry, you'd get an error saying that "pst" files are viewed internally. This is EnCase's way of saying that this file has an internal structure that needs to be parsed before you can work with it. You do that by right-clicking on the entry in the Table pane to bring up the context menu as shown in Figure 3-23.

From the Entries menu, choose View File Structure. You will be prompted for which options you want to choose for the parsing (Figure 3-24).

Figure 3-24   *View File Structure options*

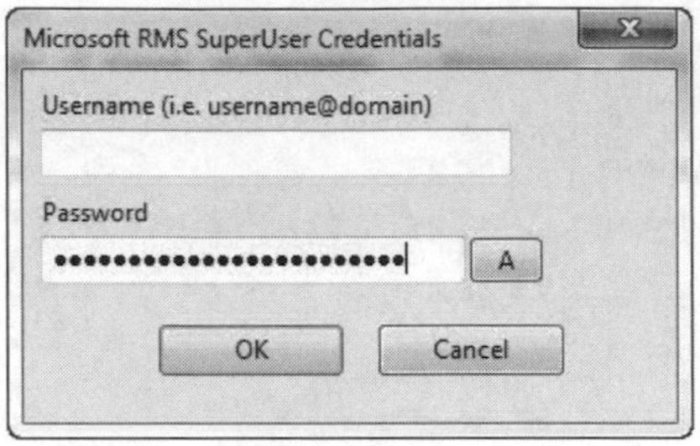

Figure 3-25 *The encryption credentials prompt*

Figure 3-26 *View file structure successful*

All of these options will not be relevant for every type of compound file, but I've chosen all of them for this example. Next, you get prompted to put in the credentials for Microsoft RMS (Figure 3-25). I tested several scenarios with this, including putting in the password to the key that I set and leaving it blank. Both worked. It isn't actually related to the encryption of the file but is due to the fact that I am working with an Outlook PST file.

If the file does not contain a PST, you will not get this prompt. I included this example so that if you see this pop-up you will know that it is not encryption related. EnCase goes on to parse the file structure regardless of what is entered in the prompt shown in Figure 3-25. For large files, this will take a while. You can see the progress bar at the bottom-right corner as usual. When it completes, it mounts the file for you. The icon next to the entry in the Table pane will change from the blank sheet of paper to one with a small green plus next to it as shown in Figure 3-26.

The name also changes to a hyperlink and you can just click on it to start looking inside this file. You've successfully opened the file your colleague sent you that he encrypted with your public and his private key.

Using Encryption in a Multi-Investigator Environment

Another thing to consider is if the file is encrypted, what if the person whose key was used is on vacation or otherwise unable to be there to decrypt the file? One option you may want to consider is having the file encrypted with multiple keys, including one that is used for all of your evidence files as an emergency recovery key. That way even if someone leaves the company or gets hit by a bus, the evidence files are recoverable. The key could be designated as the data custodian key. This is something I recommend if you are working in an environment where you keep all of your evidence files on a shared disk array where your team does not maintain the hardware. By encrypting the files, you ensure confidentiality even when system administrators have full powers on the disk array to read any file. If it is encrypted, they still cannot read it without access to the keys and knowledge of the passwords. I would further recommend keeping a copy of this shared key in a very safe place (preferably offline on alternative media, perhaps in an evidence safe). Remember, as with all of the encryption demonstrated here, EnCase will not be able to recover your files if you forget the password to the keys or if the only place you kept your private key suffers a media failure. Plan carefully how to manage the keys for your evidence.

To encrypt with multiple keys, simply import them into your Encryption Details screen as usual, and then you can blue-check multiple keys at the same time. Any of the keys you have checked will work to open the evidence file.

The alternative to using the Encryption Details screen (if, for instance, you want to import multiple keys at once, or don't want to do this in conjunction with reacquiring evidence) is to copy the keys into your key folder. This is by default under the profile of the user running EnCase (C:\Users\<profilename>\Documents\EnCase\Keys in Windows 7).

TIP

The support for encryption brings with it the need to manage both the keys associated with each encrypted file, and the passwords/passphrases that go with them. I recommend using a password manager to keep track of the passwords in addition to managing the keys. There are a number of freeware password managers available, and even commercial solutions that are specifically designed for privileged account management. Managing your encryption keys and passphrases is just another part of managing your evidence lifecycle.

EnCase Configuration (ini) Files

EnCase stores configuration information in several locations, depending on whether it is a global setting (affecting all cases) or a case-specific setting. The parameters are stored in configuration files called "ini" files (due to the file extension of .ini that these files all share). Global ini files are stored in the installation directory under \Config\. For the installation we performed earlier, that would be C:\Program Files (x86)\EnCase7.04\Config. Default files are FileTypes.ini and TextStyles.ini. File Types is how EnCase associates specific file headers and/or file extensions with applications on the system. These can be edited from the View menu choosing File Types. This brings up the File Types tab (Figure 3-27).

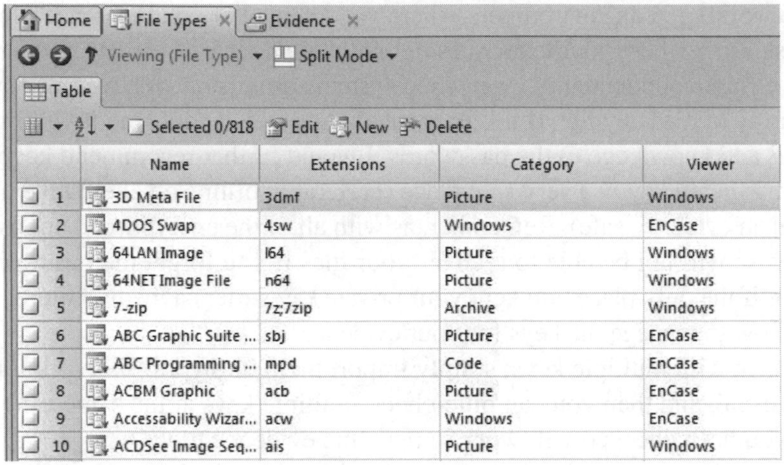

Figure 3-27 *The File Types tab*

Here you can add custom file types that your organization uses or you have encountered on other cases. Windows identifies files using the file extension (i.e., .docx is associated with Word files, .xslx is associated with Excel files, and so on). However, a common technique to disguise a file is to change the extension. So let's say I found a Word document that contained the secret formula for turning lead into gold and I wanted to steal it, but I knew that the email filters delete any file with the .docx extension. To get around this, I change the file extension to .jpg, and the email filters let the file through because .jpg is a graphics file and those are allowed. When an examiner brings up my file in EnCase, it will show the extension and identify it as a graphics file. If I perform a signature analysis, EnCase will look at the first few bytes of the file (called the header) and potentially the last few bytes (called the footer) depending on the file type and identify the file's type based on that data. This signature analysis will then show that there is a mismatch between the file's extension and the signature, and flag the file for further inspection. Signature analysis is a powerful tool in the examiner's arsenal, and the File Types tab is where you can define new signatures. Many companies write their own in-house software, and these programs frequently store their data in proprietary file structures. By writing new file types for these, the examiner can add to the abilities of EnCase to perform an accurate signature analysis.

As you can see, you can get as specific as you like—if you have information on consistent headers and footers, for example, I highly recommend putting them here, because they will be used for signature analysis during evidence processing. If all you have is the file extension, it will still allow you to associate a specific application with it, but if someone has changed the file extension to try and hide the real file type, it will not detect this behavior.

The TextStyles.ini file is for configuration of text, as the name indicates, and is where EnCase stores this information.

The case-specific .ini files are stored in the user's profile. For my installation, it is under C:\Users\<profilename>\AppData\Roaming\EnCase\EnCase-7.04.01\Config. There are a number of files under this directory, but I want to draw your attention to a few important ones. The local.ini file contains the most recent case paths and the other historical parameters that show what you last did when you go back into the Home screen. The FileTypes.ini file in this directory is where the changes you make to the File Types tab will be stored—but only after you've completed a global save. In testing, I found that a case save did not change this file. Even having performed a global save did not add the new text style I defined to the global ini file, so changes are stored here on a per-user basis.

Viewers.ini stores the customized file viewers that you have added to EnCase. These are also associated in the File Types tab. In addition to defining new file headers, footers, and extensions, you can also associate that new record with a file viewer if there is one available. You can specify the length of the file (the default used if not specified is 4096 bytes) if a footer is not available. You can associate with an installed EnCase viewer by choosing the EnCase radio button, or if you have a Windows application installed, you can choose that radio button to specify which application you want to view the data in when encountered. The installed viewers option will bring up a list of already installed viewers to choose from. Keep in mind that using these viewers will not alter the evidence file.

Case Templates

Case templates are new to version 7 of EnCase and can be quite useful to ensure that specific case types are handled the same way from start to finish. Several templates are provided, and you may customize or create new ones to suit your needs. You access the templates when creating a new case.

I typically use the Forensic template, but you can create a new template by saving an existing case as a template. From the Case menu (which when you have a case open will be the name of the case) choose Save As Template. The Save As Template dialog will open to allow you to choose the parameters you want to have as part of your new template (Figure 3-28).

As you can see, there are a number of options to choose from. I recommend if you are going to handle your templates by case type you also prepare an organizational folder structure that reflects this. For example, it would make sense to have intellectual property (IP) theft cases stored in an IP Theft folder under the Cases directory. Then preserving that path would automatically ensure that new cases using this template would be saved in the proper place.

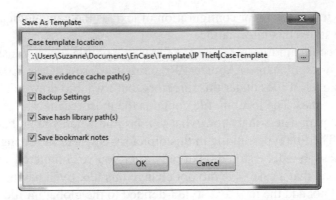

Figure 3-28 *The Save As Template dialog*

Make your choices for the new template and click OK. Now when you open a new case, you will see your new template in the list to choose from, as shown in Figure 3-29.

Figure 3-29 *New template in list*

The default templates all have the hash signs as the start to their names. These are the ones that come with EnCase standard. Right-clicking on them brings up a context menu that allows you to copy, but it only copies the name of the template—not the template itself. It would make sense for this to be the way to copy an existing template and then modify it, but it does not allow for that. Alternatively, I tried to see if I could copy a template file in Windows Explorer and rename it to get a new template (these are stored in C:\Program Files (x86)\EnCase7.04\Template in Windows 7). After Windows grumbled at me several times about needing to be Administrator, it let me copy and rename the .Template file. However, when I then launched EnCase and tried to create a new case, my new template did not show in the list. When you create your own templates, the file is stored in the profile directory of the user who is running EnCase. For Windows 7, it is C:\Users\<profilename>\Documents\EnCase\Template. Copying and pasting a template file in this directory does show up in the list when you go to create a new case, in contrast to the built-in templates.

You can select your template from the list in the Templates section and add new fields in the Case Information section. The New button will allow you to define the name and value pair for each new field you add. If you make a mistake, you can edit the fields either by right-clicking on the Name or Value field and choosing Edit, or by clicking on the field and pressing the F2 key to edit the text.

When customizing a template, it makes sense to create a new blank case and make all the changes you want to it and then save it as a template. For instance, if I took the IP Theft template that I just created and added several new fields, the changes would not be saved to the template—only to the case I was creating with it. I would have to go back and save that case as a template again with the same name to have those new fields appear in each subsequent use of the template.

Summary

We have covered the basic concepts that EnCase uses, as well as delving into how to apply some of the topics to handling your cases. With the EnCase case file backups, you can ensure that changes you make in the course of your investigation are preserved against failure of the system or storage medium. You have learned how to use encryption to protect the confidentiality of your evidence files and how to share files with others within EnCase. You have learned where the configuration files for EnCase are stored and how to customize the way that EnCase identifies files inside of the evidence container. Finally, you have learned about templates and how to customize your own set of templates based on your organization's practices.

Beginning with EnCase Forensics

U p to this point, we've been going over the basics of preparing for the forensic function, installing the software, and talking about how the EnCase interface works. Now it is time to dig in and start using the product in a case study, so you can see how to accomplish the typical tasks associated with performing a digital investigation. You are introduced to the case study we will be using and the investigative questions you will want to answer.

Chapter 4 covers adding the various forms of evidence that EnCase supports. The most common methods are covered in depth so you will be prepared to add the evidence that comes your way.

Chapter 5 digs into our case study further and shows you how to use the EnCase Evidence Processor. This is a very powerful module that automates quite a few of the preparation tasks that must be completed to facilitate later analysis.

Chapter 6 shows you where to find the results of the processed evidence and the methods of bookmarking available in EnCase Forensic. Two of the hallmark interface conventions used (the blue check and the Set Include or home plate) are covered, letting you know how to control what is being selected and displayed.

Adding Evidence

This book uses a case study approach in teaching how to use EnCase. Now that we have reached Part II of the book, it is time to introduce you to the case we will use for the rest of the chapters. You should download the evidence so you can follow along with the steps and duplicate the results. Doing so will allow you to become more comfortable with the EnCase interface before you have to apply it to an actual case. After all, trying to become familiar with EnCase in the middle of an active investigation where people are demanding answers is a much more stressful approach—I find it is easier to learn without that pressure.

Case Study: The NIST CFReDS Hacking Case

The case study in this book (www.cfreds.nist.gov/Hacking_Case.html), known as the Hacking Case scenario, is taken from the National Institute of Standards and Technology Computer Forensic Reference Data Sets (CFReDS) site (www.nist.gov) and is available for anyone to download. Here is the description of the case we will use from the NIST site:

> On 09/20/04, a Dell CPi notebook computer, serial # VLQLW, was found abandoned along with a wireless PCMCIA card and an external homemade 802.11b antennae. It is suspected that this computer was used for hacking purposes, although cannot be tied to a hacking suspect, Greg Schardt. Schardt also goes by the online nickname of "Mr. Evil" and some of his associates have said that he would park his vehicle within range of Wireless Access Points (like Starbucks and other T-Mobile Hotspots) where he would then intercept internet traffic, attempting to get credit card numbers, usernames & passwords.

> Find any hacking software, evidence of their use, and any data that might have been generated. Attempt to tie the computer to the suspect, Greg Schardt.

The scenario provides a raw image in eight parts, plus notes, and an EnCase image in two parts. There are a series of questions that we will be answering as part of our study, and while the solutions are given at the bottom of the page, they won't help much by themselves in teaching you how to use EnCase to find the answers. That is what going through the chapters in this book are geared toward—how to use the EnCase tool to accomplish the goals of your investigation. The questions are:

1. What is the image hash? Do the acquisition and verification hashes match?
2. What operating system was used on the computer?
3. When was the install date?
4. What is the time zone setting?

5. Who is the registered owner?

6. What is the computer account name?

7. What is the primary domain name?

8. When was the last recorded computer shutdown date/time?

9. How many accounts are recorded (total number)?

10. What is the account name of the user who mostly uses the computer?

11. Who was the last user to log on to the computer?

12. A search for the name "Greg Schardt" reveals multiple hits. One of these proves that Greg Schardt is Mr. Evil and is also the administrator of this computer. What file is it? What software program does this file relate to?

13. List the network cards used by this computer.

14. This same file reports the IP address and MAC address of the computer. What are they?

15. An Internet search for vendor name/model of NIC cards by MAC address can be used to find out which network interface was used. In the above answer, the first three hex characters of the MAC address report the vendor of the card. Which NIC card was used during the installation and setup for LOOK@LAN?

16. Find six installed programs that may be used for hacking.

17. What is the SMTP email address for Mr. Evil?

18. What are the NNTP (news server) settings for Mr. Evil?

19. What two installed programs show this information?

20. List five newsgroups that Mr. Evil has subscribed to.

21. A popular IRC (Internet Relay Chat) program called MIRC was installed. What are the user settings that were shown when the user was online and in a chat channel?

22. This IRC program has the capability to log chat sessions. List three IRC channels that the user of this computer accessed.

23. Ethereal, a popular "sniffing" program that can be used to intercept wired and wireless Internet packets, was also found to be installed. When TCP packets are collected and reassembled, the default save directory is that user's \My Documents directory. What is the name of the file that contains the intercepted data?

24. Viewing the file in a text format reveals much information about who and what was intercepted. What type of wireless computer was the victim (person who had his Internet surfing recorded) using?

25. What websites was the victim accessing?

26. Search for the main user's web-based email address. What is it?

27. Yahoo mail, a popular web-based email service, saves copies of the email under what file name?

28. How many executable files are in the recycle bin?

29. Are these files really deleted?

30. How many files are actually reported to be deleted by the file system?

31. Perform an antivirus check. Are there any viruses on the computer?

In preparation for working this case study, I recommend you download the evidence files (in both E01 format and in dd format—as we will use each for different sections). They are not small, so they will take some time to acquire. However, having them allows you to have access to the same files I use to illustrate how to perform the case actions. You can directly compare your results, and as long as the evidence has not been changed and the selections you make are identical to those I make, our results should look the same. NIST has multiple scenarios for educational and testing purposes, and I encourage you to further explore the site when you have a chance.

The Hacking Case scenario uses an image from a Windows XP laptop. I realize that this is a legacy operating system that is soon to reach the end of its supported life by Microsoft (although you may still encounter people and even organizations running it), but it is also a very well documented operating system, and the forensic artifacts have long since been identified by practitioners. This book is not about teaching the newest forensic techniques on the latest operating systems and applications. It is about learning to use EnCase to perform your tasks, and using a well-known operating system reduces the complexity in troubleshooting when you encounter a problem. If you know very well how the artifacts are supposed to look, you can narrow down what is happening when things are not what you expect in the tool.

Since the NIST Hacking Case evidence files are provided in EnCase evidence file format (.E01), we will not be able to show the acquisition phase for this case. This brings up an important point—an investigator needs to have experience doing various types of acquisitions because one method may not be suitable for every situation they encounter. To that end, I will walk through some of the methods provided by Guidance Software and supported by EnCase so you can become familiar with multiple methods as we move through the chapters. However, because of this limitation, much of this chapter must deal with examples that do not reflect the use of our case study.

Creating a Case Plan

A case plan functions as a roadmap or project plan for a new case. Based on the particulars of the case, the analyst maps out the involved systems and areas for investigation prior to the start of the work. Some analysts will include this plan at the start of their case log, while others keep it as a separate document. For those in consulting companies, this data is frequently used to form the statement of work that the customer signs prior to the analyst being sent to the location.

Case plans for common types of cases that an organization handles can be developed ahead of time, and will help to standardize how these events are handled by the team members. For example, a common case for the private sector is an acceptable use policy violation involving pornography. Most companies have policies that prohibit the accessing and viewing of this type of material on company-owned devices. A case plan for this type of case would include imaging the computer of the subject and inspecting the graphics files stored on it. Standard procedure may involve looking at the subject's Internet browsing history as well. For a security incident response or a more complicated case, the plan will contain all of the suspected systems and storage locations that must be checked out to determine involvement. When the event is complex, spanning numerous devices and/or subjects, the case plan serves two purposes: first, to track all of the systems and tasks involved at the outset to ensure that none are missed (which defines the scope of the incident and response); and second, to allow for sections of the work to be delegated to various team members while keeping everyone up to date on where progress has been made.

Figure 4-1 shows a sample case plan for a case with multiple subjects and systems to be imaged and specific data to be processed.

Case Name	Sample Case								
Subject/Custodian				**Acquisition Targets**					
Name	Location	Phone	Email	System Name	Live Forensics	HDD Image	External Media	Mail Server	Sharepoint
Jane Doe	Dallas, Tx	214-335-5224	jane.doe@sampleco.com	DFW10122	X	X	X	X	
John Smith	Costa Mesa, CA		john.smith@sampleco.com	SNA20114	X	X		X	
				SNA12006		X			
Fred Matthews	Houston, TX	713-694-2323	fred.matthews@sampleco.com	IAH22908	X	X		X	X
Steve Anderson	Fort Lauderdale, FL	954-329-1812	steve.anderson@sampleco.com	FLL13472	X	X	X	X	
				FLL15221		X			
John Jackson	Dallas, TX	214-335-5323	john.jackson@sampleco.com	DFW10038	X	X		X	X
				DFW21304		X			
				DFW32101		X			
Amy Wilder	Austin, TX	512-226-1934	amy.wilder@sampleco.com	ASQ13291	X	X		X	

Figure 4-1   *Sample case plan*

As you can see, the list of potentially involved systems and devices is included. Under some of these is more detail as to the locations that should be examined for evidence. There is also a designation for who is assigned to each section of the work and the status of the task.

There will be incidents where the investigator needs to deviate from the plan based on the findings. It is important to stress that when this occurs, the investigator should communicate this to the stakeholders and make sure they authorize the changes in scope or focus. As discussed in prior chapters, guidance from the legal team will help protect the analyst in the event that some action is called into question.

Adding Evidence: Acquisition with EnCase Forensic

First, let me preface this section with the caveat that you should follow your organization's procedures for documenting a scene prior to attempting an acquisition. Once that important set of tasks has been completed, the examiner can proceed to acquiring evidence using EnCase or by whatever means your organization supports.

There are a number of ways to acquire evidence in EnCase. While we can certainly use files acquired in dd format, or those that are already provided in .E01/.L01 or .Ex01/.Lx01 formats, the most common scenario we encounter as investigators is the need to acquire evidence ourselves. While EnCase has long provided LinEn as an acquisition tool, it is not commonly used anymore in favor of more current tools. So if you need to use LinEn, the EnCase User's Guide is a good reference for the steps to get that set up.

That said, there are several acquisition options listed in EnCase Forensic that aren't frequently used by practitioners to perform acquisitions. They are in the User's Guide and in the product, but are only available in their Enterprise product. EnCase Forensic does not, for example, support network-based acquisition (which requires deploying servlets); the sections of the EnCase manual that deal with that type of activity may confuse people who purchased the EnCase Forensic edition of the software. While Forensic can be configured to use a Network Authentication Server (so you don't need to have a security dongle for each machine running EnCase), the traditional use of this product has been as a standalone workstation. Many labs don't allow their forensic systems to be connected to a network—or their networks are highly restricted.

I will spend more time on those methods for acquiring evidence that are most commonly used with the Forensic edition of the product, and make a note when the options in the Add Evidence menu are either rarely used or there are better options.

Add Local Device

Using a write blocker, you can attach a confiscated hard drive to your local forensic workstation and acquire evidence that way. Once the drive is connected to the write blocker, and to power, you can connect it to your workstation. When Windows recognizes the device, it will show the dialog that asks what you want to do with the device (i.e., open files to view folders, etc.). Take note of the drive letter that the device has been given and also the volume name. You will need these to identify them later. For this example, connect any drive you have that contains files so that you can see how local drive acquisition works. If you don't have an external drive you can use, you can acquire your workstation's C:\ drive, just to get a feel for the interface.

From the Home screen, click the Add Evidence link. This brings you to the Add Evidence screen where you can choose from a number of options for bringing evidence into your case. We will choose Add Local Device so that EnCase can scan our system and determine the devices we have attached.

Figure 4-2 shows the Add Local Device dialog and the default option that is selected. EnCase supports several very important options here. First, you can tell EnCase that you are using Tableau hardware, and that it should go out and attempt

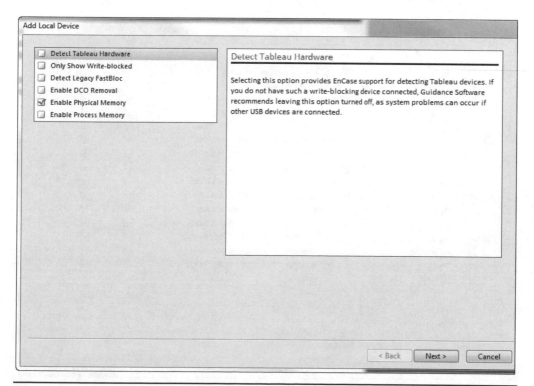

Figure 4-2   *Add Local Device dialog*

to detect it. It can also be directed to only show write-blocked devices, which is a good practice. This prevents you from accidentally choosing a device in error, or finding that the write blocker isn't working properly for some reason and you made changes to the device. If you are using a FastBloc (one of the older compatible write blockers), you can also tell EnCase to detect that hardware.

Enable DCO Removal is for when you are attempting to acquire a drive that has a device configuration overlay (which is a hidden area on the disk drive). This will make changes to the device, and it should only be checked if that is what you wish to do (the write blocker will not allow this to occur). Consult the EnCase User's Guide for further information in dealing with DCOs.

Enable Physical Memory is checked by default. This allows you to use EnCase to acquire RAM on a system. Enable Process Memory will allow you to preview memory on a running computer, potentially even conducting searches for keywords. This can cause instability, however, as indicated when you check that box in the interface.

Clicking Next will allow EnCase to scan our system and brings back a list of the attached devices (Figure 4-3).

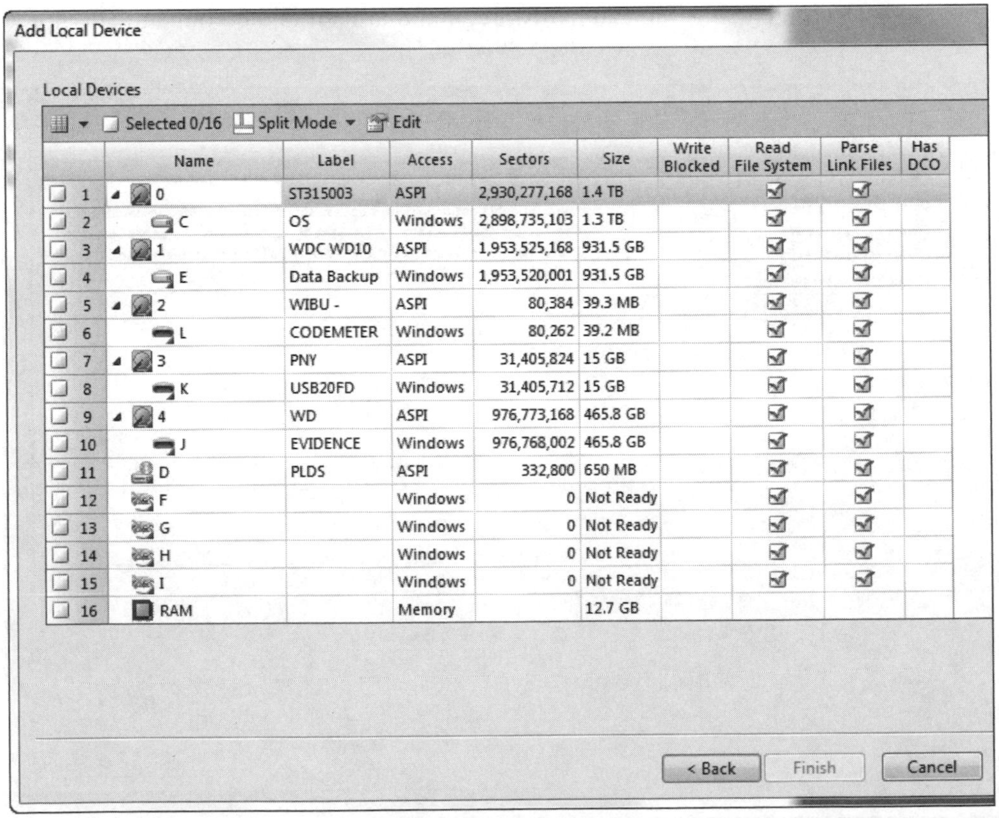

Add Local Device

Local Devices

Selected 0/16 Split Mode ▾ Edit

		Name	Label	Access	Sectors	Size	Write Blocked	Read File System	Parse Link Files	Has DCO
☐	1	▲ 0	ST315003	ASPI	2,930,277,168	1.4 TB		✓	✓	
☐	2	C	OS	Windows	2,898,735,103	1.3 TB		✓	✓	
☐	3	▲ 1	WDC WD10	ASPI	1,953,525,168	931.5 GB		✓	✓	
☐	4	E	Data Backup	Windows	1,953,520,001	931.5 GB		✓	✓	
☐	5	▲ 2	WIBU -	ASPI	80,384	39.3 MB		✓	✓	
☐	6	L	CODEMETER	Windows	80,262	39.2 MB		✓	✓	
☐	7	▲ 3	PNY	ASPI	31,405,824	15 GB		✓	✓	
☐	8	K	USB20FD	Windows	31,405,712	15 GB		✓	✓	
☐	9	▲ 4	WD	ASPI	976,773,168	465.8 GB		✓	✓	
☐	10	J	EVIDENCE	Windows	976,768,002	465.8 GB		✓	✓	
☐	11	D	PLDS	ASPI	332,800	650 MB		✓	✓	
☐	12	F		Windows	0	Not Ready		✓	✓	
☐	13	G		Windows	0	Not Ready		✓	✓	
☐	14	H		Windows	0	Not Ready		✓	✓	
☐	15	I		Windows	0	Not Ready		✓	✓	
☐	16	RAM		Memory		12.7 GB				

< Back   Finish   Cancel

Figure 4-3 *Scanned devices attached to this machine*

I scanned my local system without checking the box that shows only write-blocked drives. You can see that the list of devices includes the operating system (OS) drive and several other drives. You can also see the CodeMeter security key listed, as these always show up with the label of WIBU-. This is also true of EnCase Portable, which runs from a CodeMeter dongle, and we will discuss in Chapter 14.

The drive letter assigned is in the Name column. The icon tells you what type of device it is—disk, DVD/CD, or RAM. In this column, physical devices have numeric names, while logical volumes have a drive letter that was assigned by the operating system when it recognized and mounted the device. The Label column contains the volume label, and you can see the number of sectors and size, which are good to use to verify that you have the correct device before you begin imaging. If the write blocker is detected, you would see it indicated in the Write Blocked column, and the same goes for if EnCase detected a DCO on the device. Neither is present for our purposes. The default is to read the file system and to parse link files. We will leave those defaults.

I am choosing to image my 15 GB USB thumb drive that I purchased for this purpose. Which device you select here makes a big difference. In Figure 4-3, line 7 in the list is for the physical device—note that the icon that looks like the inside of a hard disk is the device icon. Line 8, in contrast, will image the logical volume instead of the physical device. If you want to make sure to get everything on the drive, you need the physical device and not the logical volume. Say for example that your device has multiple partitions on it. If only one of the partitions included a Windows recognizable partition (i.e., there was a Linux partition as well), then imaging the logical volume that Windows recognized will not get you everything on that device.

I selected line 7 to image the physical device by placing a blue check in the box next to the line number. Clicking Finish kicks off the imaging. When it is completed, you are returned to the Evidence Browser with the new evidence item listed at the bottom (Figure 4-4).

You can see that the device has been added to the list and that it retains the device number allotted by the operating system as its name. Clicking on the number 3 in the Name list opens the image for us, as shown in Figure 4-5.

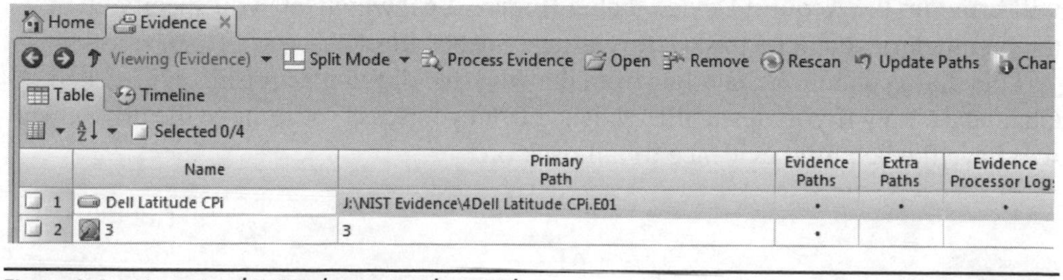

	Name	Primary Path	Evidence Paths	Extra Paths	Evidence Processor Log
1	Dell Latitude CPi	J:\NIST Evidence\4Dell Latitude CPi.E01	•	•	•
2	3	3	•		

Figure 4-4 *Acquired USB device in the Evidence Browser*

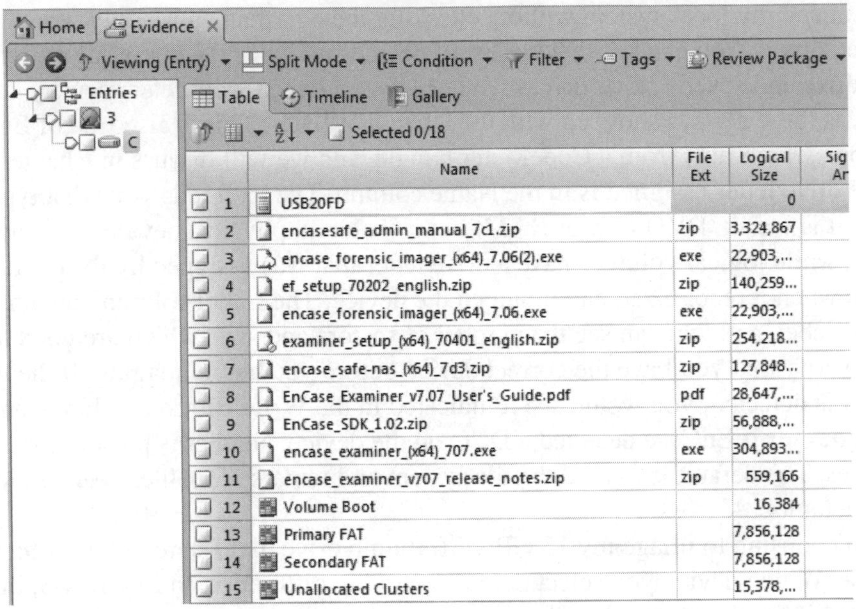

		Name	File Ext	Logical Size	Sig Ar
☐	1	USB20FD		0	
☐	2	encasesafe_admin_manual_7c1.zip	zip	3,324,867	
☐	3	encase_forensic_imager_(x64)_7.06(2).exe	exe	22,903,...	
☐	4	ef_setup_70202_english.zip	zip	140,259...	
☐	5	encase_forensic_imager_(x64)_7.06.exe	exe	22,903,...	
☐	6	examiner_setup_(x64)_70401_english.zip	zip	254,218...	
☐	7	encase_safe-nas_(x64)_7d3.zip	zip	127,848...	
☐	8	EnCase_Examiner_v7.07_User's_Guide.pdf	pdf	28,647,...	
☐	9	EnCase_SDK_1.02.zip	zip	56,888,...	
☐	10	encase_examiner_(x64)_707.exe	exe	304,893...	
☐	11	encase_examiner_v707_release_notes.zip	zip	559,166	
☐	12	Volume Boot		16,384	
☐	13	Primary FAT		7,856,128	
☐	14	Secondary FAT		7,856,128	
☐	15	Unallocated Clusters		15,378,...	

Figure 4-5   *USB drive detail in the Evidence Browser*

This shows up as a drive in EnCase of letter C, which has no bearing on what it was mounted in the system, clearly. There are several files listed, and at the bottom you see we have the Volume Boot, Primary and Secondary FAT, and Unallocated Clusters. The evidence acquisition is completed and ready for processing or analysis.

Note, these files will be available for as long as you are in EnCase and have saved your case. But it isn't the same as actually doing a full acquisition and generating an evidence file. The evidence is acquired, but not turned into an evidence file that you can remove and add to another case, or that you can remove and add later if you need it again. Once you remove it, it is gone.

To turn this into an EnCase evidence file, you would need to select the top level device in the Tree pane with a blue check. Then right-click in the Tree pane and choose Acquire from the context menu, and Acquire again from the submenu. This will bring up the Acquire Device dialog (Figure 4-6), which lets you specify all of the parameters you need to save this as an evidence file.

This dialog should be familiar from the work we did in reacquiring evidence in Chapter 3. Now if you delete the evidence from your case (or remove the drive), you will have the acquired evidence to fall back on.

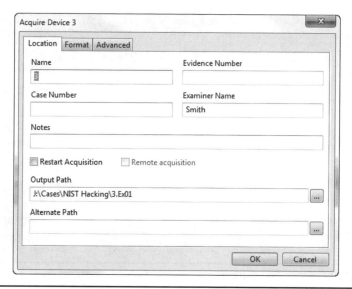

Figure 4-6   *Acquire Device dialog*

Add Network Preview

If you are logged on to an EnCase SAFE (network authentication and licensing), you can use it to handle network previewing of machines that are either connected to the SAFE or have servlets pushed out to them. This is usually done in EnCase Enterprise rather than EnCase Forensic edition.

Add Evidence File

This menu item is for adding files that are already in EnCase evidence file format—whether logical or physical. To add a file, assuming you are in the Home screen, click the Add Evidence link, and then click on Add Evidence File. EnCase brings up the Add Evidence File dialog for you to browse to the location where your evidence is stored and choose a file (Figure 4-7).

You can see in Figure 4-7 that the .E01 file is the only one shown in the list, even though if you view this in Windows Explorer, there are two files associated with this image (.E01 and .E02). This is because EnCase is programmed to just display the first in the series. You can also see that it displays the first in the series of the raw files as well. However, this is not the dialog where you would add the raw file, and trying to do so brings up the error shown in Figure 4-8.

Instead, select the .E01 file and click OK. The file is then brought up in the Evidence Browser without your having to worry about how many additional associated files it contains (.E01, .E02, etc.) as shown in Figure 4-7.

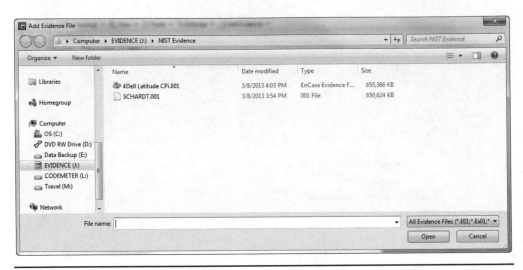

Figure 4-7   *Add Evidence File dialog*

You can see in Figure 4-9 the directory structure in the Tree pane of the Evidence Browser, with the top level Dell Latitude CPi evidence item in the Table pane.

Add Raw Image

You recall that the NIST CFReDS site has the evidence in two separate formats? Here is where we get to use that second format. In our last section, we added the EnCase format evidence file to EnCase. Now you can add the dd image format to see how that differs. From the Home screen, choose Add Evidence, and then choose Add Raw Image.

A dialog appears for you to specify the information about this dd image we are going to add (Figure 4-10). First, you know it is a disk image, so you can leave the

Figure 4-8   *Error on trying to add a raw file in the Add Evidence File dialog*

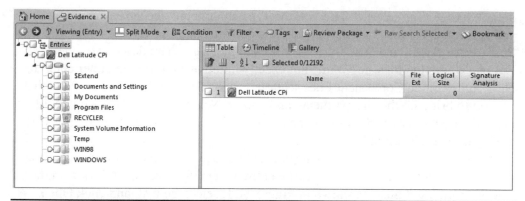

Figure 4-9 *EnCase Evidence file added to Evidence Browser*

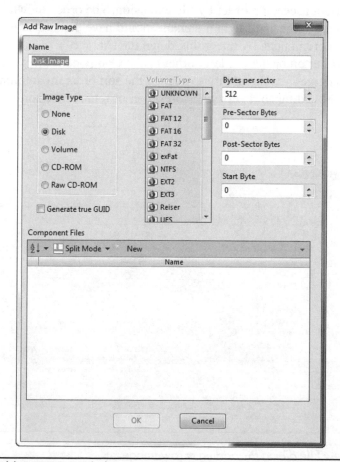

Figure 4-10 *Add Raw Image dialog*

default image type selected. The Volume Type column only becomes enabled when you select the Volume image type. Take the default values for Bytes Per Sector, Post-Sector Bytes, and Start Byte for this example. But where do you go to tell EnCase where the files are? While not exactly intuitive, you need to either click the New button in the Component Files section or right-click on the white space in that section to bring up the context menu, and choose New from that. Also, you could press the INSERT key and get the same results: a dialog that allows you to browse to the location as shown in Figure 4-11.

When adding a raw image, you need to select each file in the series. EnCase does not automatically check to associate the entire image together like it does with the EnCase formatted files. As shown in Figure 4-11, select them all and click Open.

You are returned to the Add Raw Image dialog (Figure 4-12), only this time you see that the files have been added. Check carefully to make sure that EnCase added them in the correct ascending order by file extension. The order shown in the figure is the correct order—the first file in the chain should have the .001 extension, with the extensions incrementing by one going down the list.

Note the sort button on the top left corner of the Component Files section. Clicking on this gives you the ability to change the sort order, to automatically sort ascending or descending, to reverse the sort order, or remove the sort entirely.

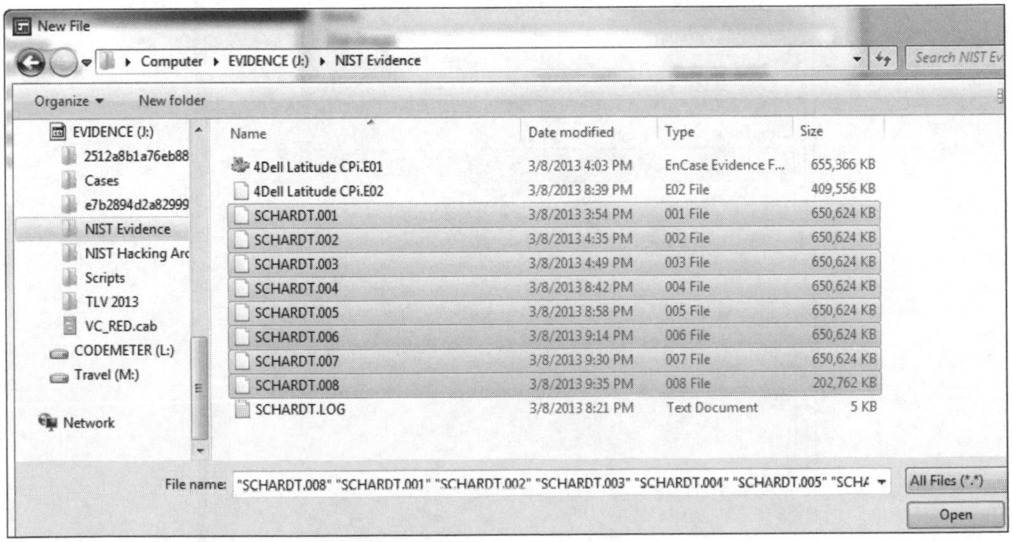

Figure 4-11   *New File dialog for adding a raw image*

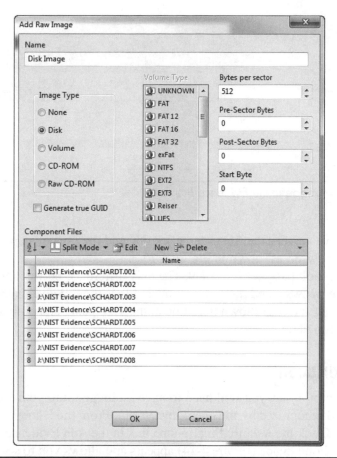

Figure 4-12   *Add Raw Image dialog with evidence files*

File Order When Adding Raw Images

For those of you who are used to working with an earlier version of EnCase, there was a time when you needed to add image files in descending order by file extension (i.e., file.008, then file.007). This is no longer the case, and all image files must be in ascending order by file extension (i.e., file.001, then file.002). If the files are in the wrong order, EnCase will not import them properly.

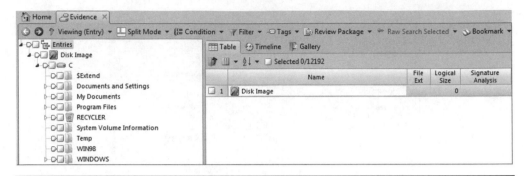

Figure 4-13 *Raw image in the Evidence Browser*

Once you have verified the file order, click OK and the image is opened for you in the Evidence Browser, as shown in Figure 4-13.

Take a quick look back at Figure 4-9. The only difference between the raw image in the Evidence Browser and the EnCase image file is the top level name of the image. The file structure is shown the same in the Tree pane, and both act the same when drilling into details.

 ## Acquire Smartphone

To acquire a smartphone, you will need to have it plugged into your forensic workstation and recognized by the operating system. From the Home screen, click on Add Evidence. Click the Acquire Smartphone link in the Add Evidence screen. The Acquire Smartphone dialog (Figure 4-14) appears and allows you to see the list of detected devices, as well as a list of the devices that are supported by the version of EnCase you are running. For our example, we will be acquiring an Apple iPhone 4S.

I will select the Apple iOS device under the Detected section. EnCase changes the message displayed in the top message section to tell you that you need to verify that Apple iTunes is installed but not running for the acquisition to work. You will also need to make sure to unlock the phone.

NOTE

EnCase can only perform a logical acquisition of an iPhone at this time—this will not be a physical acquisition. However, if you have acquired a physical image from a device using other means (such as a Cellebrite), you can then bring that image into EnCase for analysis.

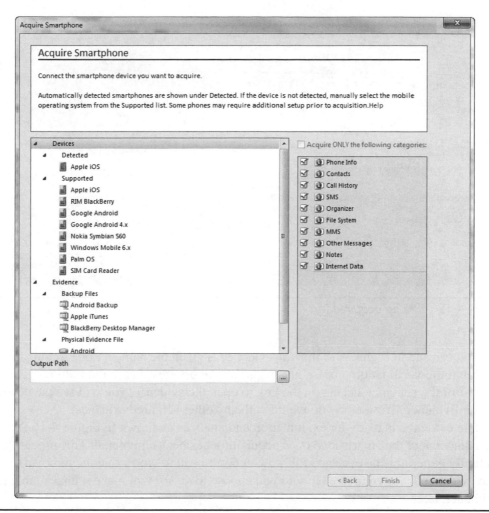

Figure 4-14 *Acquire Smartphone dialog*

I will also specify a path for the output logical evidence file. Clicking on the ellipses (...) button brings up a dialog for you to browse to the directory you want to save the file in. Note that the only option for saving the file is as a legacy .L01 file type. I accepted the default categories for collection, and clicked Finish.

A progress bar appears at the bottom of this window and shows you the progress EnCase has made in acquiring the smartphone. Once it has completed, you will be dropped into the Evidence Browser with the newly acquired smartphone as the bottom item.

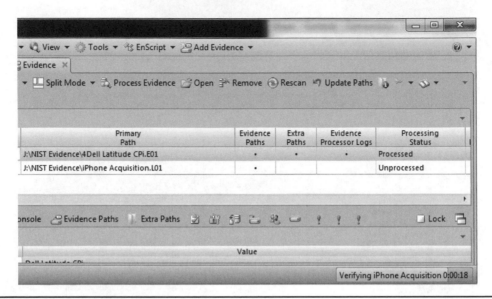

Figure 4-15 *iPhone acquired*

You can see in Figure 4-15 that the evidence is given the name iPhone Acquisition, and that the verification process has begun by the progress bar at the bottom-right corner of the screen. Clicking on the link to open the evidence, you will see the detail in the Evidence Browser as you would with any other acquired evidence.

The evidence is ready for examination and analysis as shown in Figure 4-16. You can disconnect the smartphone once acquisition has been completed. This process actually generates the evidence file, so you don't need to worry that the removal of the evidence from your case (should you choose to do so) will make it unavailable to add back later.

Add Crossover Preview

The Crossover Preview option requires both the source machine (that you want to collect from) and a forensic machine that you will use to preview and acquire the source system.

To add a crossover preview, you need to combine working with EnCase Imager and LinEn. Follow the instructions in the EnCase Forensics User Guide to burn a boot image ISO of LinEn, and then set the source computer as the target when the LinEn boot menu is displayed.

You will also need a crossover cable connecting the two machines to accomplish this, and you will need to set your imaging system as the client. EnCase Forensic

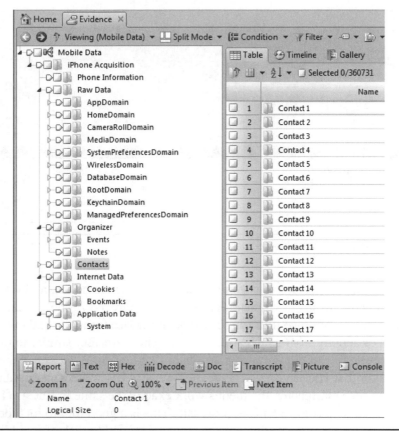

Figure 4-16   *iPhone evidence detail*

and EnCase Imager are rarely used in this way. This is actually another feature that is typically used with EnCase Enterprise. The alternative is to use EnCase Portable to do your preview (which we cover in Chapter 14, and is much more straightforward than the combination of LinEn and EnCase Forensic/Imager).

EnCase Imager

Guidance Software released EnCase Imager as a more modern tool for acquiring evidence (as opposed to LinEn). It is included in the download links that Guidance sends out with an order or an update. It is also available on the distribution media that Guidance provides. EnCase Imager is provided as an executable with the title of encase_forensic_imager_<version>.exe. Double-clicking that standalone executable launches EnCase Imager. No dongle is required to run this program.

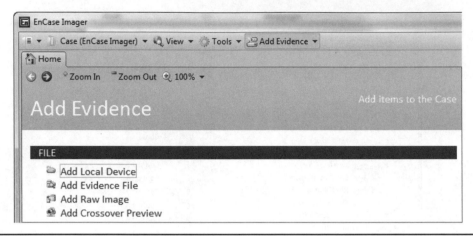

Figure 4-17   *EnCase Imager Home tab*

When EnCase Imager launches you are placed into the Home tab, and your options are all about acquisition of evidence. As shown in Figure 4-17, you can add local devices, add image evidence files (these will be in EnCase formats), add raw images (dd format), or acquire from a crossover preview. These are very similar to the Add Evidence section of EnCase Forensic in Authenticated mode. What you cannot do in EnCase Imager that you can do with EnCase Forensics is acquire a smartphone.

Other than the smartphone, the menus work exactly the same in EnCase Imager as they do when acquiring in EnCase Forensic. This is a good tool to include in your jump bag for on-scene collections, and can be burned to disk or to a USB drive easily, since it is a standalone program.

Summary

We have covered the main methods of adding evidence into a case and using EnCase to acquire evidence. You can see that it is fairly straightforward, and that the process lends itself well to Run Books. I have taken many of these and added them to Appendix C for you to use. The first thing that I usually have new examiners do is get rock solid on the methods of acquisition that my organization uses. Having easy, step-by-step instructions on the many methods they will need to become familiar with is a good way to get them started with the basics.

Next, we will get started on the NIST hacking case and dig into the Evidence Processor.

CHAPTER
5

Processing Evidence

W e have our evidence, so we can begin working on it from within EnCase. This chapter walks you through the steps to get your case created and addresses several of the questions in our case study. We add our evidence to the case and begin looking at the options for processing evidence.

Creating the NIST Hacking Case

The work we've done up to this point has been using samples and examples. Now it is time to get started processing our evidence. As I mentioned in prior chapters, we have Run Books for common procedures, which can be found in Appendix C. You can refer to those procedures, and customize them to your organization's standards to create your own set of Run Books. To refresh your memory, here is the procedure for creating a case:

If you haven't already, launch EnCase and create a new case. Choose the Forensic template and fill in your paths. Name your case "NIST Hacking", and if you wish, once the case is created, copy any additional files and folders via Windows Explorer to set up your case. Figure 5-1 shows the information I used when creating our new case file.

Once the case is created, you are dropped back into the EnCase Home screen.

Run Book: Creating a New Case

1. Launch EnCase.

2. Click New Case on the Home screen.

3. Choose case template type.

4. Fill in information on file paths, examiner, etc.

5. Save case.

6. Copy additional files/folders from template folder in Windows Explorer.

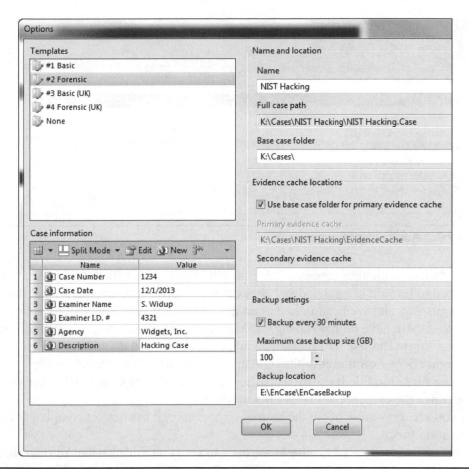

Figure 5-1   *The NIST Hacking case*

Adding and Verifying the Evidence

We have already downloaded our evidence file from the location provided in Chapter 4. We need to bring that evidence into EnCase so we can verify it, process it, and ultimately analyze it. If you have created a storage location within your case to keep your evidence organized, place the copy there.

To add our evidence to the case, from the Home screen, click on Add Evidence. You are adding an existing EnCase image file, so choose Add Evidence File from the FILE section of the Add Evidence page (Figure 5-2).

Browse to where you stored the downloaded evidence file and click on it. Click OK to add it to the case. When you add evidence to EnCase, it automatically begins

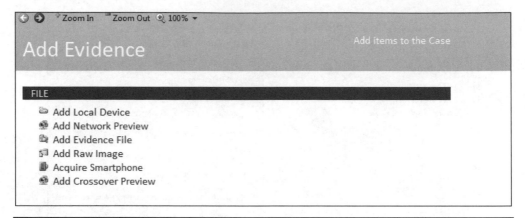

Figure 5-2 *Add Evidence page*

the evidence verification process. This runs while you work with the evidence, but you need to be sure to go ahead and check that the verification completes and that the acquisition and verification hashes on the evidence match. This will be your proof that there have been no changes to the evidence between acquisition and your bringing it into EnCase for processing and analysis. You can do this in the Evidence tab (Figure 5-3). Scroll over to the right until you come to the column on your evidence file titled File Integrity. This should have a value of Completely Verified, 0 Errors once the evidence has been fully verified.

If you see a progress bar in the bottom-right corner, it has not yet completed the verification process (Figure 5-4).

You don't actually need to have a case open to verify an evidence file. You can simply choose Verify Evidence Files from the Tools menu to start as shown in Figure 5-5.

The Verify Evidence Files dialog opens and allows you to choose the files you want to verify. Click on the .E01 file and then click Open (Figure 5-6).

Figure 5-3 *Verified evidence file*

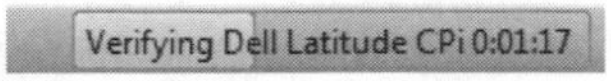

Figure 5-4 *Evidence verification in progress*

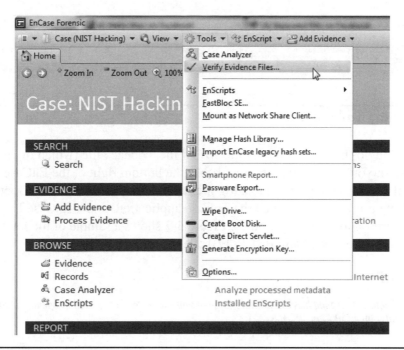

Figure 5-5 *Verify Evidence Files*

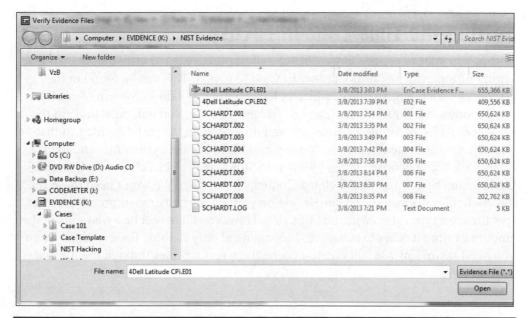

Figure 5-6 *Browse and select evidence file*

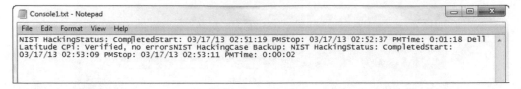

Figure 5-7 *Log file contents*

When you do this, depending on the size of the evidence file (which in our case is fairly small), you may see the progress bar at the bottom right of the EnCase screen. EnCase also writes the output into a log file, which is located in the My Documents folder of the profile that launched the EnCase application, under EnCase/Logs. They are written to Console#.txt files. Figure 5-7 shows a sample of the log from verification of the 4Dell Latitude CPi.E01 file.

> **TIP**
>
> *Some of these log files can get very large — you should get in the habit of opening them in WordPad rather than in Notepad.*

When the evidence is verified, you should check and ensure that the acquisition and verification hashes match, and make a note of it.

Setting the Time Zone in EnCase

Before you start to process any evidence, a best practice is to verify the time zone setting of the evidence file(s) and set EnCase to match. This can be found in the Windows system registry hive, which is located in C:\Windows\System32\config for Windows XP, 2000, Vista, 7, and 8. To view this file, you will need to be in the evidence file in the Evidence Browser, and drill down to the path provided so that you can see the system file in the Table pane. Highlight the system file, and then right-click it and choose Entries | View File Structure. You can choose to Calculate Unallocated Space and Find Deleted Contents if you like. We won't need these for this particular operation. You can decide on your own whether your procedures for specific case types should include this step. However, there will be a trade-off in the amount of time it takes to complete. I recommend only running these options when you need them. EnCase will create a cache file when it parses through the file and write it to disk, so if you process the file with all the options checked and need to come back to it later, it will be readily available. Once EnCase completes parsing the file structure, the file name turns to a hyperlink and the icon next to it gains a green plus sign. You can now click on it to see what is inside.

For those who are used to viewing the Windows registry in other tools, you will notice that some of the path structure is truncated. For instance, for keys in the System hive, you would normally see keys referenced as having a path beginning with HKEY_LOCAL_MACHINE\System followed by the path to the specific key. In EnCase, you won't see the HKEY_LOCAL_MACHINE portion of the path. You will see the System file as the top level of the Tree pane, and the rest of the path displayed so that you can navigate down into the specific keys to get at their values. It takes a little getting used to if you are used to working with other tools that display the full path, but after a while it becomes second nature just to navigate through the registry hive file as if it were any other file that has been parsed by EnCase. I provide the full path here for clarity in case you want to verify the findings with another tool (another best practice, particularly for critical evidence).

First, you'll need to determine which control set was active when the system was imaged. You find this in the HKEY_LOCAL_MACHINE\System\Select key. In our case, the evidence image indicates that ControlSet001 is the active set.

Therefore, to check the time zone that is active for this image, look in the active control set, and look for the values found in the TimeZoneInformation key. Specifically, the keys you are looking for are found under HKEY_LOCAL_MACHINE\System\ControlSet001\Control\TimeZoneInformation. In looking at the values in this key in the evidence file, you can determine that it is set to Central Daylight Time (Figure 5-8).

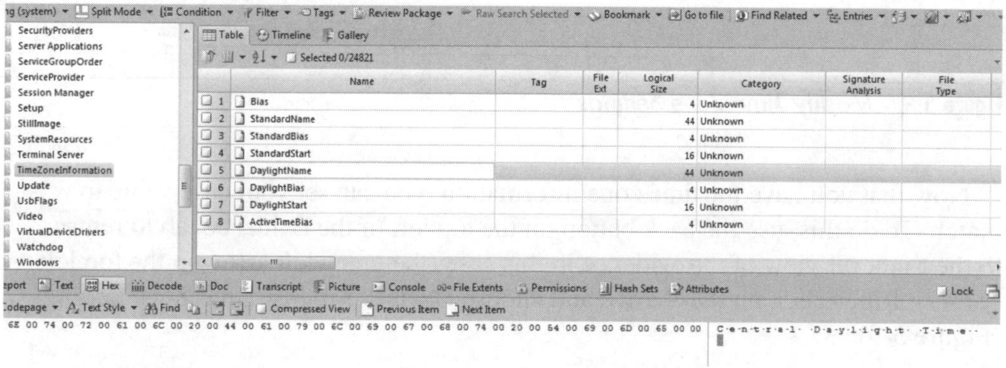

Figure 5-8   *TimeZoneInformation key*

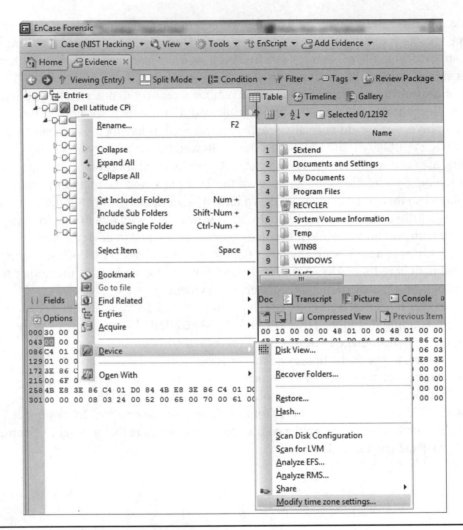

Figure 5-9 *Modify Time Zone Settings*

Now that you have the time zone information, you can set your case value to match. To do this, use the back button on the top left of the Evidence tab to return to the top level view of the evidence in this case (the green left arrow in the top left corner). Right-click on the C drive and choose Device | Modify Time Zone Settings (Figure 5-9).

This brings up the Time Properties window where you can choose the time zone that corresponds with your evidence (Figure 5-10). Choose the Central Time (US & Canada) option, and check the box next to Use Single DST Offset, since this is set to Daylight Saving Time, and click OK.

TIP

If you do not specify the time zone information from the evidence, EnCase will use the time zone settings from your examiner machine.

Note that you must set the time zone for each evidence item separately—this does not set one zone for the entire case. This is because a single case has the potential to contain evidence that span multiple time zones and you need to be able to account for that possibility.

Finally, note the check box for Use Single DST Offset. Because Daylight Saving Time has different rules depending on the evidence (due to the passing of the Energy Policy Act of 2005), EnCase gives the option of either automatically applying the rules for the proper year (the default behavior) or of overriding this behavior and choosing the year for the correct bias (by checking the box).

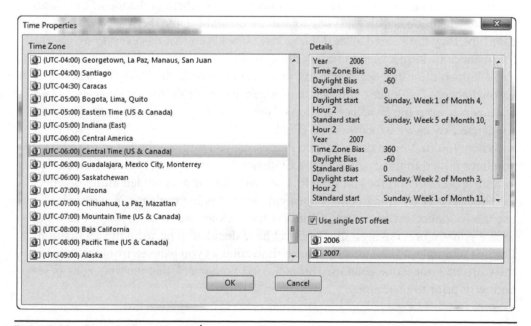

Figure 5-10 *Time Properties window*

The EnCase Evidence Processor

Now that we have our evidence added and verified, and have set our time zone for the case, we need to start processing the evidence file. We are working on an evidence file that was previously acquired. However, it should be noted that if you are working from a preview of a machine and have not yet acquired the evidence from it, you will need to do so prior to processing the evidence. The EnCase Evidence Processor can only process acquired evidence files.

When you have been doing cases for a while, you will see some commonalities in the processing you do, depending on the type of case. There are some steps that I start with just so that I won't have to stop and reprocess the evidence in the middle of my analysis. There are also some processing options that can only be run the first time you process the evidence, so if there is even a slight chance you will want them, consider having that part of your process. These options are marked with a red flag to the left of the item. We will cover the modules in more depth in just a moment.

The Evidence Processor allows you to save your settings for specific case types and use them to enforce consistency from case to case. It does this in a .EnProc file, which you can then open when you are in the Evidence Processor again using the Load Settings option. The Save Settings button under Current Processor Options will allow you to save the file wherever you choose. I save them at the top of my Cases folder to make it easy for everyone to find them, and I name them according to the case type they are geared toward. I also have one saved that has everything checked for instances where I want to run all the options.

To launch the Evidence Processor, you can either be in the Evidence tab, and click on the Process Evidence button on the Evidence tab button bar, or you can choose to launch it from the Evidence section of the Home page. Either way, the EnCase Evidence Processor window opens (Figure 5-11).

When you first open the Evidence Processor, you will see the list of the evidence you have added to the case under the Evidence Name section, and the various modules available on the bottom left. The modules are not enabled until you check the Process box on at least one of the evidence items in your case. You can also use the Evidence Processor to acquire evidence using the Acquire box for cases where you are previewing a machine and have decided to perform the acquisition. For this example, I have already set the time zone as you can see from the value in the Current Time Zone column. This is a good final check that the time zone is set correctly prior to processing.

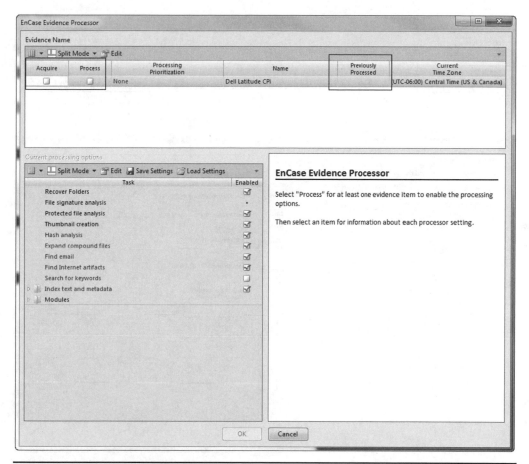

Figure 5-11   *EnCase Evidence Processor*

Checking the Process box makes immediate changes to the Current Processing Options section of the window. I've checked the Process box, and also expanded the modules to show you how they look once they're no longer disabled (Figure 5-12). To run an optional module, check the box next to it. To bring up information and options for that module, click on the module's name, which is a hyperlink.

Let's look at the options we want to use in the Evidence Processor for our case. I'll go through the modules that are run by default and have no configurable parameters first, and then discuss those we will use and the settings we want for this first run of the Evidence Processor.

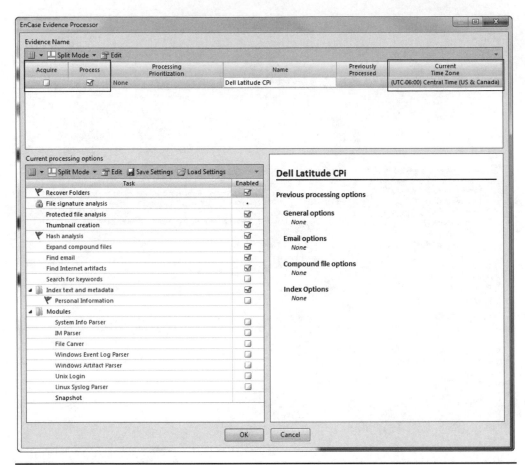

Figure 5-12 *Process evidence enabled*

Process Prioritization

In the Evidence Name section of the window, between the Process check box and the Name, you will notice a Processing Prioritization column. This defaults to None, but if you click on that hyperlink, you will bring up your options for prioritizing how you want the modules run against the evidence (Figure 5-13). Since you can work with evidence results as they become available, this can be very helpful if you want specific processes to run first, before some of the more time consuming modules. For instance, you can set this to process documents first if you want to see the results of specific operations before other processes run.

When the Process Prioritization window first opens, the Enable Processing Prioritization option is not checked. To be able to choose from these options, you

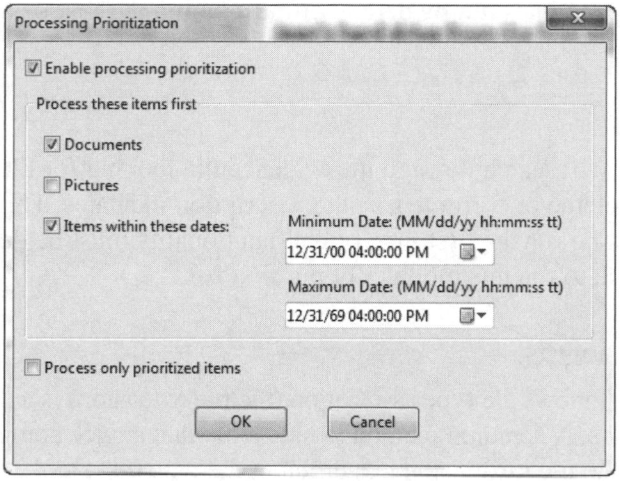

Figure 5-13   *Process Prioritization options*

must first enable it by checking the box. Then you can choose which items to process first and apply a date range if desired. You can also tell EnCase to only process those items you have checked. After making several choices, and clicking OK, when you return to the Evidence Processor window, the Processing Prioritization column shows "Multiple" instead of "None" as it did before you started making choices. We aren't going to use this feature for this processing run, but it is good to know that you have these options for cases when the order of operation matters to you. If you have saved any changes to this window, just go back into it and remove the check next to Enable Processing Prioritization to turn them off again.

Default or Red-Flagged Modules

You will notice that some of the modules have a padlock symbol next to them. This means they are locked and you cannot change the settings. These are the modules that are enabled by default and cannot be disabled—they will run each time the Evidence Processor is run against any evidence file. A red flag next to the module's name indicates that you must run this during the first processing run and it cannot be run later. Several modules have this restriction, including Recover Folders, Hash Analysis and Personal Information under the Index Text and metadata module. Guidance Software trainers stress the importance of running these at the start of the case so you don't miss important evidence. That is why they are red-flagged and must be done first.

In all modules, clicking on the module names will bring up the descriptive information in the box to the right of the Current Processing Options section, and provides general information about that module and how it performs.

The following modules run by default or must be run the first pass of the Evidence Processor.

Recover Folders

Recover Folders will search through the evidence file looking for files and folders that have been deleted or corrupted, as the description indicates. This is a red-flagged module and must be run the first time or the functionality must be done manually thereafter. Choose to run this module for our first pass.

File Signature Analysis

Relying on the Windows file type association (the file extension) is a recipe for missing important evidence. A common method to hide a file that novice computer users may use is to change the file's extension to a different file type (or remove it entirely). This will cause the file to masquerade as another file type unless you perform a signature analysis where the file's header and footer are checked against known header and footers. A step that may yield some interesting artifacts is to take a look at the results of this analysis and see if there are any mismatches that look suspicious. EnCase will show a signature mismatch for files that are masquerading as another file type, and these are worth a closer look. This module is run by default and cannot be disabled.

Hash Analysis

The Hash analysis module will generate a hash of each nonzero length file in the evidence. This module allows for the generation of either or both MD5 and SHA-1 hashes. Choose to run both of these hash types against the evidence file. Collisions—when two different files generate the same hash value—have been demonstrated with MD5, and there have been cryptographic weaknesses identified in SHA-1 as well. However, the likelihood that a weakness can be found that will render both of the hashes suspect is much less likely, and while there is a performance trade-off for running both hashes, I believe it is worth doing. Calculating just one hash is an option, as is doing none—but I don't recommend it.

Index Text and Metadata

This module creates an index to make keyword searching faster. While the description for the module indicates that you can make changes to how the index is created, this is not a place where you can do that. This module has a red-flagged module under it, so while it is not itself required, if you do not choose this module, you cannot choose to run the Personal Information module beneath it.

The Personal Information module is specifically searching for certain types of text strings. EnCase has prebuilt the filters to look for the major brands of credit cards, phone numbers, email addresses, and Social Security numbers. While this is something you can also do yourself manually in the Search section, this saves you the work of building those filters yourself. While your case may not initially have anything to do with credit cards, for example, consider running this anyway because it is an easy thing to do and you may uncover some interesting data that you didn't expect (performed within the parameters of your organization's investigation procedures).

Take the default selections for the Index Text and Metadata module, and choose to run both that and the Personal Information module with all of the options checked.

Optional Modules

The rest of the modules are optional and can be run repeatedly or during subsequent runs of the Evidence Processor. Each time the Evidence Processor runs, you will get new folders in the Records tab under the Evidence Processor Module Results folder.

Protected File Analysis

The Protected File Analysis module will identify files that are password protected or encrypted by running the built-in Passware Encryption Analyzer against them. This tool will provide information on the strength of the encryption used as part of the results. Choose to run this module.

Thumbnail Creation

The Thumbnail Creations module does just what it says—it creates thumbnail-sized versions of all graphics it encounters for display in the Gallery view. This speeds up the viewing of graphics files considerably. Choose to run this module.

Expand Compound Files

You have the option of having the Evidence Processor mount and expand compound files—such as zip archives, thumbs.db files, and other files with internal structures that must be processed before EnCase can display them. By default, Expand Compound Files is checked when you launch the Evidence Processor. However, it is one of the options that you can choose to forgo and come back to later. To have the Evidence Processor handle mounting and expanding all compound files, first launch the Evidence Processor from the Home screen, click the Process check box for the evidence you want to process, and ensure that the Expand Compound Files option is checked. You can look at the options by clicking on the name of the module, but you will see that it has only one option—Archive Files. Once it completes, you should be able to simply click on the compound file when you encounter it and have it already mounted and ready for examination. Keep in mind this also comes with a potentially large performance impact. If you have the luxury of time to spend in preprocessing, it is worth doing—but sometimes you cannot afford the time and must go back later to do further processing steps.

For this run of the Evidence Processor, choose to expand and mount all compound files so we don't have to revisit them later.

Find Email

The Find Email module allows you to look for a variety of email client artifacts. Clicking on the module brings up a list of options. You can choose which email client artifacts you want EnCase to look for based on the particulars of your case. By default, they are all checked (Figure 5-14).

Since we are processing this case and don't know for certain if data was exfiltrated, it makes sense to run this module with all of the options checked, including the option to search unallocated space as shown here. Note, this is not where you choose to look for webmail—that will be in the next section.

Find Internet Artifacts

This module collects browser artifacts, including history files and cached pages. The module's description provides a list of the browsers that are supported. If you are working with a different browser, you will have to perform the search for those artifacts manually. Choose to run this module and search unallocated space.

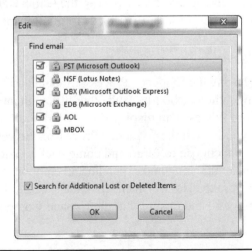

Figure 5-14   *Find Email options*

System Info Parser

The System Info Parser has many options for gathering information about the operating system and various aspects you may be interested in. Run this to document the state of the system at the time of acquisition. It gives a basic picture of the users, hardware, software, and network settings that were present on the system; many of these things become important in investigations as you try to determine who is responsible for various activities. We are running this against a Windows system, so I have unchecked the Linux related option. Figure 5-15 shows how your window should look in the Standard tab.

There is also an Advanced tab, where you can get more granularity into which commands to run and which key values to read, but we won't be using it for this run of the Evidence Processor.

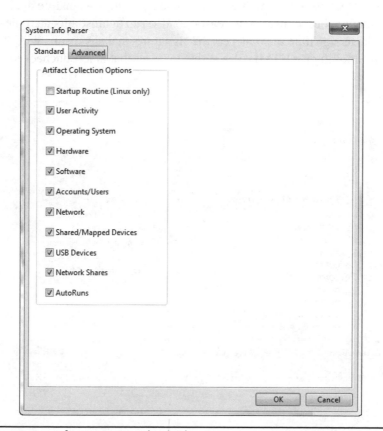

Figure 5-15 *System Info Parser Standard tab*

IM Parser

The Instant Messaging (IM) Parser will find artifacts from AOL, MSN, and Yahoo instant message clients. You can also scan the unallocated space for deleted artifacts. Check all of the options, including the unallocated scan for this module.

File Carver

The File Carver will search unallocated space and file slack to see if there are fragments or entire files that match our specifications to be found on the image. Click on the File Carver module to bring up the options (Figure 5-16).

To get a sense of what this returns, we will run this with APPLICATION and ARCHIVE checked. When you do this, the pane to the right will automatically put a blue check in all of the options for this file type. I left the default Search Options to look in unallocated space and the file slack. We are running a signature analysis against the entire evidence file, so there is no reason to also run against allocated files. If there are files that have signature mismatches, the signature analysis results will show them. We also aren't looking for HTML files at this time, so that is left unchecked.

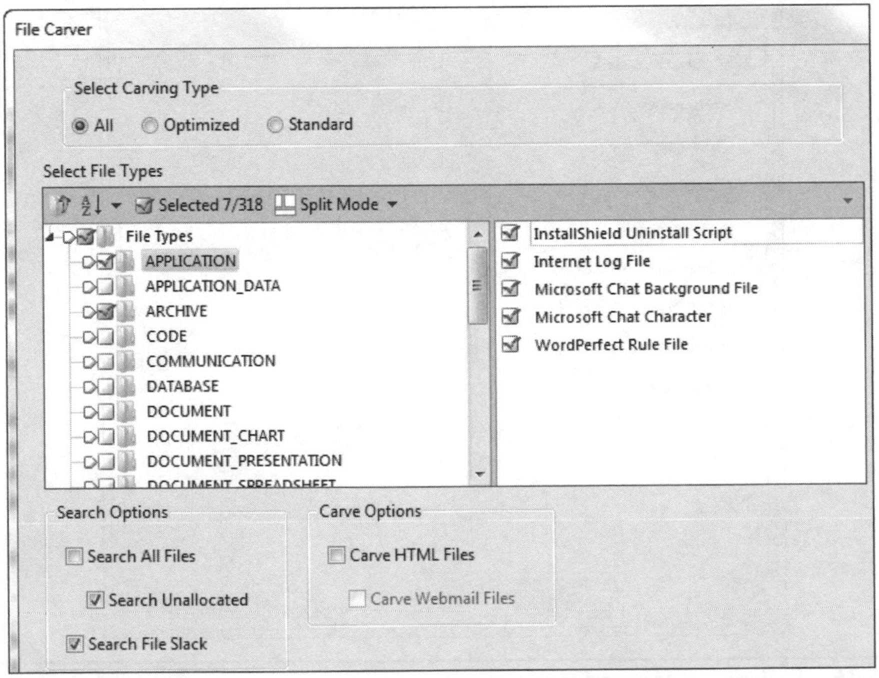

Figure 5-16   *File Carver window*

Clicking Next lets you choose whether you want to export the files it finds. You can also specify the file size and the place you want it to export these files. You can chose to export the files into the Export directory. You have the option to make a new folder under your directory structure as well if you want to keep these potentially fragmented files separate from the other files you have exported. Also, you can limit the number of folders you export if there is a very deeply nested directory tree you are dealing with. Be sure to click Finish.

Windows Artifact Parser

The Windows Artifact Parser module will process link files, recycle bin files, and MFT transactions, and put them in one location for you to inspect. It also has the option of searching unallocated space for these artifacts. Choose all of the options from this module.

 ## Our First Evidence Processor Run

That covers the modules that we will be running on this first pass through the evidence file. To circle back, let's make sure you are running the same modules that I am. Figure 5-17 shows the Evidence Processor window with the modules I have checked.

Click OK to start the processing once your selections match mine. At the bottom-right corner of the screen, you will see the Evidence Processor's progress bar. At the bottom-left corner, you may see a warning that you should stop the evidence processor before performing a case backup. Since the Evidence Processor is busy building out your cache files on disk as it processes through the evidence, it makes sense that you should not try to perform a case backup in the middle of this activity.

Once the Evidence Processor completes (which may take some time), you can view the results. They are accessed by choosing the Records option from the View menu, or by choosing the Records option from the Home page in the Browse section. Both get you to the same place.

NOTE

You don't have to wait until the processing job completes to look at the results, but keep in mind that until it does complete, not all of the items will show up.

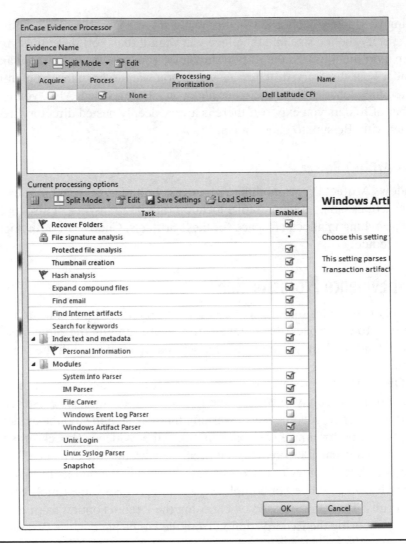

Figure 5-17   *The Evidence Processor options we will be running*

Note that when you launch the Evidence Processor after having processed your evidence at least once, it will not allow you to make changes to the modules you ran during prior runs. These will show up as checked with the same options you used before, and you will be unable to uncheck them. It is a quick way of seeing if you have already run a module that doesn't put its results in an easy to spot location, such as the Results section.

Run Book: Initial Case Evidence Processing and Preparation

1. Add evidence.

2. Once the automatic evidence verification has completed, compare acquisition and verification hashes and note that you have verified they match.

3. Determine the time zone of the acquired evidence and set EnCase to match.

4. Start Evidence Processor and choose what processes you want to run.

5. Save the case once Evidence Processor completes.

Summary

We have created our case and set the time zone for our evidence. We've also kicked off our first run of the Evidence Processor, which will do the work to prepare our evidence for further analysis. With these modules run, we will spend some time in Chapter 6 looking at the results of the processing, and go further into using EnCase to analyze evidence for our investigation.

Documenting Evidence

aving completed our initial processing run on the evidence, we can now begin answering more of the questions for the case study. Getting in the habit of documenting the details of our case and the state of the system at the outset of the case is a good practice as it provides a framework for the investigation. With these initial questions answered, moving on to answering the allegations in the case gives you a solid foundation to work from. It is better to be in the habit of noting items as you find them than to have to try and remember everything at some later date.

Initial Case Documentation

A good place for us to start is to document the basics about our case—the operating system, install date, and some of the fundamental questions associated with this evidence before we move forward with asking specifically what this laptop was used for in the context of this scenario. Here are the questions (from the NIST Hacking Case scenario) we will tackle in this initial phase of documenting the state of the system prior to delving further into event reconstruction:

1. *What is the image hash? Do the acquisition and verification hashes match?* We verified the image hash in the last chapter, but in keeping with the spirit of these questions, we can quickly revisit this. With the NIST Hacking case open, choose Evidence from the Browse section on the case Home page. This opens the Evidence Browser. Selecting Entries in the Tree pane will show the list of evidence items for this case in the Table pane. Select the Dell Latitude CPi evidence item, and click on the Report tab in the View pane. Scrolling down a bit, you will come to the section with the acquisition and verification hashes (Figure 6-1).

   ### NOTE

   There is also a Run Book for this process in Appendix C.

   As you can see, the answer to the first question for this case is that the image hash (which is the acquisition hash) is aee4fcd9301c03b3b054623ca261959a. You can also tell by inspection that the acquisition and verification hashes match each other.

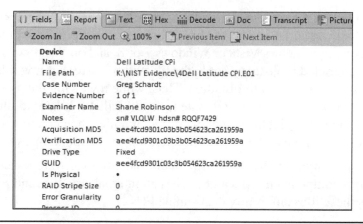

Figure 6-1   *Acquisition and verification hashes*

2. *What operating system was used on the computer?* This can be found in a couple of places. The fastest is the contents of the prodspec.ini file located in c:\WINDOWS\system32. Selecting the file in the Table pane brings us the detail in the View pane shown in Figure 6-2. You could see the same detail in several of the tabs, including Text, Hex, and Transcript. They would look slightly different, but the data displayed is the same.

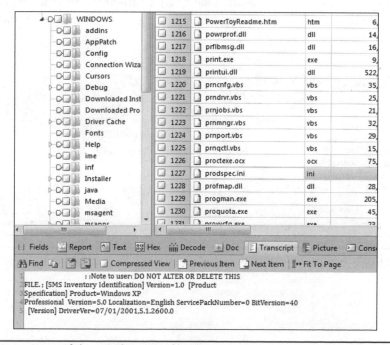

Figure 6-2   *Contents of the prodspec.ini file*

You can see by the contents in Figure 6-2 that the version of the operating system that was installed is listed here. However, the prodspec.ini file does not exist native in Windows Vista or Windows 7 or 8, and on Windows XP systems that are upgraded to Vista or 7 or 8, the file will be there, but it will list the wrong operating system information. Thus, while reviewing the prodspec.ini file is a fast way to check on XP systems, and I will use it later to illustrate a specific point about highlighting text inside of a file when creating a bookmark, it isn't the recommended method for determining the operating system.

The recommended method is to look in the Windows software registry hive, which is a compound file (meaning it has an internal structure and EnCase handles these files differently than simple files).

Files with Internal Structure

We dealt with a different type of compound file in Chapter 3 when we examined Ken Lay's .pst file from the Enron case, mounting it manually. These files are not handled by the Evidence Processor and must be expanded individually. Since we are looking for the value of a specific key inside of the software registry hive, we must first have EnCase mount the file—open and parse the internal structure of the file and display it for us. To do this, open the Evidence tab and navigate down to the C\Windows\system32\config folder (Figure 6-3).

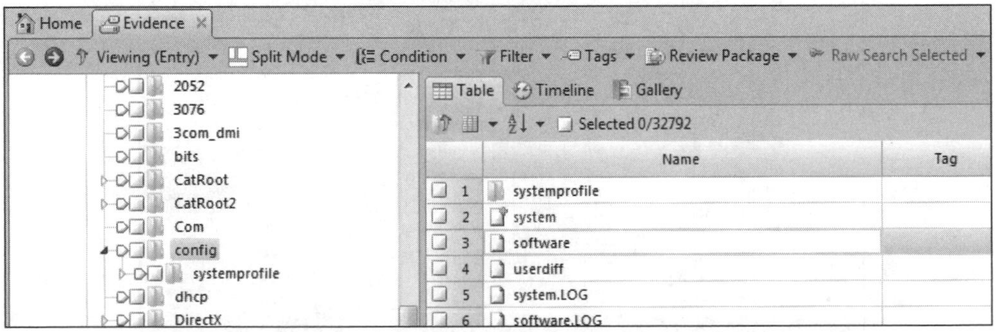

Figure 6-3 *The software registry hive*

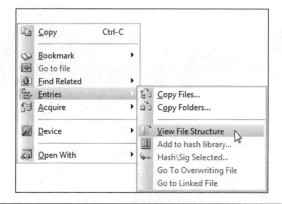

Figure 6-4   *View File Structure*

When a compound file has been mounted and parsed, you will see the plus
sign next to it, and it will become a hyperlink. The system hive in Figure 6-3 is an
example of a compound file that has been mounted. The software file below it is not
yet mounted. Right-click the software file and choose View File Structure from the
Entries context menu that displays (Figure 6-4).

EnCase will process the file structure and when it finishes, the filename will
change to have a green plus sign next to it, and it will become a hyperlink, as with the
System hive example above. Clicking on the filename will allow you to view the file.
Regardless of the type of compound file you encounter, the process for individually
mounting and processing them will remain the same.

Now that we've parsed the internal structure of the software registry hive, we need
to look under Microsoft\Windows NT\CurrentVersion\ProductName to get the value
in the Hex tab of the View pane as shown in Figure 6-5.

3. *When was the install date?* The install date can be obtained from another
   registry key in the same registry hive. In fact, it is in the same location as the
   prior key, under Microsoft\Windows NT\CurrentVersion\ but this time we look
   at the InstallDate key's value (Figure 6-6).

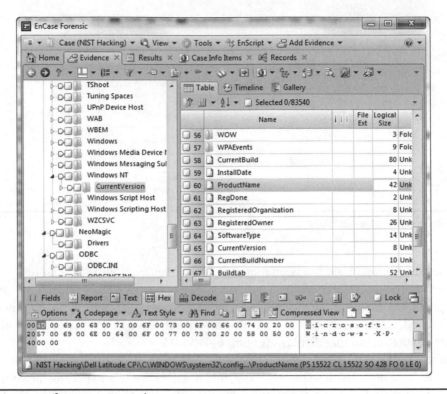

Figure 6-5 *Software registry showing operating system version*

Not exactly in human readable format, is it? We need to decode this to be able to decipher what we're looking at. To do this, first make sure you have the contents of the key value selected as shown in Figure 6-6, and then click on the Decode tab of the View pane. You will see a number of folders showing various options for decoding the data you've selected (Figure 6-7). The InstallDate value is stored in Universal Time (the number of seconds since January 1, 1970), which corresponds to the Unix Date format under the Dates folder.

So selecting the Unix Date option on the left will show you the value of the InstallDate for the operating system on the right. In our case, it decodes to August 19, 2004 at 05:48:27 p.m.

4. *What is the time zone setting?* We covered this in the last chapter as well. The time zone value can be found under the system registry hive in the current control set's TimeZoneInformation key values. If you recall, we took note of the DaylightName and ActiveTimeBias key values to help determine the settings for this image. Ours is set to Central Daylight Time.

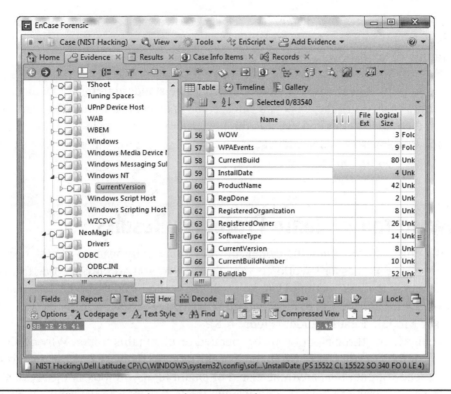

Figure 6-6   *InstallDate registry key value in Hex tab*

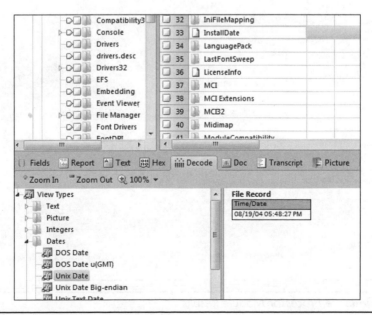

Figure 6-7   *Decode tab*

5. *Who is the registered owner?* The registered owner is also in the software registry hive under Microsoft\Windows NT\CurrentVersion\RegisteredOwner. In this case, it shows a value of Greg Schardt.

These first five questions seem like they would be standard items to document for every single case, don't they? As you can see, the answers are scattered in various places in the registry files and even on the file system. Now let's look at how the Evidence Processor's results can help us answer these and the other questions more quickly based on the options we chose.

Viewing the Evidence Processor Results

Once we finished processing the evidence, we will naturally want to see the results of the Evidence Processor's work. To view the results, you go into Records from the Home screen's Browse section. Here you will see several folders in the Tree pane under the Dell Latitude Cpi evidence item. What you are looking for is the Evidence Processor Module Results folder (Figure 6-8).

You can see the three modules that generated results in this folder. Why don't all of them put their results here? Well, that speaks more to the way EnCase displays various pieces of data than anything else. For example, if you look in the Evidence tab at the system registry hive that we used in the last chapter to determine the time

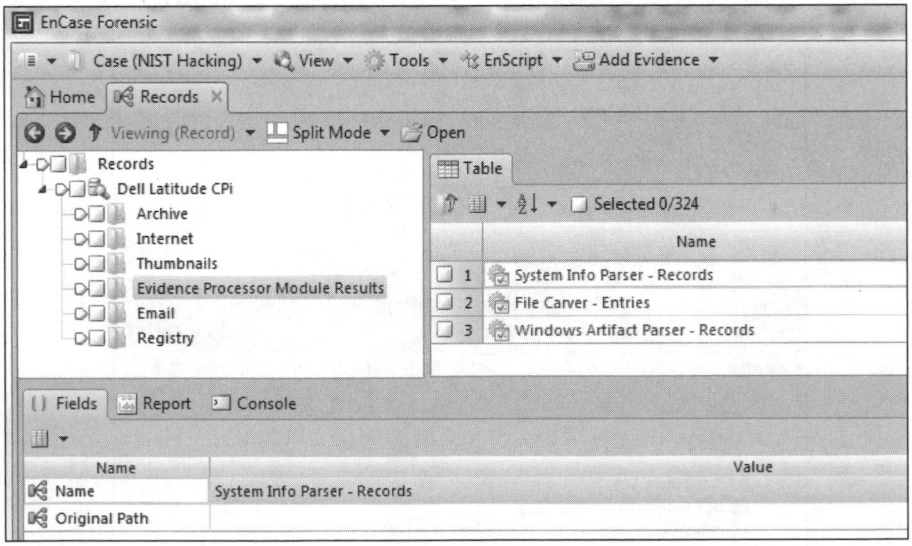

Figure 6-8 *Evidence Processor Module Results*

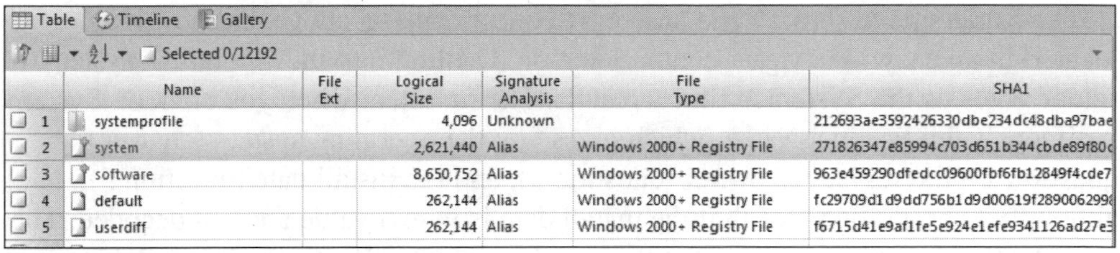

	Name	File Ext	Logical Size	Signature Analysis	File Type	SHA1
1	systemprofile		4,096	Unknown		212693ae3592426330dbe234dc48dba97bae
2	system		2,621,440	Alias	Windows 2000+ Registry File	271826347e85994c703d651b344cbde89f80c
3	software		8,650,752	Alias	Windows 2000+ Registry File	963e459290dfedcc09600fbf6fb12849f4cde7
4	default		262,144	Alias	Windows 2000+ Registry File	fc29709d1d9dd756b1d9d00619f289006299
5	userdiff		262,144	Alias	Windows 2000+ Registry File	f6715d41e9af1fe5e924e1efe9341126ad27e3

Figure 6-9 *Evidence Browser, system registry hive*

zone settings, you would see quite a bit more data than you did before. There are now values in the Signature Analysis, MD5, SHA-1, and a number of other columns that were blank before we ran the Evidence Processor (Figure 6-9). (I dragged these columns over by their column headings and dropped them in the order you see here for readability.)

So some of the modules, such as those just mentioned, will put their results in columns that are viewable in the regular Evidence view rather than making you go to a specific folder in the Records tab to see whether the signature analysis on a specific file shows a mismatch. It doesn't make sense to have to chase these types of results all over the interface—you want to see them when you are viewing that specific file. What does make sense is to group certain results together, and those are the ones that we can see have specific results folders for us to view.

The first results set under the Evidence Processor Module Results folder is the System Info Parser – Records results. Clicking on this in the Table pane gives us a view into that set of records (Figure 6-10).

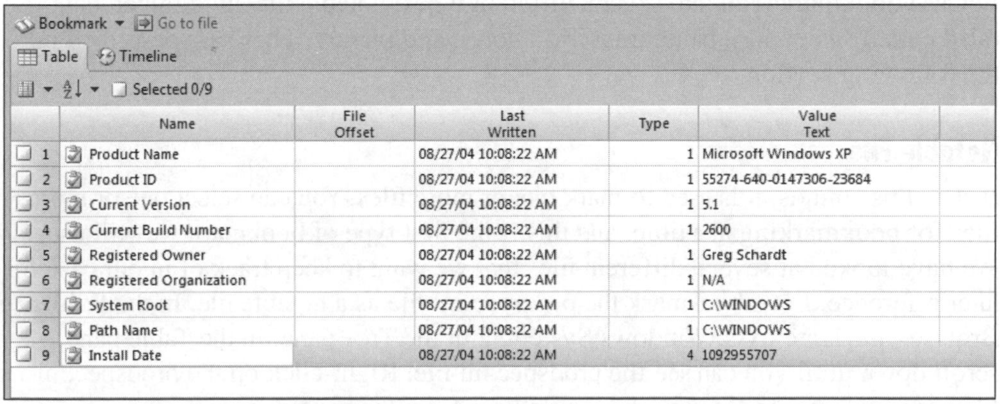

	Name	File Offset	Last Written	Type	Value Text
1	Product Name		08/27/04 10:08:22 AM	1	Microsoft Windows XP
2	Product ID		08/27/04 10:08:22 AM	1	55274-640-0147306-23684
3	Current Version		08/27/04 10:08:22 AM	1	5.1
4	Current Build Number		08/27/04 10:08:22 AM	1	2600
5	Registered Owner		08/27/04 10:08:22 AM	1	Greg Schardt
6	Registered Organization		08/27/04 10:08:22 AM	1	N/A
7	System Root		08/27/04 10:08:22 AM	1	C:\WINDOWS
8	Path Name		08/27/04 10:08:22 AM	1	C:\WINDOWS
9	Install Date		08/27/04 10:08:22 AM	4	1092955707

Figure 6-10 *System Info Parser results*

The folders have some of the answers to questions 1–5 above, but now they're located in an easy to navigate central location. Drilling into the Operating System folder gives us the System Artifacts results. The first item when you click on System Artifacts is the Product Name, which gives you the operating system (answer to question 2), the registered owner (question 5), and the install date (question 3), although it should be noted that the install date is in text value and not decoded. The Last Written column's value is not the same as the InstallDate we decoded and is not what that is showing. Rather, that is the last write date of the registry key in question.

While this won't get you a shortcut to all of the questions we've answered above, it does help to keep quite a few of the answers to those and some further questions in one convenient location. This brings us to another point, however. If you find something that is relevant and you want to include it in your report (or just make it easier to find later), you need to bookmark it.

Bookmarking Evidence Items

Much as you create a bookmark in your favorite web browsing application to make sure you can find it again easily, EnCase allows you to create bookmarks to identify evidence items of interest to your case. Bookmarks are stored in the .Case file along with any metadata and content all in the same place. Keeping your bookmarks organized into related folders will help you later when you need to present your findings in a report.

Types of Bookmarks

EnCase bookmarks fall into several different types: notable file, highlighted data (also called sweeping), table, transcript, notes, and picture. These are described in the following sections.

Notable File

Just as this sounds, it is used to mark one or more files. You can select one or more files for bookmarking at a time, and this is the first type of bookmark we will use. We have looked at several different files that we want to keep track of in our case for later reference. Let's bookmark the prodspec.ini file as a notable file. In the Evidence Browser, navigate to C:\Windows\System32 in the Tree pane. In the Table pane, scroll down until you can see the prodspec.ini file. Right-click on the prodspec.ini filename and choose Bookmark | Single Item from the context menu.

As you can see in Figure 6-11, there is a place to put a comment. The button to the right of the comment box brings up another window with a listing of the most recent

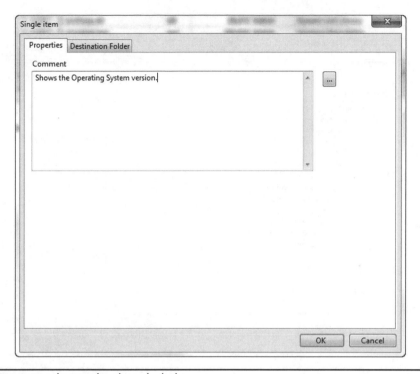

Figure 6-11 *Single Item bookmark dialog*

comments you have added to other bookmarks, so you can choose from them. Since this is our first bookmark, this is empty, of course.

The Destination Folder tab (Figure 6-12) is important because, here, you choose where to put the bookmark. EnCase provides a folder structure by default to help keep your case items organized. You can also create a new folder using the text box at the top of the window and choosing where in the folder structure to place it.

Under the Bookmarks main level, you see the Examination folder. Under that there are two sections—Examiner Notes and Report. These are expanded by default as shown in Figure 6-12. The items in this folder hierarchy are dependent on the type of case template you selected at the outset when you created your case. We chose the Forensic template, and the structure shown is the default for that.

For items you want to appear in your report, use the Report section of the tree. I've put this bookmark into the System Information folder under the Examination section.

Notable file bookmarks can also be made for multiple files. The process is much the same, but first you select the files you want (by clicking in the box to the left of each file in the Table pane to select it) and then follow the same process. When you do this with a group of files, they will all be put into a single folder, so be sure that is what you want.

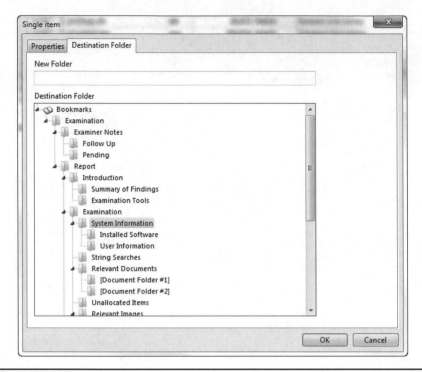

Figure 6-12   *Bookmarks Destination Folder*

Highlighted Data

Highlighted data (also called sweeping) is when you select a chunk of contiguous data, such as a paragraph of text in a document or a section in the Hex view, for example. There are two types of highlighted data bookmarks. They are:

▶ **Raw text**   You create this type of bookmark by selecting raw text in the View pane the same way you select blocks of text in a word processor. The expected mouse shortcuts exist, such as double-clicking to select a word and SHIFT-click to highlight from the cursor to your location. Raw text bookmarks are created by highlighting data in the Text tab of the View pane and saving the selection as a bookmark. The bookmark will be identifiable as a Raw text bookmark in the Bookmarks view by the icon next to the filename that matches the icon for the Text tab. This convention is consistently used for other types of bookmarks.

▶ **Data structure** This type of bookmark is for storing something from the Decode tab of the View pane. Since we have the InstallDate to bookmark, this is a good time to preserve that information for later reference. In the Evidence Browser, navigate back to the software registry hive and the InstallDate key. With the contents of the InstallDate key selected in the Hex tab, click the Decode tab and click on Unix Date under the Dates folder. You should now see the Time/Date File Record shown as before in the right pane. Right-click on Unix Date and choose Bookmarks | Data Structure. Give this a description and assign it to the System Information folder under Examination in the Report hierarchy. When you go back to this in the bookmarks viewer, you will see that it has preserved the decoding option you selected. We'll discuss that more in just a moment.

Table

There may be times when you want to bookmark everything in the Table view and keep the tabular nature of the data intact. To do this, select each entry you want to keep with a blue check, and then right-click and choose Table View from the Bookmarks menu. This opens up a Properties dialog where you can give this bookmark a name and comment, and assign where you want it to go just like other bookmark types. Then pick and choose which columns you want to include in your bookmark. When you use this type of bookmark later in your report, you get a nice table layout of the data that you selected.

We looked at the results of our Evidence Processor in the Records tab earlier, and the contents of the System Info Parser module are a good candidate for a Table bookmark, since this documents much of the information that is relevant to the state of the system when it was imaged. To create this bookmark, open the Records Browser (Home | Records), and drill down into the Dell Latitude CPi image. Open the System Info Parser hyperlink from inside the Evidence Processor Modules Results folder. You will note that as you navigate deeper into this path, the Tree pane will change the top level folder. For example, before you click on the System Info Parser – Records hyperlink in the Table pane, the view is as shown in Figure 6-13.

Clicking on that System Info Parser – Records hyperlink changes your view to that shown in Figure 6-14.

EnCase starts the Tree pane at the top of this record instead of continuing the folder hierarchy as you would expect to be able to drill down in Windows Explorer or the Evidence Browser. It does not provide the expected vertical scroll bar to allow you to

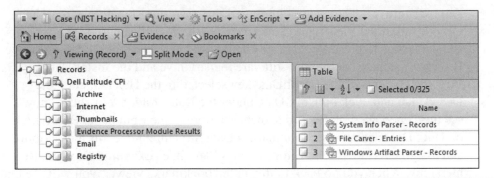

Figure 6-13   *Evidence Processor module in Tree pane*

follow the path back up again. You have to use the green back arrow button at the top left to move back along the path you just traversed. It does this again each time you click on a hyperlink to drill into the detail. Click on Operating System as shown in Figure 6-14 and then click on the System Artifacts hyperlink in the Table pane.

To create our Table bookmark, select each of the files in the Table pane with a blue check by clicking the box to the left of the Name column. Once you have selected them all, right-click and choose Table View from the Bookmark context menu. This launches a Properties dialog where you can give the bookmark a name (System Artifacts from Evidence Processor) and descriptive comment. Click Next and choose the System Information folder under the Report hierarchy. Click Next again and you will see the Add Datamark dialog (Figure 6-15). This is where you choose which columns you want to include in your bookmark.

Include the columns shown in the figure and click Finish.

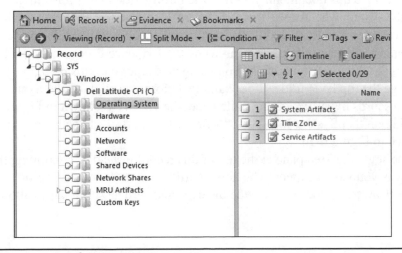

Figure 6-14   *System Info Parser view*

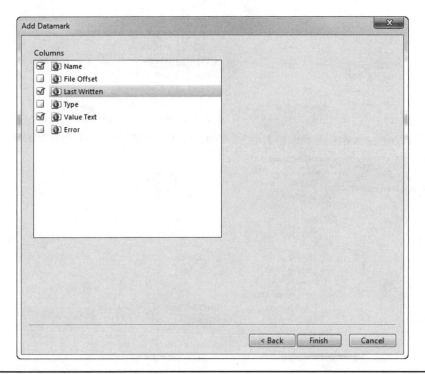

Figure 6-15   *Add Datamark dialog*

Transcript

Are you sensing a theme here? Basically the type of bookmark you create depends largely on where you are when you create it. If you are in the Text tab of the View pane and selecting data, you will be creating a Raw text bookmark. Likewise, for the Transcript tab—if you select text in this tab, your option will be to bookmark it as a transcript text bookmark.

So if we wanted to highlight a specific section of the prodspec.ini file as the most interesting bit, we can do that with this type of bookmark. To do this, in the Evidence Browser again, with the prodspec.ini file in the Transcript tab of the View pane, select the third and fourth lines of text (or whatever portion of the file you find most interesting) and right-click. From the context menu, choose Bookmark and then Transcript Text (Figure 6-16).

Include a description of the data you've selected and put it in the same folder that we used before for the single file bookmark.

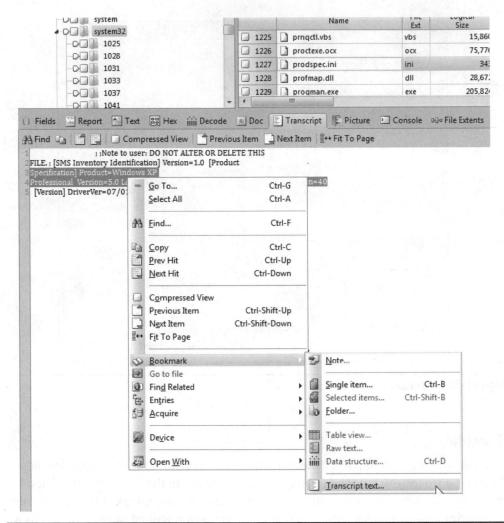

Figure 6-16 *Transcript bookmark*

Notes

You can include notes in your bookmarks—they aren't tied to specific evidence items, but more for description and comments—think of them as a virtual sticky note. The size limit for a notes bookmark is 1,000 characters. They can be especially useful in the Examiner Notes section of the folder structure where investigators make notes to themselves as the case progresses. You can include them in your report or not, as you choose.

> ### TIP
>
> *Use the follow-up section to keep track of things you want to revisit at a later date. This section is great for items that reminded you of a lead you want to follow up, but don't want to take the time away from the current path you are investigating.*

Remember when we verified that the acquisition and verification hashes matched? A notes bookmark is a good thing to create when you do this. So with the Dell Latitude CPi image open in the Evidence Browser, looking at the Report tab, note the date and time and create a notes bookmark to indicate that you completed this step (Figure 6-17). Put the bookmark in the Examination top level folder of the Report hierarchy.

Picture

You can bookmark pictures either individually or as multiple files, much like any other file. The Gallery view makes it easy to browse through all of the pictures on a system quickly, and you can bookmark them from there was well as from the Table pane. These will be notable file bookmarks.

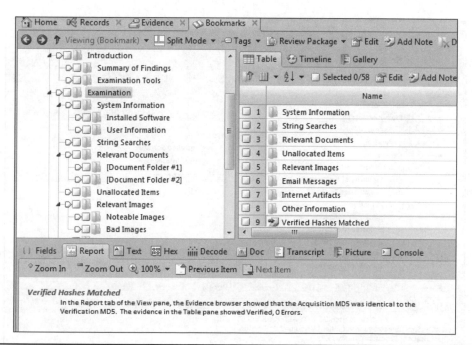

Figure 6-17   *Notes bookmark*

Viewing Bookmarks

Once you have created bookmarks, you may need to go back and look at them (whether to revisit the evidence item quickly, or to rearrange or edit them). To see your previously saved bookmarks, choose Bookmarks from the View menu. You will have the folder structure of your bookmarks in the Tree pane, with the details accessible in the Table and View panes. Figure 6-18 shows the single file bookmark we created for the prodspec.ini file earlier.

The Bookmark template structure is tied into the Report template structure, which we will discuss later. While you can create new folders in your bookmarks hierarchy in the Tree pane, you will also need to mirror those changes in your Report template for consistency. This is also something to keep in mind when you are creating new case templates—plan out the Bookmarks and Report templates at the same time to ensure that you are providing the tools to keep your cases consistently organized from start to finish. The alternative is to have the Report template inherit the Bookmark template folder structure as a workaround.

You can create new Bookmarks folders either when you create a new bookmark or in the Bookmark view using the Tree pane. To do this, right-click on the parent

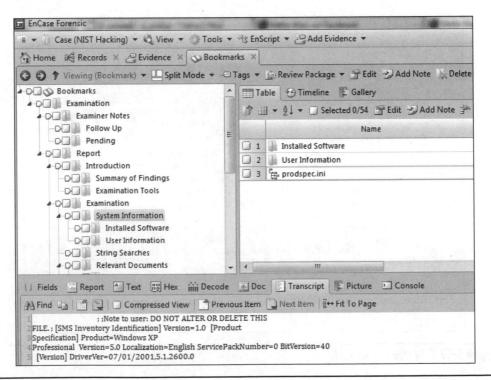

Figure 6-18 *Viewing bookmarks*

folder under which you want your new folder to be created and choose New Folder from the context menu. You will be presented with a new folder that has a default name of "folder##", with the number being the count of existing folders plus one for this new folder. You can change the name (and should) either using the F2 shortcut or choosing Rename from the right-click menu. You can also drag the folder to another folder should you wish to change its location in the folder hierarchy.

Remember earlier when we made a single file bookmark for prodspec.ini and then later made a highlighted data bookmark for text inside the same file? This does something interesting in the Bookmarks view. If you look under the folder where you put the two bookmarks, you now see the two different types of bookmarks that you created (Figure 6-19). In the Table pane, item 3 is a file type bookmark, and you can see the tree hierarchy symbol next to it. Item 4 is the highlighted data bookmark we created, and it has the same symbol as the Transcript tab where we made it. Clicking on item 4, you can see in the View pane our highlighted text, as you would expect. However, if you click on item 3, the same text is still highlighted, even though we made this bookmark before the highlighting was done.

The highlighting in the file is now permanent unless you delete that bookmark—clicking elsewhere in the pane will not remove it.

Remember that data structure bookmark we made earlier for the InstallDate? Look at it in your bookmarks viewer. When you first click on it, it brings up the

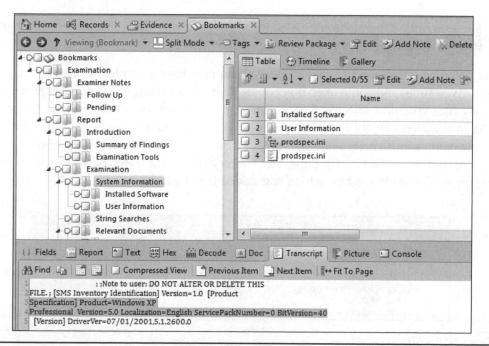

Figure 6-19 *Prodspec.ini in the bookmarks viewer*

Report tab and shows you the decoded date value, correct? If you go back into the Decode tab of the View pane with this bookmark selected, EnCase will allow you to choose another option, but even if you do, clicking back on the Report tab still shows the value that you originally bookmarked.

The Blue Check

When you need to select multiple files at a time, you do this in EnCase by checking the box next to the item (in either the Tree or Table pane). This is called "blue checking" the item, named after the blue check mark that appears inside the box. We used this earlier when we selected multiple files for the Table bookmark. Since we still need to make one more bookmark with the time zone information, we can use that to illustrate more about blue checking.

When you place a blue check in the box next to an item in the Table pane, you may have noticed that the Tree pane shows a blue check in the folder where that evidence item exists, plus all folders up the tree to the top folder. This lets you know at a glance if a folder has an item selected (checked) in it from the Tree pane, and gives you a sort of path to follow if you selected something earlier and can't remember exactly where it was in the folder structure.

The Selected Box

As you navigate around in your evidence, you may have a number of files checked at a given time, and sometimes it becomes a bit of a challenge to figure out how many files you have selected. That is where the Selected box (known as the Dixon box in prior versions of EnCase) comes in. The Selected box can be found in the Table pane, and it keeps a running tally of how many files you have blue checked. It is present in the Table, Timeline, and Gallery tabs of the Table pane, as shown in Figure 6-20 (inside the box, which was added for emphasis).

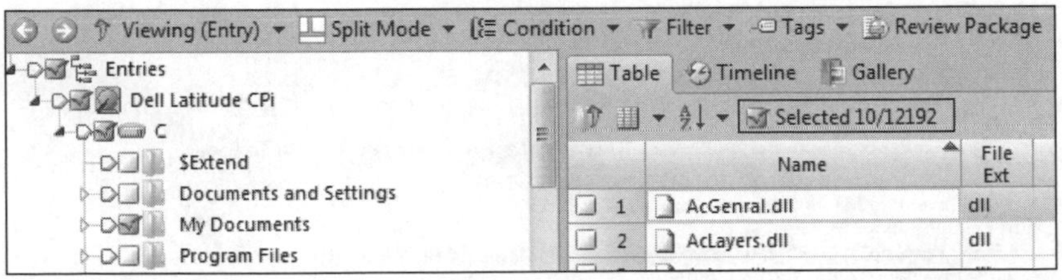

Figure 6-20 *The Selected box*

	Name	File Offset	Last Written	Type	Value Text
☐ 1	Standard Time Bias		08/19/04 12:20:02 PM	4	0
☐ 2	Standard Time		08/19/04 12:20:02 PM	1	Central Standard Time
☐ 3	Standard Time is set to chang...		08/19/04 12:20:02 PM	3	Month: 10 - Sunday: 5 - Time: 02:00
☐ 4	Daylight Time Bias		08/19/04 12:20:02 PM	4	+1
☐ 5	Daylight Savings		08/19/04 12:20:02 PM	1	Central Daylight Time
☐ 6	Daylight Savings is set to cha...		08/19/04 12:20:02 PM	3	Month: 4 - Sunday: 1 - Time: 02:00
☐ 7	Active Time Bias offset from G...		08/19/04 12:20:02 PM	4	-5
☐ 8	Current Time offset from GMT		08/19/04 12:20:02 PM	4	-6
☐ 9	Display		08/19/04 12:01:58 PM	1	(GMT-06:00) Central Time (US & Ca...

Figure 6-21   *Time zone records*

In this example, I have 10 out of 12,192 files selected. This is very useful in determining how many files you are about to run an action on—such as applying a filter or condition. You can also use it as a toggle to select or deselect all of the files in your case by clicking inside the box.

We still have one more bookmark to make—we haven't created a bookmark showing the time zone information yet. Navigate back into the Records tab and down into the Evidence Processor module results to get to the System Info Parser – Records results. You can either drill into the folders until you get to the Operating System folder by hand or you can right-click in the Tree pane and choose Expand All to expand all of the folders so you can go right to the directory. Either way, once there, click on the Time Zone hyperlink.

Note the Selected box at the top of the Table tab (Figure 6-21)? It has changed from showing the files selected in the case to just showing the files selected in this result set. Selecting items in this view also does not change the number selected if you were to go and look at the Selected box in your Evidence Browser. These are just showing the items selected in each section of the records you are looking at.

For our bookmark, select all of the items in the Table pane, and create a table bookmark with the columns that have values in them. Save this under the name Time Zone Setting Key Values in the System Information Bookmarks folder.

The Set Include (Home Plate)

The other way to select files that you should know about is called "home plating," named after the symbol that looks like the shape of a baseball home plate in the Tree pane. The official name is the "Set Include," and you will hear it referred to both ways.

Clicking on the home plate symbol displays all items below that in the Table pane, regardless of type. EnCase also turns the home plates and all those below it in the Tree pane green to show the folders that are included. This is especially useful in the Gallery view when you want to see all of the pictures in the image in one place. You can put a Set Include on the top level of the evidence item in the Tree pane, and then click on the Gallery tab in the Table pane and you will see all of the graphic images for the evidence you selected.

It should be noted that images in the Gallery view are included based on their file extension rather than a signature analysis by default. So if a graphics file has an incorrect extension (i.e., someone has tried to use an alias and changed it to a .dll extension to have it masquerade as an operating system file to hide it), the file will not show up in the Gallery view before you use the Evidence Processor to run a signature analysis against the evidence.

You can see how this is a powerful way to see all of the graphics in your evidence in one easy to browse interface. If you want to see all of the graphics across multiple evidence files, simply home plate the Entries item at the top of the folder tree. Clicking on a specific picture in the Gallery view will allow it to be displayed in the Picture tab in the View pane (Figure 6-22). Hmm…looks like someone has been looking into books on wireless networking. Let's make a quick picture bookmark on that file. Right-click the item in the Table pane and choose Single Item from the Bookmark menu (note, choosing Selected Items now would have bookmarked the 10 items that are shown as selected in the Selected box at the top of the Gallery tab) and put it in your Follow Up folder under Examiner Notes. Click OK to save the bookmark.

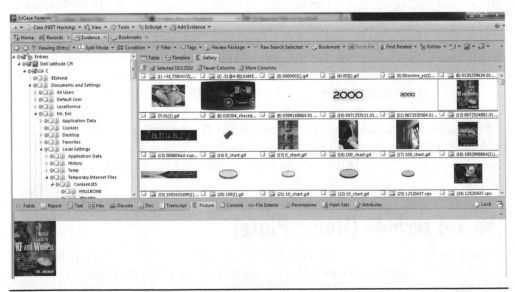

Figure 6-22   *The Set Include and the Gallery view*

TIP

Speaking of saving, have you saved your case lately? Even though there are case backups occurring automatically, it is always a good practice to save early and often.

Tagging

EnCase allows you to assign high level category names or tags to evidence items. You can create your own tags or use the ones already defined. Predefined tags include Review, Add to Report, Follow Up with Submitter, Ignore, and Important. To add a tag to an evidence item, which can be done from the Evidence, Bookmarks, or Records tabs, you can either choose Tags from the top menu bar, or use the CTRL-T shortcut key. Since we are in the Gallery looking at this potentially interesting file, let's give that file a tag.

With the graphic of the book (*The Essential Guide to RF and Wireless*) selected, I chose Tag Selected Items from the Tags menu. The Tags dialog pops up and I can choose which category to put this in (Figure 6-23). Choose Review and click OK. Now we can look at that graphic file in the Table pane to see our new tag (Figure 6-24).

Figure 6-23   *Tags dialog*

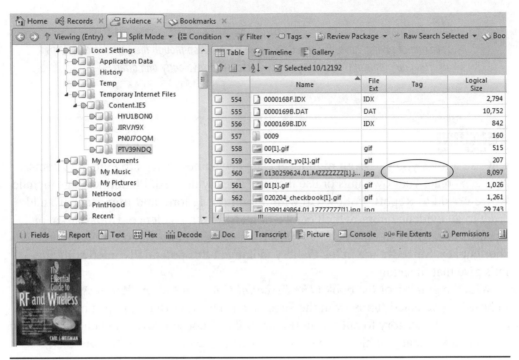

Figure 6-24 *Graphic file in the Table pane*

The tag(s) associated with the file will be displayed in the Tag column of the Table pane. What happened to our tag? Remember when we talked about the Selected box? Tagging works on selected files, not on highlighted files. It even says so in the menu item I used—Tag Selected Items. No blue check means no tag will be applied to this, even though I had it highlighted in the Gallery tab. So what did we just tag? Every evidence item that did have a blue check—10 items according to Figure 6-24. What to do now? Well, there isn't an Undo in EnCase, but we can do the next best thing. We still have the same number of files selected, so we can delete the tags we just added accidentally. Go back to the Tags menu, choose Untag Selected Items, and click OK. Note in that dialog, at the top, it says the number of tags you are affecting. It said the same thing when we tagged them, so paying attention to this is a good idea.

Now that we have removed the tags we didn't want, we still need to create the tag that we do want. This time, in the Gallery tab or the Table tab—it makes no difference—put a blue check in the box next to the file's name instead of just clicking on the file to highlight it. Now that it is selected, look at the Selected box at the top of the Gallery tab to make sure it only shows one file. Choose Tag Selected Items from the Tags menu, and this time when the dialog comes up, it shows only one item will be tagged at the top title bar. Choose to assign this the Review tag and click OK.

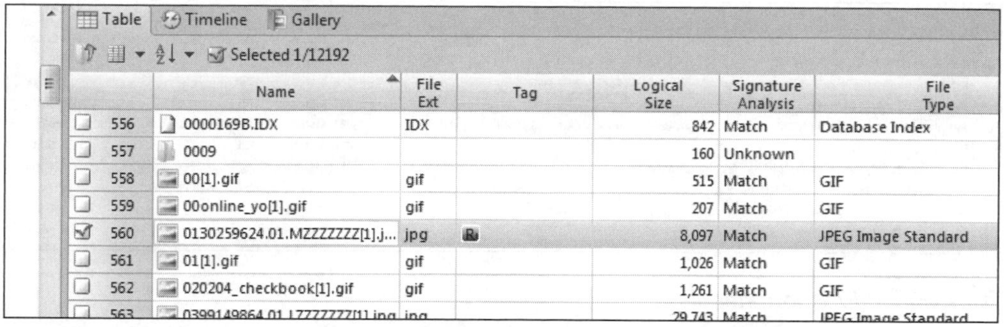

Figure 6-25 *Graphic file in the Table pane showing tag*

Now you can see the tag in the Tag column for this file (Figure 6-25). Another way to tag a file is actually to click in this Tag column. The tags are positional, which means if I visually divide the Tag column into as many columns as I have defined tags, each one only shows up in its column. To illustrate this, remember all of the tags that showed up in the predefined list when we were tagging a file? Each of those has its own place in the column, and, in fact, if you expand the Tag column, you can see that the graphic shown in Figure 6-25 is really a color-coded tag button with the name of the tag inside (see Figure 6-26).

If you clicked in any of these other file's Tag columns, you could toggle on and off any of these by clicking where the tag would be positioned. Figure 6-27 shows an example (not part of the case, just to illustrate the point).

Click the blank space under one of the tags for another file to see the Tag turn on and off. Clicking on an existing tag will turn it off. Once you have finished, just leave the Review tag on the file we tagged earlier.

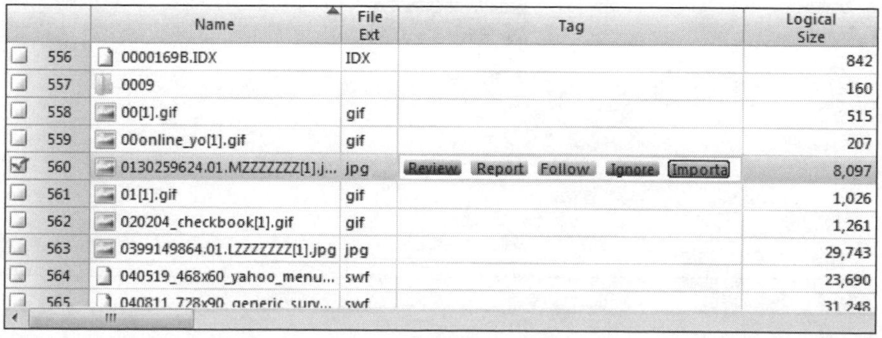

Figure 6-26 *Tag column expanded with all tags assigned*

		Name	File Ext	Tag				Logical Size	Signature Analysis	File Type	
☐	556	0000169B.IDX	IDX				Importa	842	Match	Database Index	a0b686f
☐	557	0009						160	Unknown		867a58a
☐	558	00[1].gif	gif	Report				515	Match	GIF	86ec4d6
☐	559	00online_yo[1].gif	gif					207	Match	GIF	540711c
☑	560	0130259624.01.MZZZZZZZ[1].j...	jpg	Review Report Follow Ignore Importa				8,097	Match	JPEG Image Standard	2ea46a5
☐	561	01[1].gif	gif					1,026	Match	GIF	37f8ab4
☐	562	020204_checkbook[1].gif	gif	Review				1,261	Match	GIF	241d4f9
☐	563	0399149864.01.LZZZZZZZ[1].jpg	jpg		Ignore			29,743	Match	JPEG Image Standard	b8aec0b
☐	564	040519_468x60_yahoo_menu...	swf		Follow			23,690	Bad signat...		44f446d
☐	565	040811_728x90_generic_surv...	swf					31,248	Bad signat...		67e8d97

Figure 6-27   *Tags in other files*

Managing Tags

You are not limited to the tags that are included by default with EnCase nor are you stuck with the default colors. If you want to make changes, you do so by choosing Manage Tags from the Tags menu (or using the CTRL-~ keyboard shortcut). This brings up the Manage Tags window (Figure 6-28).

Double-clicking on the Frame Color box of a tag will allow you to make changes to back and foreground colors. You can also hide and show tags with the Hidden boxes. This dialog also allows you to add and delete the tags that you can assign to your case items.

	Name	Display	Frame Color	Hidden
☐	Review	Review	F:White B:Blue	☐
☐	Add to Report	Report	F:White B:Comment	☐
☐	Follow Up with Su...	Follow Up	F:White B:0-128-255	☐
☐	Ignore	Ignore	F:White B:Red	☐
☑	Important		F:Black B:255-0-0	☐

Figure 6-28   *Manage Tags window*

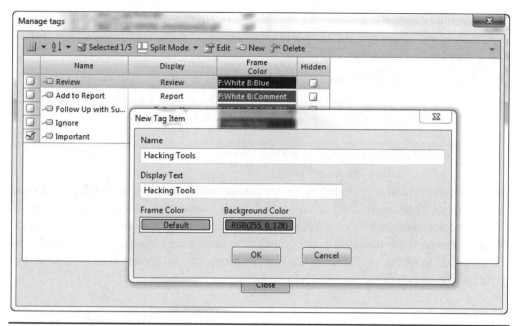

Figure 6-29   *Hacking Tools tag*

For this case, create a new tag called Hacking Tools. Click the New button and add the name and display text as shown in Figure 6-29.

Give it a color of your choice and click OK to create it. You can now see it in the Manage Tags window, and assign it as needed to evidence items in your case.

Summary

In this chapter, we've learned about viewing the results of the Evidence Processor, and have created bookmarks for the first five questions in the NIST Hacking Case. You should have also created the following bookmarks:

▶ A notes bookmark indicating you verified by inspection that the acquisition and verification hashes match on your evidence.

▶ A notable files bookmark on the prodspec.ini file.

▶ A highlighted data bookmark (transcript) on the prodspec.ini file showing the operating system information.

▶ A table bookmark showing the operating system (product name) with additional details about the version and build information, plus the registered owner and other basic system data.

▶ A second table bookmark showing the time zone data for this image.

▶ A single item picture bookmark showing the book cover about wireless network saved for follow-up in the Examiner Notes section.

You should also have the picture we bookmarked tagged for review, and have created a new tag called Hacking Tools.

Finally, the end of this chapter also concludes Part 2 of the book. We have covered quite a lot of ground, starting from scratch with a new case, we have covered a number of acquisition methods, created our first case and populated it with evidence. We have covered the basics of processing our evidence and completed the initial case documentation of the evidence. In the next section, we will move on to looking at the artifacts in more depth using the EnCase Forensics tool.

Looking for Artifacts

This section is all about using EnCase to help you get to the artifacts in your case that most matter to you. In some instances, this is done using the Evidence Processor, which was introduced in Chapter 6 and is continued in Chapter 7.

We look at the Case Analyzer in Chapter 8, where artifacts from multiple different areas can be put together to give you a picture of what is happening on the system. We also dig into creating your own custom Case Analyzer reports for artifacts that are not associated already for you in the EnCase interface.

Finally, Chapter 9 is all about searching—which is a big part of a number of cases. We cover logical versus physical searching, and the different ways to search, including an in-depth section on using GREP. You are shown how to get to the results of the searches, and how to handle some of the common occurrences where you need more complex search terms.

Further Inspection

In the last chapter, we started out looking at the modules that the EnCase Evidence Processor provided. We began the process of looking at the results and documenting the basic elements of the case. We continue the initial documentation of the system as we go through the modules that we've processed. Even if you don't find that everything you document is directly relevant to reconstructing the events in question, it is a good practice to document the basic state of the system when it was imaged. Sometimes this provides good leads to work on later down the road. It is a sign that the investigator has done a thorough job of the basics before moving on to look at the more advanced stages of the case.

More on the Evidence Processor Modules

There are interesting artifacts in several other modules that we haven't looked at yet. You should always at least review the contents of the modules once they have finished processing to ensure that you haven't missed anything of note. The three modules that we have to work through are:

▶ The System Info Parser, which we have already begun working through

▶ The File Carver

▶ The Windows Artifact Parser

The System Info Parser (Continued)

We started working through the System Info Parser module in Chapter 6. However, we have barely begun to scratch the surface of what this module has to offer in terms of initial system documentation. Some of the information that should be included in any case documentation includes:

▶ What user accounts are on this machine?

▶ What software is installed?

▶ What hardware has been connected to the system?

▶ What network interfaces are present?

▶ Are there any network shares configured?

These are questions that we can answer using the System Info Parser results. When we left off, we were looking at tagging and bookmarking evidence, so you may not be in the System Info Parser module. Open it up again by choosing Records from the Home screen of your case, and clicking on the Evidence Processor Module

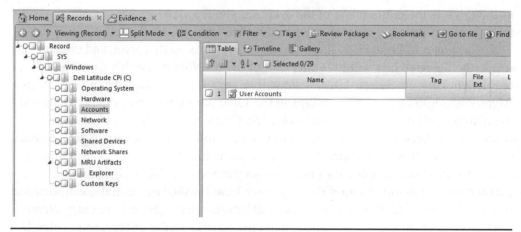

Figure 7-1 *The System Info Parser level*

Results under the Dell Latitude CPi evidence item. The System Info Parser – Records link appears in the Table pane, and you can drill into it from there. This brings us to the main level of the System Info Parser.

First, we will document the user accounts from this image. Expand the Dell Latitude CPi directory in the Tree pane and click on the Accounts folder (as shown in Figure 7-1). Click the User Accounts link, which appears in the Table pane.

We want to add these to our report, so create a bookmark with all of the accounts (Figure 7-2). In the Table pane of the Records tab, the Selected box acts differently than it does in the Evidence Browser. We can click every record in the current view by clicking on the Selected box above the Name field, and it won't put a blue check next to records in the hierarchy above this, as it would if we were blue checking in the Evidence Browser. Instead, each level of the Records tab you drill down into acts

		Name	File Offset	User Name	Full Name	Comment
☐	1	Administrator		Administrator		Built-in account for ad.
☐	2	Guest		Guest		Built-in account for gu
☐	3	HelpAssistant		HelpAssistant	Remote Desktop Help ...	Account for Providing .
☐	4	Mr. Evil		Mr. Evil		
☐	5	SUPPORT_388945a0		SUPPORT_388945a0	CN=Microsoft Corpora...	This is a vendor's acco..
☐	6	ProfilesDirectory				
☐	7	DefaultUserProfile				
☐	8	AllUsersProfile				
☐	9	S-1-5-18				
☐	10	S-1-5-19				
☐	11	S-1-5-20				

Figure 7-2 *User Accounts*

as though it is the entire scope of the evidence you are viewing. This is why you see the number of possible records change with each level you drill into.

So as shown in Figure 7-2, there are only 11 records on this level, and clicking inside the Selected box will blue check all of them. (Note, since this works as a toggle, clicking the Selected box again will remove the blue check from all of them.) Right-clicking on any of the accounts in the Table pane once you have blue checked them all will allow you to create a bookmark. Create a table view bookmark and name it User Accounts. Store it in the Bookmarks folder under Examination | Report | Examination | System Information | User Information. Include all of the columns.

A cursory glance at this list of users shows the account "Mr. Evil." Flag the account for follow-up at a later time, once we have finished our initial documentation of the evidence state. Create a note bookmark of just that user account entry. Name it Mr. Evil User Account, and save it in the Bookmarks folder under Examination | Examiner Notes | Follow-Up folder.

Now that we have the currently defined user accounts bookmarked, let's go look at the software that has been installed. Navigate back up to the main System Info Parser level and this time click on the Software folder in the Tree pane. You see three options there: Installed Applications, Installed Microsoft Applications, and Uninstalled Applications (Figure 7-3).

First, let's drill into the Installed Applications link. This provides us with a list of 34 applications that are installed. Blue check those and create another table view bookmark. Call this one Installed Software and save it in the Bookmarks folder under Examination | Report | Examination | System Information | Installed Software folder, including all the columns. Repeat this step for the Installed Microsoft Applications section. Name that table view bookmark Microsoft Installed Applications and save it in the same folder with all of the columns. Finally, repeat this for the uninstalled applications, saving them in the same folder with the same options under the name Uninstalled Applications.

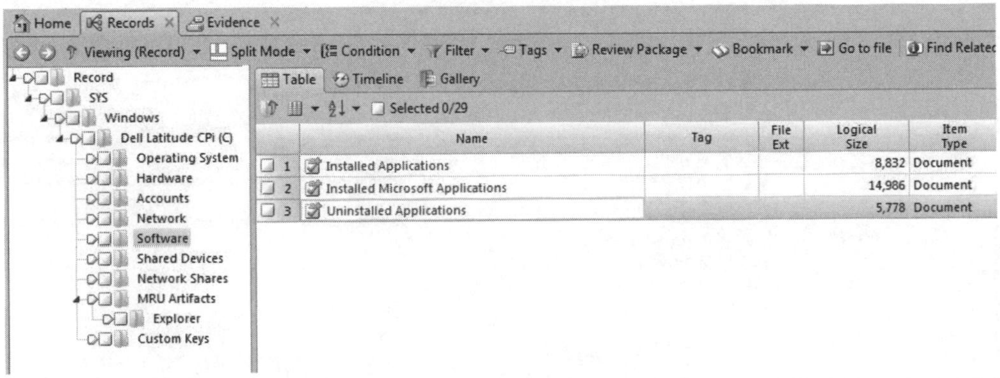

Figure 7-3 *Software folder*

The uninstalled applications are interesting, in that there are several applications that point to hacking and network discovery. As a matter of continuous learning, if there are applications you are not familiar with and suspect may be relevant to the case, it makes sense to do some research on what the software capabilities are. It may be as simple as typing the name of the application into a search engine to get an idea of whether this is likely to be useful to someone with malicious intent. The applications here show several tools that can be used for legitimate network administration, such as Ethereal or WinPcap, but if they are in the hands of someone who does not do that type of work for the organization, then they should raise a red flag for the inspector. These should also be marked for future follow-up. Create a notes bookmark for the entries as shown in Figure 7-4.

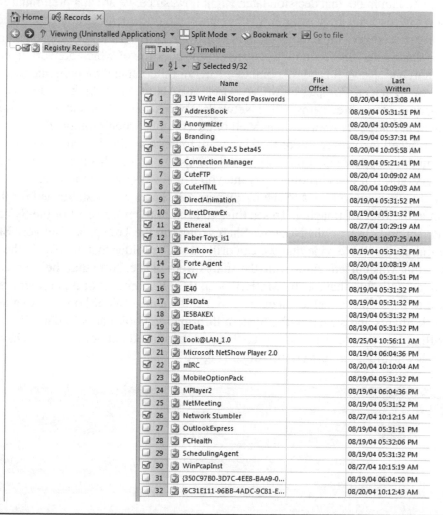

Figure 7-4 *Uninstalled applications for follow-up*

Name the bookmark Uninstalled Software and place it in the same Follow-Up directory you just used for the Mr. Evil user account bookmark. In doing this, you will ensure that once we finish our initial documentation, you have a good place to start digging further into the artifacts of this evidence image.

Now that we have the software artifacts documented, we can move onto the hardware state of the system. Navigate back up to the main level of the System Info Parser module and click on the Hardware folder. You will see two links in the Table pane: Devices and Miscellaneous. First let's look at the Devices link. This gives you 251 entries of the various devices in the system. Create a table view bookmark of these results and store it under the System Information bookmarks folder. While this may not be something you want to include in your report, due to the volume of the results, you can make that decision later. Right now, since we are at a preliminary stage and don't necessarily know what might be important, documenting it is good standard operating procedure. Name the bookmark Hardware Devices and include all columns.

Note that inside this section we can answer the question of which network interfaces the system had. Rows 38 and 39 point to a Xircom Ethernet and modem interface card, while row 47 lists a Compaq PCMCIA wireless LAN PC card. Make a table view bookmark of these three items called Network Devices and save it under the System Information folder. As always, include all of the columns when prompted.

The Miscellaneous section of the Hardware folder contains information about the number and specifics of the computer's CPUs. Including this is probably not necessary, and if it does become relevant, you can always go back to this.

Finally, we want to look and see if any network shares were established for this system at the time of imaging. To see this, go back to the main level of the System Info Parser and click on the Network Shares folder in the Tree pane. Network Shares is the link in the Table pane that we can drill into. The folder that appears is the IP address that was current at the time the shares were in use. Note that the user name associated with this share is the Mr. Evil account. The contents of this folder are of interest to us, so place a blue check next to it and create a folder bookmark called Network Shares and save it in the System Information bookmarks folder.

Drilling into that folder, we can see there are two listed network shares. They are the top level folder and the \Temp folder (Figure 7-5).

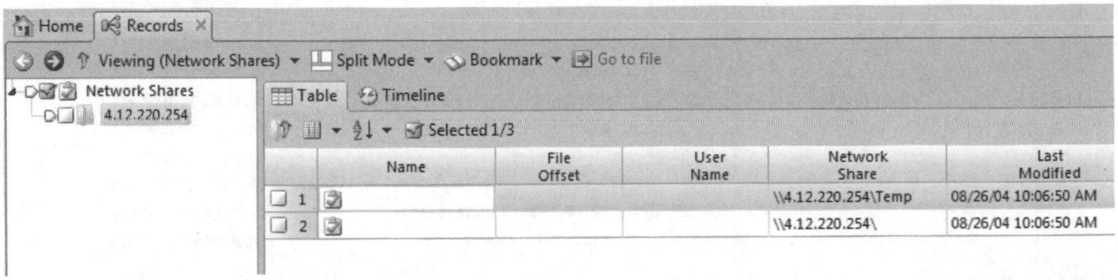

Figure 7-5   *Network shares*

There are a number of other folders in the System Info Parser that I will leave as an exercise for you to look through and bookmark anything that looks significant. The next Evidence Processor module we will look at is the File Carver.

The File Carver

The File Carver module contains the results of the efforts of EnCase to carve out identifiable records from unallocated space based on their defined header/footer combination. In our case, we chose to look for archive files. To access the results, click on the File Carver – Entries hyperlink in the Table pane.

When EnCase is able to carve out a file and then successfully parse through it as expected, you see a hyperlink for the filename (Figure 7-6). When this doesn't work as expected (the file may be a fragment or have some other issue), you can see the name, but it is not a hyperlink. However, just because the name has changed to a hyperlink doesn't mean that all is automatically well with this file. In our case, clicking on the hyperlink for either of those two files will show you that the logical size is 0 length. That wasn't very helpful, was it? This illustrates how sometimes we can have EnCase perform the file carving operation, but that doesn't guarantee the files will be anything useful. This is not due to anything EnCase is doing—it is a hazard of working with unallocated space. The files may have been overwritten or corrupted, or there simply wasn't anything to recover as far as content goes.

It should be noted that these hyperlink entries also show up in the archive section of the Records tab. The items in the list that do not contain hyperlinks do not appear in the other location, however.

The Windows Artifact Parser

Navigate back up to the top level of the Records tab and into the Evidence Processor module. This time we will focus on the Windows Artifacts Parser – Records link.

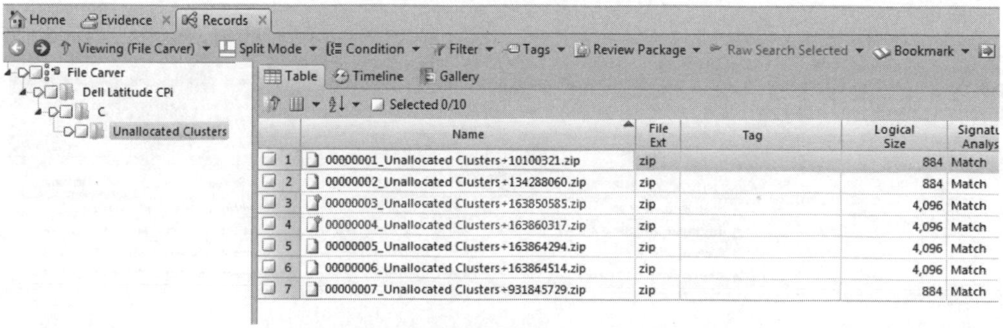

Figure 7-6 *Archive files from Unallocated Clusters*

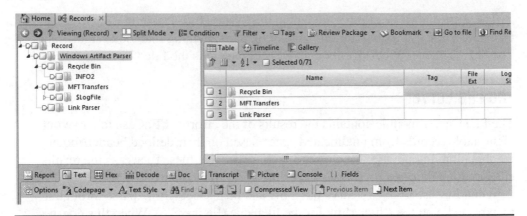

Figure 7-7 *Windows Artifact Parser*

You can see in Figure 7-7 that this module provides several good places to look for artifacts. Given the results from our prior inspection of the Uninstalled Software section, it makes sense to look at the contents of the INFO2 file to see what has been deleted, but may be recoverable. The Windows Artifact Parser automatically recovers the recycle bin for us and we can start there. Clicking on INFO2 folder in the Tree pane then allows us to follow the INFO2 hyperlink in the Table pane (Figure 7-8).

These are some of the files we saw in the Uninstalled Software module, and all are relevant to the case.

Filename	Application	Usage
lalsetup250.exe	Look@LAN	Network discovery
netstumblerinstaller_0_4_0.exe	NetStumbler	Wireless access point discovery
WinPcap_3_01_a.exe	WinPcap	Network packet capture

In our case scenario, we don't know if the subject of the investigation is a network administrator or some other type of role that would legitimately have tools that assist

Figure 7-8 *Contents of the INFO2 file*

with network discovery and packet capture on their system. However, since the tools can be used for good or evil—someone with no business having these tools would use them for discovering the assets they wanted to attack, for example—these are directly relevant to the case and should be documented. Create a table view bookmark for them called INFO2 Contents. This time we are going to make a new folder under Examination | Report | Examination | Other Information called Hacking Tools and store this bookmark there.

Going back to our Windows Artifact Parser top level, we will examine the MFT Transfers folder next. If you expand the folder, you see the $LogFile and under that, three more folders (Figure 7-9).

Drilling down into the Mft Artifact folder, and into the MFT Artifact link in the Table pane, you see the list of entries for what is essentially a transaction log of the file system for a period of time. Scrolling down the list of entries provides some interesting items. For example, row 42 lists a filename of wardriving[1], with the content path in one of the temporary Internet folders of the user name Mr. Evil. There follows a number of entries showing further Internet browsing activities, and we see the NetStumbler installer downloaded on row 80. Row 118 shows the download of Ethereal, and row 120 shows WinPcap downloaded, all on Mr. Evil's desktop. Further down, row 133 begins the section of entries showing NetStumbler being installed in the Program Files directory. Continuing down, we can see the other programs installed as well.

Following the installation activities, our Mr. Evil was very busy. In fact, there is so much of interest in this file, that I'm inclined to create one big bookmark and save it off for later revisiting. You may choose to only bookmark those items in the list that are of interest to you. I called this table view bookmark $LogFile Artifacts and saved it under the System Information bookmark folder.

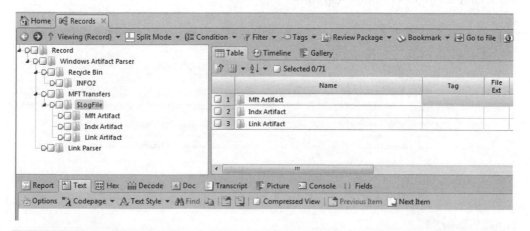

Figure 7-9 *MFT Transfers folder*

There are a couple of other folders in the MFT Transfers | $LogFile section. The Indx Artifact folder contains a number of entries that are hyperlinks in the Table pane. You can click on them and inspect their contents. The Link Artifact folder was more interesting, particularly in the Share Name column where you can see the name of the shares that were associated with some of these files. The computer account name is listed for the Temp share that we identified earlier rather than just the IP address. It is N-1A9ODN6ZXK4LQ as shown in Figure 7-10 (which is question 6 for the case study).

As before, I reordered the columns for readability by dragging their headers over until I had them where I wanted them. Remember this is always an option to make your life easier. However, EnCase does not remember the column order settings if you leave and return to the section.

The link files also show us the \\ANDREWS-1 share that Mr. Evil accessed. These bear further examination later to see if data was exfiltrated. I created two bookmarks for this section—first a table view bookmark with all of the entries, stored in the User Information section.

> **TIP**
>
> The User Information section has quite a number of columns, so remember that when you get to that window instead of individually clicking each of the check boxes, you have the option of clicking the first one and scrolling down to the bottom to SHIFT-click the bottom box. This selects the entire group so you don't have to do it manually (you can also hold down the SPACEBAR while clicking and it will select the entire group as well—these are typical Windows software behavior conventions that are supported by EnCase).

Second, I created a note bookmark of the \\ANDREW-1 share rows and put it in the Examiner Notes | Follow-Up folder.

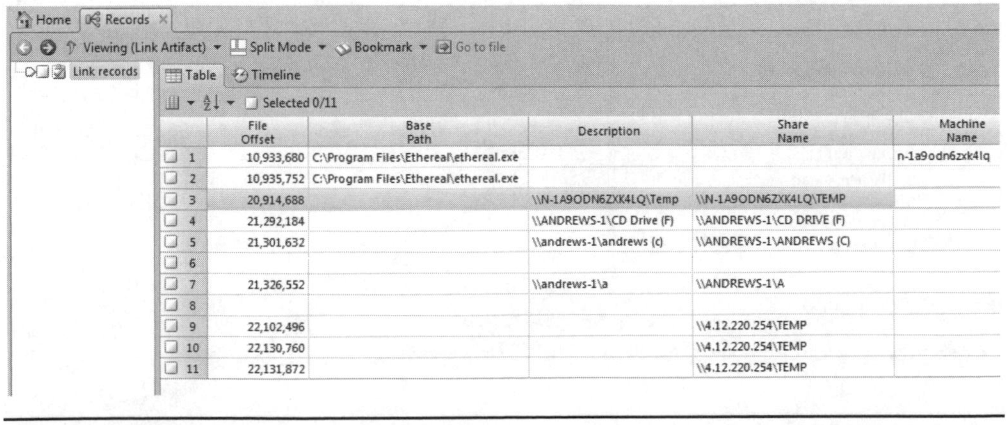

		File Offset	Base Path	Description	Share Name	Machine Name
☐	1	10,933,680	C:\Program Files\Ethereal\ethereal.exe			n-1a9odn6zxk4lq
☐	2	10,935,752	C:\Program Files\Ethereal\ethereal.exe			
☐	3	20,914,688		\\N-1A9ODN6ZXK4LQ\Temp	\\N-1A9ODN6ZXK4LQ\TEMP	
☐	4	21,292,184		\\ANDREWS-1\CD Drive (F)	\\ANDREWS-1\CD DRIVE (F)	
☐	5	21,301,632		\\andrews-1\andrews (c)	\\ANDREWS-1\ANDREWS (C)	
☐	6					
☐	7	21,326,552		\\andrews-1\a	\\ANDREWS-1\A	
☐	8					
☐	9	22,102,496			\\4.12.220.254\TEMP	
☐	10	22,130,760			\\4.12.220.254\TEMP	
☐	11	22,131,872			\\4.12.220.254\TEMP	

Figure 7-10 *Computer account name*

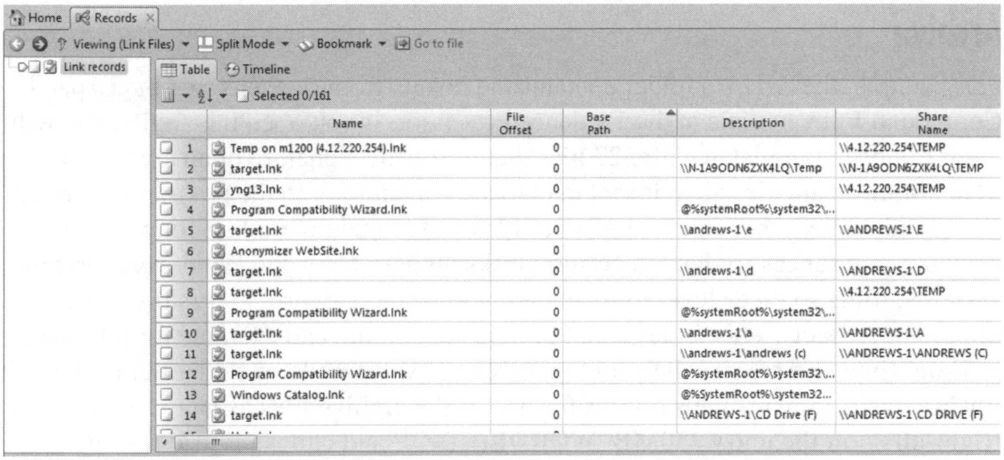

Figure 7-11   *Link records sorted by base path*

The final folder in the Windows Artifact Parser section is the Link Parser. Clicking on that folder in the Tree pane shows us the Link Files hyperlink in the Table pane. Drilling into that, we can see all of the .LNK files that EnCase found during processing. This is one handy place to view them all, and while you can alternatively sort by file type in the Evidence Browser after placing a Set Include on the top level of the evidence item, this is a simpler method of accessing the same data.

I placed a sort on the Base Path column by double-clicking the column header (note the red up-arrow at the top of the column indicating the ascending sort). This immediately shows a number of interesting items (Figure 7-11).

Just looking in the Description and Share Name columns, we can see more of the activity that involved the ANDREWS-1 share. Further down (not shown in Figure 7-11), you can find link files for Cain v2.5, Ethereal, Look@Lan, mIRC, Faber Toys, NetStumbler, CuteFTP, and CuteHTML. At the bottom of the list, there are also items with base paths of D: that look interesting. Bookmark any of the items that are relevant to the case in a table view bookmark and place them under our Hacking Tools bookmark folder.

Other Modules

If you look at the top level of the Records tab after running the Evidence Processor, you will see a number of other folders that have been populated in addition to the Evidence Processor Modules Results. They contain more artifacts that have been categorized into folders to help keep them organized.

Archive

For example, the Archive folder contains the results from our selecting the Expand Compound Files module in the Evidence Processor. If you open this folder, you will see it has been populated with 327 files that fit the file signature of an archive file. Many of these are directly relevant to our case. In addition to the programs we have already identified, there are a number of files that contain word lists for password cracking, references for how to perform tasks on both Unix and Windows operating systems, tools to clear logs, tools to enumerate the network, and many other important artifacts. This folder is full of items to explore and examine for relevance.

From time to time, it is helpful to be able to export a file or folder out of the EnCase environment. Let's do this for one of the archive files as an example. Right-click on the entry 250MB_WORDLIST.ZIP and choose Entries | Copy files from the pop-up menu. The Copy Files dialog appears with several selection options (Figure 7-12).

Since we only have one file highlighted, the option of exporting all selected files is disabled. Note the option to merge multiple files into one file as well—not what we are interested in right now, but good to know we have that option. This is particularly useful if you have a selection of related items and want to make them into one combined file.

You can change the default character to replace for deleted files, but we don't need to for this example. Click Next to tell EnCase more about how you want to export this file.

By default, we will export just the logical file, and not use a character mask. Click Next.

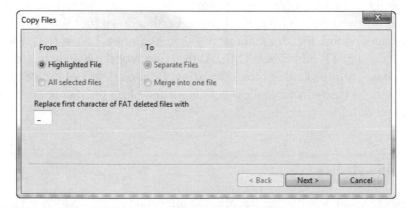

Figure 7-12 *Copy Files dialog*

If the Right-Click Menu Does Not Show Copy Files as an Option

Artifacts presented in the Records tab act differently in some contexts than they do in the Evidence Browser. This is one of those times—if you right-click on the hyperlink name and all you see is the Copy option, left-click on the hyperlink instead. This will open the file in the Table pane, and you can right-click on that and choose Go To File. This will bring the file up in the Table pane of the Evidence Browser. Here you can right-click on the hyperlinked name of the zip file and be able to choose Copy Files. This is one of the quirks of the EnCase interface and may be addressed in later versions.

TIP

I always keep the Show Errors check box activated, because I want to know if there is a problem (Figure 7-13).

Finally, you are asked to provide the path to where you want this file export (Figure 7-14). Note the Split Files Above option—this is mostly used for making sure files will fit on specific-sized media or for when there is a limit on file size based on the file system. I don't like to split files up without good reason, so I make sure that this number is higher than the number of the file size.

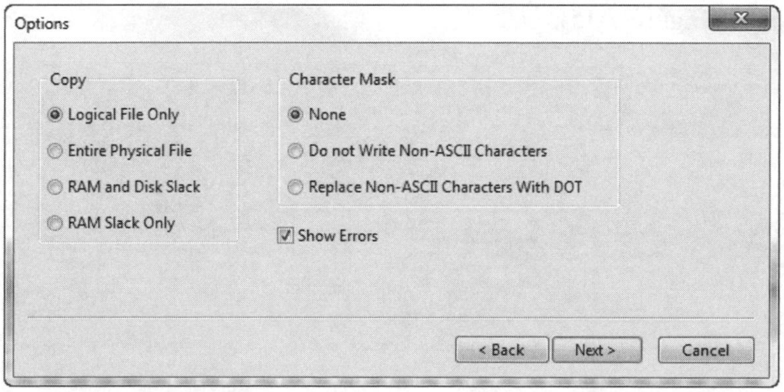

Figure 7-13   *Copy Files options*

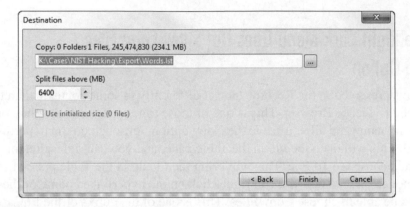

Figure 7-14 *Destination for the Export*

NOTE

If you put a 0 value in the Split Files Above (MB) field, EnCase with neither split nor compress the output.

Be sure to add bookmarks to all of the files you deem significant. If you don't have time for this right now, consider putting a note bookmark for later follow-up on what these tools do.

Internet

The Internet folder is where EnCase places the Internet artifacts it recovers during processing. Clicking on the folder allows EnCase to display the Internet hyperlink in the Table pane (Figure 7-15).

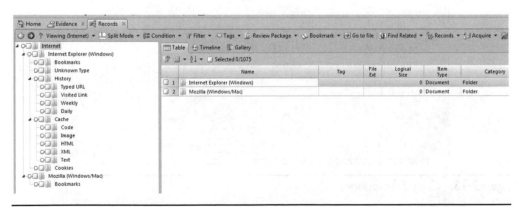

Figure 7-15 *Internet artifacts from the Evidence Processor*

The folder structure is based on the browser used when the artifacts were created. The Internet Explorer artifacts are arranged for easy examination. What is not apparent is what directory path these are from. While clicking on a specific artifact will show the path on the bottom bar of your EnCase screen, when you are in the Visited Link folder, for example, all of the files are called "index.dat", but which one do you need? There are potentially a large number of index.dat files on a given system. To find out which one you are looking at, you can right-click on the artifact and choose Go To File from the pop-up menu. This will take you to the file's location in the Evidence Browser so you can see which part of the image you are working with. To get back to where you were in the Records tab, you can just click on the green left-arrow (the back arrow) on the top left of the tab you are in to step backwards.

Drilling into these folders, EnCase has arranged the history, cache, and cookies into a single location interface. For example, if we drill into the History folder and click on Typed URL, we see 11 entries all with the name of NTUSER.DAT (Figure 7-16). If you click on each of these in the Table pane, you can see the value in the View pane using either the Text, Hex, or Transcript tabs as you prefer. The way EnCase arranges these columns by default requires you to click on each row to see

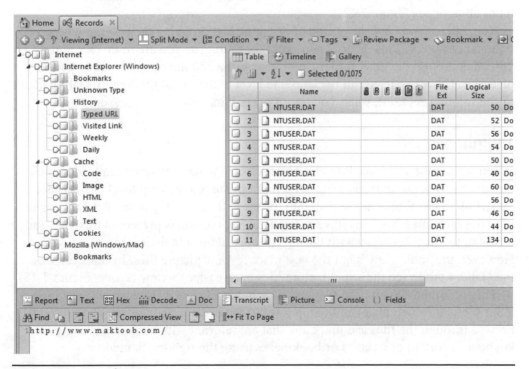

Figure 7-16   *Typed URLs*

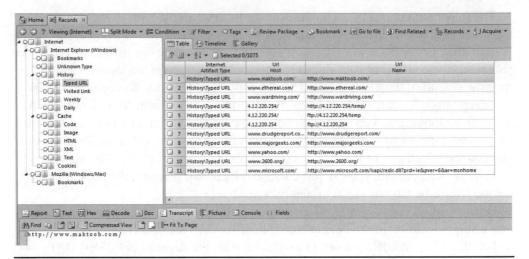

Figure 7-17 *URL Name column*

the value. However, if you scroll all the way to the rightmost columns, you can see them all at once (Figure 7-17).

Remember, you have the option of dragging and dropping the column wherever you want to see it. This order is persistent for as long as you are in this section. If you click around the other folders in this view, the column remains where you've placed it. However, if you go back up one level to the top of the Records tab (and out of the Internet section), when you return the column order is not preserved.

Thumbnails

When we ran the Evidence Processor and selected to have all thumbnails identified, the results were put into this folder. Again, from the Records top level tab, it is a hyperlink in the Table pane to drill into the view. By default, you see the Table view with the filenames. You may have noticed the Tag column is present in this view (as it was in the Internet view) with the tags that are defined in their respective positions. However, the Table view is not the best place to view picture files. Instead, click on the Gallery tab to see the actual picture files in an easier-to-view layout (Figure 7-18).

This is similar to using the Gallery view in the Evidence Browser and placing a Set Include (home plate) on the top level of the evidence container. You can now browse through the files and mark any that are relevant with either tags (using the keyboard shortcut of CTRL-T) or bookmarks using the right-click menu.

Figure 7-18 *Gallery view of thumbnails*

Email

EnCase overhauled the way it handles email artifacts from prior versions. The interface is more intuitive and you can follow conversation threads much more easily. The Email section at the top of the Records tab is populated with a number of .dbx files that EnCase found during processing, which are associated with Outlook Express. They are displayed as hyperlinks in the Table pane, and you can click on them and inspect them as you like. We'll be spending more time on email in Chapter 8.

Registry

The Registry folder provides the system, software, and SAM registry hives already parsed for you. Remember that in the Evidence Browser EnCase had to mount and parse these before being able to access them? This is taken care of for you in the Evidence Processor module. If you are looking at these files in the Evidence Browser, they will also show as having been mounted and parsed, so it is not dependent on being in the Records tab and viewing the results of the Evidence Processor. Evidence is processed once and available throughout the EnCase interface.

Summary

In this chapter, we continued exploring the output from the Evidence Processor. We completed our inspection of the results in the System Info Parser, the File Carver, and the Windows Artifact Parser.

We documented the user accounts on the system and the software artifacts we found that were either relevant to the case, or required further follow-up later. We also learned how to export the content of specific files for viewing outside of EnCase.

Finally, we looked at the Internet artifacts and learned how to use the Set Include (home plate) to view all of the graphic files in our case in the Gallery view of the Table pane.

In Chapter 8, we will inspect the Case Analyzer and learn to customize the reports that are generated from that tool. We will get a quick primer on SQL, and then move on to looking at email.

8

Analyzing the Case

W e've looked into the Evidence Processor and the results that it provides. Now we're going to focus on the Case Analyzer. This tool is a good companion to the Evidence Processor and provides another view into the artifacts. Run the Case Analyzer after you have finished with your evidence processing. It is particularly useful in that it will analyze multiple evidence items in your case and correlate them to provide a more holistic view.

The Case Analyzer

The Case Analyzer is a powerful tool to present the evidence that you have processed in one location. The Case Analyzer can be run at any time, but since it pulls its data from the SQLite database that EnCase builds during Evidence Processor runs, it makes sense to finish your processing first. This SQLite database only contains artifact metadata from the Evidence Processor results—it does not contain actual file content. This is an key distinction, because this means that you can share this database file between examiners or other interested parties and you share only the data about the artifacts—not the artifacts themselves. This is of particular importance when the artifacts in question are contraband, such as with child pornography. While the artifacts themselves are not part of the database, care should be taken when sharing some of the metadata, since even the filenames can be offensive to some.

The Case Analyzer is located under your case directory in the EnScript folder and is called Case.sqlite. It comes with a large number of standard reports, which will be run based on the contents of the artifact database. These reports can also be customized to suit your particular case or organization's needs, which we will discuss in a moment. It is particularly useful for drawing connections between multiple artifact locations to paint a picture of the actions performed on the system.

To begin, with our case open, choose Case Analyzer from the Home screen under the Browse section. This will launch the Case Analyzer page (Figure 8-1). The Case link is the only item on the page for us under the View Reports section, but if you had an EnCase Portable collection plugged in, it would show up as a portable device and you could analyze that as well.

Case is a hyperlink, and clicking on it launches the Case Analyzer tab after the Updating Reports progress bar completes (Figure 8-2).

If you had launched the Case Analyzer prior to processing your evidence, you would find that there were no reports with data available in the Case tab, but the Unavailable Reports button on the Case tab would have a list of all the reports that would be populated if data were available.

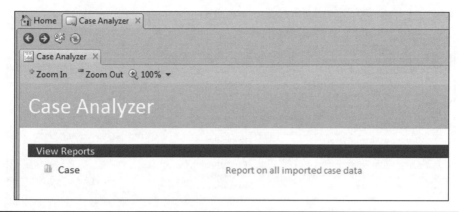

Figure 8-1   *Case Analyzer page*

> **TIP**
>
> *If you run the Case Analyzer and get something that looks like Figure 8-3, with no data returned in your reports, check back and make sure you've actually completed running the Evidence Processor on your evidence. The progress bar at the bottom right of the screen will indicate if the Evidence Processor is still running.*

Once the evidence has been processed, the Status column (Figure 8-3) will change in this window. For example, if you are running the Case Analyzer against all Windows images, you will see messages in the Status column like "no such table: OSX_Install_Log" under the report that looks for the Mac OSX Installation log. Only when no evidence has been processed at all do you see the "No Data Returned" error on every report possible.

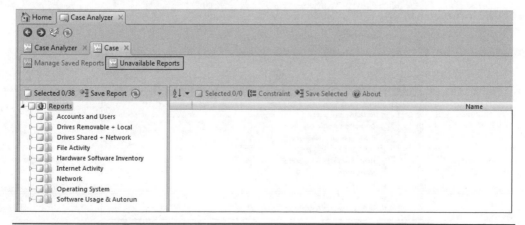

Figure 8-2   *Case Analyzer*

	Report	Status
1	Accounts and Users\Users - Snapshot	No data returned
2	Collected Files\AcquisitionStatus	No data returned
3	Accounts and Users\Account Change Event	No data returned
4	Drives Removable + Local\Known USB Devices\Devices His...	No data returned
5	Accounts and Users\Linux Users	No data returned
6	Drives Removable + Local\Known USB Devices\Drives Over...	No data returned
7	Accounts and Users\Users - Comprehensive	No data returned
8	Accounts and Users\Users - Registry	No data returned
9	Drives Removable + Local\Known USB Devices\Files Seen	No data returned
10	Accounts and Users\Users - Snapshot	No data returned
11	Drives Removable + Local\Drives Overview	No data returned
12	Collected Files\AcquisitionStatus	No data returned
13	Drives Shared + Network\Drives Overview	No data returned
14	Drives Removable + Local\Known USB Devices\Devices His...	No data returned
15	Drives Shared + Network\Seen on Net Drives	No data returned
16	Drives Removable + Local\Known USB Devices\Drives Over...	No data returned
17	Drives Removable + Local\Known USB Devices\Files Seen	No data returned
18	Drives Shared + Network\UNC Files Seen	No data returned
19	Drives Removable + Local\Drives Overview	No data returned
20	Drives Shared + Network\UNC Folders Visited	No data returned
21	Drives Shared + Network\Drives Overview	No data returned
22	Drives Shared + Network\User Mapped Shares	No data returned

Figure 8-3   *Unavailable Reports*

When the Case Analyzer is run against a case with processed evidence, in contrast, you will get reports listed where data was returned. They appear in the Tree pane as high-level folders with the related reports organized under them as HTML files (Figure 8-4).

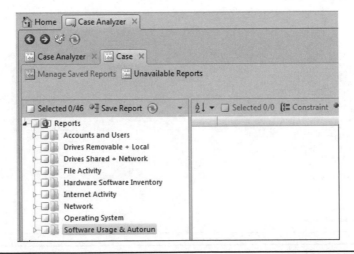

Figure 8-4   *Case Analyzer reports*

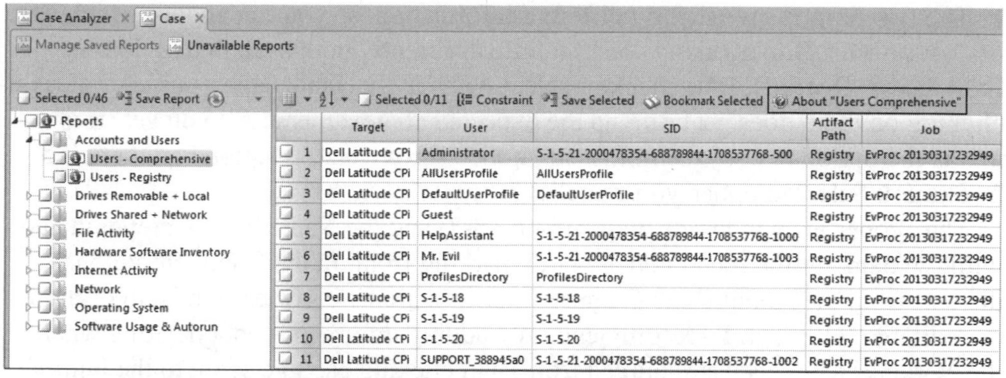

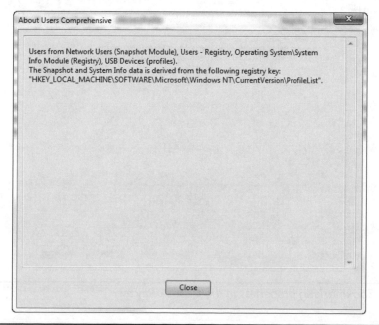

Figure 8-5   *Accounts and Users folder*

Looking first at the Accounts and Users report, we can see two options for Users—Comprehensive and Registry (Figure 8-5).

What is in each of these? Well, up at the top of the Table pane, there is an About section (see the box at top right of Figure 8-5) for each of these reports. If you click on that, you will get information on where the data in each report was drawn from (Figure 8-6).

As you can see, it lets you know the exact registry key the data came from, so if you should need to verify the results of this analysis for any reason, you know exactly where it originated from.

Figure 8-6   *About Users Comprehensive*

The two reports give slightly different information, so you can choose which best fits your needs. Bookmarking works a little differently in this tab than it does in Evidence or Records. Blue check or select items in the Table pane as usual, but right-clicking on them does not bring up the expected context menu. All you get from that is the option to copy them. Instead, notice across the top button bar, there is a Bookmark Selected option you can click.

The Properties window displays (Figure 8-7) and the Name field is prepopulated with the name of the report you are bookmarking from. In the Comment field is the text from the About Users Comprehensive section we saw earlier. Both of these are editable (although I'd recommend only adding information, not deleting where the evidence artifacts were sourced from) and clicking Next gets you to the familiar interface to choose where to store this bookmark in the regular Bookmarks folder structure. The next window allows you to choose the columns you want in the bookmark.

You could also use the Save Selected option on the button bar, which gives you the option to save an entire table and change the title as you like (Figure 8-8).

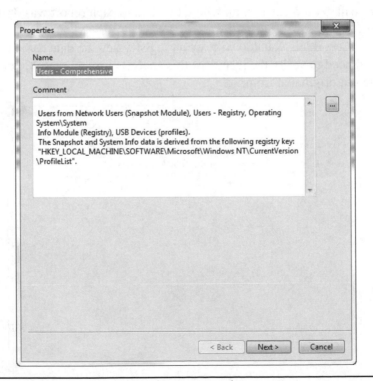

Figure 8-7 *Bookmarking properties in the Case Analyzer*

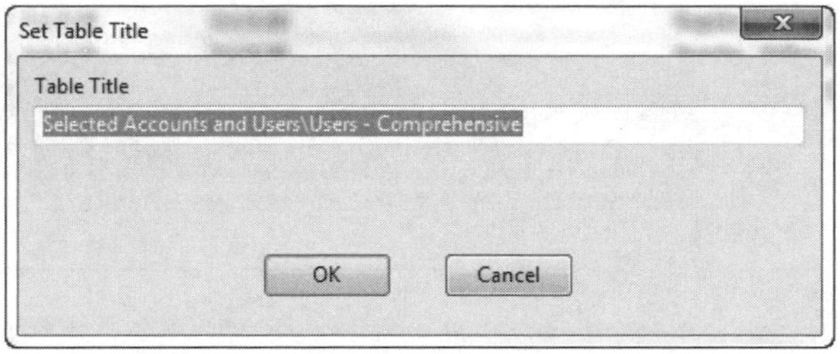

Figure 8-8   *Set Table Title dialog*

This does not give you an option of saving this as a bookmark in the folder structure, however. There is far less control over what data you save and where it ends up with this option.

Windows Artifacts

The Case Analyzer reports cover quite a lot of area. One of the more useful features is in their highlighting of the Windows operating system artifacts. They pull the values from several registry keys and put related results together to easily show you information that you would otherwise have to go and hunt down individually. A good example is the Drive Shared + Network report.

I've captured both the pop-up explanation and the items in the report in Figure 8-9. Incidentally, if you are not already a forensic ninja, and are interested in honing your skills, seeing where these items are taken from gives you a good place to start researching to see what additional information sources you don't normally use can provide. Many people are not familiar with the shellbags and their use in forensics. Figure 8-9 gives you an example that you should look into if you don't normally use these artifacts in your examinations. They can be quite useful in reconstructing user activities.

Another example of the way these reports can shorten the time to compile data from multiple locations is the Recent Files report (Figure 8-10).

You can see from the About data that this report is compiled from a number of registry keys and contains some potentially relevant data. This would be a good table to create a follow-up bookmark for later inspection of the individual contents.

The Internet Activity module also contains some useful reports. The Operating System section has the time zone information all laid out for you (although it is important to be able to determine that yourself).

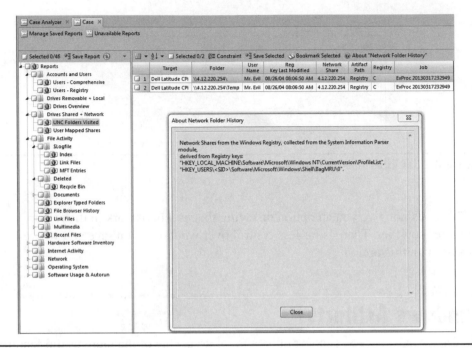

Figure 8-9 *UNC Folders Visited*

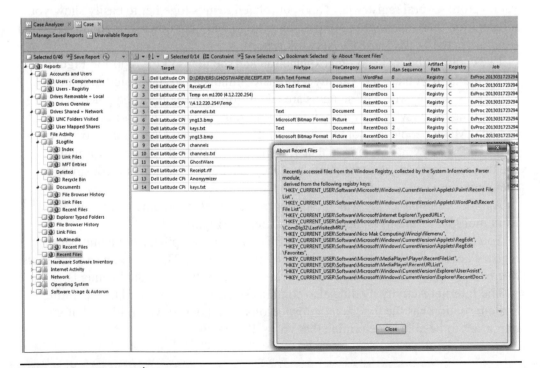

Figure 8-10 *Recent Files report*

Scan through the various reports and bookmark what looks relevant to you. Since we have covered how to create these bookmarks, we are now just populating them so that our report will have data in it to work with when we get to that section. The Case Analyzer is a good example of how to easily and quickly gather important data so that you have time to go and dig into the more complex portions of the investigation that can't be automated—parts that require your expertise.

Some of these reports can be quite large and a bit unwieldy. You have the option of filtering the data using the Constraint button. For example, look at the File Activity folder, and the $Logfile folder under that. The MFT Entries has 808 entries. Let's say we are looking specifically at the Ethereal tool and want to filter for that result.

I want to look at only those entries where "Ethereal" occurs in the file path. So, as shown in Figure 8-11, I clicked on the File Path column (note that the interface does not highlight it well and could use a better contrast). I clicked on the Contains option in the Operator window and typed "Ethereal" (no quotes) in the Text box. I clicked Add and it appears in the WHERE window. I then clicked the Test button, and it indicated that I would have 129 rows back from this constraint—much better than scrolling down through all 808 rows. Clicking OK then applies the filter to my data.

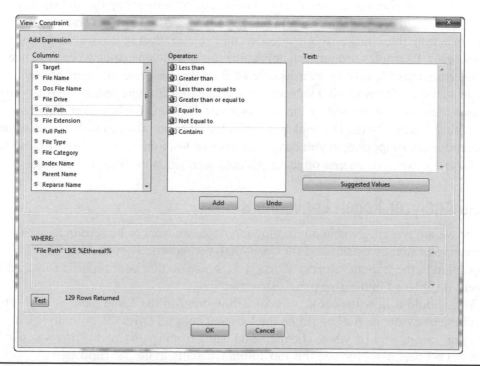

Figure 8-11   *Adding a constraint*

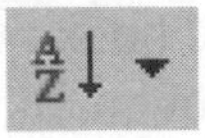

Figure 8-12 *The Sort button*

Fine, but how do I get back to the original full result? By clicking on Constraint, not applying anything, and clicking OK. That brings back the full result (or you can click on another report and then click back to this one—that also clears constraints).

You can also sort columns in the Case Analyzer reports by double-clicking on them or using the Sort button at the top left of the Table pane as shown in Figure 8-12. The sort drop-down will also give you more options (such as removing the sort).

If you are working within the Case Analyzer reports and want to make sure you are working with the most recent data, you can click on the Refresh button, which is next to the Save Report button at the top of the Tree pane.

Customizing the Case Analyzer

You can customize reports in the Case Analyzer. Once you have tested them, you can even export them and offer them on Guidance Software's App Central store. If there are certain sets of artifacts that you typically associate to prove evidence of a certain action, these make excellent reports that you can then reuse over and over in other cases. Examples that immediately come to mind include cases where you need to determine the file activity on a specific USB device, generate Internet browser usage statistics, determine if a subject downloaded files from a specific website—the possibilities are only limited by the use cases you devise. Customization requires becoming familiar with SQL, which is useful for other purposes as well. The common operations are supported, so you can select from tables, join or combine them, and perform the expected queries on the metadata contained in the SQLite database.

Case Analyzer Report Conventions

Since we are working within an existing interface, we want to be certain to use the conventions already established for Case Analyzer reports. They include what is populated in the "About <Report Title>" text, how you title your report's name, and where it is placed in the Tree pane's structure.

You should follow the convention of listing order in the Table pane as well. The machine or evidence file should be the leftmost column (with the column titled "Target"), followed by where the metadata came from (path), and if this was used in Sweep Enterprise, include the Job column, usually at the far right.

SQLite Manager (Firefox)

An easy way to interact with a SQLite database is via the Firefox plugin called SQLite Manager. A quick Google search can get you the current URL, which at the time of this printing is https://addons.mozilla.org/en-us/firefox/addon/sqlite-manager/. Click on the Add to Firefox button to install; this will require a restart of Firefox. (Alternately, you could go to the Add-ons page from the Firefox menu drop-down, search for SQLite, and click on the Install button next to the SQLite Manager item.)

Once Firefox restarts, you can launch SQLite Manager using the Firefox menu and choosing SQLite Manager from the Web Developer menu (Figure 8-13).

SQLite Manager will launch in a new browser window without a database by default (Figure 8-14).

Now we need to open our Case.sqlite file. Remember, it is located under your case directory inside the EnScript folder.

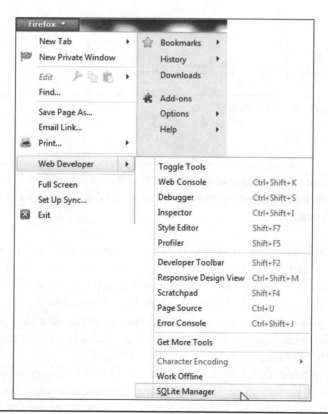

Figure 8-13 *Launching SQLite Manager from Firefox*

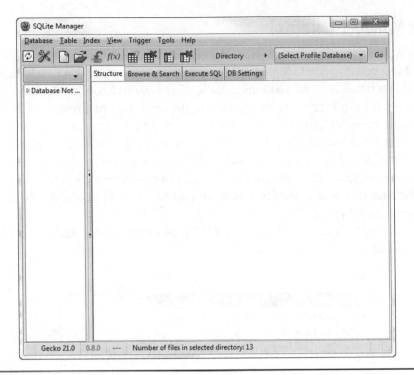

Figure 8-14   *SQLite Manager opens*

> ### NOTE
>
> *If you have not run the Case Analyzer at least once, this file will not exist. Be sure to have completed both the evidence processing and running the Case Analyzer reports first before moving into this section.*

Choose Connect Database from the Database menu on the top left. Browse to the EnScript folder under your case directory and choose the Case.sqlite file.

In the left pane you see the names of the tables in the database (Figure 8-15). In the right pane, you have several options, including an important tab called Execute SQL. This is a good place to test your statements to make sure they provide the results you anticipate. I spend most of my time on this tab, and it is where we will be working in this section as well.

Expanding the table names in the left pane lets you see the individual fields each table has. This will be very important in building your queries, since you need the table names to build them. Under the Structure tab, you see the field types of each item. This information is important for when you are performing table joins and other operations that expect the same data type in the fields.

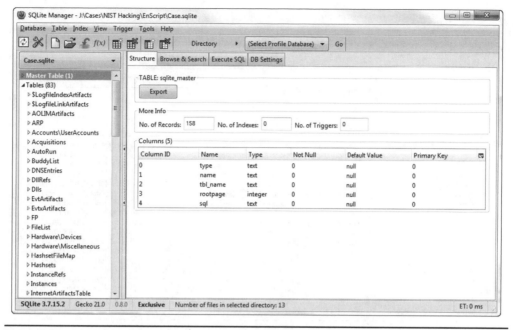

Figure 8-15   *SQLite Manager with Case.sqlite open*

The Browse & Search tab is also useful, as it gives you a quick view of the data in the table in a columnar format. This can give you a sense of how the columns are populated and is an additional tool for when you are trying to determine what the data structures look like in a database. If you scroll over to the right on this tab and expand the sql column's size, you will see the SQL used to create each view as well, which can be a helpful syntax reference.

Note the other tabs across the top of the right pane—be very careful when you are in this interface, because you could cause data destruction (Figure 8-16). While this won't alter the evidence, and should be recoverable by rerunning the Evidence Processor, I highly recommend staying away from the Create/Alter, Data Manipulation, and Drop buttons entirely.

In the event you do make a change or something else goes wrong, you have the option of deleting the Case.sqlite file. EnCase will then regenerate the database for you—however, you will lose any customization of the reports that you may have done. If you exported the reports to your hard drive, you can hit the Refresh button to have them pulled back into the Case Analyzer—just make sure to do this before you export reports.

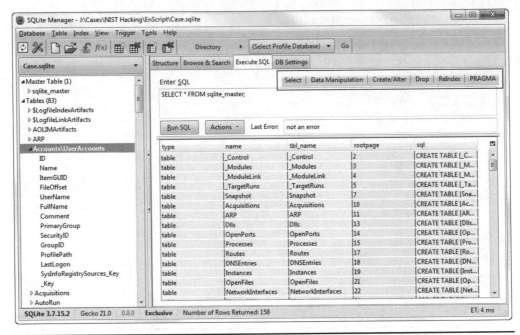

Figure 8-16 *Be careful: you have a DBA level account.*

Run Book: Regenerating the Case.sqlite database

1. Close EnCase (if open).

2. Remove the Case.sqlite file from the EnScript folder in your case directory.

3. Start EnCase.

4. Click on Case Analyzer from the Home screen.

5. Click Case. EnCase will regenerate the contents of the database and you will have a Case.sqlite in your EnScript folder again.

SQL Basics

The Select button is your friend. If you click on it, you see three options where it will generate a skeleton statement so you have the syntax in the Enter SQL box. The first two are fairly simple, but the last option SELECT (general) provides the syntax for all of the SELECT statement options. If you get stuck on the syntax of the SQL for what you are trying to do, choose SQLite Syntax Help from the Help menu, and you will be directed to a web page that is a SQLite language reference.

The SELECT Statement

The most common statement you will use is the SELECT statement. The basic syntax is:

```
SELECT columnname FROM tablename;
```

where *columnname* and *tablename* are variables that you fill in with the appropriate values.

Remember to end your statement with a semicolon—that is the end of statement marker in SQL. So if I wanted to select all of the names from the Accounts\UserAccounts table, I'd enter:

```
SELECT Name FROM Accounts\UserAccounts;
```

I bet that didn't work for you, did it? I picked this table on purpose because it has a backslash (\) in the name and that causes problems with the SQL syntax. Figure 8-17 shows the error message the above code generated for me:

To "protect" the backslash character from being interpreted as part of the command we are sending rather than as part of the table name, we need to enclose the table name in square brackets:

```
SELECT Name FROM [Accounts\UserAccounts];
```

You can see in Figure 8-18 we now have just the values from the Name column displaying. If you want all of the results from this table, you could use the * wildcard rather than having to list all of the columns individually:

```
SELECT * FROM [Accounts\UserAccounts];
```

You can also list specific columns separated by commas:

```
SELECT Name, UserName, PrimaryGroup FROM [Accounts\UserAccounts];
```

The next thing we want to do is limit the results returned based on conditions we define. We do this using a WHERE clause.

Figure 8-17 *SQL syntax error*

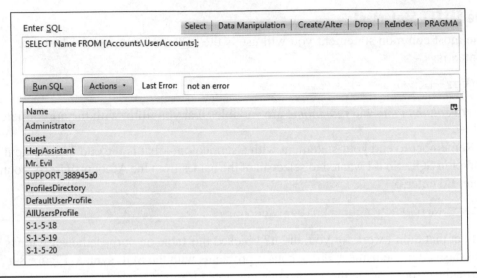

Figure 8-18 *Results using square brackets*

WHERE Clauses

When using a WHERE clause, the expression is evaluated for each row as a true/false (Boolean) value. That is to say that each row will either match the WHERE clause criteria and be included, or not match and be excluded from the results returned by the database. We can filter by exact matches or matches that are similar to what we are looking for. For exact matches, here is a syntax example:

```
SELECT Name FROM [Accounts\UserAccounts] WHERE GroupID != 513;
```

For similar results rather than exact matches (used most frequently on text), use the `like` syntax:

```
SELECT Name, SecurityID FROM [Accounts\UserAccounts] WHERE Name like
'%User%' ;
```

Run each of these statements in the SQLite Manager interface to see how the results change.

Changing the Order of Results

Sometimes we want to change the order in which the results are displayed. Of course, changing the column order is simply a matter of moving them up or down in the list of the SELECT statement. However, changing the results themselves to be alphabetized, for example, requires an `order by` clause. To change the previous statement to have the results in alphabetical order by the Name field's value, you would do the following:

```
SELECT Name, SecurityID FROM [Accounts\UserAccounts] WHERE Name like
'%User%' order by Name;
```

Also note that SQL ignores white space—so having the space between the last character and the semicolon has no effect on the results. The same can be said for putting in new lines and indents for readability. None of these make any difference to how the SQL is interpreted.

Joins

You can also join tables together on a specific field where the values are equal. You can see an example of that later in Figure 8-23. Joins require some knowledge of the data in the database as well as the table structure. Basically, if you want to join two tables, they need to have a field in common. It doesn't have to be named the same, but the data type should be the same. An example of a join would be to have two tables joined on an ID number that they both use—the name of the field in the example is not the same, but the type of data will be the same and when the tables are joined on the equal values inside the fields, the results still make sense.

Aliases

Finally, the Case Analyzer reports use aliases. When you see the first column of the reports is titled Target, that is independent of the field name the value actually came from. It is a convention used in these reports and should be followed. To use aliases, you select something as the alias name. Here is the syntax example from the prior SELECT statement we used, with the first column aliased to "Target" and the second column aliased to "Bogus Name":

```
SELECT Name as "Target", SecurityID as "Bogus Name" FROM [Accounts\
UserAccounts]
WHERE Name like '%User%'
ORDER BY Name  ;
```

You can see that the column headers have taken the alias names (Figure 8-19). So you can basically think of aliasing in this context as changing the names of the columns to what you want reflected in your report.

A complete treatment of SQL is beyond the scope of this book, and in fact there are books out there devoted entirely to the topic. However, this small introduction should be enough to give you an idea of how you can customize reports in the Case Analyzer. Use the syntax reference provided in the Help menu to further explore changes you might want to make to reports. Now let's get to making our own changes to a report.

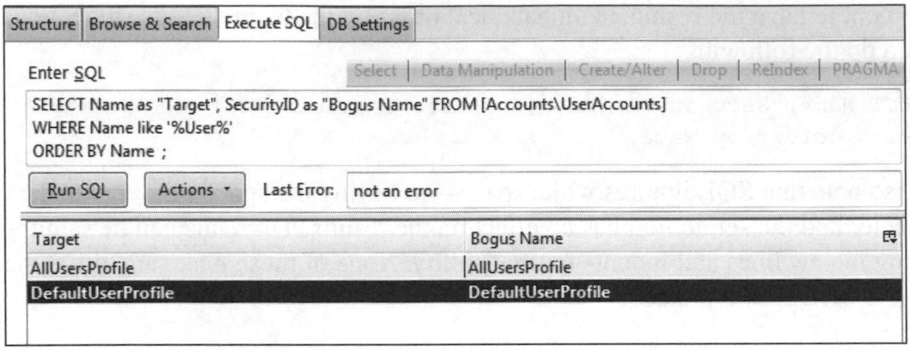

Figure 8-19 *Results of the aliases*

Customizing Our Report

The easiest way to begin is to copy an existing report and modify it to suit our needs. Remember when we were looking at the MFT Entries report under File Activity | $Logfile before and used a condition to narrow what we saw down from the 808 entries originally provided? Let's say we want to make that into a custom report instead of having to perform that action each time. First, we have to export the report definition file. So click on the MFT Entries report in the Tree pane and then use the down arrow menu on the top of the Case tab on the right as shown in Figure 8-20.

Choose Export Report Definitions. Once you do that, the quickest way to get to the definition files is to choose Open Export Folder from the same down arrow menu. This will open a Windows Explorer window to the installation directory of EnCase on your system. The path you want is C:\<*install directory*>\EnScript\ Analysis Reports\Advanced\Standard\File Activity\$Logfile. There you will find a copy of the MFT Entries.xml file. Make a copy of that file and rename it to Ethereal MFT Entries.xml. You may be prompted for administrator permission for the copy and rename operations by Windows. I always like to work from a copy and preserve

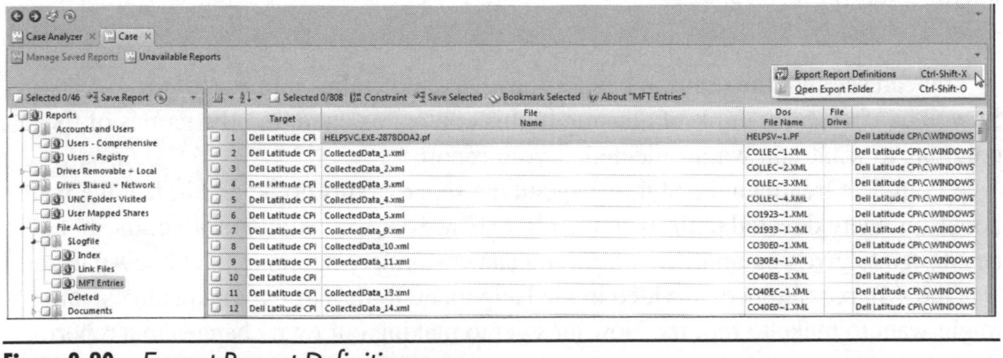

Figure 8-20 *Export Report Definitions*

Figure 8-21 *The Refresh button*

the original, and I recommend you do the same. One thing of importance to note is that by performing the Export Report Definitions, EnCase copies all of the current reports each time you execute this command. This means that if you have made customizations to a report and not changed the name, and perform this export again, your changes will be overwritten.

That said, changes are snarfed up (technical term) into the EnCase interface by hitting the Refresh button (Figure 8-21) at the top of the Tree pane in the Case tab. After you have refreshed the navigation view, you should now see the new report we made (Figure 8-22).

Of course, all you did was rename the old report, so it looks exactly like the MFT Entries report and shows all 808 entries. To change that you need to alter the xml file for your new report. Open the Ethereal MFT Entries.xml file in the editor of your choice.

For our report, I changed the following fields: title, description, help, and select. Figure 8-23 shows the altered report.

The title and description changes were just a matter of adding the word "Ethereal". I also clarified the help text so that the user would know how I am filtering out the data. The final change is to the SELECT statement. I recalled from before that the file path contained the term "Ethereal", so to change the SELECT statement, I needed to put my change in the WHERE clause. This report's SELECT statement is fairly complex in that it has a JOIN and a WHERE clause. In those cases it is important to get the right location to put your changes, and to test them in SQLite Manager prior to committing them to your report. You can see from the SELECT statement that the column we want to use to key the value off of is the FilePath column. Then it was just a matter of determining how to represent the "contains" filter option in SQL. There isn't a direct correlation—there is no Contains

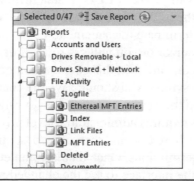

Figure 8-22 *Case tab after refresh*

Figure 8-23 *Changes made to new report*

keyword in SQL. Instead, there is a `like` keyword, and the percentages on either side of the word indicate that I don't care what characters come before or after the word we are filtering on. The single quotes allow it to be interpreted correctly and not throw a syntax error.

To test your syntax, copy the whole SELECT statement from your editor into the Enter SQL window of the SQLite Manager interface and be sure to add that semicolon (;) at the end to terminate the statement. Click the Run SQL button and you will either get a syntax error or you will get rows of data (Figure 8-24).

As with the filtered version earlier in this chapter, you get 129 rows back. After you have verified the syntax, you should save the changes to your report xml file. You may be denied the ability to overwrite your file, depending on your configuration (remember it requires administrator level privileges), in which case you can copy the file somewhere else and then copy/paste in Windows Explorer with an account that has those permissions. Once that is completed, go back into the Case tab in EnCase and refresh the interface to see the changed report.

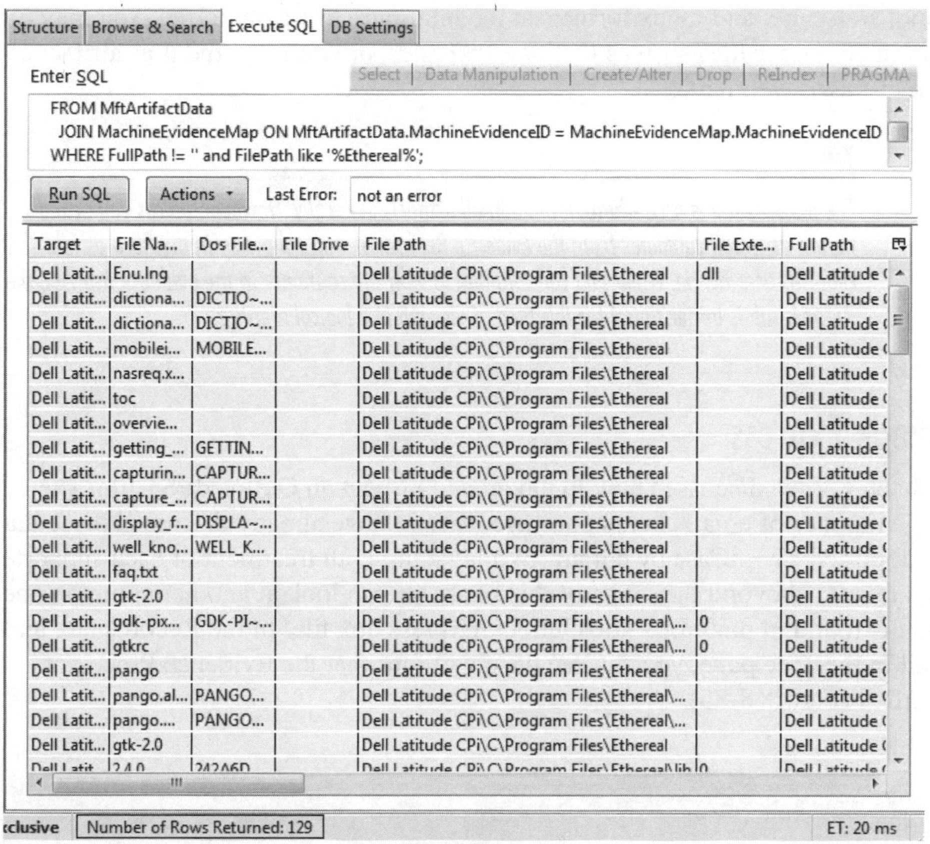

Figure 8-24 *Rows returned when syntax is correct*

As you get more comfortable with the SQLite database, you can potentially do some very powerful things with it—for example, export data on Indicators of Compromise from your case into a central database storing those across cases. This would allow for a better reuse of data across cases in an organization and also potentially facilitate data sharing.

Parsing Email

We ran the email module from the Evidence Processor earlier when we went through our case. There are a number of supported email file types, and they are listed in the User Guide for the version you are using, but generally you can expect the Microsoft products (Exchange, Outlook, and Outlook Express), Lotus Notes, AOL, Hotmail,

Yahoo, Netscape, and mbox formats at the minimum to be supported. You may find email in container files such as Outlook PST files, or you may find it as artifact of Internet-based webmail.

> ### TIP
>
> *The Records tab is used when viewing email artifacts generally. However, unless you actually mount an email container from the Evidence Browser, it won't show up in the Records tab. That requires user action. While you can continue to view the container in the Evidence Browser, the Records tab is better suited for this type of viewing in a logical manner.*

Outlook Express

In Chapter 3, we discussed how to mount and inspect an Outlook PST file. There are a large number of email clients out there, and we have already discussed those that are supported by EnCase by default. While an in-depth treatment of each supported email client is beyond the scope of this book, we can look at another common one which is found in our case—the Outlook Express dbx file. In the Records tab, under Email in the Tree pane, you can see the email files that the Evidence Processor identified (Figure 8-25).

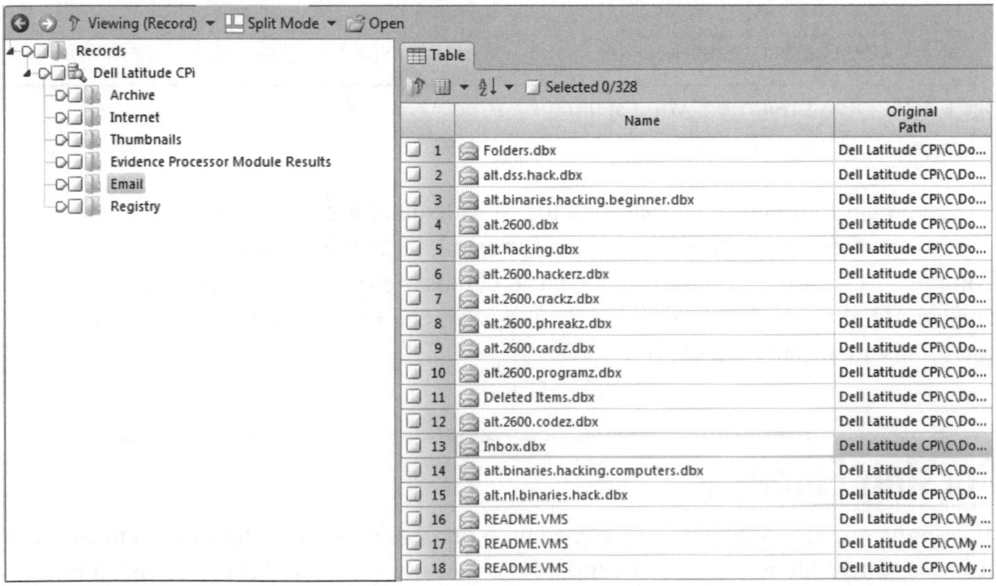

Figure 8-25 *Email files in the Records tab*

		Name	Original Path
☐	1	Folders.dbx	Dell Latitude CPi\C\Do...
☐	2	alt.dss.hack.dbx	Dell Latitude CPi\C\Do...
☐	3	alt.binaries.hacking.beginner.dbx	Dell Latitude CPi\C\Do...
☐	4	alt.2600.dbx	Dell Latitude CPi\C\Do...
☐	5	alt.hacking.dbx	Dell Latitude CPi\C\Do...
☐	6	alt.2600.hackerz.dbx	Dell Latitude CPi\C\Do...
☐	7	alt.2600.crackz.dbx	Dell Latitude CPi\C\Do...
☐	8	alt.2600.phreakz.dbx	Dell Latitude CPi\C\Do...
☐	9	alt.2600.cardz.dbx	Dell Latitude CPi\C\Do...
☐	10	alt.2600.programz.dbx	Dell Latitude CPi\C\Do...
☐	11	Deleted Items.dbx	Dell Latitude CPi\C\Do...
☐	12	alt.2600.codez.dbx	Dell Latitude CPi\C\Do...
☐	13	Inbox.dbx	Dell Latitude CPi\C\Do...
☐	14	alt.binaries.hacking.computers.dbx	Dell Latitude CPi\C\Do...
☐	15	alt.nl.binaries.hack.dbx	Dell Latitude CPi\C\Do...
☐	16	README.VMS	Dell Latitude CPi\C\My ...
☐	17	README.VMS	Dell Latitude CPi\C\My ...
☐	18	README.VMS	Dell Latitude CPi\C\My ...

Figure 8-26   *Choose an archive with content*

As you can see, all of these have been parsed by EnCase and are hyperlinks that you can further drill into. Obvious places to start would include the Inbox.dbx and Deleted Items.dbx, but you will notice that there is no content there apart from the welcome email. One feature that is new with EnCase 7 is the ability to follow threaded conversations as you would see them in an email client. To show this, we need an email conversation that has responses.

For this example, choose the alt.2600.programz.dbx file by clicking on the hyperlink in the Table pane (Figure 8-26). You will see that there are any number of good candidates for inspection in this archive (Figure 8-27).

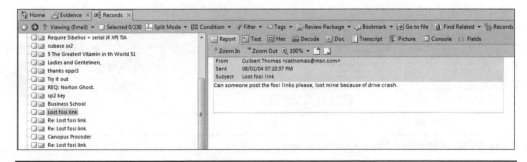

Figure 8-27   *Email thread of interest*

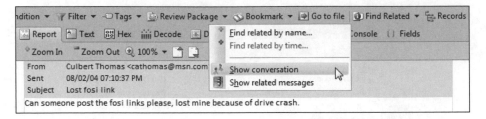

Figure 8-28 *Show Conversation*

I chose the Lost fosi link thread in the Tree pane. You can click anywhere in the thread—it doesn't have to be the first email. Then click on the Find Related drop-down menu and choose Show Conversation (Figure 8-28).

If it is a long and complex thread, it may take some time to parse. However, once EnCase finishes, you will see the conversation in a new window by itself (Figure 8-29).

You can bookmark threads from this window as well—just blue check the items of interest in the Tree pane and create a bookmark from there.

Web-Based Email

In many cases, the subject of the investigation may not use a standalone email client such as Outlook or Notes. In these cases, when email is handled in the cloud by an email provider such as Yahoo or Gmail, the artifacts will be found in the Internet artifacts. While the email providers have done significant work to reduce the amount that can be found in cache folders, it is always worth looking at the contents (or searching with keywords) to be thorough. For our case, while the Internet folder is present in the Records tab. Clicking on the hyperlink in the Table pane shows that there were no records placed in this section by the Evidence Processor.

If we look in the Evidence tab, however, we can see some items in the Mr. Evil Temporary Internet Files folder (Figure 8-30).

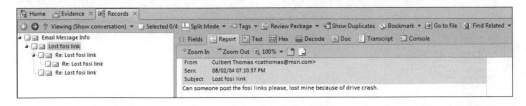

Figure 8-29 *Results of Show Conversation*

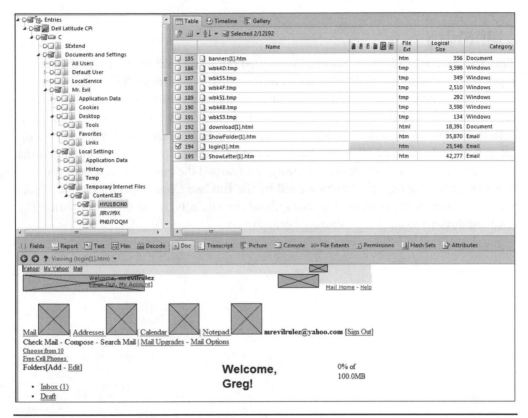

Figure 8-30   *Internet artifact from Yahoo Mail*

You can see the full path in the Tree pane of the Evidence Browser, and I sorted the columns on Category. The page I have selected shows that this is a page from the logged-in email account of mrevilrulez@yahoo.com, and it welcomes "Greg" when he logs in. Since our registered owner is Greg Schardt, this gives us a nice link between the Mr. Evil user, this email account, and the registered owner.

Create a Selected Items bookmark for all three of the pages marked Email in the Category column and save them under the Report | Internet Artifacts | [Internet Explorer] folder. While we are in the neighborhood, there is another email item you can look at in the PN0J7OQM folder under the Content.IE5 folder, which has the same association, so bookmark that in the same location.

Summary

This has been a productive chapter. We started out looking at the Case Analyzer reports and how to use their contents to more quickly determine the basics of our case. We learned how to determine the original locations the evidence inside these reports are sourced from and how bookmarking the results inside the Case Analyzer differs from bookmarking in other locations of the EnCase interface. We went on to learn how to customize our Case Analyzer reports and build new reports that suit the needs of our organization or case. Finally, we learned the basics of SQL and how to work inside the SQLite database used by the EnCase Case Analyzer, and the fact that since it only contains the metadata about the artifacts, it can be shared among investigators without fear of sharing contraband.

Keywords and Searching

W e've spent time reviewing the Case Analyzer and the Evidence Processor modules. These are great for helping you get an initial feel for what was going on with the case. However, when faced with the volume of evidence that many of today's cases involve, the examiner also needs other tools to find clues. When looking for needles in such a large haystack, we have a number of tools at our disposal. They include performing keyword searches and building filters and conditions. We will look the search options in depth in this chapter, and filters and conditions in the next chapter, so that you will have a thorough understanding of how to use them within the EnCase interface.

Keywords and Searching

It is quite common to have cases that require extensive searches for a set of keywords. How you build the list of words to search varies between examiners and even between cases. Usually there will be a list of terms that are relevant to the case—the company involved, the subject of the investigation and their associates' names, phone numbers, and other particulars are obvious candidates. In e-discovery cases, the search terms are frequently topics of negotiation between the opposing parties, and while the person performing the analysis may have input into what terms are used, they may not make the final decision. Since we have been using the NIST Hacking Case study, words associated with hacking and computer technology are also of interest.

There are two ways to search for instances of keywords: logical raw keyword searches are conducted against allocated files, while physical searches, in contrast, are against the unallocated space from the disk. This is an important distinction, because a physical search will miss a keyword if it is fragmented between noncontiguous clusters, while a logical search will find that same keyword. In EnCase, you can search for keywords in the Evidence Processor or from the Evidence tab.

Logical vs. Physical Searches

EnCase can perform both a logical and a physical search. What is the difference? A logical search looks at all the logical data of a file in performing the search regardless of the physical characteristics of how it is stored. Think of this as if you are reading a word processing document—do you know how it is stored on the hard drive? No, and you don't care. You only want the logical data associated with the file and don't need to be bothered with the physical locations.

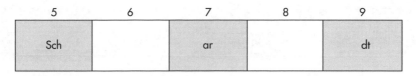

Figure 9-1   *Noncontiguous data stored on disk*

A physical keyword search is run against the raw file data—it is not searching against the metadata of the file, which is an important distinction to keep in mind. A physical search will look at data cluster by cluster, and if the file is not stored contiguously, it may not find the match. Figure 9-1 shows an example of how data might be stored.

You can see that if the keyword "Schardt" was stored in several different locations rather than one after another, a physical search will not find it. When searching unallocated space, this should be kept in mind.

Searching in the Evidence Processor

Keyword search results that are created from within the Evidence Processor are placed in the device's evidence cache files. They are available once the module has completed processing.

TIP

Search terms can be used across multiple cases if desired, so part of your case management process should include harvesting keyword search terms that are useful globally. You may wish to build keyword lists for common case types that you handle to help streamline your process as well.

Creating a New Keyword

We are going to do our first set of keyword processing from the Evidence Processor. The Search for Keywords module can be run on evidence at any time. Launch the Evidence Processor from the Evidence tab by blue checking our evidence and choosing Process Evidence from the toolbar on the Evidence tab. In the EnCase Evidence Processor, place a blue check in the Process box in the Evidence Name section to enable the Current Processing Options. Clicking on the Search for Keywords module in the Evidence Processor brings us into the Keywords editor (Figure 9-2). Here, you can either create a new keyword or import a keyword list. First, we will create a new keyword, and later we will see how to bring in a keyword list.

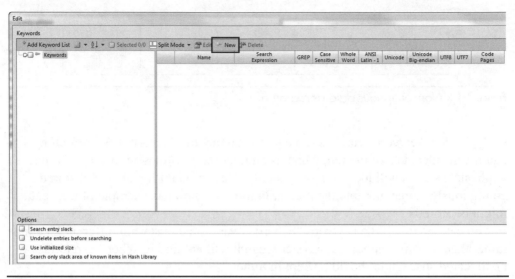

Figure 9-2 *Keywords editor*

Click the New button on the Keywords toolbar to open the New Keyword dialog (Figure 9-3). This interface is the same, regardless of whether you get to it by creating a new keyword in the Evidence Processor or if you are searching from outside the Evidence Processor.

If you've used prior versions of EnCase, this keyword dialog should look quite familiar. The Search Expression text box is where you enter the keyword you want to search for. If you are using a GREP expression, it also goes here. As we get into the GREP expressions later, you will see that they can become rather complex, and since they are frequently made up of many symbols, they can take some time to decipher. To help you remember what they are for at a glance, there is also the Name text box. While you may not always want to put in something for a straight text keyword, you will almost certainly want to put some kind of descriptive name in there for GREP keyword expressions.

What would make a good keyword for our case? Well, we know that the name of the person we suspect is Greg Schardt, and we know that there was a user account called Mr. Evil as well as an email account mrevilrulez@yahoo.com. So all of these would make good keywords for our case. Also, we know that this case is about suspected hacking, so we should also build some keywords around that topic. Remember some of the graphics we found in Chapter 6? Also, some of the tools that we saw installed might be good keywords to see if there is any other related material to find there.

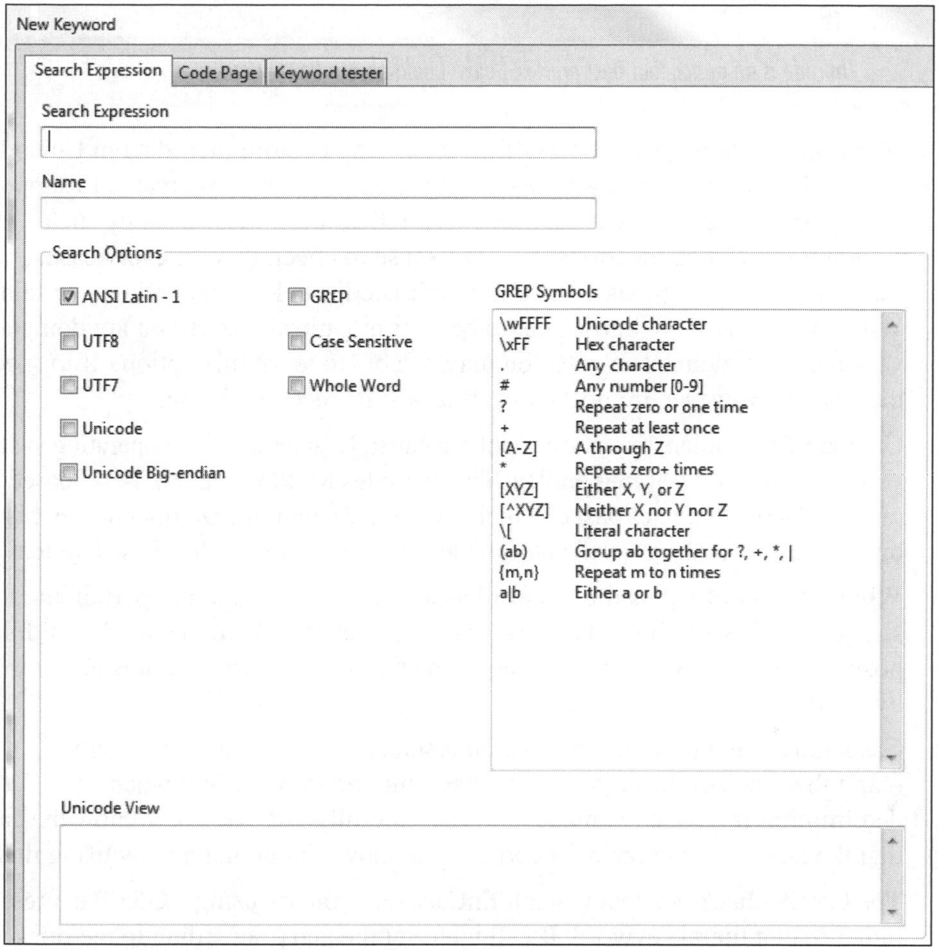

New Keyword

| Search Expression | Code Page | Keyword tester |

Search Expression

```
|
```

Name

```

```

Search Options

☑ ANSI Latin - 1   ☐ GREP

☐ UTF8   ☐ Case Sensitive

☐ UTF7   ☐ Whole Word

☐ Unicode

☐ Unicode Big-endian

GREP Symbols

\wFFFF	Unicode character
\xFF	Hex character
.	Any character
#	Any number [0-9]
?	Repeat zero or one time
+	Repeat at least once
[A-Z]	A through Z
*	Repeat zero+ times
[XYZ]	Either X, Y, or Z
[^XYZ]	Neither X nor Y nor Z
\[	Literal character
(ab)	Group ab together for ?, +, *, |
{m,n}	Repeat m to n times
a|b	Either a or b

Unicode View

Figure 9-3 *New Keyword dialog*

So, our first keyword will be Schardt. Type "Schardt" in the Search Expression text box (without the quotes), and give the keyword the same name. Now look at the search options.

Search Options   The default checked option is ANSI-Latin-1. This is the standard code page that Windows is using, and unless you are doing a non-English language search, this should be fine. UTF-8 is primarily used for non-English language searches, and is not checked by default.

> **TIP**
>
> *Unicode is an option that best practice holds should always be checked.*

▶ Many applications (Microsoft Office, for example) store their data in Unicode format. Unicode stores characters in 2-byte lengths and was created to support non-English language character sets. Given that it is widely used by such a common set of applications, it makes sense to check this for every case. That said, there are times when you won't need to select this option—certain Windows artifacts are known not to be kept in Unicode, so if you are doing a very narrowly defined search, you may be able to leave this option off to speed the search. However, in most cases, it is best to check Unicode.

▶ Unicode-Big Endian, by contrast, only needs to be selected if the operating system you are searching is in big endian. This includes Motorola and SPARC based processors (unlike Intel based, which are all little endian). Do not choose this option unless you have verified the evidence is from a big endian based system.

▶ Whole Word only finds the keyword as a word by itself and not part of another string. This is something that is typically applied to reduce the number of false positives on a keyword that is likely to be part of other words but is also a word by itself.

▶ Case Sensitive will force your search results to take the case sensitivity (capitalization) of the keyword you have entered into account when determining if a match is made. Use this carefully—if you don't know the case that the keyword will have for certain, you may miss actual hits by using this.

▶ The GREP check box lets you tell EnCase that you are using a GREP expression rather than a literal keyword. It will interpret the entry according to the rules we will cover later.

So, with all that in mind, we keep the ANSI-Latin-1 option checked, and add Unicode. Nothing else is checked. Once you have finished creating the search expression, click OK. Our keyword shows up in the Table pane in the Keywords editor now.

> **TIP**
>
> *Did you notice the Unicode View changing at the bottom of the dialog as you typed in your keyword? That is the value of the keyword you have entered as it would appear in Unicode. This is useful to pay attention to if you are going to be creating Unicode-specific GREP expressions at some point—you can use this feature to determine what your Unicode should be based on the value this displays.*

Adding a Keyword List

You don't have to enter all of your keywords manually. They can be imported from a keyword list that you have built outside of EnCase. This is very useful for when you have GREP expressions you want to bring into a case that you have tested before and know they work. Click on the Add Keyword List button at the top of the Keywords editor and the Add Keyword List dialog appears (Figure 9-4).

To add your list, copy it to the Windows clipboard from the list you have developed (usually in a word processor) and paste them into the Keywords box by right-clicking inside the box and choosing Paste. You have the same options for each keyword you enter that you would if you were entering them manually. However, if you select any of these options, it will affect the entire list. Once you have finished adding your entire keyword list, you can make changes to individual keyword values in the Table pane of the Keywords editor by right-clicking in the column of the keyword's attribute you want to change.

Incidentally, if you happen to finish adding your list and realize that you neglected to set an attribute you wanted on all of them, you can highlight the whole column— say the Unicode column—and right-click on it to bring up the context menu. From there you can choose the Invert Selected Items option to change the values of all of the items in that column from False to True.

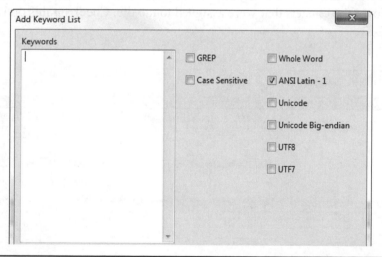

Figure 9-4 *Add Keyword List Dialog*

For our purposes, add the following keywords into our case using whatever method you like best:

▶ Greg

▶ Mr. Evil

▶ mrevilrulez

▶ Hacking

▶ Wireless

▶ Ethereal

Once you have created them and are back in the Keywords editor, look at the Options box at the bottom of the dialog (Figure 9-5). These are options that control where in your evidence you will be searching. The Search Entry Slack option tells EnCase to search the slack space between the end of the logical data to the end of the physical file. Click on that option.

The next option is Undelete Entries Before Searching. This will perform a logical undelete of files before searching them. This will only work on files that have been deleted but have not been overwritten. How does this work? During the search, EnCase encounters a deleted file. It attempts to recover that file by reading the assigned starting cluster and determining how many clusters were used to store that file. EnCase then tries to recover the clusters that were assigned to the file. Check on this option as well and click OK.

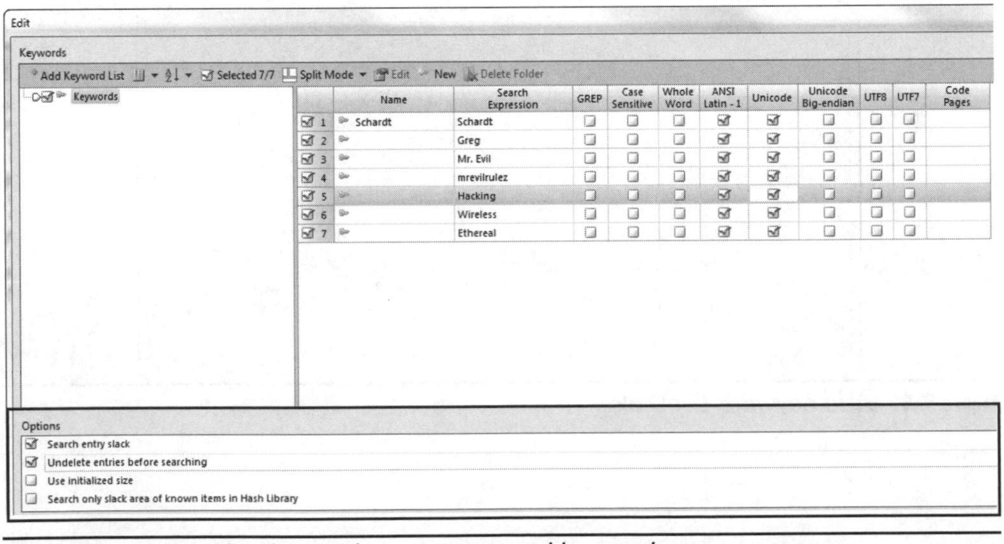

Figure 9-5   *Keywords editor with our options and keywords*

You should see the progress bar in the bottom-right corner as EnCase performs the search. This can be a time consuming process.

Viewing Search Results

Once the Evidence Processor completes, you will naturally want to see your new search results. You can see these by opening the Search tab (choose Search from the View menu) and then clicking on the Keyword tab. If you have the tabs close together, it will show as a small key icon and the word "Keywords" will be hidden (Figure 9-6). Expanding the border between the Table and Tree panes will show the labels for these subtabs.

Here you can see that EnCase has each result labeled (these are hyperlinks) and gives you statistics in terms of how many items (files) and how many hits (instances of the search term) they contain. You can click each of the terms and drill into the detail in the Table and View panes.

Another behavior worth noting when searching within EnCase is the fact that you can also view the currently selected results in the Results tab under Search as shown in Figure 9-7. However, this only displays the most recent results. So, for example, if you clicked on the mrevil result in the Search tab shown in Figure 9-6, and then clicked over to the Results tab and clicked on Search line item as shown in Figure 9-8, you would see exactly the same thing displayed in both locations.

Note, however, that there is no indication in the Results tab what this search term was. This can be quite confusing if you don't realize that this just reflects whatever search result from the Table pane you had clicked on in the Search tab.

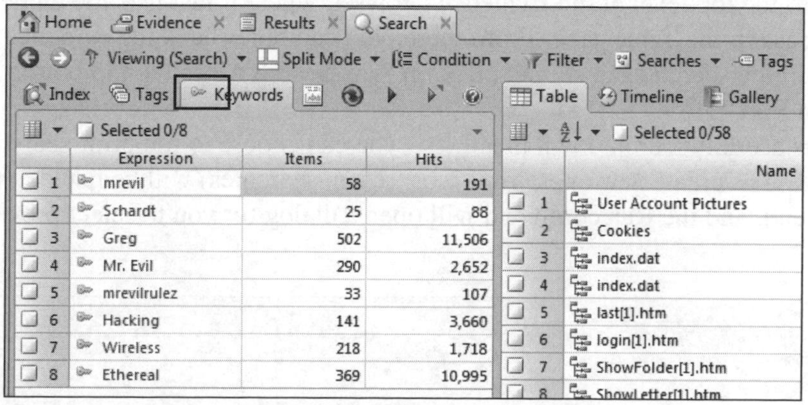

Figure 9-6 *Keywords subtab of Search tab*

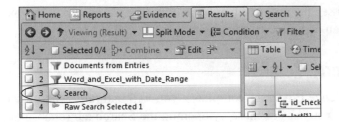

Figure 9-7 *Results tab, Search row*

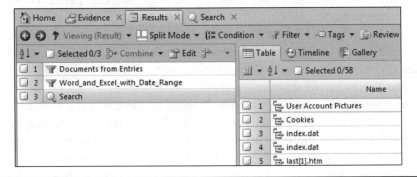

Figure 9-8 *Current search in the Results tab*

Searching in the Evidence Browser

EnCase provides for searching outside of the Evidence Processor. The easiest way is to go to the top level of the Evidence Browser, where it just lists the evidence in your case in the Table pane. From there, you can blue check the evidence you'd like to run the search against, and click on Raw Search All in the top button bar as shown in Figure 9-9.

This is actually a drop-down menu, and you can choose to run prior searches from here as well as create new ones. Your most recent search(es) will be listed at the top of the menu, and the Run command will open a dialog for you to select previously

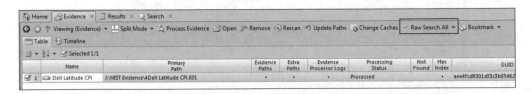

Figure 9-9 *Raw Search All from the Evidence Browser*

saved searches as well. If you want to make changes to one of those previously saved searches, choose Edit. For our purposes, choose New Raw Search All from the menu and you will see the same familiar Keywords editor from when we created keywords for the Evidence Processor. Since we covered this already above, you can go ahead and click Cancel here.

You can also drill into the evidence you have listed and run your raw keyword search against just certain images in your case, or even just a subset of a specific image. Click on the Dell Latitude CPi hyperlink to get into the Evidence Browser—you can see if you don't have anything blue checked, the Raw Search Selected button is grayed out. Once you select something, that becomes an available option, and the same interface you have seen in prior examples is available for building keywords.

> **TIP**
>
> *If you choose to perform keyword searches outside of the Evidence Processor, you should note that the results will not be in the device's evidence cache files and would have to be handled separately if you want them available to other cases.*

Evidence and Cache Locations

I'd like to cover an important point about the processed evidence and where the evidence cache is stored. You can see when you open the Evidence Browser that there are buttons across the top that let you manage the evidence in your case. Specifically, I am referring to the Rescan, Update Paths, and Change Caches buttons (Figure 9-10). The Rescan button will simply rescan the evidence you had previously included in your case, and open it in the Evidence tab when it completes. The Update Paths button is used for when the path to your evidence has changed and you need to let EnCase know where it is now stored. The Change Caches button is similar, in that it allows you to point EnCase to a new path if it has changed, but you can also use it to have EnCase reprocess evidence whose cache has become corrupted.

Troubleshooting the Evidence Cache

The latter case is what I encountered midway through the prior chapter—I started seeing strange behavior from EnCase. When I processed keywords in the Evidence Processor, there would be no results, even though the processing had completed successfully. Likewise, when I tried to use the index search, similar strange behavior occurred, leading me to think there was something wrong going on with the evidence. This could happen to anyone if there is an issue with the evidence processing—there were no error messages in the EnCase interface, just behavior that made no sense. I want to cover this because it may help others who run into similar issues.

The first step was to see if there was anything going on in the logs. If you recall, these are located in C:\<*profile of user running EnCase*>\Documents\EnCase\Logs. I found messages indicating that the system could not find files in the evidence cache—not a good sign. Sure enough, Guidance Tech Support confirmed that the problem was due to problems with the disk I was using to store the case data and evidence cache files.

How is this fixed? Actually, the solution is not too painful (compared to what I feared it might be). I was advised to change the evidence cache location and reprocess the evidence. But how do you change the cache location? You cannot make this change in the Home screen's Options dialog—that path is grayed out. Instead, you need to go to the Evidence Browser where you can see your evidence listed but you haven't clicked into the detail view of it yet, as shown in Figure 9-10.

Clicking on the Change Caches button will bring up the Change Caches dialog, where you can make your adjustments (Figure 9-11). The "Use base case folder for primary evidence cache" option is checked by default. Since I knew there was a problem with the primary evidence cache and wanted to create a new one, I needed to uncheck that box. This allowed me to make changes to the Primary Evidence Cache text box.

Make the changes to the path as appropriate and click Next. The Evidence Cache Preview dialog opens. You can see that the Cache Status is Missing in Figure 9-12.

This is because I created a new folder for the evidence cache to be placed into, so EnCase notes that there are no existing cache files in the directory I pointed it to.

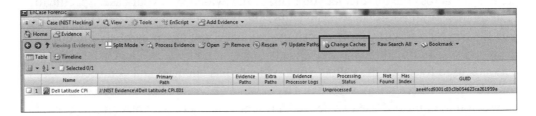

Figure 9-10   *Evidence Browser, Change Caches button*

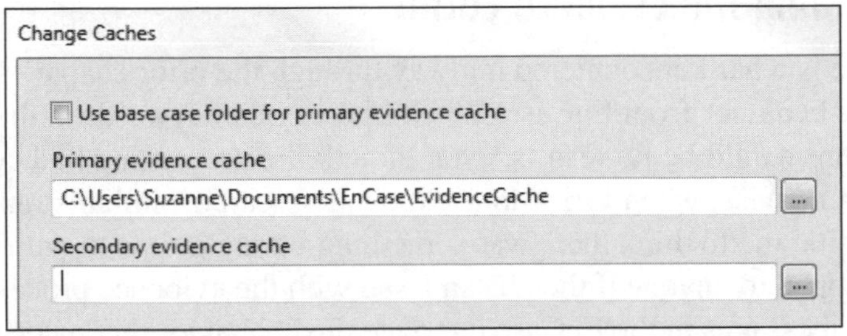

Change Caches

☐ Use base case folder for primary evidence cache

Primary evidence cache

C:\Users\Suzanne\Documents\EnCase\EvidenceCache   [...]

Secondary evidence cache

[   ] [...]

Figure 9-11   *Change Caches dialog*

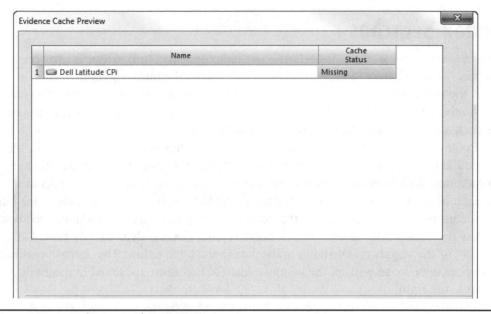

Figure 9-12   *Evidence Cache Preview*

If I had used a directory (for example, if I changed the directory to my secondary evidence cache that had been defined when the evidence was processed), then it would show that this was ready to be primary instead.

Since that was not the case, and I was pointing to an empty directory, I also got a warning after clicking Finish, as shown in Figure 9-13.

This is EnCase letting me know that it will be creating a new cache in the new location, which is just what I want to happen. Now that I have a new location for the evidence cache files, I kick off the Evidence Processor again with all the same modules checked and keywords specified and let it rebuild the evidence cache for the case. Note, rebuilding the evidence cache can be time consuming, depending on the size of the evidence to be processed, so only do this if you are trying to fix the problem I have described, or have been directed to by EnCase Technical Support.

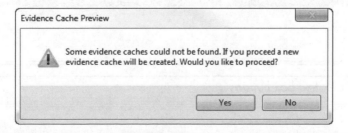

Figure 9-13   *Evidence Cache Preview warning*

Index Searches

The Search tab is where you perform your index searches in EnCase. When you process your evidence, EnCase builds an index from the transcript data of the file plus the metadata, and this is what you are running index searches against. You can get to the Search tab in one of two ways: either from the Home page by clicking on Search, or by choosing Search from the View menu.

In the Search tab, the first subtab is Index. Note, the smaller your window is, the more likely the buttons on the button bar as shown in Figure 9-14 may be either turned into their icons without the text shown or not show at all. As it shrinks this section of the window, EnCase will start hiding buttons from the right side of the bar to accommodate smaller sizes of this section. Type your search terms in the text box below the button bar. As soon as you begin typing, EnCase dynamically brings up the list of the variations available in the data in the table below. These are hyperlinks, and clicking on one will get the results related to that term displayed in the Table pane to the right.

The text field where you type your terms has a button bar of its own above it. There you will find the very powerful options that allow you to control the results with significant granularity to reduce false positives (Figure 9-14).

From left to right, these buttons are:

▶ **Field**   This is a drop-down menu that lets you choose specific fields to constrain your search. It gives you an easy way to make sure you have the right field name without having to look up the syntax. Once you have added the field name, type the value that you want to find in the index text box next to the name with no space after the bracket.

▶ **Patterns**   This is a drop-down menu that has a list of several predefined numeric patterns to choose from. Choosing one will embed it in your search term.

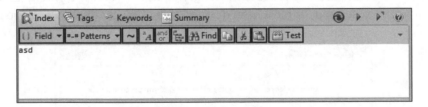

Figure 9-14   *Index text box buttons*

▶ **Stem**   This displays a list of possible stemming alternatives to the currently selected term. Stemming is basically alternate endings to a core term you have entered in the text box. If you want to see an example, type "want" without the quotes and click the Stem button. You can delete alternatives from the list if you don't want them to be included by right-clicking on them in the list and choosing Delete. You can also add new variations to the list. Finally, you can change the locale selected for the term—but you can only choose one item from that Locale list.

▶ **Case**   This lets you toggle between either case sensitive (capitalization is considered and enforced in the results) or case insensitive (return results regardless of their capitalization).

▶ **Logic**   This inserts an AND or an OR logical operator at the point of the cursor. It also will toggle the logic back and forth between these two options if they already exist. To change a specific logic operator, highlight it first and then click the button (or you could just type it).

▶ **Expand**   This opens the highlighted term in the Expand interface, which has three tabs. The Text tab shows you the search term as entered. The Terms tab shows a hierarchical view, and the Report tab shows how the term will be displayed in the Report module.

▶ **Find**   This lets you find search expressions within the search term.

▶ **Copy, Cut, Paste**   These are standard Windows interface buttons that act as you would expect them to allow you to copy, cut, and paste text into the Index text box.

▶ **Test**   Test will let you check your syntax—it displays an error if there is a problem. This is particularly useful when crafting the more complex search terms.

Search Operators

In addition to the above options, you can also include search operators that EnCase provides to make a more complex query. There are several terms, and for a complete list, it is best to consult the EnCase User Guide for your version of the product. However, here are some common examples and how to use them.

Proximity

To do a proximity search (which is to say if you are looking for a word within X number of words distance from each other), you use the w/ operator:

```
apple w/4 orange
```

This will give you occurrences where apple is within four words of orange.

Not Proximity

For keywords that are *not* within X number of words distant (so the opposite of the above example), you would use the `nw/` operator:

```
apple nw/4 orange
```

This will give you results where apple is *not* within four words of orange.

Word X Before Word Y

If you are looking for one word to occur before another (so the order is important here), and to specify by how many words the first term should precede the second, use the `pre/` operator:

```
apple pre/4 orange
```

This will return results where apple precedes orange by no more than four words.

Grouping and Variables

You can specify multiple options in parentheses to group them and then use search operators to modify them:

```
apple pre/4 (orange or grape)
```

This will return results where apple precedes either orange or grape by no more than four words. You can group on both sides of the operator, so if you wanted to put additional values in with apple, you would just include them in their own set of parentheses.

You can also nest terms, for example:

```
((apple and pear) or kiwi) pre/4 (orange or grape)
```

Pay attention to the opening and closing parentheses so that you always have matched sets. This is where that Test option on the button bar of the Index text box can be helpful as you build more complex search terms.

Searching Within Fields

By default, EnCase will search within all the fields unless you choose to restrict the search scope. You can do so with the Field drop-down discussed in the above list. Once you select a field from that drop-down menu, EnCase places the field in square brackets in the Index text box. You can now just type the value you want to search directly after (no spaces between the ending square bracket and your search term).

```
[To]mrevilrulez
```

The above would return results where the email field included the value "mrevilrulez" in it. You can also use the same grouping and logic operators in combination with the field names.

Searching with Dates

You can use dates in your search terms. They must be entered in ISO 8601 format, and surrounded by a hash tag (#) on either side. You can use as much detail as you need—for example, you can just specify the year if you want to restrict only that, but you can also be much more complex:

```
[Modified]#2005-01-24...2006-12-24#
```

The above example uses the Modified field. When you choose the field, EnCase inserts the field name surrounded by square brackets, and then two hash tags. You type in your date value between the two tags. The ellipses (...) represent a range between the first and second dates. You can see that the ISO 8601 format is yyyy-mm-dd.

Other numeric values also follow the same syntax—you enter them between two hash tags, and ellipses are used to indicate a range. Note, if you include an ellipse before a number alone, or after a number alone, it serves as a less than/greater than indicator:

```
[Logical Size]#...5000#
[Message Size]#1500...#
```

Using GREP Operators

GREP is an acronym that stands for *Globally* search for a *Regular Expression* and *Print* it.

GREP originates from the Unix operating system, but the implementation in EnCase is not a standard Unix GREP. (EnCase documentation keeps GREP in all uppercase, but I'm old school—I learned it during my years as a Unix system administrator, and we don't do caps lightly in an operating system that is case sensitive. If you encounter it elsewhere outside of EnCase, expect to see it all lowercase.) If you are used to using standard Unix GREP, you need to pay even closer attention because some of the GREP operators mean quite different things in EnCase's implementation.

GREP is very powerful for creating search expressions that only find what you are looking for—used correctly it reduces false positives. However, GREP is cryptic, and complex search expressions can seem quite daunting to people just starting out with it. To get us started, Table 9-1 lists the GREP commands that EnCase supports and their usage.

Syntax	Usage
`\wFFFF`	The `\w` indicates you want GREP to treat this as a Unicode character and not its ASCII equivalent.
`\xFF`	The `\x` indicates you want GREP to treat this as a hex character and not its ASCII equivalent.
`.`	A period (.) will match any single character, even nonprinting characters like line feeds and carriage returns. The period is a wildcard character that will match once and only once, whether the character is alphabetic, numeric, symbolic, or nonprinting.
`#`	The hash (#) or pound symbol will match any single numeric character of zero through nine. When you are looking for numbers only, this is your friend.
`?`	A question mark (?) after a character/group of characters will match one or zero occurrences of that character/group.
`+`	A plus sign (+) after a character/group matches any number of occurrences of that character/group at least once.
`[A-Z]`	The dash or hyphen (-) within a set indicates GREP should treat the set as a range of values. This is used both with alphabetic and numeric character sets.
`*`	An asterisk (*) after a character/group matches any number of occurrences of that character/group, including zero times.
`[XYZ]`	The square brackets hold the place of just one character—so if you have a set of characters enclosed in them this acts as an OR statement. To hit on a search term, one member of the set must be present, but not more than one.
`[^XYZ]`	The circumflex or caret (^) is the GREP NOT operator. When used in a set, it means "NOT any of these".
`\[`	The backslash character (\) is used to "protect" or "escape" the following character and effectively tell GREP to ignore it as a GREP operator and use it as a literal string for searching. You need to do this any time you want to search for a character that is a GREP operator (i.e., those listed in the left column of this table).
`(ab)`	Parentheses are used for grouping characters together for use with other GREP commands such as wildcards or the logical operator pipe (l).
`{m,n}`	The curly braces repeat the character/group between *m* and *n* times (so this is treated as the start and end of the range) up to 255 times.
`a|b`	The pipe (l) symbol is used as a logical OR in GREP. You use it to separate groups of characters where you want to see one group OR the other.

Table 9-1 *GREP Commands*

What are all of these symbols and how can you use them? The best way to learn to use GREP expressions is to dig in and start building some. Our table is in the same order that you will find these expressions in the New Keyword dialog so that you can easily find the definition here when you have that window open. However, the order doesn't lend itself well to teaching how to use GREP expressions, so I'll go over them in a more functional order.

This is best taught interactively, so I have created a file with the GREP expressions we discuss, and another one with sample data for us to use to search through so we can see how each of these behaves. They can be found on the McGraw-Hill Professional Computing download page, www.mhprofessional.com/templates/computing. The files are called grep-expressions.txt and grep-datafile.txt.

The GREP Wildcards

First, let's start with the wildcard symbols (. # ? + *). Each one acts a bit differently and is used in cases where you need specific characteristics.

The Period (.)

The period matches any single character or noncharacter (space, tab, nonprinting characters, etc.). So what does using it look like?

```
li.e
```

The above example will find "live", "like", "line", but not "love" because the wildcard is in the third position of the expression, and the first two letters must match "l" and "i". GREP will also find it in the middle of a string, such as "sliver" and "Livermore", although it will only highlight the "live" portion of the word in the results. Note also that since we did not force the keywords to be case sensitive when we built them, Livermore will be a match. If we had forced case sensitivity, that would not have been a match.

The Pound or Hash Sign (#)

The # sign is all about numbers, which makes it easy to remember. This is commonly used to look for phone numbers, credit cards, Social Security Numbers (SSNs), and other numeric combinations.

Here is an example of a U.S. phone number pattern without the area code:

```
###-####
```

This will match any three digits (including 0), followed by a hyphen, followed by four digits. Here is an example:

```
025-6375
```

Does that make sense in the context of this being a phone number? Maybe, but not if the first digit is 0. GREP will do exactly what you tell it to do—whether or not it makes sense in the context, it is all about whether the pattern matches. The other consideration is whether the locale your evidence uses separates numbers using hyphens—some do not use this form at all. There are things you can do to cope with that, such as using certain types of wildcards to represent the expected string formatting of the keyword you are looking for. We will get into more complicated forms of looking for number combinations further down as we build our expressions into more complex patterns.

The Question Mark (?)

Next, the question mark (?) matches zero or one instance of the character (or group of characters if you use the parentheses). So for our phone number example above, if you weren't sure the hyphen was present or not, you could use the question mark.

```
###-?####
```

This would match on all these:

```
223-3426
4585286
665548831
555-448-5618
```

The Keyword Tester

One really nice way to test what your search terms will find is to use the Keyword Tester tab in the New Keyword dialog. You can create a file with the example data of what you do and don't want to be caught by the search and tweak your GREP expression until you get just the results you are looking for. For the above example, I loaded a file with the results you see and entered the keyword as usual in the Search Expression tab. Then I clicked over to the Keyword Tester tab, and loaded the test data from grep-datafile .txt. You can see the results in Figure 9-15, although to see specifically which text is highlighted is difficult in a black and white book. I strongly recommend that you load the two files I am using into EnCase and follow along with each example.

Right away, I can see if my keyword expression is working as expected, and make adjustments to the expression until it behaves as I need it to before I waste time running it against large volumes of evidence.

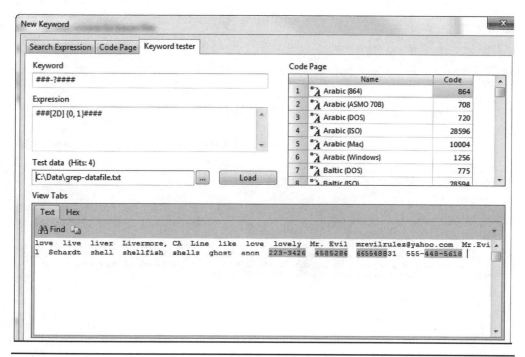

Figure 9-15   *Keyword Tester*

Grouping and GREP

Many times, you will need to group characters to show that you want an entire group repeated or to use them as a range. Several of these wildcards are best shown in combination with groups, as it can change their behavior, depending on the choices you make.

The Plus Sign (+)

The plus sign (+) matches one or more of the character or group that appears before it. This operator can be used a number of ways other than just by itself. First, let's show it by itself.

```
abc+
```

This will match the letters "ab" followed by one or more "c" characters as shown in Figure 9-16.

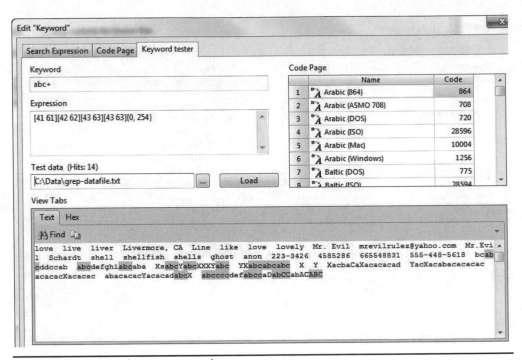

Figure 9-16 *GREP plus sign example, no grouping*

Parentheses (abc)

Now say you want "abc", and it can be repeated one or more times, but only together. We'd represent this in GREP by grouping them inside of parentheses:

```
(abc)+
```

In Figure 9-17, you can see we get a very different set of keywords highlighted when we run this through the Keyword Tester.

Square Brackets [xyz]

Now assume you want to find this group in the middle of another expression, you can nest them. If I wanted to have the letters X or Y followed by the group "abc", I would use this:

```
[XY](abc)
```

You can see in Figure 9-18 that it hits on the Y or the X prefacing the group, but does not take both. This is because letters in the square brackets have an implied logical OR between them. Think of the items in square brackets as having a "pick one of me" property.

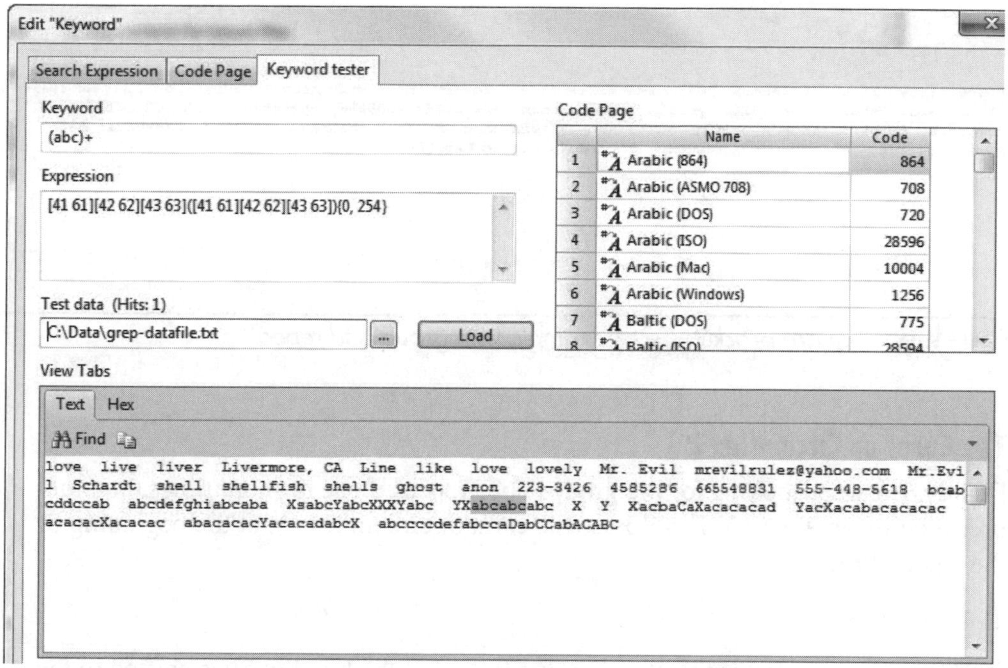

Figure 9-17   *GREP plus sign example with grouping*

If I were looking for the letter X or the letter Y, followed by my (abc) group repeated, I would represent this way:

[XY](abc)+

This matches "abc" prefaced by either X or Y, and "abc" can appear once or more repeated, as shown in Figure 9-19.

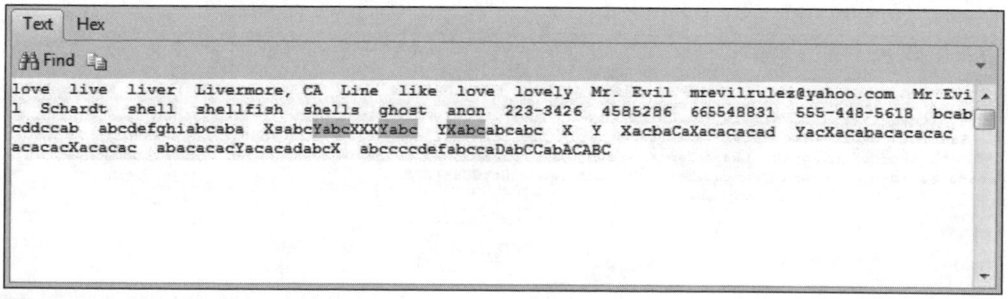

Figure 9-18   *Square brackets GREP example with group*

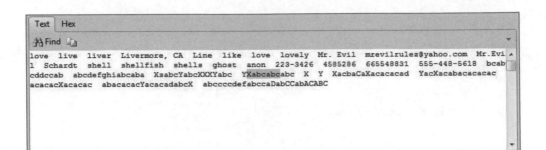

Figure 9-19   *Square brackets GREP example with group and repeat*

The Carat or Circumflex (^)

Finally, if I were looking for the group "abc" repeated one or more times, but *not* preceded by an X or a Y, I could use the carat or circumflex (^) at the beginning of the square brackets.

```
[^XY](abc)+
```

You can see from the results in Figure 9-20 that the highlight has shifted to the right compared with the previous figure. The X character is no longer included in the keyword hit.

The Asterisk (*)

The asterisk after a character or group of characters will match any number of occurrences of that character/group—including zero times. Let's start with just the two letters "a" and "c".

```
ac*
```

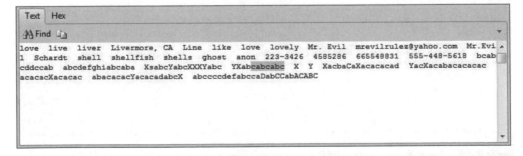

Figure 9-20   *Square brackets GREP example with group, repeat, and carat*

love live liver Livermore, CA Line like love lovely Mr. Evil mrevilrulez@yahoo.com Mr.Evi
l Schardt shell shellfish shells ghost anon 223-3426 4585286 665548831 555-448-5618 bcab
cddccab abcdefghiabcaba XsabcYabcXXXYabc YXabcabcabc X Y XacbaCaXacacacad YacXacabacacacac
acacacXacacac abacacacYacacadabcX abccccdefabccaDabCCabACABC

Figure 9-21   *Asterisk GREP expression example*

As you would expect, there are a lot of matches in this data file, as shown in
Figure 9-21. Now we can add the parentheses to show the difference that grouping
makes on this keyword.

```
(ac)*
```

Figure 9-22 shows far fewer results for this keyword expression, and we only see
instances where the two letters both appear at least once.

```
[XY](ac)*
```

As before, this will match the X or Y character, followed by "ac" repeating zero or
more times (Figure 9-23).

Note that while the asterisk is supposed to hit on the group even when it is zero
times, it is only showing here when it is at least once. If zero times were actually
the behavior, we'd see hits on X and Y by themselves, but that is not the case. Also
note that we see the asterisk only showing hits when the group appears once—those
strings have multiple occurrences of the "ac" group—why is it not showing those
selected? What we are seeing here is a function of the square bracketed group prior
to the "ac" group.

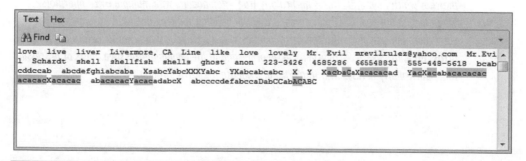

Figure 9-22   *Asterisk GREP expression with grouping*

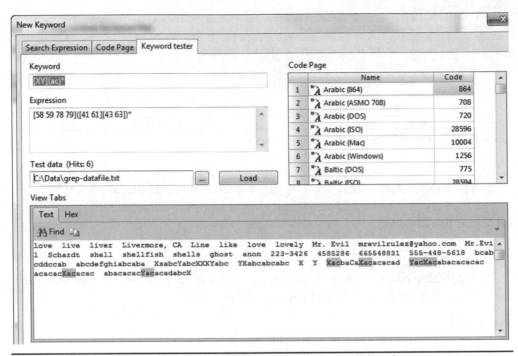

Figure 9-23 *Asterisk GREP example with grouping and square brackets*

You can see in Figure 9-24 that when I remove the [XY] group, the asterisk behaves more like we would expect it to. This influence that the square bracketed group has on the way the asterisk behaves should be kept in mind when crafting your GREP expressions.

TIP

When you have a number of search hits in a file, it is sometimes difficult to determine which hit matches which keywords. This is particularly true when dealing with multiple GREP operators. When testing out your GREP keywords, it is worth building some examples of keywords as you want them hit, and also some counter-examples to test how your syntax works before applying it across an entire evidence collection. Some pretesting at the beginning can save hours of processing time, particularly in cases with terabytes of evidence to search through.

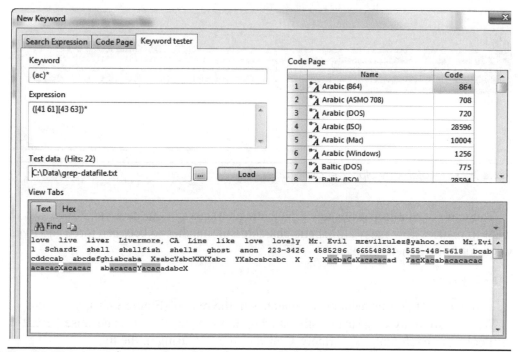

Figure 9-24 *Asterisk example without the preceding square brackets*

Ranges and Logical Operators

The final operators we will cover include curly braces and the pipe symbol. These are both quite useful in controlling how many times, or even if, an expression will return matches.

The Curly Braces {m,n}

Curly braces are used to restrict the range of matches to between the beginning value (m) and the ending value (n). Contrast this with the asterisk, which accepts repeating matches without restriction. This is best illustrated with a before and after example. Consider this expression:

```
[A-Z]
```

This matches any alphabetic characters, regardless of case (because I didn't choose the Case Sensitive option). Figure 9-25 shows the result from our data file in the Keyword Tester.

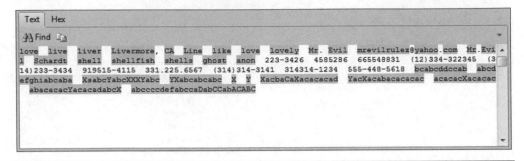

Figure 9-25 *Match any alphabetic characters*

You can see that it matches any alphabetic characters in our data file. Now if we want to restrict how many alphabetic characters it matches to between three and five, we would make these changes:

```
[A-Z]{3,5}
```

You can see that this reduces the matches in the results (Figure 9-26).

Why do so many long strings still show up in the results? This is because GREP will consider each match separately. Consider the last string in the file:

```
abccccdefabccaDabCCabACABC
```

We have a minimum match length of three, which this string obviously has, and a maximum length of five letters. So GREP will parse through the string matching the maximum letters until it gets to a point where the minimum required are not present. The following illustrates how GREP is breaking the string up into five-character chunks:

abccc	cdefa	bccaD	abCCa	bACAB	C

GREP matches the first five characters, then looks at the next chunk of five and since they are also all alphabetic, matches those. Then it continues onto the next

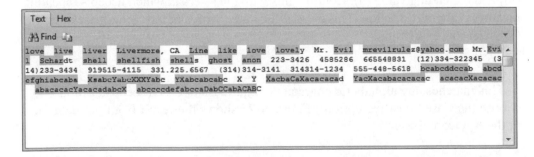

Figure 9-26 *Match only three to five alphabetic characters*

five, and the next five. Then it gets to the last chunk of letters. It matches bACAB (five alphabetic characters), and since that leaves the last "C" all by itself, it is not a match. If there were two more letters, it would have met the minimum criteria of three letters and matched the entire string.

Escaping Reserved Characters with the Backslash (\)

There are cases where you will be looking for a symbol that is a GREP reserved symbol, and you need to wave your hand and tell EnCase that "these are not the symbols I am looking for." This is called "escaping" the characters, and you do this with the backslash character (\). Using this character will protect it from being interpreted as part of the GREP expression. You need a backslash character for each reserved GREP operator you use in an expression.

So if I wanted to look for a phone number, but I didn't know that I needed to escape the parentheses in my search expression:

(###)###-#####

You can see in Figure 9-27 that EnCase found something, but not the number we are looking for. In fact, that hit isn't likely to be a phone number at all. You can see in the data file that we have some different separators between these phone numbers. How about if we use the backslash to escape the parentheses?

\(###\)###-####

The backslash characters in front of the open and closed parentheses keep EnCase from interpreting them as GREP operators, and so it finds the literal open and closed parentheses, with three numbers inside, followed by three numbers, a hyphen, and four numbers (Figure 9-28).

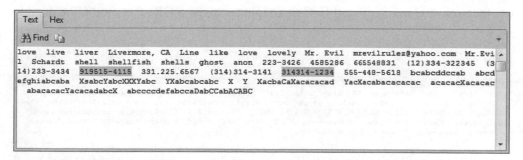

Figure 9-27 *Looking for a phone number*

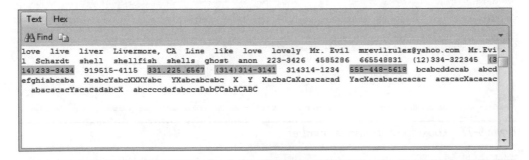

Figure 9-28 *Using the backslash to escape the parentheses*

The Pipe Symbol: Logical OR (|)

The data file we're using has a number of common ways that phone numbers can be written. Consider the case where periods can be used to separate sections, or hyphens, or parentheses, or some combination therein. How would we adjust our GREP expression to handle these cases?

We can use the logical OR symbol, which is called a pipe (|). It is commonly found on the same key as the backslash, and you use SHIFT to access it. We still need to make sure that our parentheses are escaped, but wc also need to let EnCase know we want matches where either a hyphen or a period is used in between the numbers. Here is the expression; the results it produces are shown in Figure 9-29:

```
\(?###(\)|.)###(-|.)####
```

You can see that this gets us those phone numbers where the dots are separating the numbers, as well as those where the parentheses are present. Look at the last string highlighted in Figure 9-29, though—why is it hitting on that when they are separated by hyphens? It is because we are looking for a literal period, but we didn't use the escape character to tell EnCase to ignore this as a GREP operator. We need to

Figure 9-29 *Phone number with a period or a hyphen*

```
Text   Hex
🔍 Find ▐🐱                                                                    ▼
love  live  liver  Livermore, CA  Line  like  love  lovely  Mr. Evil  mrevilrulez@yahoo.com  Mr.Evi ▲
l  Schardt  shell  shellfish  shells  ghost  anon  223-3426  4585286  665548831  (12)334-322345  (3
14)233-3434  919515-4115  331.225.6567  (314)314-3141  314314-1234  555-448-5618  bcabcddccab  abcd
efghiabcaba  XsabcYabcXXXYabc  YXabcabcabc  X  Y  XacbaCaXacacacad  YacXacabacacacac  acacacXacacac
  abacacacYacacadabcX  abcccdefabccaDabCCabACABC
                                                                                                  ▼
```

Figure 9-30   *Phone number with the periods escaped*

escape those periods, because EnCase interprets them to match any single character. This is fine if we want to include hyphen-separated phone numbers, but that isn't what we were trying to achieve.

\(?###(\)|\.)###(-|\.)####

Once we put in our escape characters to protect the periods in the expression, the results are what we were trying for (Figure 9-30).

Summary

You can see from these examples how powerful GREP can be when used properly. I can't stress enough how important it is to test your keywords on both positive examples and negative ones before you process evidence with them. The Keyword Tester is an excellent tool for this type of testing, since you can build a file with both types of keywords to refine your expressions before turning them loose on your evidence. It is possible to get "too fancy" with your GREP expressions, and introduce cases where you see false negatives because you have tuned the expression too tightly. Guidance Software recommends in their training that you keep these expressions only as complex as necessary to get the job done. One expression should not be stretched to cover too many contingencies.

This chapter has covered quite a bit of ground, and you should now have some comfort in crafting your own search terms and GREP expressions to ensure that you minimize the number of false positives in your searching. In Chapter 10, we will go into detail on dealing with filters and conditions to even further narrow your results to just those that are relevant.

Putting It All Together

In Part IV, we cover quite a lot of ground. First, Chapter 10 introduces conditions and filters and their uses. The differences between the two are discussed, and you are shown how to run existing conditions and filters, as well as how to make edits to create your own.

Chapter 11 deals primarily with hash libraries and hash sets. You are shown how to create new hash libraries and sets, as well as how to import legacy sets from older versions of EnCase. We also walk through importing the NSRL hash library for use in your cases. Finally, there is a brief discussion on using the timeline function in EnCase.

Chapter 12 is all about reporting. If you've used the reporting function in EnCase, you know it frequently needs adjustments made to have the reports appear how you need them. We walk through how to make changes to the reporting templates to suit your organization's needs, and how to change how the evidence you've bookmarked is displayed in the document.

Finally, Chapter 13 deals with the end stage of the case—and considerations for managing the evidence lifecycle. This chapter is particularly important as it raises the types of questions you need to have addressed as an organization. The best way to get into trouble and find that evidence has been destroyed improperly or without permission is to "wing it" when it comes to evidence and case lifecycle management.

N ow that you are comfortable building your own keywords and performing searches in EnCase, we can look at more complex options for narrowing down our results. By combining the various options available for searching with the ability to include specific criteria and programming logic, we can get quite granular in our results while maintaining confidence in their quality.

In addition to keyword searching, EnCase provides two powerful methods to design your own criteria for finding and reporting results—conditions and filters. Conditions and filters are similar, differing primarily in the way you build (new) or modify (existing) ones. EnCase provides a point-and-click graphic interface for working with conditions, while filters are created and edited inside the EnScript programming environment. If all you are doing is running them, they will appear much the same to you in practical use.

Conditions

Conditions allow you to narrow your search result set based on criteria that you define. They are written in EnScript (as are filters), but EnCase provides an interface that allows you to build them without having to be fluent in EnScript (EnCase's built-in programming language, which we cover in Chapter 15). This user interface is very powerful and allows you to build your conditions based on a number of parameters.

The other main difference between filters and conditions in EnCase is that there are no conditions included by default with the product. They must be built by the examiner or copied from a condition built by another person.

Running an Existing Condition

You can run a condition by choosing the Run command from the Condition drop-down menu in the Evidence browser. This will bring up a dialog that allows you to browse to where the condition is stored. Conditions are stored in C:\Program Files\<*install directory*>\Condition by default. Putting conditions that you have received from other examiners in this directory will allow you to easily run them. The Edit command from the same menu will allow you to make changes to conditions you have already defined or copied from others. Again, I recommend always working on a copy of the original, both to preserve the original for later use and in case something goes wrong with your edits.

Creating a New Condition

You can create new conditions from scratch by choosing the New Condition command from the Condition drop-down menu. Note the Path text box (Figure 10-1).

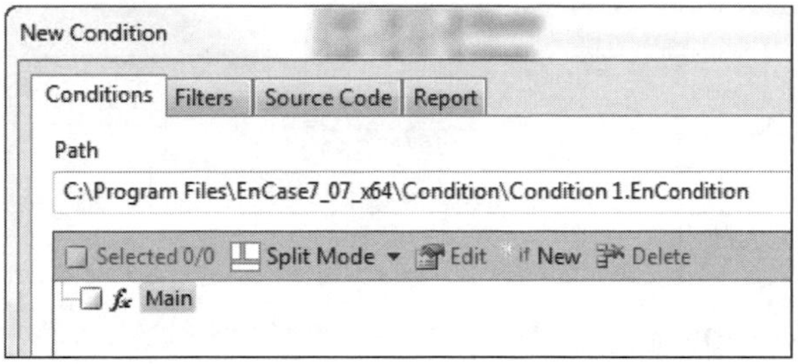

Figure 10-1 *New Condition dialog*

This shows both what EnCase is going to call your new condition and where it will be stored. This filename is what shows in the list of conditions to choose from as well. If you don't give your condition a name here, EnCase will name it "Condition#" with the # incrementing a counter each time you create a new condition without a name specified. Since this isn't very descriptive when choosing from a list of conditions to run, I recommend a more descriptive name based on what the condition is designed to do. For your new condition, call it "Office Files with Date Range".

You are provided with the Main clause of the new condition. As you add new terms to this condition, they will appear under the Main clause. This is where you can change the logic of the condition once you have built your terms. The New Condition dialog (Figure 10-1) provides you with the interface to build new complex conditions. To get started, either click the New button, press the INSERT key, or right-click on the Main function and choose New. All of these accomplish the same thing, which is to display the New Term dialog (Figure 10-2). Here is where you really start to build your criteria for the condition.

You have the option of naming each term in your condition. This is largely personal preference, because if you choose not to name the term, EnCase will display it in the New Condition dialog as the attributes, operators, and values you chose. If you do choose to name it, you will see the name you chose instead. Figure 10-3 shows an example of what I mean.

Both of the terms do the same thing. The first term is the one I gave a name to, and this illustrates the need to make that name descriptive if you choose to use a name instead of the standard display method shown in the second term.

In the New Term dialog (Figure 10-2), the Properties box contains a list of the various options you can choose to build your condition upon. These are the attributes (column headings) you will see in the Table pane when viewing evidence items. The icons next to the property items show you what data type they are. For example, Name is a string data type; Logical Size is an integer type; IsFolder is a Boolean data type (so values will be true or false). The File Created attribute has a calendar icon, which indicates it is a date/time attribute. If you scroll down to find MD5, you can

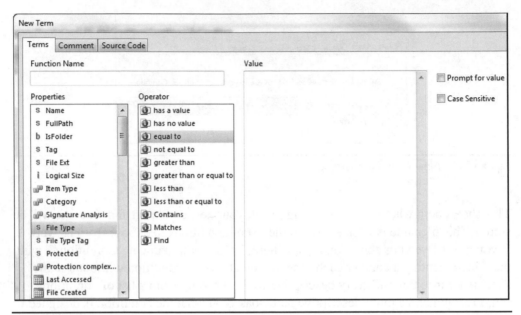

Figure 10-2 *New Term dialog*

see the hash property icon. Knowing what data type the attribute will be helps you determine the value that you should search on. Obviously, if this is an integer data type, you shouldn't be putting alphabetic values in the Value box. For our condition, let's say we're just looking for basic Excel and Word documents—not template files or anything else. We're going to look at file extension for simplicity. You could also put in a term that looks at signature analysis, of course.

The operators and values you are given to work with are context sensitive and change depending on what you clicked in the Properties list. You can see in Figure 10-2 that I have the File Type property selected, and that you can use the values in the Operator list to narrow your search criteria. You then add a value in the Value text box. Operators that allow you to enter values in the Value box also allow GREP expressions to be entered here. Remember, also, to test those expressions in the Keyword Tester to verify that they function as planned before making them part of a condition.

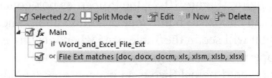

Figure 10-3 *Two identical terms*

Another point to be careful of is when you are entering values into the Value box—make sure you don't have any trailing characters such as a space or tab at the end of what you type or copy/paste into this box. Some of the comparison operators, such as Matches, will do a literal string comparison based on what you entered, so if you have trailing spaces or tabs, those will become part of the search term, and may return results that don't actually capture what you were trying to achieve.

TIP

Make it a point to ensure there is nothing after the entry that might throw off your results—even if you aren't using that type of comparison operator, it is a good habit to have.

Finally, choose if you want to either have the criteria prompt you for a value each time it is run (which makes it more flexible for reuse) and if you want the search criteria to consider the capitalization of letters when it processes evidence. Figure 10-4 shows the values for this first term of our condition.

In the example in Figure 10-4, I chose File Ext in the Properties box, and Matches in the Operator box. In the Value box, I listed the extensions I am interested in matching. I don't want this search to be case sensitive, since the extensions may be in a combination of uppercase and lowercase. I am limiting this condition to look at just Word and Excel files, so I'm not having it prompt for a value. If I wanted to make just a generic condition to search on any file extension, then I'd have checked

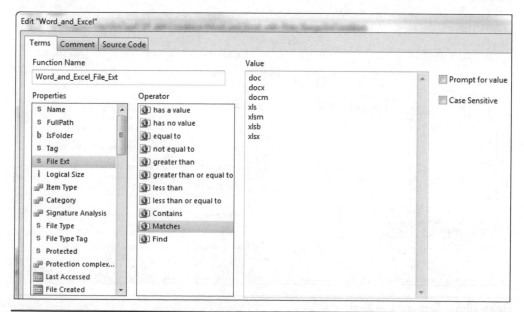

Figure 10-4 *Word and Excel file extensions*

that so the examiner could provide their own values. Clicking OK gets you back into the New Condition dialog. Under the Main clause there now should be an If statement with the term name showing there, like the first term in the example in Figure 10-3.

You need to create your date range term now, so again, click the New button in the New Condition dialog (Figure 10-1) to get you into the New Term dialog. Give this the name of "Last_Accessed_Date_Range" and make your choices match Figure 10-5.

> ### *NOTE*
>
> *I use a convention of underscores in my condition names to make it more readable. Spaces are not allowed in these names by EnCase, so this is an alternative.*

Note that I'm not specifying an initial value, but rather prompting the examiner for a date range. The Examples box shows the values you could put in there if you chose. Click OK to save this term. Now you are back at the New Condition dialog, with your two terms showing.

I find it helpful when building a new condition to just read out loud what actions this will perform. It makes it easier to catch logic errors. In this case, based on our condition as shown in Figure 10-6, I would be saying, "If it matches the file extension

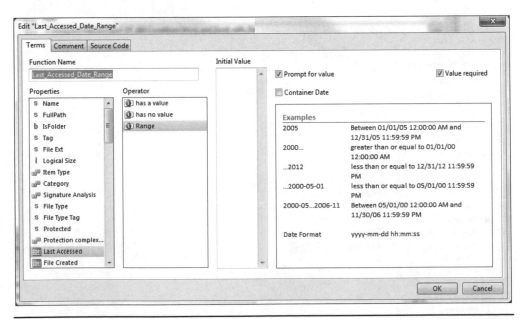

Figure 10-5   *Date range term*

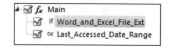

Figure 10-6   *Condition terms*

for Word or Excel, or it matches my last date range…" Wait a minute, we want it to match both conditions, don't we? Of course we do, or we would return a set of files that are *either* Word/Excel files, *or* they have a last accessed date within our date range. How do we fix this? We change the logic. To do this, right-click on the Main clause and choose Change Logic from the context menu (Figure 10-7).

You are returned to the New Condition dialog, and now the logic operator reads And instead of Or. Your criteria will match Word and Excel file extensions within the date range specified by the examiner. Notice the Not logic operator on the same menu where you changed the logic (Figure 10-7). This will allow you to exclude items based on your term instead of including them. This is a very useful feature when you know what you don't want rather than what you do want.

One more thing—let's reverse the order of these two terms by dragging the bottom one up. You can see the results in Figure 10-8.

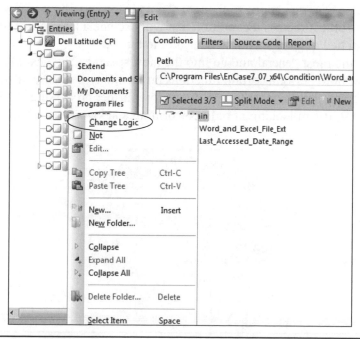

Figure 10-7   *Changing the logic*

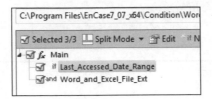

Figure 10-8 *Logic and order correct*

Why did I change the order? It is more productive to first reduce the result set to only those files that fall within the date range specified and then whittle it down further by file extension than it is to do this in reverse order. Click OK to save our condition.

> **TIP**
>
> *The order in which a condition's statements are evaluated can make a huge difference in performance.*

Condition Logic

Conditions are evaluated from top to bottom. This can be very important to the performance of your condition, so thought should be given to how you want your condition to work. If there is a condition that will exclude a large percentage of the evidence searched quickly, it should be nearer to the top.

Start with the most general and go into the most specific if you can. For example, if you only want to perform certain functions on the file types that you are interested in, make sure you first find that type of file before further processing. As illustrated by Figure 10-9, if I'm looking at only performing a keyword search inside Word

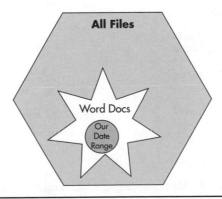

Figure 10-9 *From general to specific*

documents within a specific date range, it will be much faster to first eliminate all non-Word documents, and then eliminate any that are not within my date range and only perform a keyword search on the remaining much smaller number of files. You want to do the most time-consuming processes on the smallest subset of results you possibly can.

Nesting Terms

Conditions can be as complex as your ability to create them. You can group terms together so they do not affect the terms around them by creating folders and dragging terms into them. In this manner, folders act like parentheses in a math equation—they group items together so they are treated as one unit in terms of logic and order of operation. This is also how you can control the logic between groups of terms. You can create a folder by right-clicking in the New Condition window and choosing New Folder. Give the folder a name and then start either creating terms inside it directly or create them in the Main clause and drag them into your folders.

You can also use the Not operator to affect entire folders of terms in this manner. This will act to exclude any terms you have defined in that folder—so if there is a group of characteristics you want to exclude, place the definitions in a folder and then change the logic to Not to apply to all of the contents. This can be quite useful if you have a number of applications that you know you won't want to collect.

Running the Condition

Now that you have saved your new condition, run it against your current view to see how it works. Click the Condition button and choose your condition from the menu. Alternatively, you can choose Run from the same menu and browse to the condition.

You can see in Figure 10-10 that EnCase pops up the Edit Conditions dialog asking the examiner to enter the date range for the Last Accessed value you specified. If you click on the question mark to the right of the field, it will pop up a help section that lets you know how the values should look.

The image we are using for this case dates back to 2004, so if you choose a date range that includes between August 2004 and December 2005, you'll get a good number of results. Enter the format like the fifth value in the list in Figure 10-10, "2000-05…2006-11", (so our range would be "2004-08…2005-12") and click OK. You'll be returned to the Evidence Browser and should see the progress bar at the bottom right for your condition (Figure 10-11).

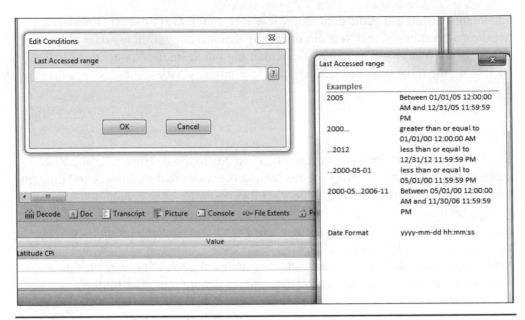

Figure 10-10   *Edit Conditions dialog*

The results are displayed in the Table pane by default. I get 24 results based on that filter and the date range selected. The name of the condition will appear across the top bar of the Table pane, although EnCase calls it a filter. This further illustrates that conditions and filters are the same—just the interface in which you work with them is different.

Take a look at some of the results—did you notice Overview.doc in your results? I have it circled in the Results, and the Transcript tab of the file showing in Figure 10-12. It is relevant to the case, so it should be bookmarked. I created a Selected Files bookmark for the Overview.doc and the readme.doc files, as they both are part of the Brutus remote password cracking tool installation.

Figure 10-11   *Condition progress bar*

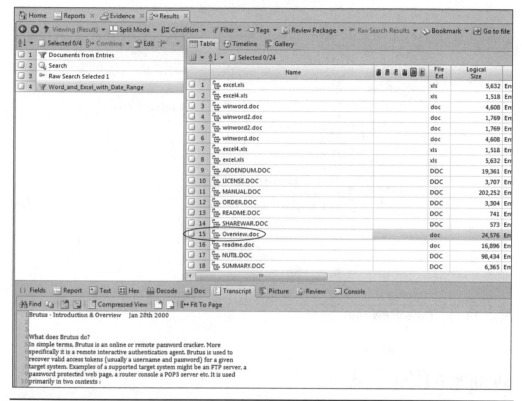

Figure 10-12 *Results of condition*

Filters

EnCase provides a selection of default filters for narrowing the view of your evidence (EnCase does not provide default conditions, as indicated previously). Like conditions, filters do not remove anything from your evidence, they simply change what artifacts are displayed based on your specified criteria. Since filters are created and edited in the EnScript programming language, you have the ability to perform much more complex logic. While the conditions graphic interface will accommodate many needs, sometimes a full programming language that supports complex logic and looping constructs is the only way to accomplish the task.

To bring up the list of default included filters, in the Evidence Browser, click the Filter button on the button bar. This is a drop-down menu from which you can see the list of filters at your disposal.

The list of default filters provided by EnCase are shown in Figure 10-13, along with any filters you have run recently.

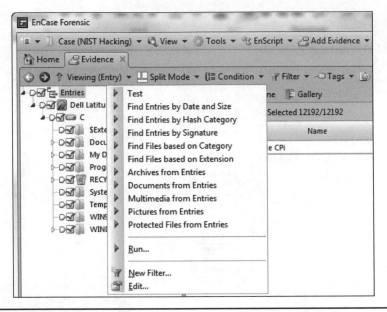

Figure 10-13   *Default filter list*

 ## Running a Filter

To run a filter, choose it from the menu if it is in your list. If not, choose Run from the Filter button's drop-down menu. You are presented with a dialog to browse to the location of the filter you'd like to run. You will also be presented with the dialog that asks for the scope you want to run against (Figure 10-14).

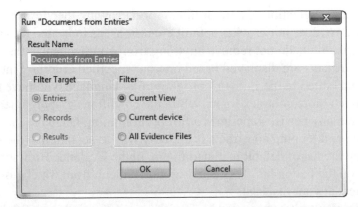

Figure 10-14   *Running a filter*

The filter target is predefined—and depends on where in the interface you are when you choose to run it and the type of filter you are running. In our case, we were in the Entries view of the Evidence Browser and thus it will automatically be run against Entries—this is grayed out and cannot be changed. If you wanted to run against records or results, you would need to be viewing them when you run the filter. You can change your scope to run the filter against the following:

▶ **Current View**   To run against the evidence in the current Tree/Table pane that is showing when you launched the filter. Results are displayed in the Table pane of the tab you were on. This is the only option that does not display in the Results tab.

▶ **Current Device**   To run against the device you have currently selected. This displays in the Results tab rather than the tab you launched the filter from.

▶ **All Evidence Files**   Filters through all the evidence you have added to the case and displays in the Results tab.

Some of the filters will bring up further dialogs to allow you to specify parameters to use. When run in Current View, EnCase will drop you directly into a view with the results in the Table view still within the Evidence tab, as shown in Figure 10-15. The example is the result of running the Documents From Entries filter—and should look familiar, since it is the same interface you were dropped into from running your custom condition earlier. The Filter: Documents From Entries button shows you both

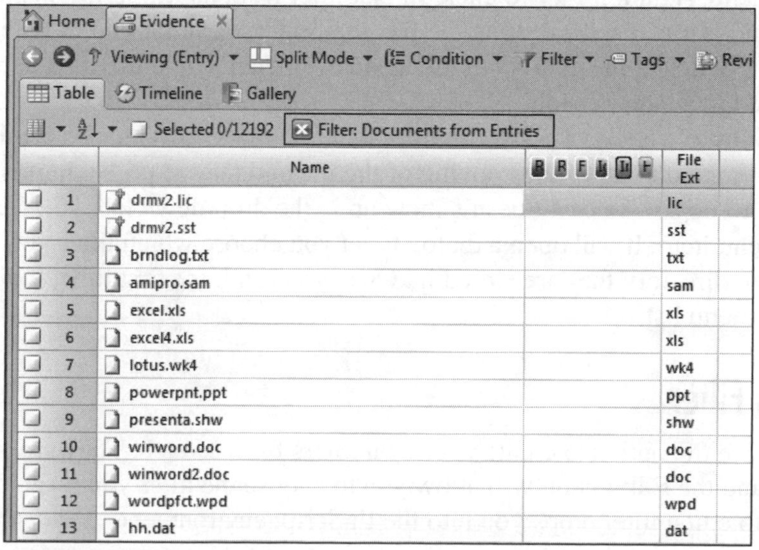

Figure 10-15   *Running a filter in Current View*

the name of the filter you have applied and how to turn that filter off. By clicking that button, EnCase will remove the filter and drop you back into the Evidence tab.

If you want to turn the filter back on, the Table pane in the Evidence tab now shows a button with that filter's name on it to the right of the Selected box. That button will change as you apply different filters and will always show the last filter you ran as the option to reapply.

Note the Test filter at the top of my Filter menu list in Figure 10-13. This is because I added this as a filter, which brings us to our next point—you can create your own filters or modify the existing ones. They can be found in C:\<*install directory*>\Filter if you want to edit the default filters. They are stored in two folders based on the type of data they are meant to be run against. The filters in entries will be those displayed when you are in the Entries view in EnCase. I recommend that you work on a copy, of course, and not change a default filter.

Another thing to note is that the contents of the Filter drop-down are not built dynamically from the filters in the default directory. I created the Test filter you see in the menu, but then I went into the directory where it was and manually deleted it in Windows Explorer. Even after exiting EnCase, the filter still showed in the menu until I actually tried to run it—then EnCase deleted it out of the menu. There was no error message indicating it could not find the file. So if you try to run a filter that is in the list and get no actual change at all, verify it still exists in the directory where it should be as your first troubleshooting step. Incidentally, that filter name will also now be included as a menu item in the EnScript menu, and when EnCase deleted the Test filter from the Filter drop-down after I deleted it, it did not remove it from the EnScript menu. Again, if I try to click on that filter from the EnScript menu, nothing happens—no errors display despite the fact that EnCase cannot find the file. In this case, it did not delete the filter from the menu even then. Hopefully this behavior will be addressed in a later version.

If you want to work on a copy of a filter that you made in Windows Explorer (you are prompted to allow the copying of the file and may require administrator credentials to do so), since it doesn't show up in the drop-down list, you can choose the Run menu item. It will open a dialog to let you choose which filter you want to run from the directory they are stored in. Once you run it the first time, it will show up in your menu list.

Editing a Filter

You also have the option to create your own filters from scratch. They are written in EnScript, and the Edit option will allow you to choose the filter you want to modify. Choosing to edit a filter drops you into the EnScript environment.

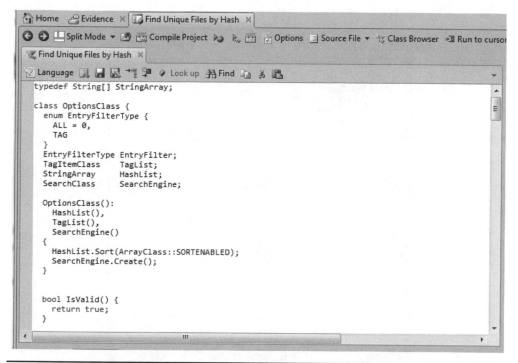

Figure 10-16 *Editing a filter*

As you can see in Figure 10-16, this method is for someone who is comfortable in the EnScript programming language. The enum value on the third line lets you know what type of filter this is. The EntryFilterType indicates this will be run against items that are entries as opposed to records or results.

Adding a New Filter

Adding a new filter also drops you into the same EnScript programming environment, but with the minimal code to get you started writing a filter (Figure 10-17).

Again, remember we are in the Entries view, so the type of filter EnCase brings up to create is an Entry type (as evidenced by the fact that the class of the parameter to Main is an EntryClass type). If you had been in the Records view, the type would have been a RecordClass instead. We cover the EnScript language in Chapter 15, and that should go a long way toward getting you comfortable with both the EnScript environment and the language.

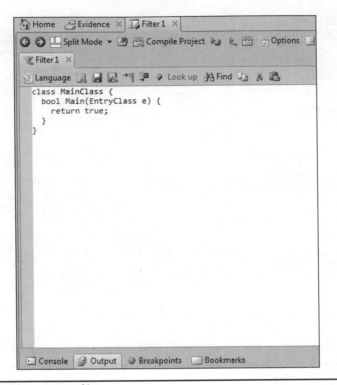

Figure 10-17 *Adding a new filter*

Sharing a Filter

You have the option of sharing filters among examiners. You do this in EnCase by choosing Edit from the Filter drop-down menu on the button bar. It will display a dialog to let you browse to where your filter is located on your computer. Right-clicking on any of the filters in the list will allow you to choose Copy from the context menu. This is not something provided by EnCase—this is normal Windows behavior. You could also just copy and paste the filter file from where it is stored to where you want to place it in Windows Explorer. When you do this in EnCase, and you've selected Copy, you then navigate in the same dialog to where you want the new file placed, right-click and choose Paste. However, you're still left in the Edit Filter's Open File dialog. What do you do now? It turns out that it doesn't really matter what you do now in this dialog. If you choose Cancel, the filter has already been copy/pasted to the location you chose, so this doesn't actually cancel what you've done. If you choose OK, you are dropped into the code for editing the filter you chose.

Summary

We have covered conditions and filters, and have even added some new bookmarks to our case. I am sure that you can see the potential use for these—whether you build your own custom conditions and filters or use those shared by others. If you haven't already visited the site, Guidance Software's App Central is a good place to look for EnScripts, but also people may be sharing conditions and filters on the site that will be of use to you. There are also resources available on the Customer Portal.

Hash Analysis and Timelines

We briefly discussed the use of hashes when we talked about performing evidence processing. Now we are going to get into more detail on how to use hashes to include or exclude files in your case. There are publicly available hash libraries you can use, and your organization may also maintain certain standard image files that you can generate hash libraries from. We will cover the most common use cases for how examiners can use hash libraries and hash sets to increase productivity in their casework.

Working with Hash Sets and Libraries

The Evidence Processor has a hash analysis module that generates MD5 and/or SHA-1 hashes depending on your choices. Another feature of EnCase is the ability to build your own hash library—these are good for either including or excluding files in your case as noteworthy. There are three very common scenarios for using hash sets that I want to cover here. They are:

▶ Creating a new hash set from hashes of files in a case.

▶ Importing one of the publicly available hash libraries—such as the one provided by the National Software Reference Library (NSRL). EnCase distributes the NSRL with the email notification of updates to your software. It is a large file (over 4GB), but can be a useful place to start when you want to begin using hash libraries. It should be noted that the version that Guidance Software distributes is RDS 2.32 March 2011 which they have converted into EnCase Version 7 format. You can always check the User Guide to see what version is being distributed with the software.

▶ Importing legacy hash values into your case.

You may wonder what the difference is between a hash and a hash library set. A hash library is contained in a folder and stored in a database-like structure by EnCase. There is a specific format for EnCase to be able to use these—an example is the NSRL library that has been converted to EnCase-compatible format. You can run queries against these libraries, much like you would a database. Hash libraries contain one or more hash sets.

Hash sets are collections of hash values. You will likely want to keep them in groups to differentiate them, since EnCase allows you to include/exclude them from your case. An example of a hash set would be a group of malware hashes that you have collected from prior cases and would use to identify bad files in a new case.

Creating a New Hash Library

EnCase provides an interface for creating your own hash library. To begin, choose Manage Hash Library from the Tools menu. Recall that one of the properties of a hash library is that it is contained in a folder. This means you either need to create a new folder for it, or if you are going to use an existing folder, it must be empty.

CAUTION

EnCase will delete the contents of your existing folder when you create a new hash library. Be careful if you are using an existing folder that it does not contain data that you want preserved.

To create your new hash library, choose New Hash Library from the toolbar. You will be presented with a dialog that allows you to browse to where you want the hash library stored. I made a directory called Hash Libraries, and a subdirectory under that called Widgets Hash Libraries. This way I can keep the company-specific libraries separate from something like the NSRL or other libraries I received from other examiners. Once you finish this process, you will see a pop-up indicating that the library was created successfully. You are dropped back into the same Manage Hash Library interface, but there are now many more buttons available, and the Hash Library Path shows the location you selected for the new library (Figure 11-1).

If you go to the folder that you created for your new hash library, you can see that EnCase has populated the folder with the hash database files, although they are mostly quite small because you have an empty database at this point. While you created the container for the hash library, you haven't populated it with hash sets.

Now you have an empty library created—so you need to create a hash set inside of it before you can add hash values to it. To do this, choose New Hash Set from the button bar. The Create Hash Set dialog is displayed.

NOTE

There does not seem to be a way to delete hash sets once they are created. Edit will allow you to modify them, but actually removing them seems to be something that EnCase does not allow.

Create a hash set as shown in Figure 11-2. You can add known good files to this over time. Since we are compiling a group of executables that we are going to associate with this hacking case—which would likely be useful in future hacking cases—also create another empty hash set called "Hacking Tools".

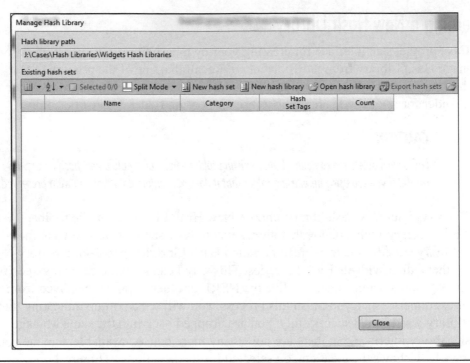

Figure 11-1 *Manage Hash Library with Hash Library Path populated*

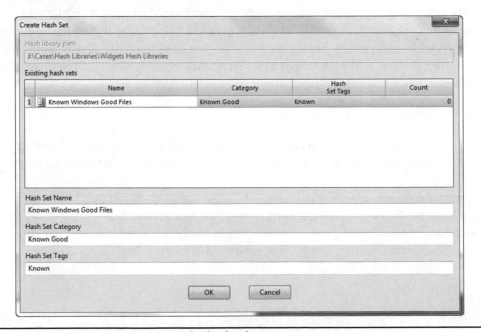

Figure 11-2 *Known Windows Good Files hash set*

Adding Case Results to Your Hash Library

You can add results from your case to your hash library once you have created it. We have several examples of hacking tools to add to our hash set. In the Evidence Browser, navigate to \My Documents\EXPLOITATION\NT\Pwdump directory. In the Table pane, select the file(s) you want to add, right-click, and choose Add To Hash Library from the Entries option (Figure 11-3).

You could also have selected Add To Hash Library from the Entries button on the Evidence tab's button bar. Either method will bring up the Add To Hash Library dialog where you can choose which library to add the selected files to (Figure 11-4). Note, both hash sets currently are empty, with their counts showing as having zero entries.

The default list will be from your Primary hash library. You can also click on Hash Library Type and access what you have defined as your secondary hash library, or choose Other and browse to additional libraries you may have to choose from.

By default, EnCase adds the Name, Logical Size, and the two hash values fields to the library. You can optionally select the other fields in the list. If you want them all, click the first, scroll down to the bottom, and use SHIFT-click to select them all.

Another useful option to avoid putting entries into your hash library that don't actually have hash values is to check the "Skip items with no MD5 or SHA1" check box at the bottom left.

For our purposes, blue check the Hacking Tools hash set, take the default fields, and click OK.

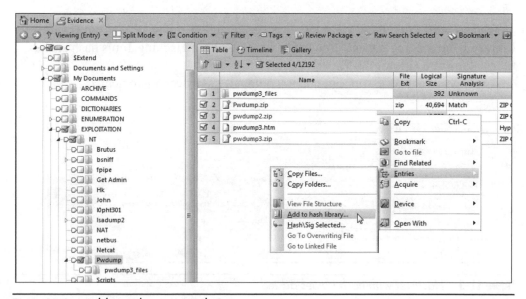

Figure 11-3 *Adding Files to a Hash Set*

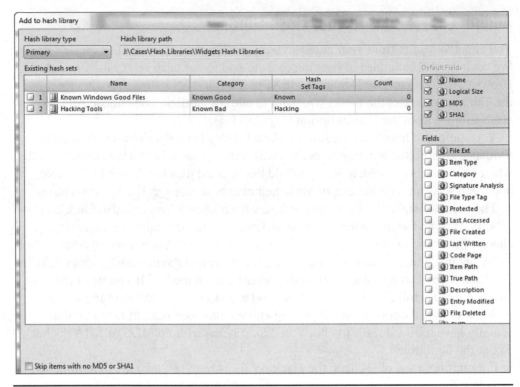

Figure 11-4 *Add To Hash Library dialog*

We can verify that these values were added by again choosing Manage Hash Library from the Tools menu. You can now see that our Hacking Tools hash set has four values in it (Figure 11-5).

If this was not successful, our count would not have been incremented.

		Name	Category	Hash Set Tags	Count
☐	1	Known Windows Good Files	Known Good	Known	0
☐	2	Hacking Tools	Known Bad	Hacking	4

Figure 11-5 *Hash set with hash values added*

Importing the NSRL Hash Library

EnCase provides a link to download the NSRL hash library that has been converted to EnCase 7 format. As I mentioned before, this is a very large file, but it can be quite useful. The NSRL when compressed is over 4GB and once decompressed expands to over 18GB. To use this library, you need to first decompress it under the directory where you store your hash libraries. I put it under my Hash Libraries folder, but not under Widgets Hash Libraries, since those are specific to my organization's cases. You will need to decompress the file you have downloaded from the Guidance Software link (which should be in the email they sent you with your license and download links), using 7-Zip or some other compression utility. The NSRL libraries decompress to NSRL<*version*> so you know which version you are working with and can keep subsequent versions separate should you wish to. If you decompressed it elsewhere, you can just move the directory tree to where you need it.

In Figure 11-6, you can see the files for the hash library from the NSRL directory once they have been downloaded and decompressed. To start using them, you will need to let EnCase know about them using the Manage Hash Library option from the Tools menu. This opens the Hash Library Manager. Next, you need to open the NSRL library by clicking the Open Hash Library button on the button bar.

When you have opened the library, you will see EnCase has populated a list of the hash sets that are contained within it (Figure 11-7).

Name	Date modified	Type
CFGS.bin	4/22/2013 7:11 AM	BIN File
HashRoot.bin	4/22/2013 7:11 AM	BIN File
HIDT.bin	4/20/2013 6:27 PM	BIN File
HILS.bin	4/22/2013 7:11 AM	BIN File
HIMT.bin	4/20/2013 6:27 PM	BIN File
HITL.bin	4/20/2013 6:27 PM	BIN File
HSDT.bin	4/20/2013 6:27 PM	BIN File
HSHD.bin	4/22/2013 7:11 AM	BIN File
HSHT.head.bin	4/20/2013 6:27 PM	BIN File
HSHT.tail.bin	4/20/2013 6:27 PM	BIN File
HSTL.bin	4/20/2013 6:27 PM	BIN File
HSTR.bin	4/20/2013 6:27 PM	BIN File
MPFS.head.bin	4/20/2013 6:27 PM	BIN File
MPFS.tail.bin	4/20/2013 6:27 PM	BIN File
SPFS.head.bin	4/20/2013 6:27 PM	BIN File
SPFS.tail.bin	4/20/2013 6:27 PM	BIN File

Figure 11-6 *NSRL hash library files*

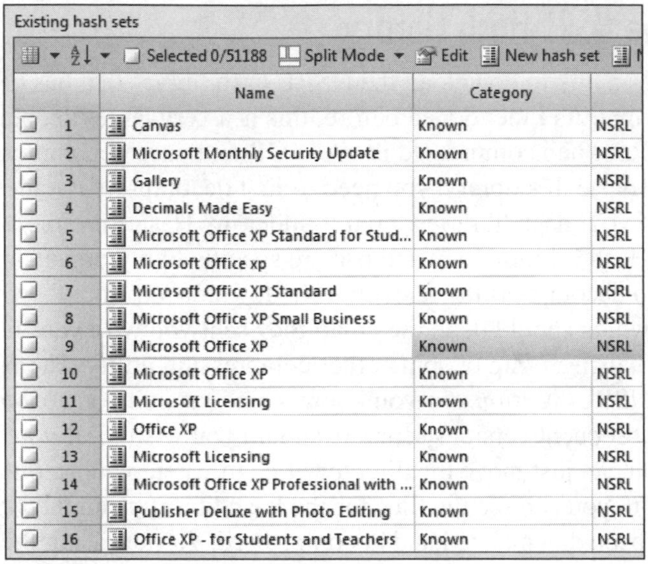

Existing hash sets

Selected 0/51188 | Split Mode | Edit | New hash set

	Name	Category	
1	Canvas	Known	NSRL
2	Microsoft Monthly Security Update	Known	NSRL
3	Gallery	Known	NSRL
4	Decimals Made Easy	Known	NSRL
5	Microsoft Office XP Standard for Stud...	Known	NSRL
6	Microsoft Office xp	Known	NSRL
7	Microsoft Office XP Standard	Known	NSRL
8	Microsoft Office XP Small Business	Known	NSRL
9	Microsoft Office XP	Known	NSRL
10	Microsoft Office XP	Known	NSRL
11	Microsoft Licensing	Known	NSRL
12	Office XP	Known	NSRL
13	Microsoft Licensing	Known	NSRL
14	Microsoft Office XP Professional with ...	Known	NSRL
15	Publisher Deluxe with Photo Editing	Known	NSRL
16	Office XP - for Students and Teachers	Known	NSRL

Figure 11-7 *NSRL hash library opened*

You can also set this to your secondary hash library path for EnCase to use, which will allow easy access when adding hashes in the Evidence Browser as discussed earlier. You do this from the Home tab, by clicking on the Hash Libraries link in the Case section.

While I didn't call it out specifically, this is much the same procedure you would use if you have a hash library that you've built from a golden image that contains the hashes of all known files in your organization's standard operating system build. (A golden image is an IT term for the standard system image the organization is currently deploying on a specific class of hardware, and it will have the standard applications as part of the build. There are typically different golden images depending on the function of the hardware—that is, the golden image for laptops wouldn't be the same as the golden image for servers.) You can use these to exclude files from analysis as well.

Importing Legacy Hash Results into Your Hash Library

If you have hash sets from versions of EnCase prior to version 7, you can import them. From within the Manage Hash Library window, choose Import from the button bar. Then choose EnCase Legacy Hash Sets from the drop-down. You are provided with a dialog that will let you browse to where those hash sets are stored on the computer. Clicking Finish will prompt EnCase to convert them to the new version's format.

TIP

If you use both versions of EnCase in your organization, you may want to work on a copy of the hash set to preserve the old version for use in earlier versions of the software — a good practice anyway in case something goes wrong.

Running Queries Against Your Hash Libraries

EnCase provides an interface for you to run queries against your hash library. There may be occasions where you want to determine if a particular hash value exists in it, particularly if you maintain a hash library across all of your organization's cases. This is very useful to combine with results obtained from any information-sharing groups you belong to that share indicators of compromise between members.

You must first open the hash library by selecting Manage Hash Library from the Tools menu and then choosing Open Hash Library. You can then query the database using the Query button from the button bar.

For example, say we wanted to look for the MD5 hash value from one of the Pwdump executables from our case, and we wanted to query the NSRL library. First, you need to copy the hash value of the file. In the Evidence Browser, navigate to the C:\My Documents\EXPLOITATION\NT\Pwdump directory, and click on the hyperlink for Pwdump.zip. This brings up pwdump.exe in the table pane, and you can scroll over to the MD5 column. Right-click inside that column and choose Copy.

Next, bring up the Manage Hash Library interface again from the Tools menu. If you don't already have the NSRL library open, choose Open Hash Library and browse to it. Once open, click the Query button on the button bar. This opens the Hash Library Query dialog.

In Figure 11-8, I have pasted the hash value from our file into the Hash Value text box and clicked the Query button. The matches are populated, and you can look at each entry. You also have the choice to show either the metadata about the record or the hash sets they are from. You can see how this could be quite useful in researching files you encounter in the course of investigating a case.

NOTE

You can only query one database at a time — whichever one is open. This means that if you have multiple hash libraries, you will need to perform this query on each one individually.

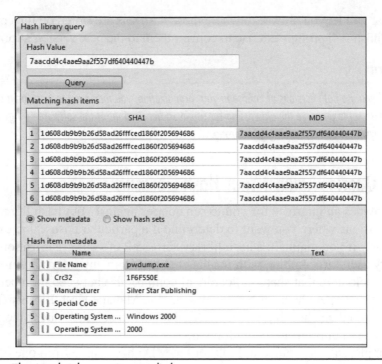

Figure 11-8   *The Hash Library Query dialog*

Using Hash Libraries for Hash Analysis

Now that you know how to work with your hash libraries and populate them with values, the other powerful thing you can do with them is to apply them to your cases to include or exclude files. You do this from the Home screen, using the Hash Libraries option under the Case section. You can see, when the Hash Libraries dialog opens, you have two options for applying libraries to your case—a primary and a secondary. While you can perform queries against any number of hash libraries, you can only perform hash analyses using two libraries.

To use the libraries in a hash analysis, you must make certain they are blue checked as shown in Figure 11-9. You also have the option of only using one of your libraries, depending on what you have checked. Once you have selected your libraries, clicking OK applies them to your case.

To see how this affects our evidence, look again at the Pwdump executable in the table pane of the Evidence Browser. Once you have clicked on that hyperlink to get to the executable as we did before, select the Pwdump.exe item in the Table pane, and then click the Hash Sets tab in the View pane.

You can see in Figure 11-10 that we have hits on this file now for a number of hash sets. Notice that the only hits we have are from the NSRL library—didn't we

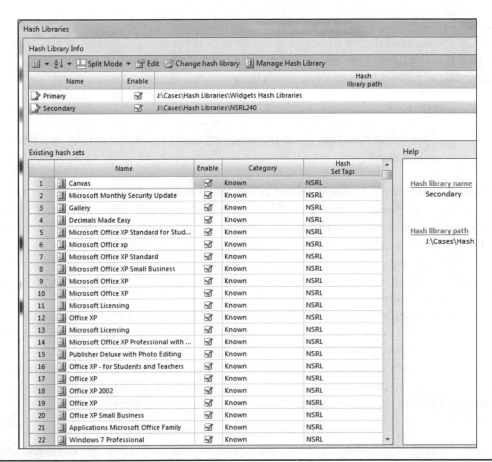

Figure 11-9   *Hash Libraries dialog*

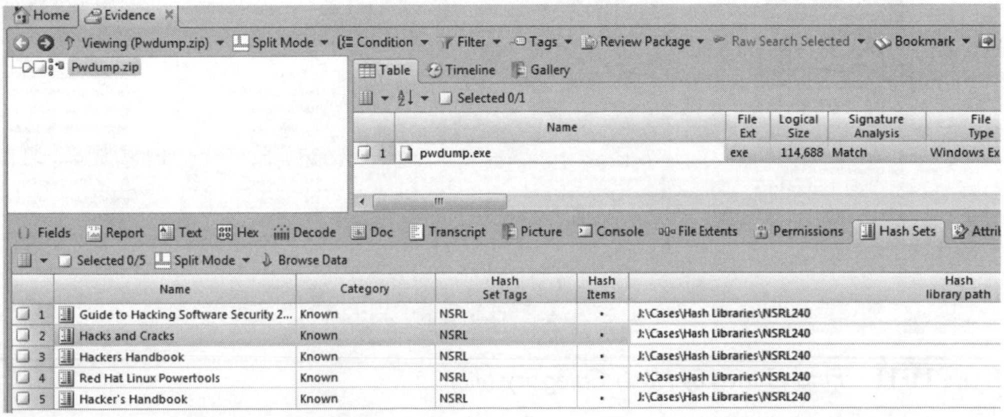

Figure 11-10   *Pwdump hash analysis*

add this to our Hacking Tools library? If you recall from before, we blue checked the files at the level of the zip files, not at the level of the decompressed contents. This means that the hashes for the individual files contained within the archive are not automatically included when you blue check.

TIP

If you have compound files like an archive, you will need to go into them and blue check their contents as well.

Can you use the Set Include (home plate) function instead? Unfortunately, if you home plate the Pwdump top-level folder in the Tree pane and then try to either right-click or click the Entries button on the button bar, you'll notice that the Add To Hash Library option is grayed out. The only option is to do it by hand.

So how can you use this to include or exclude categories of files in your case? You do that using a filter. In the Evidence Browser, click the Filter drop-down on the button bar and choose the Find Entries By Hash Category option (Figure 11-11).

You are presented with the usual dialog asking if you want to run it against the current view and so on. Take the default and continue. Finally, it asks which category you want to filter against. The choices are those we have defined in our library—Known or Known Good. I chose Known Good and applied the filter. The progress bar in the bottom-right corner lets me know that EnCase is working on it. Once it finishes, EnCase drops you into a Results tab with the filtered results.

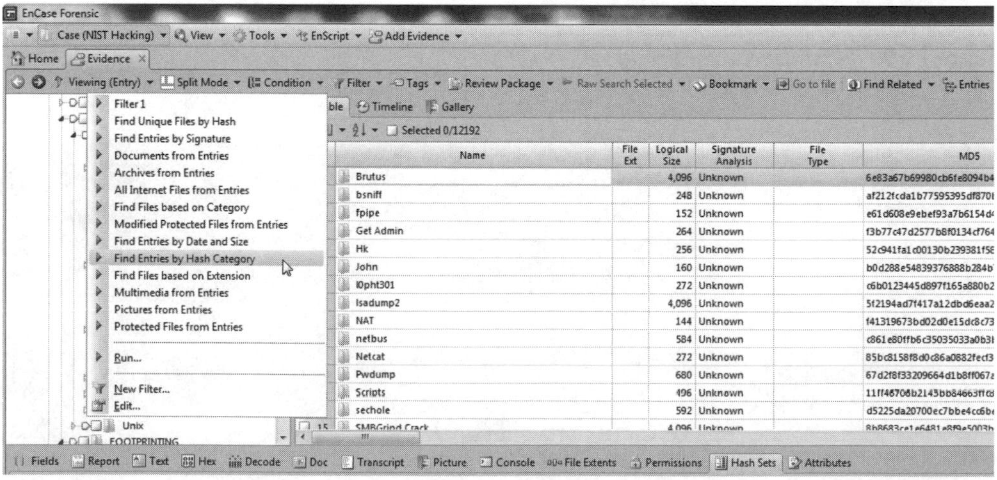

Figure 11-11   *Find Entries By Hash Category filter*

Viewing Timeline Data in EnCase

EnCase provides a way to show the evidence items on disk arranged in a timeline for analysis by the examiner. Sometimes it helps to determine what occurred by putting it in a temporal context. To view items in the timeline, you need to be in the Evidence Browser, and you need to place a Set Include (home plate) on the items you want included in the timeline view. So, for example, if you wanted to see when all those hacking tools were installed in the C:\My Documents folder in the evidence file, you would place the Set Include there. You can now click on the Timeline tab in the Table pane to show your timeline. As you can see, EnCase arranges each year into a grid with the months across the top and the days of the month down the side. Files are represented as squares inside each cell to indicate where in time they belong. You can change the default color of the file squares by clicking the Option button, and also raise/lower the resolution to get more detail.

By default, all of the date types are checked. We are interested in this example in narrowing it down to just the created date, so click on the Date Type drop-down in the button bar of the Timeline tab and uncheck every option except the Created check box. This will give us a smaller subset to illustrate how to use this feature. You should now have entries in the grid for just 2004—specifically, August 2004.

Figure 11-12 shows two dates that have items showing. August 18 has one box, but August 20 has ellipses, indicating that there are a number of files present.

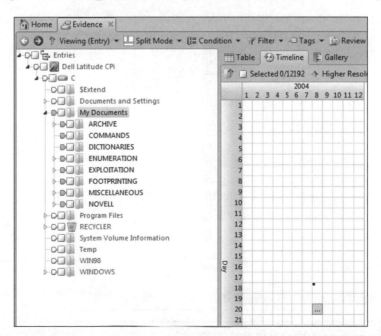

Figure 11-12   *Created dates in the Timeline tab*

Double-clicking on that cell will increase the resolution, taking you to monthly sections with the days across the top and the hour of the day across the side. Scrolling back over to August, you can see that on August 18 at 9:00 a.m., the desktop.ini file was created. However, the files on August 20 are still just shown as ellipses. Drilling in further on that cell gives you a number this time—786 files were created on Friday, August 20, beginning around 8:00 a.m. (Figure 11-13). You can continue to drill into this until you get to the level of detail you need.

While drilling into the 8:00 a.m. hour gives you more detail, it is still so much that it is tedious to click on each square to get details. Continued drilling in results in somewhat fewer choices (Figure 11-14).

Finally, we get to the highest resolution that EnCase provides. Clicking on the squares will highlight the folder that contains it in the Tree pane, and you can see the detail in the View pane.

Unfortunately, when you make a bookmark of this type of data, it does not remain in timeline format. If you want to be able to include data arranged as a timeline, you will need to use another tool outside of EnCase.

Most people use an array of tools during the course of an investigation, and this is an example of where another tool will provide more functionality. Some open source tools that are popular include Plaso and 4n6time. The Forensics Wiki is a good place to go and see what tools are available as well.

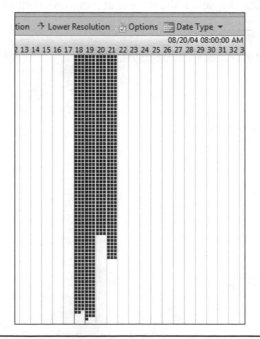

Figure 11-13 *Detail by second at 8:00 a.m.*

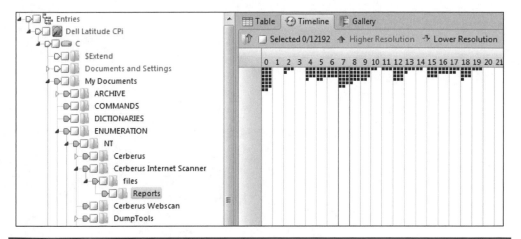

Figure 11-14   *Splitting the detail into seconds and smaller*

Summary

Hash sets and libraries can be extremely useful in both removing known good files and flagging known bad ones. As such, it makes sense for the examiner to be familiar with how to import these into their cases to increase efficiency. Why spend time looking at a large number of files when you can eliminate them with high confidence using a hash library?

Likewise, looking at the timeline data can be very useful in event reconstruction and in giving the examiner clues as to what actions took place around a date/time in question to see how events unfolded. While the timeline function in EnCase doesn't provide as many features as some of the open source options, it can provide valuable clues as to where to look in the evidence for further information. Being able to narrow the window that is in scope for an investigation is very valuable for when you need to go to other groups and get data from outside sources. An example is if you want someone to pull network firewall logs for you—if you can give them a specific date range, your work will be much reduced, as will the volume of data that comes back from your request.

Our next chapter will get into reporting, including how to build or customize your reports for your organization.

The examination report is the work product that is most often viewed by the initiator of the case—be they a client, an internal customer, or a court of law. As such, this document must represent your organization's commitment to professionalism and be presented in a way that will communicate your findings most effectively. EnCase provides an interface for associating your findings into organized sections, and will allow you to make changes and customizations to suit your needs. You will learn how to work within the reporting interface to make these customizations so that your data will be presented in a manner that best suits the needs of your organization.

Generating Your Report

Once the questions have been answered and the investigation is completed, you will want to generate a report. You can view your report at any point in your case, of course, and do not have to wait until the end. Reports can be accessed from the Home screen in the Report section by clicking on the Reports hyperlink, or you can choose Reports from the View menu. Either way, the default report opens in the Reports tab (Figure 12-1). You can see that it has a title page with the EnCase logo, title text, and the Case Information section on the first page. Following that are the default sections that EnCase provides. Our report has two tabs— Examination Report and Pictures. Note that they have two different layouts—the examination report is in portrait layout for printing, while the Pictures tab has a landscape layout.

Now, if this format looks fine to you and is everything you have ever wanted in a report, feel free to use it as-is and go on from there. However, most people will want to make some customizations to the default report template. For example, they frequently want to display their own organization's logo on the title page. If you try to click on the report in this view to make a change, however, you are unable to make modifications. The Reports tab is an interface for viewing the report as it currently stands. The way you can get in and make changes is to click on the Go To Template button in the top left corner of the Examination Report tab. This will allow you to customize the report's structure and content.

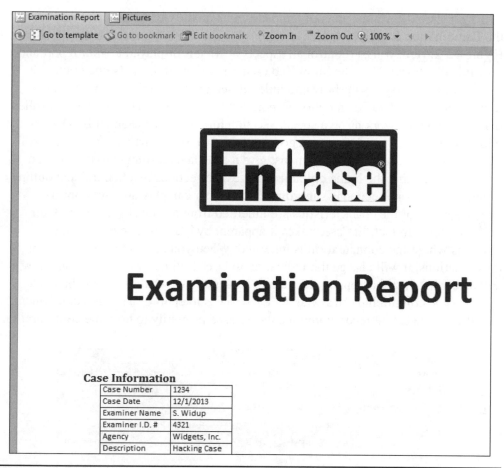

Figure 12-1 *EnCase default report*

Customizing Existing Report Templates

It makes sense to spend some time developing a standard report template for your organization so that there is consistency from case to case and examiner to examiner. Since this is usually the only work product that your customer will see, it is critical that it look professional and have commonality in both substance and style between engagements. Keeping things organized in a standard manner makes generating a report so much easier, as you'll see in a moment.

TIP

You can make the report template part of the case templates as well, so that the folder structure you put in your case template supports the needs of your report template.

To get started customizing your template, click on the Go To Template button on the Examination Report toolbar. This opens the Report Templates tab as shown in Figure 12-2. Here you can control all aspects of what is displayed in your report and how it is displayed. Note the Show Tab column to the left of the Name column. Checking these boxes will show and hide the section tabs in the report viewer—remember that we had Examination Report and Pictures tabs? This is what controlled that. So if you are working on a specific section for quite a while and it is smack in the middle of the report, each time you go back to the viewer, you aren't forced to scroll back down to that section—you can just give it a tab and go straight to that section.

You can see that the Name column arranges the sections in a hierarchical outline order. Whether one section is subordinate to another can play an important part because many of the characteristics are inherited from top-level sections to their child sections. In fact, EnCase makes it apparent by indicating in each of the columns where the configuration is inherited. When you make changes to any of these sections, it will change the indication to User Defined, which lets you know at a glance what is still accepting the default values versus what has been changed.

The Type column indicates whether each row is a report or a section component. The difference is that report components are used primarily to hold the configuration

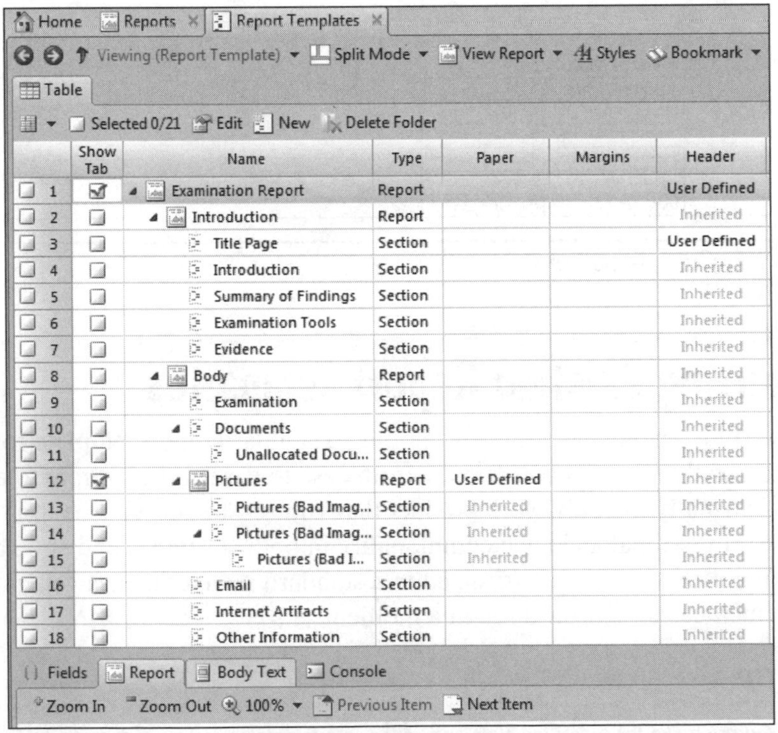

	Show Tab	Name	Type	Paper	Margins	Header
1	☑	▲ Examination Report	Report			User Defined
2	☐	▲ Introduction	Report			Inherited
3	☐	Title Page	Section			User Defined
4	☐	Introduction	Section			Inherited
5	☐	Summary of Findings	Section			Inherited
6	☐	Examination Tools	Section			Inherited
7	☐	Evidence	Section			Inherited
8	☐	▲ Body	Report			Inherited
9	☐	Examination	Section			Inherited
10	☐	▲ Documents	Section			Inherited
11	☐	Unallocated Docu...	Section			Inherited
12	☑	▲ Pictures	Report	User Defined		Inherited
13	☐	Pictures (Bad Imag...	Section	Inherited		Inherited
14	☐	▲ Pictures (Bad Imag...	Section	Inherited		Inherited
15	☐	Pictures (Bad I...	Section	Inherited		Inherited
16	☐	Email	Section			Inherited
17	☐	Internet Artifacts	Section			Inherited
18	☐	Other Information	Section			Inherited

Figure 12-2 *The Report Templates interface*

that you want inherited down to the child components. The section components will contain the formatting relevant to that particular section as it changes from the standard parent template.

The Paper column lets you specify how the section will be printed. You have control over each row in your template this way, which brings up an important point—when you are defining various options in these sections, in true EnCase fashion, the right-click is used to bring up a context menu and perform further action.

CAUTION

Where you have your cursor pointed is extremely important. Your choice will affect the section of the cell you have selected—not necessarily the cell you have your mouse positioned over.

The Margins, Header, and Footer columns all act in much the same manner and have their own specific configurations to explore. We will cover them further as we create our own report template. The Body Text column is quite important, as you do most of your formatting of the actual content of the report in this section.

However, first we will do some customization of this existing template.

Report Object Code

Before we get into the actual customization, I wanted to introduce the language that these templates are written in—Report Object Code (ROC). There is a reference in the EnCase Examiner User Guide that contains all the reserved words and goes into this more in depth, but what you need to know is that ROC is used to specify the formatting of all the components in the template. While the intent is that you be able to access all of the elements that are described and controlled using the ROC via the EnCase Report Template interface, it is a good idea to get familiar with the basics of the language to make tweaking the templates easier and faster as you gain experience. We will be looking at the Body Text tab in the View pane when we work with these sections and reports, since that is where you can see what the code is that EnCase is generating and gain some understanding of how it works.

Changing the Graphic on the Title Page

The first thing we're going to change is the logo on that title page—unless you work for Guidance Software (in which case they probably use their corporate logo and not the product logo), this is likely the most immediate change you'll want to make.

This graphic is on the title page, so you need to click on row 3 in the Report Templates tab. When you do this, note the View pane below. The Fields tab shows you the same information that you see in the Title Page row, but as a column of data.

The Report tab lets you view what your report looks like as you make changes. The Body Text tab is where you can see the ROC that is used to specify the formatting for this section.

As you can see in Figure 12-3, there is a reference to the image path on the second line. You can also control the width and height measurement.

> **NOTE**
>
> *Width and height are measured in twips, which are screen-independent units used to keep the proportion the same across all display systems. A twip is defined as 1/1440 of an inch. (Thank you, Wikipedia.)*

You can make edits to the code directly in this pane, which is quite handy. The alternative is to click on the Body Text column for that row, right-click, and choose Edit. This will open a dialog that gives you more options for editing, including the other columns in the row if you like. The Body Text tab of that dialog is identical to the one in the View pane, so if you only want to make changes to this one section of body text, using this tab is faster.

So how do you change the image? You could just edit the ROC directly from the Body Text tab, but do you know what the correct twips measurement for your logo is? We will instead delete the line with the image, and insert a new picture using the Picture button on the View pane toolbar. Alternatively, you could comment out the line by adding "//" to the beginning of the line (without the quotes).

In the Body Text tab of the View pane, select the second line (starts with the word "image") and delete it. Now click the Picture button from the toolbar on the View pane.

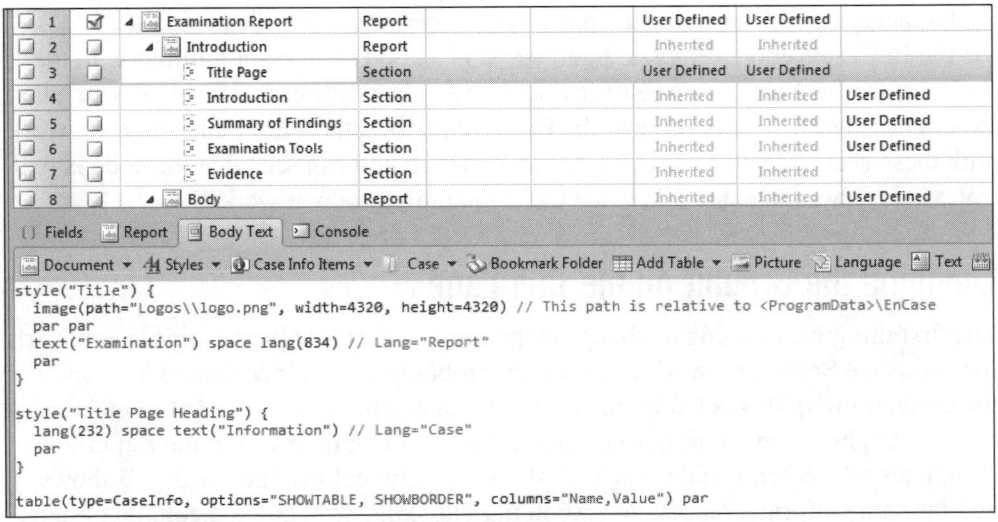

```
style("Title") {
  image(path="Logos\\logo.png", width=4320, height=4320) // This path is relative to <ProgramData>\EnCase
  par par
  text("Examination") space lang(834) // Lang="Report"
  par
}

style("Title Page Heading") {
  lang(232) space text("Information") // Lang="Case"
  par
}

table(type=CaseInfo, options="SHOWTABLE, SHOWBORDER", columns="Name,Value") par
```

Figure 12-3 *Body text for the title page*

The Picture dialog opens, which will allow you to navigate to the file you want to insert. The default value is 1 inch. You can change that to the appropriate size, but note that the interface does not enforce scaling the height and width—you need to do that. When you have the values you need, you can click OK. I chose the logo for Widgets, Inc. and kept the default of 1 inch square. EnCase handled the conversion to twips for me. This is why I recommend using this dialog unless you are quite familiar with making the conversion.

Clicking over on the Report tab for a quick look, I see that the logo is in place now, but I also want to add the company name. The third line in the Body Text code starts with par, indicating a paragraph new line. I will add the company name after that first par by pressing the ENTER key (to make some more white space just for readability.

TIP

White space in this interface doesn't translate to white space in your report, you must use ROC for that).

Click the Text button and you are presented with a text box to enter whatever you want displayed here—in this case, the company name. Looking back on the Report tab, it looks good, but I want to make sure there isn't a pagination problem going on with the rest of the page. The Report tab shows you what is in that specific section, but not how it will look when it is set up to print. In this case, I could have gone to two pages with the Case Info items that are also included in the title page. Take a quick look at the Reports tab of EnCase (not the Reports tab of the View pane, but the one next to your Home and Report Templates tab if you still have it open). This shows the pagination and it looks like I'm good to go.

Figure 12-4 shows what my body text looks like when I have completed those two changes. Your path, picture name, and other details will of course vary.

```
{} Fields   Report   Body Text   Console
 Document ▾  Styles ▾  Case Info Items ▾  Case ▾  Bookmark Folder  Add Table ▾  Picture  Language  Text
style("Title") {
image(path="C:\\Data\\Book\\Investigations with EnCase\\Artwork\\Ch12\\Widget2.jpg", width=1440, height=1440)
  par
text("Widgets, Inc.")
  par     par
  text("Examination") space lang(834) // Lang="Report"
  par
}

style("Title Page Heading") {
  lang(232) space text("Information") // Lang="Case"
  par
}

table(type=CaseInfo, options="SHOWTABLE, SHOWBORDER", columns="Name,Value") par
```

Figure 12-4 *The title page body text contents*

TIP

You may find that you get to the point where you have customized the report as best you can, but there are some things that you just can't do as effectively in EnCase, particularly if your organization uses more than one forensic tool and you need to display data from other sources. I have some good news for you—the styles that ROC uses are named the same as some of the styles in Microsoft Word, which means that you have the option of saving the report to RTF format. From the report viewer, right-click on the report and choose Save As from the context menu to bring up the dialog. Choose RTF and you can then open the resulting document in Word. Many of the styles will directly translate, making your work much easier.

While we could spend more time learning how to tweak things in the existing default report, I think we will gain more by creating a new report from scratch and making it look just how we want it to.

Creating a New Report Template

To create a new template, click the New button on the Report Templates button bar. In the New Report Template dialog (Figure 12-5), you are prompted for a report name and whether you want to create a new section or a new report. The default name is Report Template# where # increments with each template you create. I recommend a more descriptive naming convention. I changed the name in mine to "Widgets, Inc. Investigation Report."

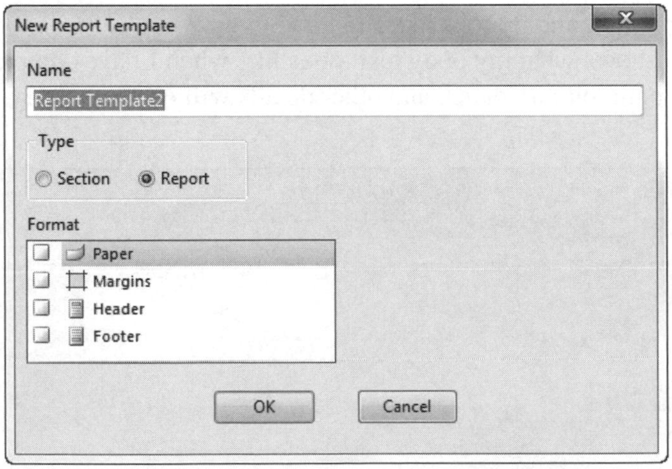

Figure 12-5 *New Report Template dialog*

We are creating a new report, so that selection is fine. Double-clicking on any of the items in the Format section will bring up your options in a dialog. Paper is where you define the printing information such as paper size and orientation. Margins are what they sound like—where you define the top, bottom, left, and right margins. The Header and Footer sections are more complex, although they use identical interfaces (Figure 12-6).

This interface should look familiar, since it is the same as the Body Text tab interface in the View pane of the Report Templates tab. For now, accept the defaults and click OK. You can now see the new template in the Table pane of the Report Templates tab. The columns for all except the Type column should be blank since you haven't done any defining of formats.

Using Styles

I mentioned earlier in the chapter that report sections inherit properties from their parent sections. You have the choice of accepting those properties or changing them with custom properties for each section—you are not required to use the inherited properties unless they work for you in that section. Let's define the header and footer so they are consistent throughout the report.

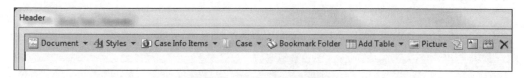

Figure 12-6   *The header format dialog*

Customizing the Header

To start with, let's put the agency name in the header and the date of the report. Double-click on the cell in your new report's row that corresponds to Header to launch the Edit dialog.

Later, when you have multiple sections under the top level, double-clicking on these columns will just expand/contract the other sections. If you want to change something in these, you will have to instead right-click and choose Edit from the context menu. In our case, this would be done with the mouse positioned over the cell shown in Figure 12-7.

Figure 12-8 should look familiar, as it is similar to the dialog you were presented when creating your new template. This dialog has more tabs and thus more options. Here, you can edit any of the properties in the Format section, as well as changing your current report to a section.

Double-click on the Header option in the Format section to bring up a dialog that allows you to make changes to the Header. You can see the empty window with your options across the top. This is where you define what you want in the Header section. EnCase uses styles for controlling how your items will be formatted. They work similarly to the way Microsoft Word styles do, and as indicated earlier, they make it easy to also pull the report into Word for further tweaking.

The Style we want to use in this case is the Header style. In the Header dialog, click on the Styles drop-down and choose Header. This inserts the wrapper ROC code for the Header style with an area where it indicates that text should be added. Select that "// text here" line, and this time choose Header Title from the Styles drop-down. This will insert the Header Title style within the Header style. The text line that you replaced when you first selected it and then chose to add another style was just a placeholder for adding text. While you can type here, it will give you an error because it expects all text to be wrapped in report object code. I like to get rid of these placeholders because I find them distracting and they are misleading—you can't just type there, and if you keep the "//", the text will be treated as a comment and ignored. They are, however, a good way to ensure your nested styles are inserted in the right place.

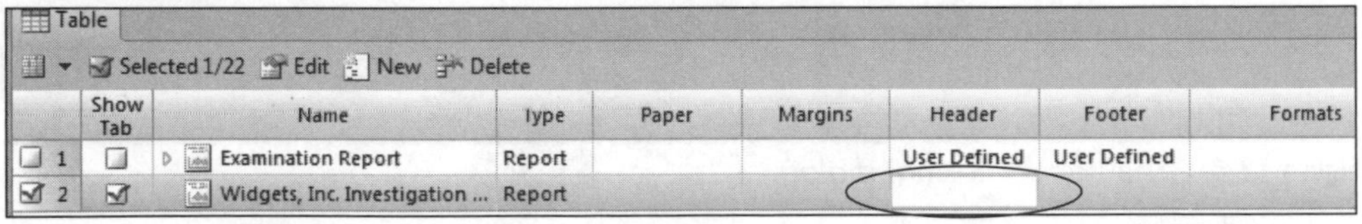

	Show Tab	Name	Type	Paper	Margins	Header	Footer	Formats
☐ 1	☐	▷ Examination Report	Report			User Defined	User Defined	
☑ 2	☑	Widgets, Inc. Investigation ...	Report					

Figure 12-7   *Edit Header cell*

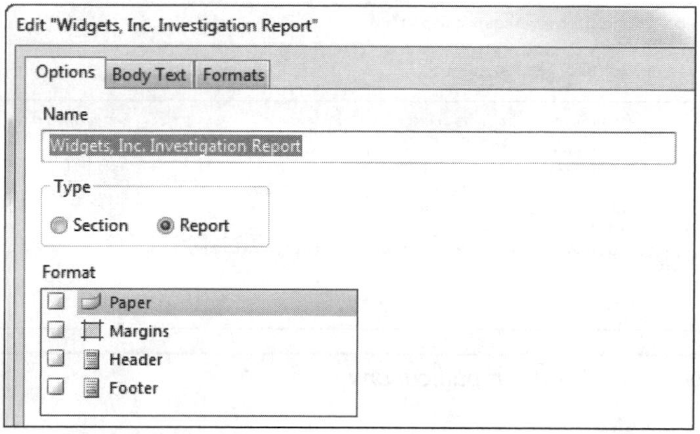

Edit "Widgets, Inc. Investigation Report"

Options | Body Text | Formats

Name

Widgets, Inc. Investigation Report

Type

○ Section   ◉ Report

Format

☐ 🗋 Paper
☐ 🏛 Margins
☐ 📄 Header
☐ 📄 Footer

Figure 12-8   *Edit report dialog*

Now that you have your Header Title style in place, you want to add your first field—the Agency. This data is brought in from the Case Info Items, which we defined at the start of the case. To insert the value, again select the "// text here" line and then choose Agency from the Case Info Items drop-down. You will see that it inserts the value of the cell from Case Info with the node name of "Agency" and that it will take the value of that associated field.

If you were to click OK and return to your Report tab in the View pane, you would now see the name of the agency you defined and an underline below it. Again, use this view to see generally how the specific section you are in will display, but keep in mind that if you are working on multiple sections, it is a good idea to actually look at the full report in the Reports tab now and again to see how the sections are interacting with each other.

Back in the Header editing interface (double-click the Header cell for your report and go to the Body Text tab), you still need to add your report date to your header. This is also taken from the Case Info drop-down. Make sure your cursor is on the line after the cell statement you inserted before, and choose Case Date from the Case Info Items drop-down. Click OK to accept these changes and then go and look at your Report tab in the View pane.

The two values are bunched up next to each other, and that isn't what we want. Go back into your Header editor and add a new line after the first cell statement. White space in this interface is ignored, so this is just for readability. Now you can just type the word "tab" as many times as you like. However, I also want to add a label to that field. Specifically, I want to add "Report Date: " before that date shows. Back in header editing dialog, I drop another new line after the tabs I inserted. The button

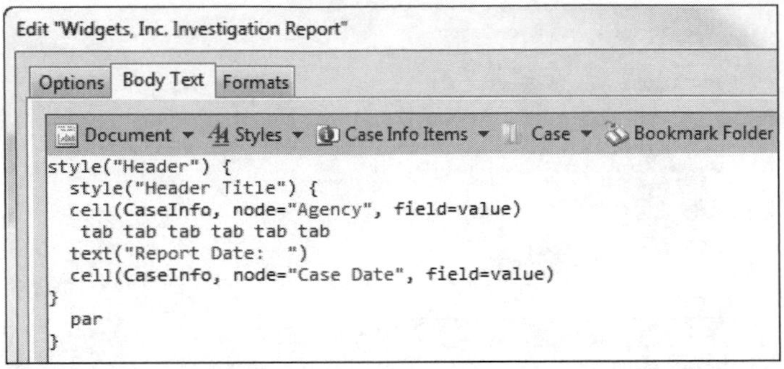

Figure 12-9 *Header code after modifications*

that will allow me to add plain text is two to the right of the Picture button, and looks like a document with a large A at the top. If you hover your mouse over it, it will say "add plain text". Clicking on that button brings up a window where you can type what you want to have displayed. Once again, click OK and verify the way this is displaying—do you like where the placement is now? I found that six tabs put the case date next to the right margin where I wanted it.

Figure 12-9 shows what my Body Text contents look like once I added these modifications to the header. The par statement indicates to EnCase that you want a new paragraph added—effectively this is a new line.

Figure 12-10 shows how this looks in the Report tab of the View pane. This shows you how easy it is to insert values from your Case Info section to the report's headers, footers, and even as content. The basic process is the same—the styles and how they behave will change depending on what you want displayed. Now that we have this defined in the top level of the report, all of the subsequent sections we create will have inherited these properties and we won't have to define them again.

Customizing the Footer

For the footer, we will list the name of the examiner who prepared the report, the text "CONFIDENTIAL", and the page number. Right-click on the cell for Footer in our report in the Table pane (row 2, Footer column) and choose Edit. This time, we will choose Footer from the Style drop-down. Selecting the commented text line as we did before is optional, but will overwrite it—click on the Add Plain Text button on

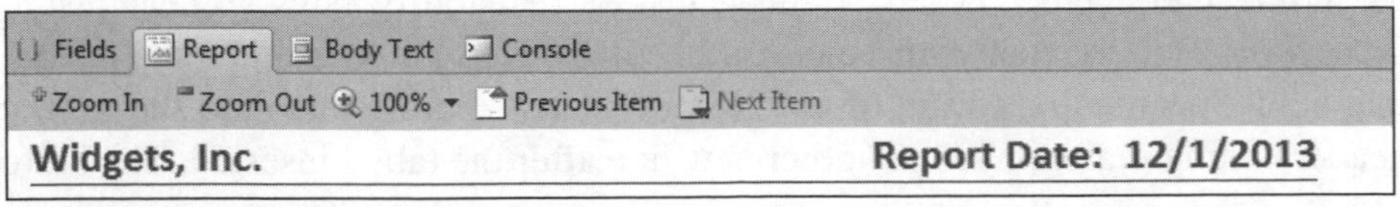

Figure 12-10 *Header with modifications*

the button bar and type "Prepared by: " without the quotes (note I have added two spaces after the colon) and click OK. This should add your text statement. Drop in a new line after that statement for readability.

To add the examiner's name, choose Examiner Name from the Case Info Items drop-down. Add another new line after that, and type "tab" without the quotes, and a new line. This will separate the examiner name text from the confidential label. Click again on the Add Plain Text button and this time, type "CONFIDENTIAL" and click OK. Add another new line and then another tab and new line.

Next, we need the page number and the label before it. Add the text "Page: " the same way you have added all your other text, and with another new line after it. The page number comes from the Document drop-down, choosing Page Number.

Figure 12-11 shows what this should look like when you have finished your footer edits.

Building the Report Tree Hierarchy

Now that we have finished formatting our header and footer, we can move on to building the structure of our report. If you look at the examination report that comes default with EnCase, you can see there are three top-level sections—Introduction, Body, and Addendum. First, let's create our top-level sections, although I don't want to use the same ones. I want to use Introduction, Body, and Appendices instead. Each of these are considered reports in their own right because they contain sections within them.

To create them, select our report, and click the New button. Give each report a name that corresponds to the three we will use.

You can see in Figure 12-12 that they are created independent of the report we had selected, despite our having selected it before clicking the New button. To associate these reports as being under the Widgets report (as shown with the Examination Report above—see how they are indented under the main report title?

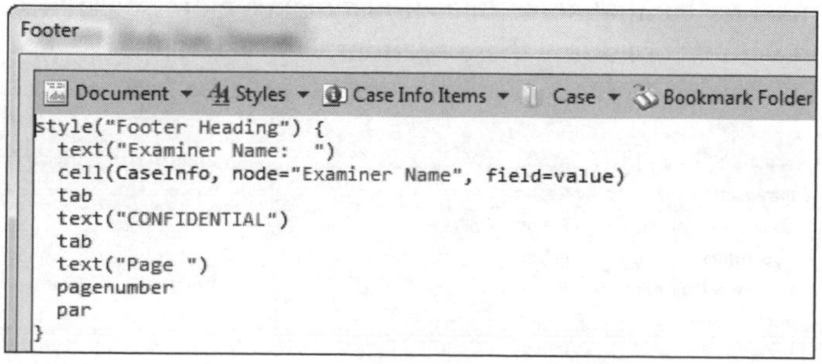

Figure 12-11 *Footer ROC*

	Show Tab	Name	Type	Paper	Margins	Header	Footer	Formats
☐ 1	☐	◢ 📄 Examination Report	Report			User Defined	User Defined	
☐ 2	☐	▷ 📄 Introduction	Report			Inherited	Inherited	
☐ 3	☐	▷ 📄 Body	Report			Inherited	Inherited	User Defined
☐ 4	☐	▷ 📄 Addendum	Report			Inherited	Inherited	
☐ 5	☑	📄 Widgets, Inc. Examination R...	Report			User Defined	User Defined	
☐ 6	☑	📄 Introduction	Report					
☐ 7	☑	📄 Body	Report					
☐ 8	☑	📄 Appendices	Report					

Figure 12-12 *New reports created but not part of top-level report*

That indicates they are subreports of the top level), we can drag them onto the main report. We do this by grabbing them with our mouse at the row number to the far left. So for example, to drag the Introduction, you would position your mouse on the 6, and drag it on top of the 5 to make it subordinate to that row (Figure 12-13). You must do these individually.

> **TIP**
>
> *Reordering reports is painful. My advice is to drag them in the order you want them to be when they are inserted. Otherwise, trying to drag them into a different order will result in them becoming subordinate to the report you wanted them to be peers with. You can drag each one back down to the bottom again to reset the hierarchy and start again if this occurs.*

Now that we have our hierarchy sorted out, we will start defining what we want to include as far as sections go.

Adding the Remaining Sections

This will be good practice for you to apply what you have learned above. You will need to pay attention to the cell you have selected when you click on the New button to make sure you keep the tree structure correct. Remember you can drag them around if you need to, but that sometimes it just makes more sense to start again. Take the default values for adding these sections.

	Show Tab	Name	Type	Paper	Margins	Header	Footer	Formats
☐ 1	☐	◢ 📄 Examination Report	Report			User Defined	User Defined	
☐ 2	☐	▷ 📄 Introduction	Report			Inherited	Inherited	
☐ 3	☐	▷ 📄 Body	Report			Inherited	Inherited	User Defined
☐ 4	☐	▷ 📄 Addendum	Report			Inherited	Inherited	
☐ 5	☑	◢ 📄 Widgets, Inc. Examination R...	Report			User Defined	User Defined	
☐ 6	☑	📄 Introduction	Report			Inherited	Inherited	
☐ 7	☑	📄 Body	Report			Inherited	Inherited	
☐ 8	☑	📄 Appendices	Report			Inherited	Inherited	

Figure 12-13 *Subreports in order under the main report*

Under the Introduction section, add the following as sections:

1. Title Page
2. Executive Summary
3. Background

Under the Body section, add the following as sections:

1. Findings
    a. System Information
    b. Installed Software
    c. User Information
    d. Hacking Tools
    e. Graphics
2. Conclusions
3. Recommendations

Under the Appendices section, add the following as sections:

1. Investigative Tools
2. Glossary of Terms

Once you have completed your additions, they should look like Figure 12-14. While you may not want each of these sections in your report, they are common to many organizations' standard reporting formats.

Some of these sections are not going to be something you want to populate inside of EnCase. The Executive Summary is an example, but it will serve as a placeholder for those who are importing the finished report into Word for further additions. Another bonus to this approach is that if you use Word to generate your Table of Contents, your sections are already marked.

Don't get me wrong, however: you absolutely can add quite a lot of your content if you set up your report template to display it. If you look in your Bookmarks section (select Bookmarks from the View menu), you can see the Report folder has a large hierarchy of folders where you can insert appropriate verbiage. For example, if you look under the Introduction folder, there is a Summary of Findings folder that contains numerous bookmarks. These are largely just placeholders with Names and Comment text boxes where you can insert what you want this section to say. Many of the default report sections are set up to display items from here, so if you populate

		Show Tab	Name	Type	Paper	Margins	Header	Footer
☐	1	☐	▷ Examination Report	Report			User Defined	User Defined
☐	2	☑	◢ Widgets, Inc. Examination R...	Report			User Defined	User Defined
☐	3	☑	◢ Introduction	Report			Inherited	Inherited
☐	4	☑	Title Page	Section			User Defined	User Defined
☐	5	☐	Executive Summary	Section			Inherited	Inherited
☐	6	☐	Background	Section			Inherited	Inherited
☐	7	☑	◢ Body	Report			Inherited	Inherited
☐	8	☐	◢ Findings	Section			Inherited	Inherited
☐	9	☐	System Information	Section			Inherited	Inherited
☐	10	☐	Installed Software	Section			Inherited	Inherited
☐	11	☐	User Information	Section			Inherited	Inherited
☐	12	☐	Hacking Tools	Section			Inherited	Inherited
☐	13	☐	Graphics	Section			Inherited	Inherited
☐	14	☐	Conclusions	Section			Inherited	Inherited
☐	15	☐	Recommendations	Section			Inherited	Inherited
☐	16	☑	◢ Appendices	Report			Inherited	Inherited
☐	17	☐	Investigative Tools	Section			Inherited	Inherited
☐	18	☐	Glossary of Terms	Section			Inherited	Inherited

Figure 12-14   *Report sections added*

these sections it will make life much easier. At the very least, those sections that are repetitive from report to report (such as standard verbiage about your examination tools and a Glossary of Terms) are good candidates for populating once and just including in your sections.

The Title Page

The sections in the Introduction are largely going to be entered by the examiner as text, rather than displaying items from within your EnCase case. So while we won't spend time on those sections, I do want to go over our title page.

To edit your title page, double-click on the Name cell for that section. The Edit "Title Page" dialog comes up. From now on, you're mostly going to be doing your work in the Body Text tab of this dialog, so click on that. The first thing you want to do is add your report's title. Mine will say "Widgets, Inc. Examination Report". To add this, first select Title from the Styles drop-down. You may notice there is a Title Page Heading there as well, but if you use that, you will find it is a small font, which is not what we're looking for. The Title style is a much larger font, as befits our title page.

Once again, the commented text line is dropped into the window with the wrapper ROC for this style. Select that with your mouse and click on the Add Plain Text button. Put your report title in there and click OK. Your ROC should look similar to mine:

```
style("Title") {
  text("Widgets, Inc. Examination Report")
  par
}
```

If you look at the Report tab in the View pane, you should see the title page.

If you recall earlier, we modified the graphic on the default reporting template to include a more appropriate logo. I will also do that here using the Picture button and browsing to the location where my logo is stored. Here is what my ROC looks like once I added the logo:

```
style("Title") {
  image(path="C:\\Path\\to\\Picture\\Widget2.jpg", width=1440,
height=1440)
  par
  text("Widgets, Inc. Examination Report")
  par
}
```

Note the double back slashes in the path? This is because the back slash character is a reserved character, so it must be escaped the same way you learned to escape characters in GREP. I encourage you to experiment with different styles, and how either nesting them like we have here within the Title style (since the boundaries of that style statement are everything between the two curly braces), or putting certain items before or after a style. This is particularly true of the header and footer items—where you put them and what style precedes them can make a big difference in how they display.

Finally, we can see if we look at the Reports top-level tab (not the one in the View pane) that there is a header and footer printing on our title page. This isn't what we want, and we know from the values in the Header and Footer columns that this behavior is inherited from the top-level report where we defined them. To turn them off, double-click on the header (or footer, it doesn't matter) to bring up the Edit "Title Page" dialog. There you can blue check the boxes next to Header and Footer. Doing so tells EnCase to use what you define there—but since we aren't going to define anything, it effectively turns that inheritance off.

We now have a title page with the logo centered, and our title in large print also centered. I would like to add a few more items, however, to make this title page more useful at a glance. Specifically, I want to add the rest of the case information items, and I also want a separate page with the list of evidence items for this case.

You do not always have to work in the pop-up dialog for the report, you can just work in the Body Text tab of the View pane when you are working on the main body of that section. We are constrained to use the pop-up dialogs when working with the Header, Footer, Margins, and Paper columns, but for regular content inside the body of the section, I find the Body Text tab a bit more useful. For one thing, the Compile button is rather handy for checking for syntax errors. While this is an option from the down arrow drop-down on the far right in the dialogs, it is not a convenient button like it is in the View pane.

To add the Case Info items, we will start at the bottom of our current text. You recall from earlier that we had a Title style defined. Now we will add two additional par statements to the line before the last curly brace. Then drop your cursor down after that curly brace and add a few blank lines to separate them (remember, white space is ignored). Choose Normal from the Style drop-down (it should be the top style). Select the add text comment line so that our changes overwrite it, and now we are going to add a table. From the Add Table drop-down, choose Case Information. Blue check both the name and the value in the columns section, and in the View Options tab, select Table, Border, and Header. Click OK, and compile your ROC. Switch to the Report tab to check how this is displaying and if you want to adjust the vertical spacing at all (using the par statement).

The Evidence Items are to go on a separate page, so we need to add a pagebreak statement next. You can either type it on the line after the table you just inserted (as shown in Figure 12-15 with no spaces), or you can insert it by choosing Page Break from the Document drop-down.

Next, after the last curly brace, add some more blank lines for readability and then choose Heading 1 from the Styles drop-down. Select the commented text line and add another table, this time choosing Evidence from the Add Table drop-down. This time we get a Columns tab where you can choose which columns you want included in the table. Choose Name and Primary Path, and on the View Options tab, choose Table, Border, and Header. Following that, add another page break.

NOTE

If you view this in the Report tab of the View pane of you will see that the page break is not shown. This is one of the reasons you need to also periodically view it in the top level Reports tab to see it more true to how it will actually display.

Figure 12-15 shows the final contents of the Body Text tab in the View pane of the Title Page section for your reference.

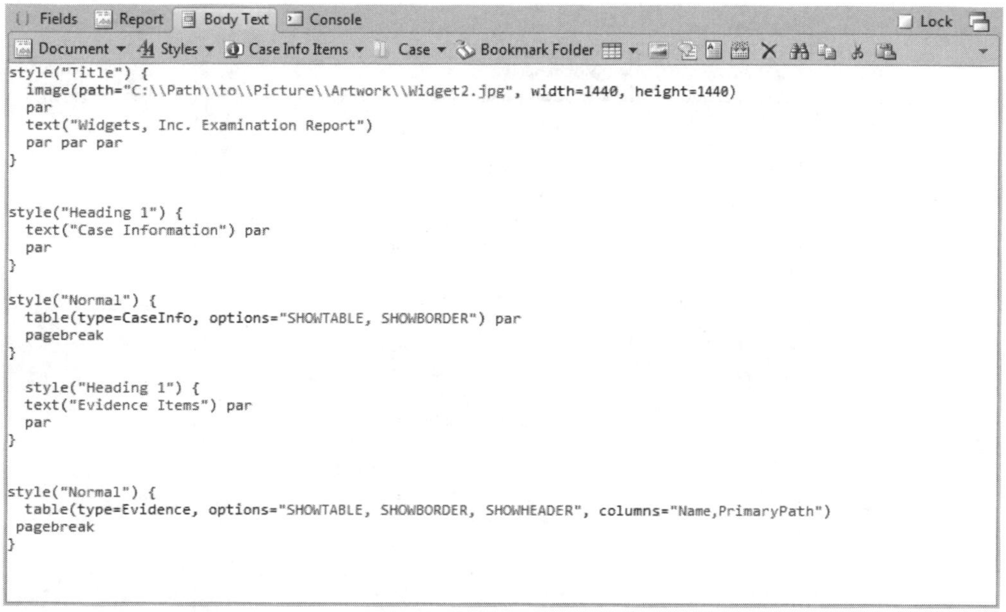

```
() Fields  [=] Report  [=] Body Text  [>] Console                                              [] Lock  [=]
[=] Document ▼  [4] Styles ▼  (1) Case Info Items ▼  []] Case ▼  [>] Bookmark Folder []] ▼  [=] [=] [=] [=] X [=] [=] [=] [=]         ▼
style("Title") {
   image(path="C:\\Path\\to\\Picture\\Artwork\\Widget2.jpg", width=1440, height=1440)
   par
   text("Widgets, Inc. Examination Report")
   par par par
}


style("Heading 1") {
   text("Case Information") par
   par
}
style("Normal") {
   table(type=CaseInfo, options="SHOWTABLE, SHOWBORDER") par
   pagebreak
}

   style("Heading 1") {
   text("Evidence Items") par
   par
}

style("Normal") {
   table(type=Evidence, options="SHOWTABLE, SHOWBORDER, SHOWHEADER", columns="Name,PrimaryPath")
   pagebreak
}
```

Figure 12-15   *Final Body Text for Title Page*

Associating Bookmark Folders with Report Sections

Now we can start looking at the sections where we found items of interest during the course of our examination. Have you guessed that some of the bookmarking we did was to ensure we'd have something good to work with in this chapter? It's true, I confess.

We can associate the contents of bookmark folders with sections of the report. We will be working in the View pane's Body Text tab for these sections.

System Information

Click on System Information and move onto the Body Text tab in the View pane. From the Styles menu, choose Normal. As usual, select the commented text line, and click on the Bookmark Folder drop-down.

As shown in Figure 12-16, the Bookmark Folder picker dialog opens for you to navigate to the appropriate folder you want to have displayed. In this case, choose the System Information folder under Examination. The Show Folders option lets you show the contents of the folder and any associated comments you entered with it—it treats the folder itself as something that may have data to be displayed rather than just a container. Click OK. Look at how this populates in the View pane's Report tab.

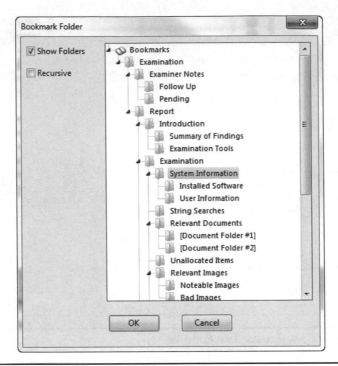

Figure 12-16 Bookmark Folder picker dialog

Installed Software

For installed software, repeat the basic steps—insert the Normal style, highlight the text line, choose the Bookmark Folder drop-down and this time select the Installed Software folder. Choose both the Show Folders and Recursive options. This will allow you to show the subfolders underneath Installed Software. If you look at the folder in the Bookmarks tab, you will see that you have both Installed and Uninstalled Software folders.

User Information and Hacking Tools

Repeat the same steps as above; check both the Show Folders and Recursive options here as well.

Graphics

For Graphics, follow the same steps to insert the style and associate the bookmark folder with both options again checked. If you recall, we put some images of interest into our Relevant Images bookmark folder structure. In this section, we are going to change the paper orientation to display in landscape rather than in portrait. Click in the Paper column associated with this section and right-click. Choose Edit and the Paper dialog opens. Click in the Landscape box. Keep in mind, if you wanted to make the entire report's orientation landscape, you could have done so by defining the paper cell in the top level so that all the children would inherit those properties. As it stands, if you made report sections under this Picture section, those would by default inherit this setting of landscape.

Formats

Now that we have our graphics associated with the report, and our paper orientation defined, what if we wanted to add the checksums associated with the graphics files? We would do this using the Formats column. Right-click on the Formats column in the cell corresponding to our graphics row and select Edit. The Formats dialog opens (Figure 12-17).

This dialog is for controlling the way the bookmark output will display. Remember, like the paper formatting we did, anything you do here will be inherited by the children, so if you want to control the formatting of a specific bookmark type for the entire report, define it at the top.

By default when nothing is selected, all of the entries in the Format column are grayed out. If you mouse over one of the rows in that column, however, you will get a box showing the contents that would be applied if you chose them. To start working with them, double-click the desired category.

Since we are working with image files, double-click on the Image category (either column, both will do the same thing). The Format: Image dialog launches with the default ROC already generated for you (Figure 12-18).

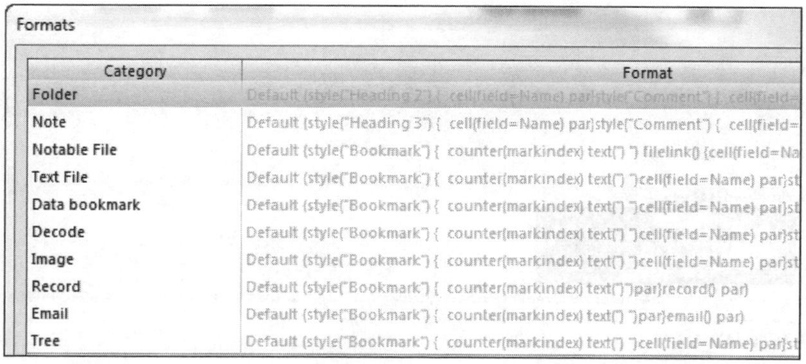

Category	Format
Folder	Default (style("Heading 2") { cell(field=Name) par)style("Comment") { cell(field=
Note	Default (style("Heading 3") { cell(field=Name) par)style("Comment") { cell(field=
Notable File	Default (style("Bookmark") { counter(markindex) text(")) filelink() {cell(field=Na
Text File	Default (style("Bookmark") { counter(markindex) text("))cell(field=Name) par)st
Data bookmark	Default (style("Bookmark") { counter(markindex) text("))cell(field=Name) par)st
Decode	Default (style("Bookmark") { counter(markindex) text("))cell(field=Name) par)st
Image	Default (style("Bookmark") { counter(markindex) text("))cell(field=Name) par)st
Record	Default (style("Bookmark") { counter(markindex) text(")par)record() par)
Email	Default (style("Bookmark") { counter(markindex) text(")par)email() par)
Tree	Default (style("Bookmark") { counter(markindex) text("))cell(field=Name) par)st

Figure 12-17 *Formats dialog*

```
Format: Image

  Document ▾   ⚊ Styles ▾   Item Field ▾   Entry Field ▾   Record Field ▾   Picture
style("Bookmark") {
  counter(markindex) text(") ")
cell(field=Name) par
}
style("Image") {
  image(width=2880, height=2880) par
}
```

Figure 12-18   *Format: Image dialog*

This is the default code for this image format. However, we want to add our checksums. Add a new line to the bottom of the code so we start outside of the existing styles that are already defined. It would probably display, but sometimes you get strange behavior when certain styles have their default font set to white. When that happens, you can't see the content because the background is also white—so if you run into a situation where you have nested styles and don't see it displaying like you would expect, check to see if this is the culprit.

As usual, we start with a style—in this case, use the Metadata style. You will note that when you pull down the Styles menu, they aren't in alphabetical order. This is something I'm hoping Guidance will remedy, because having to hunt for the style you want in the list is a bit tedious. Select the "text here" commented line and this time, note that you have some different picker menus in this dialog than you had in the regular Body Text dialog. You now have Item Field, Entry Field, and Record Field pickers where we can choose from those menus depending on the type of data in our bookmark. For our purposes, choose MD5 from the Item Field drop-down. That gives us our first checksum associated with the file. Add a new line for readability.

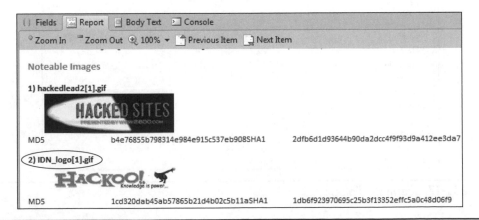

Figure 12-19   *Notable images in View pane*

Now choose SHA1 from the Item Field drop-down. Click OK twice to get back to our report template. Take a look in the Report tab of the View pane—does this look good?

Well, I'm not fond of how the SHA1 label is jammed up against the end of the MD5 checksum (Figure 12-19), so we need to address that. Go back into the Formats and drop a new line after the MD5 fieldname statement. Add a par in there and another new line for readability and click OK twice. Your code for our Metadata style should look like this:

```
style("Metadata") {
  fieldname(field=MD5Hash) tab cell(field=MD5Hash)
 par
fieldname(field=SHA1Hash) tab cell(field=SHA1Hash)
  par
}
```

Take a look again in the Report tab and you will see that our graphic looks much better, with both checksums displaying separately (Figure 12-20).

You can see how powerful formats are to allow you to customize exactly what fields you want associated with each bookmark type. You can choose from the pickers all of the specific items you want displayed, and how they will display based on the ROC you define.

Reverting Changes

You may find that your section isn't behaving properly and you want to undo the changes you've made. There are a couple of ways to revert changes. First, the nuke approach—if you right-click on a column with User Defined displaying, you will usually have the option to choose Use Default Settings. That will remove all the customization you have put into a specific section's column. An exception to this is the Body Text column, where this does not come up as an option.

However, the Body Text section has its own version of an undo type of function. If you make changes to the code in the Body Text tab of the View pane (or in one of the dialogs), you should see the Revert button become enabled. It is the black X between the Compile and Find buttons. This is an all or nothing revert—it will remove all of the

Figure 12-20   *Graphic file with checksums*

changes you made since the last compile. If you made changes without clicking the Compile button, it will wipe out all the changes you made since entering the tab.

Controlling Which Sections Display

If you scroll all the way over to the right side of the Table pane in the Report Templates tab, you will see that you have an Excluded box. This allows you to switch off various sections of the report so they will not be included. This feature is quite useful since some types of reports have different flow requirements. Not all sections will be necessary for each case, and you don't have to create a new report just for a smaller subset of the data you want to display. Checking the box will allow you to keep sections from displaying in your report. This also means that if you standardize on a report template, you should ensure it has definitions for each section you typically need—it is better to be inclusive in the design of your templates and then disable the parts you don't need than to require people to reinvent the wheel each time they need a section that is not included in the standard template.

Summary

We've covered quite a bit of ground with reporting in EnCase. Put some thought into making your organization's templates and associate them with the case template folder structure and bookmark structure to help enforce consistency from case to case and examiner to examiner. It is also important to realize that not everything may be accomplished inside of EnCase and that the use of styles translates directly to pulling the report into Microsoft Word for further manipulation. With practice and experimentation, you should be able to build templates that get you through as much of the process using the built-in functions to control the way your findings and evidence are displayed.

Wrapping Up the Case

In Chapter 1, we discussed the phases of an investigation, which ended with the case closure phase. In this phase, evidence is disposed of according to the lifecycle process identified by the organization for their evidence. Likewise, the original equipment is also disposed of according to established retention policy. In this chapter, we will discuss some of the considerations for how to manage the lifecycle of evidence and specifically, the types of things that should be done as part of case closure and final disposition.

If you haven't already defined all processes around the evidence lifecycle—from collection to destruction—this chapter is for you. While numerous organizations (such as law enforcement) will have already had this mapped out and procedures outlined, there are many other organizations where evidence is gathered (primarily in the private sector) who have largely focused on the beginning phases of the case. While it is certainly important to ensure that the evidence was properly acquired and chain of custody maintained, there will eventually come a time when decisions about how to manage evidence as a whole must be made.

Evidence Lifecycle Management

Most resources that talk about evidence lifecycle management have the process ending with the presentation/delivery of evidence, and rarely touch on what happens after that step. However, for forensic labs, this is absolutely not the end of the road. This is particularly true when the evidence library is for just one organization—for those who must manage evidence across multiple cases involving the same people. This is a regular challenge for labs that handle both forensic investigations and e-discovery matters for litigation support. Many cases may involve the same custodians time and again, so when is it safe to dispose of the evidence collected? If you have a handful of custodians, such as the company's officers or board of directors who are the most likely to be named in litigation, do they need to have a different set of rules from the regular custodian/subject?

For example, can you dispose of an image from your CEO's computer because Case A has settled, even though she is a named custodian in Case B? Should you use that image for two cases or take a fresh one as a point in time from when you had a duty to preserve for that second matter? These are questions that should be explored with your legal counsel. In fact, I strongly recommend incorporating into your disposal process their sign-off on all evidence destruction.

Once a forensic lab has been functioning for some time, cases will inevitably close and the volume of evidence under management will grow. Sooner or later, questions must be asked: What do I do with evidence after the case has closed?

How do I plan for growth of more evidence? What about disaster recovery planning—do I have a plan in place if the worst happens? How do I account for evidence in legacy formats or hardware?

All of these questions should be explored as a matter of developing your processes for your organization. Finally, if you have cases that contain indicators of compromise, do you have a method for capturing them and comparing them across cases for evidence of activity by the same actors? This is the type of data that can prove very useful for an organization to determine patterns of attacks they are facing, as well as for information sharing across industries or in public/private partnerships.

A good place to start making your plan is with the Scientific Working Group on Digital Evidence (SWGDE). They published a paper called "SWGDE Data Archiving v1.0" (April 12, 2006), and while technology changes rapidly, it raises points that should be considered regardless of the medium chosen or the technology that is currently in use. They also published "SWGDE Model Quality Assurance Manual for Digital Evidence Laboratories" (September 13, 2012), which is a much more comprehensive document dealing with these and many more lab management issues. Both documents can be found at www.swgde.org on the Documents page through the Current Documents and SWGDE QAM and SOP Manuals links.

The Digital Evidence Lifecycle

The digital evidence lifecycle comprises six phases that govern the management of evidence from case initiation to the final disposal of the evidence and original media. Like the phases of an investigation, these can be iterative as the case progresses and you find more sources of evidence that need to be acquired, processed, and analyzed. These six phases are shown in Table 13-1.

Let's take a look at each of these phases and how they interact with each other.

Acquisition Phase

The acquisition phase is where you get most of your intake for the lab. You will frequently need to be able to accommodate storage and imaging of various types of computers and devices. If the image is taken in the field and the original computer is not going to be preserved, then the storage consideration becomes how to preserve the original and facilitate access to validated working copies for your examiners.

This is frequently an ongoing process, as new sources of evidence may be uncovered during the course of the case, and new acquisitions provided to the lab for management.

Digital Evidence Lifecycle Phase	Description
Acquisition	The collection and preservation of the initial evidence from the original media along with the storage requirements for maintaining custody of the original devices as applicable.
Processing	All of the activities done to prepare the evidence for analysis; examples include keyword searches, hashing evidence, expanding archives and compound files, as dictated by the policies of your organization.
Analysis	Performing the analysis to determine the merits of the case. This includes all of the topics we've covered in prior chapters, plus any others you perform based on where the investigation leads.
Presentation	The delivery of the evidence to stakeholders in the process, and/or presentation in a court of law.
Archival	This begins after the acquisition phase when a working copy is made of the evidence, but is iterative as the case progresses. Original images are archived and preserved in a dormant state unless otherwise needed. For the rest of the work products of the case, including any working copies of evidence, any analysis materials and associated artifacts generated as part of the lifecycle of the investigation, archiving is frequently done after the presentation phase.
Disposal	If original media or devices were obtained as part of the acquisition phase, this includes their return to the owner(s). All digital evidence that is in archival state is also disposed of at this time, subject to the rules governing this phase of the evidence lifecycle for the organization.

Table 13-1   *The Digital Evidence Lifecycle*

Processing Phase

Once you have provided a working copy for processing, the case work begins and the processing phase will generate new artifacts that must also be managed. This includes any results of the processing phase, exported artifacts, case files, and reports. All of these become part of the data that must be managed for the case and should be kept track of as part of your inventory.

Analysis Phase

The analysis phase may also produce more artifacts. New sources of evidence may be identified as leads are followed based on the artifacts on the systems being analyzed. An incident response activity that began with looking at hard drive images from a server may grow in scope to encompass firewall logs and other sources of information to help reconstruct the events in question.

Presentation Phase

Materials that are produced for presentation should also be recorded and managed, in case they need to be revisited at a later time. If a particularly effective method was developed to present a key piece of evidence, then this should be discussed and presented in the inactive case review. Likewise, if a presentation method was problematic, suggestions for how to improve it should be solicited among the team members.

Archival Phase

Archiving is woven throughout the case process. The goal is the preservation of the original media and equipment, plus the secure preservation of any case evidence or work product over time. So when original equipment is brought in for acquisition, the image is generated, and the original equipment is either placed into storage or returned to the owner (per the organization's policies).

Original images taken from the source media are preserved and working copies are used for subsequent phases of the investigation. As sections of the investigation are completed, the evidence associated with that phase can be incrementally archived as well. In this way, archiving should be made a part of the normal processes of your investigations.

One of the considerations for this phase is whether or not to use encryption. If you are using the EnCase .Ex01 format, you can have these encrypted, but that only protects the data in those files. You may instead choose to encrypt the entire media prior to putting it into long-term storage. Many tape vendors offer an encryption option as well. The management of encryption keys then becomes a matter that must be given serious consideration, so that your data does not become so secure that you cannot access it yourself.

When weighed against the potential for the data contained in cases either falling into the wrong hands or becoming public, the case for encryption becomes more and more compelling. With so many states (and countries) having data breach disclosure laws on the books, the loss of your backup tapes in transit when a case may have contained data that would invoke the duty to report makes the safe haven of encryption that most of these laws provide look quite attractive.

Disposal Phase

This is the end stage of the case. After all the closure criteria have been met, and the sign-offs from appropriate groups have been documented, then the secure disposal of the surrounding evidence can be achieved. Original equipment may be returned if it has not already been, and secure wiping of media should precede any disposal of hardware that contained case data.

Wiping a Drive with EnCase

EnCase has a built-in process to facilitate the secure wiping of your disk media. With the media plugged in and recognized by the forensic workstation, choose Wipe Drive from the Tools menu. You are presented with the Wipe Drive dialog. Click Next to have EnCase scan the drives attached to the system. I would recommend only having the drive you are planning to wipe attached at this time.

Figure 13-1 shows the results on my computer. In the Name column, physical devices are given numeric names, while logical volumes are given the drive letter assigned by the operating system when the device was recognized. You need to select the physical device to ensure that all of the disk is wiped and not just the filesystem that Windows mounted. If you had a drive that had more than one partition, just choosing the logical volume would not wipe the data from the other partition.

Clicking Next brings up the Drives dialog as shown in Figure 13-2. Here, you can verify that the sectors are really wiped, and you can choose the character used to overwrite. The default is 00, but you can choose something else if you wish.

Wipe Drive

Local Devices

▦ ▾ ☑ Selected 1/14 ▯ Split Mode ▾ ☞ Edit

		Name	Label	Access	Sectors	Size	Write Blocked	Has DCO
☐	1	▷ ▨ 1	WDC WD10	Windows	1,953,525,168	931.5 GB		
☐	2	◢ ▨ 2	WIBU -	Windows	80,384	Not Ready		
☐	3	▬ L	CODEMETER	Windows	80,262	39.2 MB		
☑	4	◢ ▨ 3	PNY	Windows	31,405,824	15 GB		
☐	5	▬ K	USB20FD	Windows	31,405,712	15 GB		
☐	6	◢ ▨ 5		Windows	0	Not Ready		
☐	7	▨ F		Windows	0	Not Ready		
☐	8	◢ ▨ 6		Windows	0	Not Ready		
☐	9	▨ G		Windows	0	Not Ready		
☐	10	◢ ▨ 7		Windows	0	Not Ready		
☐	11	▨ H		Windows	0	Not Ready		
☐	12	◢ ▨ 8		Windows	0	Not Ready		
☐	13	▨ I		Windows	0	Not Ready		

Figure 13-1 *EnCase scan of attached drives*

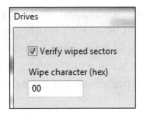

Figure 13-2 *Drives dialog*

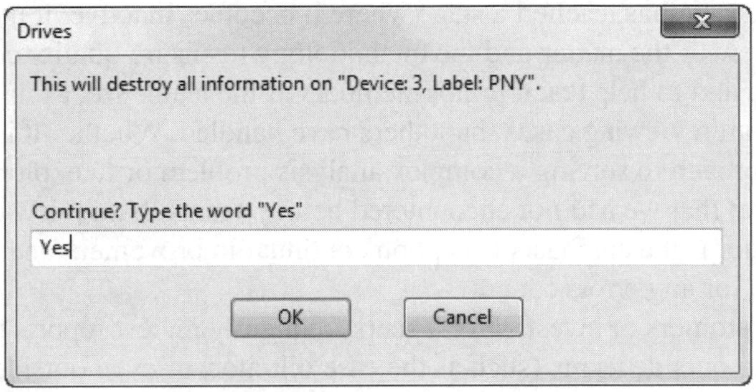

Figure 13-3 *"Are you sure?" dialog*

> **NOTE**
>
> *Verifying that the sectors are really wiped is a recommended practice, although it does add time to the process. It should also be noted in your log that the wiping was verified.*

Clicking Finish will bring up a final "Are you sure?" style dialog (Figure 13-3). The OK button will not become enabled until you type "Yes" in the text box. Verify that the information on the device you have chosen is correct, type the required confirmation, and click OK to begin the wiping process.

Case Closure Criteria

When do you close a case? Is it when you deliver the report of findings to the entity that initiated the investigation? Is it after the case has been tried and settled or resolved fully in court? Are there a set of criteria that have been established for your organization that governs when a case can be closed, and what steps should be taken as part of that process? If not, this is something you should focus on defining as soon as possible.

At the very least, I recommend having the entity that initiated each investigation and your legal counsel sign off on any case closures to ensure there are not additional regulatory requirements that should be followed in the process. Have this type of sign-off prior to your disposal process, since there could be additional litigation matters where evidence must be preserved for linked cases.

Inactive Case Review

Finally, once a case has reached a stage where it becomes inactive, it makes sense to hold peer review of the matter and the methodology to ensure quality controls have been observed and to help teach junior members of the team. We, as investigators, can benefit from reviewing cases that others have handled. Whether it is to see a different approach to solving a complex analysis problem or to explore a new forensic artifact that we had not encountered before, teams that review cases together become stronger if the emphasis is kept on continual improvement and not on placing blame for any errors found.

In larger customers of investigators, peers frequently review reports before they are provided to outside teams (such as the case initiator) or even outside or opposing counsel. Having another set of eyes on the material can make all the difference in catching errors before they become an embarrassment or in pinpointing language that is ambiguous or imprecise.

Archiving a Case

In the course of a lab's existence, cases will go through many stages, including the end stages where they either become dormant pending the actions of others (i.e., agencies or departments) or are ready to be closed. The archiving of evidence and case-related files is necessary to make room for the active cases. While storage continues to become less expensive over time, it is not free—and as a finite resource, it should be carefully managed. The long-term storage of case data must be planned for just like any other function of a digital forensics lab so that the data is stored in such a way that facilitates access when it is necessary. The ease of access may be lessened (with data stored less in readily accessible online storage, and more frequently moved to near line backup tapes or some other medium), but the integrity must be preserved against future need. Offline archiving medium has a shelf life, and that must also be taken into account in the plans for the maintenance of the evidence over time.

Also, while many organizations use tape archives as their long-term storage solution, it is important to periodically test the restore function to ensure that the backup has not encountered a problem that wasn't immediately evident. Documentation of the restore process also should not be neglected and cannot rely on one specific person being present. For many labs, the archival function also serves as a disaster recovery function if the tapes are stored in an offsite secure location.

TIP

Your backups are only as good as their ability to facilitate a successful restore. If you have a backup process and have not tested the restore process that this relies upon, you don't have any degree of confidence that it will be workable. It is only through testing (as part of regularly scheduled activities that verify your archival processes are reliable) that you can ensure that if there are any problems that arise, they can be remedied before the situation becomes unrecoverable.

Ultimately, this is something that each organization has to determine for itself. If the lab handles a high volume of evidence and a large number of cases, they will need to have sufficient online storage to handle the load. If they are an organization that provides forensics as a service, for example, there may be policies in place to pass the cost along to the client. This is particularly true for longer-term storage or litigation cases where the window of time can stretch into the years or even decades, depending on the case. If your organization is a small shop that just handles cases in-house, you may be able to get by on a much smaller scale of hardware. Either way, though, the life span of the media and the need for backwards compatibility with legacy data and hardware must be addressed.

Hard disk drives have an effective life span of around three years. Tape life span is longer but also a finite number. In addition to your storage plan, you need to have a plan in place for these devices/media aging in your evidence inventory. If the drive or the tape is nearing mean time to failure, steps should be taken to move the data onto fresh media. Keeping an inventory of what case data and evidence you have is a basic requirement for a forensic lab; accompanying that data should be both a measure of when the data should be moved onto new media and a workflow that kicks off and initiates that process. This can be as simple as an alert that sends email on a regular basis (to a group alias, not one person, to allow for turnover and vacation time) listing what media is nearing end of life, or as complex and automated as your systems and processes allow.

Preparing a Case Package

In EnCase, when the case is ready to be moved to storage that is less expensive than the primary storage used for active cases, the way to ensure that you have the entire contents associated with the case is to prepare a case package. As part of the process, EnCase packages up everything about the case, including the evidence files, cache files, and various folder structures that you have developed during the course of your investigation.

> **NOTE**
> *A case package is completely unrelated to EnCase review packages, and should not be confused with a review package despite the similarity of names. A case package is used for archiving; a review package is used for parties who do not have EnCase to be able to access and review search results from the case.*

To archive our case, choose Create Package from the Case menu. The Create Package dialog opens with the default values selected.

The Case Package feature also facilitates sharing the case with others or porting it to a different environment if needed. To that end, there are several options to choose from in the Purpose For Packaging section of the dialog.

They include:

▶ **Copy**   Only archives the required items and the primary evidence cache

▶ **Archive**   Takes all items included in Copy, plus evidence files and even the secondary evidence cache

▶ **Customized**   Allows you to specify which of the four choices in the Packaged Items section you want to package up

For our purposes, since the goal of this exercise is to create a complete archive of our case, choose the Archive option. EnCase shows the total size of the package based on the choices (the individual sections are shown as well in the Packaged Items section of the dialog). Finally, you have the option of choosing where you want this archive package to be saved. Figure 13-4 shows the options I've chosen.

Clicking Create will launch the process. The progress bar shows the steps that EnCase is going through to complete the packaging process.

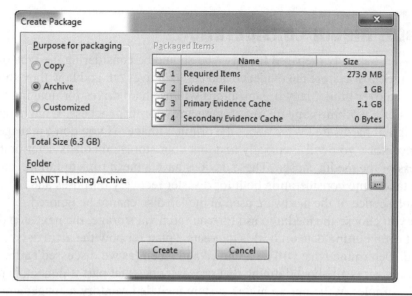

Figure 13-4   *Create Package dialog*

Once the package creation completes, you will see that a comprehensive folder structure has been set up under the location you designated (Figure 13-5). You can now compress this or move it to another location as you like.

Name	Date modified	Type
Email	11/17/2013 7:54 PM	File folder
Evidence	11/17/2013 7:54 PM	File folder
EvidenceCache	11/17/2013 7:56 PM	File folder
Export	11/17/2013 7:54 PM	File folder
Results	11/17/2013 7:55 PM	File folder
Searches	11/17/2013 7:54 PM	File folder
Tags	11/17/2013 7:54 PM	File folder
Temp	11/17/2013 7:54 PM	File folder
NIST Hacking.Case	11/17/2013 7:54 PM	EnCase Case File

Figure 13-5   *Package folder structure*

Physical Media Considerations

If you haven't already prepared for this, you should be considering the type of physical media you store the evidence and case archives on, and how they should be managed over time. Many organizations will use hard drives for imaging and then transfer a working copy up to a storage array for team access. What happens to the original hardware? What about the original image? If you don't manage the media inventory, you will eventually find that your storage media is deteriorating—regardless of the media chosen. These devices have a mean time to failure, and that must be taken into consideration both for disaster recovery purposes and for archive. The obsolescence of the hardware used in the lab also cannot be ignored.

Once you choose the media to use for your archival storage, the next step (before you start even putting data onto it) is to create a plan for how the archive is to be managed. Determine what will be archived and when (as we discussed earlier in this chapter—it is all about defining that process; once that part is done, this part is relatively simple). Will your archiving system include inventory management of the data stored? Will there be a way to mark specific files for deletion once they have met the criteria for disposal? What remains when they are deleted—do you have a way to preserve the sign-off that permitted that deletion? Make sure it isn't deleted as part of the disposal process.

Understand the expected lifetime of that archive system and make sure there is a migration plan in place when the system is nearing its end of life. As time goes by and technology changes, this may force a migration to ensure that the hardware and operating system level remains under support by the vendor as well.

Ensure that there is a disaster recovery plan in place that has been tested for the archive system (because if you haven't tested it, you don't really know if it will perform as expected). Ideally, this should allow for an offsite startup should the primary facility be compromised.

Finally, ensure that there is a plan for securely wiping the media prior to disposal of all media involved in the case lifecycle. Many organizations focus on the devices they used to capture an image and not the working copies or the archive system when they plan for secure deletion. You don't want your case data showing up on eBay.

Summary

We've followed the investigations process from start to finish, ending with the final stages of preparing your case for archiving. You should now have a good idea of how to accomplish the tasks needed to perform digital investigations using EnCase Forensics. So what is next? The final section of this book gets into the options you have for automating some of those tasks. While it is essential for investigators to be able to articulate how to perform the tasks involved in their investigation, there is no reason all of the steps must be done manually. In Chapter 14, I will cover EnCase Portable and how you can use that to facilitate remote collections in areas where you do not have a trained investigator geographically close by but still need to gather evidence. In Chapter 15, I will give you a primer on EnScript, EnCase's built-in programming language, which allows for the automation of tasks within the software.

Automation in EnCase

The final section in this book is dedicated to showing you the resources at your disposal for automating tasks in EnCase. Chapter 14 introduces EnCase Portable, which is an additional product and not included with EnCase Forensic, although Guidance Software has priced the product so attractively that it should be considered seriously for any EnCase shop. EnCase Portable allows forensic personnel to be freed up from having to be physically present at every collection, and facilitates allowing people who have not been forensically trained to perform evidence collection according to sound forensic practices. The collection jobs are programmed onto the EnCase Portable USB device and sent out with the field personnel ready to go.

We also discuss EnCase App Central, which is where you can go to find scripts written in EnCase's EnScript programming language for use or purchase. Many are freely available and submitted to help solve common problems. App Central is worth registering with and visiting just to see if there are any scripts already posted that you can use to solve an issue you are facing.

Finally, Chapter 15 is an EnScript primer. It is a chapter devoted to introducing the basics of how to use the scripting language and get you to the point where you can continue to study and use EnScript to automate tasks in your own environment. Learning EnScript has the potential for being extremely valuable, enabling you to automate processes your organization uses routinely in certain types of cases. Once an EnScript is written and vetted, you can share it across all of your examination machines to help standardize processes as well.

CHAPTER 1

EnCase Portable and App Central

When you have a collection that must be performed in person, but your trained forensic examiners cannot be freed up from other commitments, you quickly realize there is a need for a product that will allow you to "deputize" other people without having to give them a full education in forensic theory and practice. Many corporations, for example, have an established group of people who are tasked with keeping the desktop and laptops for their employees up and running. These are good candidates for leveraging when the need for a collection arises, but you cannot send your forensics team.

While it is certainly possible to prepare various tools for them, EnCase Portable is very nice to equip groups who have not been trained as forensic examiners to handle collections of various types in the field. The forensic examiner can program the EnCase Portable device with the specific collection jobs they need run (or use the standard built-in jobs that come with the product). The collection will be completed following sound forensic practices, and the data can be either previewed at the site or delivered back to the forensic lab for further analysis.

You can use this product to automate your collections to the extent possible (given that knowing exactly what your field people will encounter is a challenge) but also provide sufficient flexibility to handle most situations.

EnCase Portable Basics

To begin with, you need to install the product. As with other products, Guidance Software typically sends you an email with links to download the latest and greatest version of the product when you have purchased it. However, EnCase Portable also comes with an installation DVD. I am working with EnCase Portable version 4.05 for this chapter.

What Is Included

When you receive the physical product from Guidance Software, EnCase Portable comes with several components

- ▶ The CodeMeter USB dongle/EnCase Portable USB device. This is both the product and additional storage. It provides the license security key on board and has a capacity for 2.5GB of data storage. This is referred to interchangeably as the CodeMeter dongle and the EnCase Portable USB device in the Guidance Software training and documentation.

- ▶ The Installation DVD, which in addition to containing the product installation files includes the Quick Start Guide, the User's Guide, and Release Notes.

► The Field User Training DVD, which when launched plays a DVD movie geared toward training your field user who is going to be performing collections.

► The EnCase Portable Boot Disk (CD), used for booting a computer into the interface to facilitate collection. This is used for machines that have already been powered off or cannot boot from a USB device.

► The laminated EnCase Portable Quick Reference Field Guide, showing procedures for using EnCase Portable in the field, including a very handy reference with the key combinations required to interrupt the boot sequence of a number of different manufacturers' computers.

We will look at how to use each of these components as we go through the use cases for EnCase Portable.

NOTE

There is a User's Guide for EnCase Portable, and this chapter is meant to give an overview of the product's use, but not to replace an entire User's Guide. Guidance Software also offers a download link to their offline training for this product in the email they send out, which goes into detail and is quite useful.

Installing from the Downloaded Product

If you choose to download the product from the email link provided by Guidance Software, the process is quite simple. The installation file is named ef_portable_ setup_<*version*>_<*language*>.exe, with the version and language varying as appropriate. To launch the installation, double-click the executable from inside Windows Explorer. You may be prompted by the operating system to confirm that you do want to run this program. Once confirmed, the installation screen displays, as shown in Figure 14-1.

As you can see, first comes the EnCase Portable End User License Agreement, and you will need to check the "I agree and accept" check box to proceed. The Target EnCase Folder contains the default folder for EnCase installation, and you can browse to your specific installation folder location using the ellipses (…) button to the right. It is important to set this to your EnCase Forensic installation directory, because this product installs on top of EnCase Forensic. If you don't point it to your installation directory where it can find the expected content, you will get the error shown in Figure 14-2. You will also get this error if the version of EnCase Forensic you have installed is not compatible with the version of EnCase Portable you are trying to install.

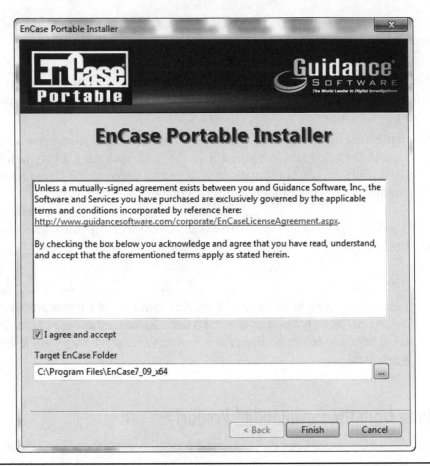

Figure 14-1   *EnCase Portable installation screen*

Once you have the correct location in the Target EnCase Folder box, click Finish to proceed with the installation. The progress bar appears, and EnCase Portable installs. You will see the Installation Successful message when it has completed.

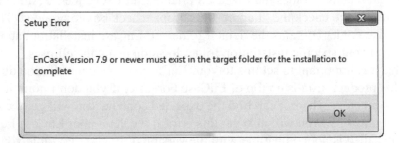

Figure 14-2   *Error message on install screen*

Installing from the DVD

Installing from the DVD is a little different to begin with. First, of course, you must insert the DVD into your forensic workstation's drive. If you aren't prompted to do so by the operating system, run the Setup.exe file found on the DVD. This launches the DVD menu screen.

Figure 14-3 shows that there are two large buttons to the right, as well as several links on the left. For our purposes, we will click the Install EnCase Portable button. A window may appear indicating that the installer is being launched. Once the installer is launched, you will find yourself in the same window shown in Figure 14-1, and the process continues in exactly the same manner.

Finally, once you finish installing, you may be given a notice by the operating system that the program may not have been installed properly and asking you to confirm if it has, as shown in Figure 14-4.

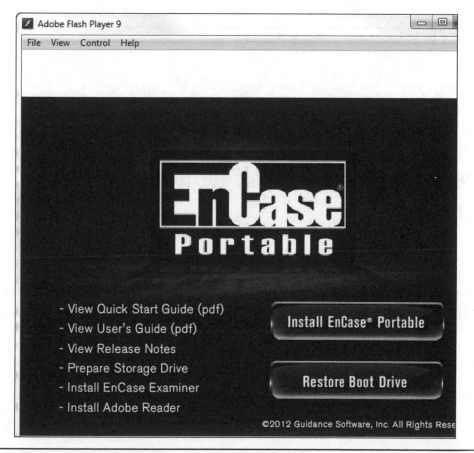

Figure 14-3 *DVD menu screen*

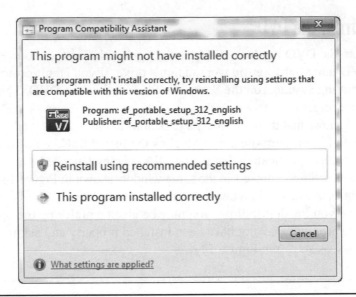

Figure 14-4 *Program Compatibility Assistant*

This indicates that Windows can't confirm this installation worked, but I had no problem with the install and chose "This program installed correctly."

Preparing EnCase Portable for Redeployment After Use

When you first get your EnCase Portable USB device, it has not been used on a case yet (obviously). However, having used it once, and returned to the lab and pulled off the data, you will eventually need to send it out to the field again to be used. Before this happens, you should follow good forensic practice, and wipe and reformat the device to avoid any potential for cross-contamination between collections. Having done this, you will need to restore the device with a fresh installation.

This step may also be used to ensure that you have the most recent software on the dongle, or to address a problem that resulted from the operating system on the dongle having become corrupted. In any case, the process for restoring the device remains the same.

CAUTION

Prior to restoring the EnCase Portable device, ensure that you have made a copy of any license or cert files required. The EnCase Portable User's Guide has directions for those situations where a license or cert file may be required for EnCase Portable to work. It lists the locations where you can find the current copy the device is using and also where they need to be placed after the restore process. You should always keep a backup copy of these files somewhere safe other than the EnCase Portable device in case they become corrupted or the device fails or becomes lost.

Restoring Using EnCase Forensic — Requires Forensic Dongle

The dongle restore process begins on your forensic workstation where you installed Portable. First, you need to have EnCase Forensic running. To be able to complete the activities required for restoring this device, you must also have the EnCase Forensic dongle plugged in and recognized by the operating system.

Once you have launched EnCase Forensic, you will need to create a new case by clicking on the New Case link from the Home screen. You will not actually be saving this case, so don't worry too much about what you enter for the details about the file paths. You will need a name for the case, and I used "EnCase Portable Restore" as shown in Figure 14-5.

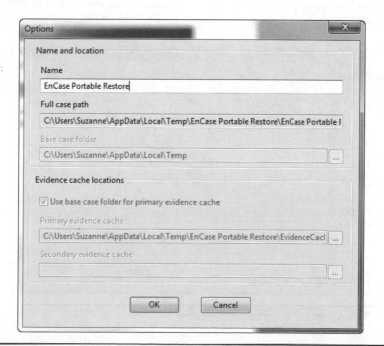

Figure 14-5   *Create a new case*

Once your case is created, add the evidence file you use to restore the Portable device. Click the Add Evidence link from the Home screen and then click the Add Evidence File link to bring up the dialog where you can browse to the storage location for your file.

You can see from Figure 14-6 that EnCase creates a new directory under your install directory called Portable. There, you will find the .E01 evidence file included with the product—EnCase Portable.E01. Select that file and click Open to bring the file into EnCase Forensic. You will see the verification process kick off in the progress bar at the bottom-right side of the interface.

Click on the link in the Name column where your evidence was added (the file is named with the version number of EnCase Portable you installed). This will open your evidence file in the Entries view of the Evidence tab. You can see the file system structure of the device, and the contents. During the restoration process, the contents of this evidence file will be copied onto the EnCase Portable device.

Blue check the evidence file in the Table pane, and then click the Device menu drop-down from the Evidence tab's button bar. From that drop-down, you now have the Restore option. This option allows you to restore your Portable dongle with the

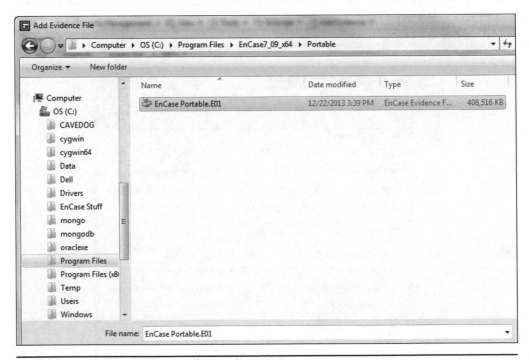

Figure 14-6   *Browse to the installation directory*

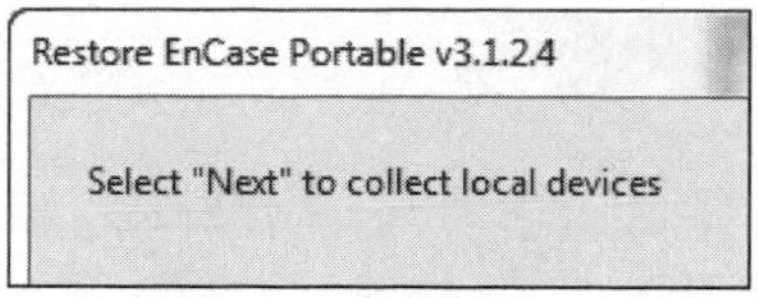

Restore EnCase Portable v3.1.2.4

Select "Next" to collect local devices

Figure 14-7   *The Restore EnCase Portable dialog*

most current software version (since this evidence file is refreshed with each new installation). This brings up the Restore EnCase Portable dialog (Figure 14-7).

The dialog is empty and instructs you to click Next so that EnCase can scan for attached local devices attached to your computer. If you didn't already have the EnCase Portable device plugged into the system, you need to make sure it is done prior to clicking Next. EnCase will not see the device if it is inserted after the scan. Also, the device must be detected by the operating system, so leave sufficient time for that if your system takes a while—or if there are issues that you need to go and troubleshoot.

Once the scan is complete (this should be fast), EnCase displays the detected devices (Figure 14-8). It automatically excludes the operating system drive from the list as a security feature to keep you from accidentally installing over top of your workstation's primary drive. You can easily locate the EnCase Portable device, because the device label will be WIBU- by default, combined with the volume label of EP_WIN. Also verify the physical size is as expected as an extra precaution. This habit is a good one to have, particularly when preparing additional storage devices. Note that the Name column shows the physical device name as a number. This is the standard naming convention that EnCase uses—numbers in the Name column indicate it is a physical device. Letters in the Name column indicate that it is the logical volume built on top of the physical device by the operating system.

When you restore the physical partition of the device, the logical partition—which is a part of the physical image—will also be restored. Highlight the physical device associated with the WIBU- label and click Next.

The Drives dialog is displayed, and you have the option to do several things here. First, you can wipe remaining sectors on target. You can verify the wiped sectors, you can choose to specify a wipe character (the default is 00), and you can have EnCase generate verification hash(es).

Do you want to wipe and verify the remaining sectors? That is up to you—if you have already prepared this device by wiping and formatting it, then this is redundant. However, you may want to include it in the process just in case a mistake is made and the device was not prepared first. It will ensure that, regardless, you can be certain no data remains on the device from the prior collections by choosing these options. Verifying that the remaining sectors have been wiped is an extra precaution.

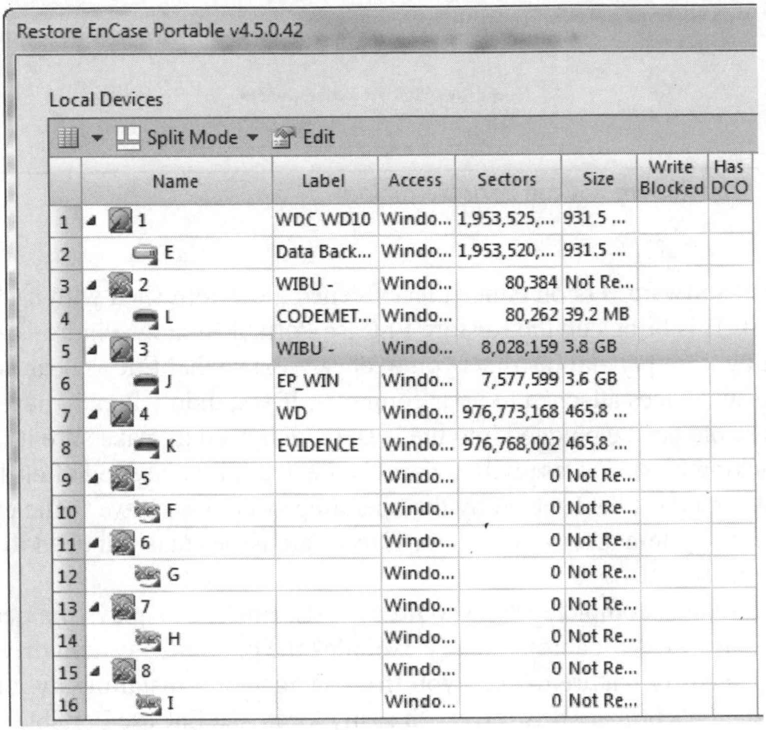

Restore EnCase Portable v4.5.0.42

Local Devices

Split Mode Edit

	Name	Label	Access	Sectors	Size	Write Blocked	Has DCO
1	1	WDC WD10	Windo...	1,953,525,...	931.5 ...		
2	E	Data Back...	Windo...	1,953,520,...	931.5 ...		
3	2	WIBU -	Windo...	80,384	Not Re...		
4	L	CODEMET...	Windo...	80,262	39.2 MB		
5	3	WIBU -	Windo...	8,028,159	3.8 GB		
6	J	EP_WIN	Windo...	7,577,599	3.6 GB		
7	4	WD	Windo...	976,773,168	465.8 ...		
8	K	EVIDENCE	Windo...	976,768,002	465.8 ...		
9	5		Windo...	0	Not Re...		
10	F		Windo...	0	Not Re...		
11	6		Windo...	0	Not Re...		
12	G		Windo...	0	Not Re...		
13	7		Windo...	0	Not Re...		
14	H		Windo...	0	Not Re...		
15	8		Windo...	0	Not Re...		
16	I		Windo...	0	Not Re...		

Figure 14-8 *Result of device scan*

TIP

Generating a verification hash is a good practice so that it can be compared to the acquisition hash to be certain that nothing has changed with the restored image. While deselecting any of these options would serve to speed up the restore process, they are good forensic practice, and Guidance Software recommends leaving them all checked.

Clicking Finish, you see the final "Are you sure?" type message—remember, you are going be overwriting any existing data that is on the drive you selected, so EnCase displays the device name and label and requires you to confirm they are correct and that you want to proceed. It is a good practice to only have the device you want to restore attached at the time you perform this so you don't risk other devices due to human error.

Type "Yes" in the text box and the OK button will be enabled. Click it to kick off the restore process. You will see the restore operation progress in the bottom-right corner. It cycles through the wiping process if you have selected that option, and then the verification process after that as well. Once the progress bar disappears, the process is complete, and you can safely remove the EnCase Portable device. You can also exit EnCase Forensic without saving the case.

If you require license or cert files for EnCase Portable to run, this is the time to restore them according to the directions provided in the User's Guide.

Restoring Using the DVD — Does Not Require a Forensic Dongle

You can also perform a restore of the device using the Installation DVD (you will again need to run Setup.exe) to launch. Once the EnCase Portable DVD menu has displayed, choose Restore Boot Drive. This will open EnCase Forensic in Acquisition mode. It creates the case for you (titled Restore) and loads the evidence file—so this is a simpler process than using the forensic workstation and EnCase Forensic. Note that since you are in Acquisition mode, you cannot see the directory structure of the evidence file, as you could with the prior process. Since you don't need to actually view this structure, it won't matter for this purpose.

The rest of the process continues the same as our prior process. You don't need to select the evidence file, since there is only one possibility with the automatic procedure on the DVD, but it doesn't hurt to do so. Choose Restore from the Device menu.

Again, you must have the EnCase Portable device plugged in prior to clicking Next when EnCase will scan the attached devices. Again, identify the correct device (remember the labels WIBU- and EP_WIN) and then click Next. Accept the default options on the next screen, and continue until the process completes. Verify the drive name and click OK to kick off the restore process.

The progress bar at the bottom right of EnCase once again indicates where in the restore process EnCase currently is. Once complete, exit the DVD menu, which should also close your running copy of EnCase. Remember, you will need to restore any license or cert files, as mentioned above.

Restoring Using an Update File — Does Not Require a Forensic Dongle

Periodically, Guidance Software sends registered users update emails when new product versions are released. You will find a link to the restore file in that email as well, to get the newest version of the restore image.

You launch the installation by double-clicking the file once it has downloaded. It will be named ef_restore_portable_*<version>*_*<language>*.exe. The rest of the process is exactly like the DVD installation—EnCase is launched in Acquisition mode and you can proceed from there to do your restore.

Preparing Additional Storage Devices for Use with Portable

Once EnCase Portable is installed on your forensic workstation, you will want to prepare for the use case where the amount of data that needs to be collected is larger than the 2.5GB of space provided on the EnCase Portable USB device. There are two ways to accomplish this. You can do the scripted method, which requires you to create a case in EnCase Forensic, and then there is the quick method—just using Windows Explorer. While the quick method is probably the one you will use, it is important to know the manual steps as well, so we will go over both.

Regardless of which method you use, the first steps are always to wipe and format the drive to eliminate any data that might already be present both in allocated and unallocated space. You can choose to wipe the drive using EnCase Forensics. In the Tools menu, the Wipe Drive option will walk you through wiping the drive of your choice. The interface for this is actually using many of the same dialogs we saw in the restore processes we just covered. The initial screen requires you to click Next, which kicks off a scan of attached devices. The resulting devices are displayed in the same dialog we saw before, only this time you do not select the volume you want by highlighting it—you must blue check it instead.

Until you blue check at least one item, the Next button is disabled. As you can see in Figure 14-9, you can blue check multiple items if you have a number of devices you want wiped. Clicking Next gets you to a screen that lets you choose if you want to verify the sectors have been wiped afterwards and change the wipe character if you like. Clicking Finish will get you the confirmation dialog and then you can kick off the process. As before, EnCase will show the progress on the bottom right.

There are any number of drive-wiping utilities out there if your organization does not want to use EnCase for this. Many of the hardware acquisition devices will also have a wiping feature and may be quicker. Having wiped your drive, you next need to build a filesystem on it. Refer to your operating system documentation for that process.

Preparing Storage Devices with EnCase Forensics—Scripted Method

Once you have built the filesystem on the wiped drive, you are ready to start this process. Make note of the drive letter and volume name that the operating system has assigned to the device—you'll need this later. Also insert your EnCase Portable device, as it has what you need to prepare additional storage devices. Open Windows Explorer and navigate to the EnCase Portable device. Specifically, you want the folder named Utilities. There you will see two files: Prepare Storage.vbs and Shutdown.cmd. Prepare Storage.vbs is the file you want—it is a Visual Basic

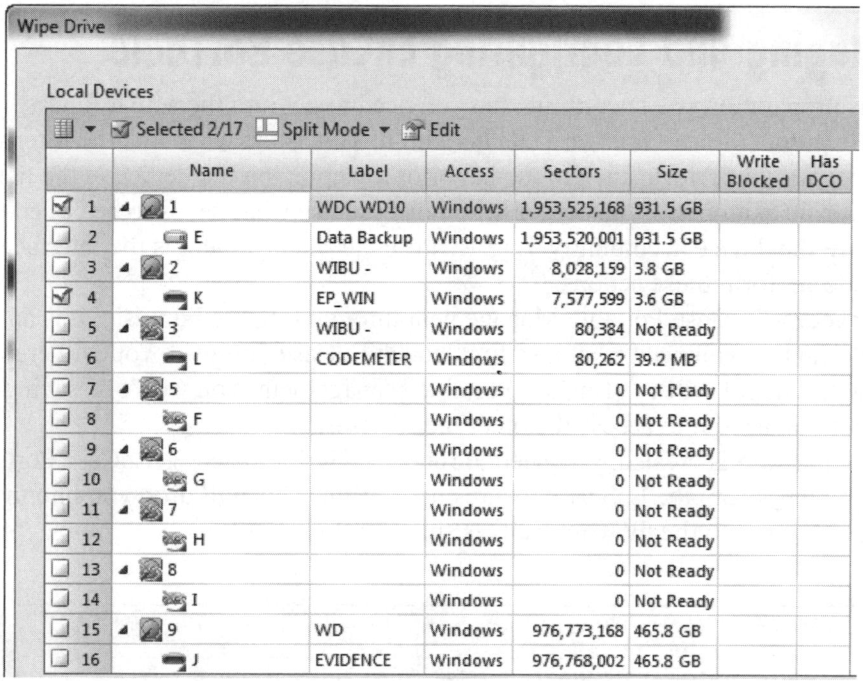

Figure 14-9 *Wipe Drive scan results*

script that automates preparing the storage device. To launch Prepare Storage.vbs, double-click it. A dialog will open that asks the drive letter of the drive you want to prepare for use with EnCase Portable. Provide the drive letter (the dialog is not case sensitive) and click OK. The process completes quickly and you see the dialog indicating the process was successful on the volume you specified.

Now if you go into the storage device you just prepared using Windows Explorer, you will see that there are two directories created.

Preparing Storage Devices with Windows Explorer — Quick Method

The previous process created two directories on the new storage device: EnCase Portable Evidence and, within that directory, Source Processor. You could simply create these two directories yourself to prepare the drive instead of having to use the Visual Basic script. If you don't want to create them manually, even having a directory somewhere with this hierarchy that you could copy/paste in Windows Explorer is likely faster.

It is a good idea to verify after a version upgrade that this script has not changed to provide additional steps.

Managing and Configuring EnCase Portable

All this preparation is a good thing, but you need to get into the actual EnCase Portable product to see what you can do with it. This is the work that the forensic examiner would perform back in the lab prior to deploying the device in the field. The forensic examiner is the person who must specify what needs to be collected and configure the device accordingly. EnCase Portable Management is the interface that is used to perform these actions.

You access EnCase Portable Management through EnCase Forensic. It is an EnPack file that you need to run, so first launch EnCase Forensic. You will create a new case, which I will call EnCase Portable Management. You won't be saving this case, but you need it to access the other menu items.

Once the case is created, you need to run an EnScript to access EnCase Portable Management. From the EnScript menu, choose Run. This will drop you into the dialog to browse to the file you want, as shown in Figure 14-10.

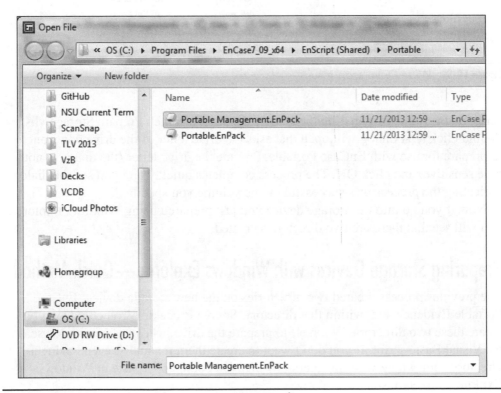

Figure 14-10   *EnCase Portable Management EnPack*

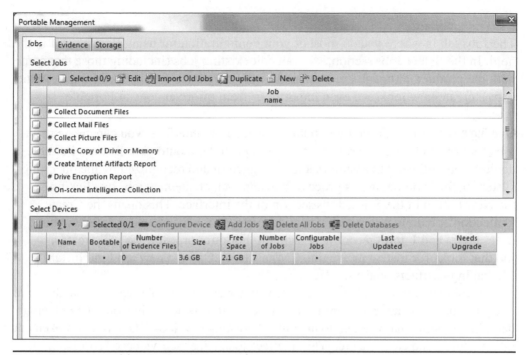

Figure 14-11   *Portable Management interface*

You are dropped into the EnScript (Shared) folder as you can see on the breadcrumb bar at the top of Figure 14-10. I have navigated to the Portable folder that was created here when we installed EnCase Portable. The file we want is the Portable Management.EnPack. Click on that file and click Open. This will launch the Portable Management interface (Figure 14-11).

The Portable Management Interface

Portable Management has several tabs as you can see in Figure 14-11. It opens to the Jobs tab by default and contains the list of default jobs included with the product. These jobs are all designated with a hash (#) symbol as the first character in their names. You can take a look inside the jobs to see what they are configured to do by clicking on the job and then clicking on the Edit button. However, the default names are good descriptors, and give you at least a general idea of what the job is designed to do. Most of them are based on the file category (i.e., the # Collect Document Files job will collect files that have been designated by EnCase as having the file category of Document). It is a good idea to investigate exactly what the definitions of the job are to make sure they match what you need prior to using them in a collection.

The Jobs Tab

The Jobs tab is where you do most of your configuration for using Portable out in the field. In the Select Jobs section, you can edit existing jobs (including those that come with the product, although I recommend duplicating them first and working from the copy), create new jobs, and even import jobs from prior versions of Portable.

Creating a New Job   From the Portable Management interface, you can create new jobs for your field users to run. To be able to push them onto your EnCase Portable device, you will need to ensure that it is plugged in and recognized by the operating system before you begin this process. You can then create new jobs by clicking on the New button in the Select Jobs section of the interface. This opens the Create Collection Job dialog, in which you give your new job a name. The default is not descriptive, and I don't recommend using it. For our purposes, we will create a job that looks for instant messaging (IM) artifacts. Call the new job Find Instant Messaging Artifacts, and click Next.

You are now dropped into the Create Collection Job dialog. You can see that there are many options you can choose from, and I recommend spending time on each of them to get familiar with what you can do in terms of creating new jobs. The jobs are broken out into modules, and each is a link. This interface looks like the Evidence Processor.

Click on the IM Parser link. The IM Parser dialog opens, and you can choose among the three types of IM clients that EnCase supports: AOL, MSN, and Yahoo. You also have the option to scan unallocated space for these artifacts. These are all selected by default, and we will leave them as-is. Click OK to accept these options.

This puts you back in the Create Collection Job dialog. Click Next to show the compound file options (Figure 14-12).

This section lets you choose how to handle the compound files that you encounter. You have these options:

▶ **Do not mount (fast)**   This option tells EnCase not to bother with mounting and searching through compound files. EnCase will just ignore them when they are detected and move on, which is why it is the fastest option.

▶ **Mount – detect extension (slow)**   This option will mount compound files as identified by their file extension. This means that if it encounters a file with the extension you blue check in the File Types section (that becomes enabled when either of the mount options arc chosen), it will mount and search through those files. Choosing this option means that you will not search through any compound files that do not have these file extensions—so if someone is trying to disguise the nature of the file by changing the file extension, this will effectively keep that file from being searched. This option is slower because it must perform the additional step of mounting the file, plus all the time searching through the compound files.

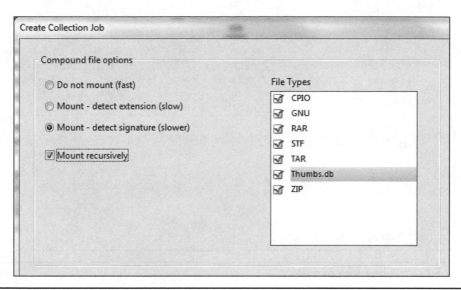

Figure 14-12 *Compound file options*

▶ **Mount – detect signature (slower)**   This is both the slowest option and the most thorough. This uses the file signature to determine if the file in question is a compound file, rather than the file extension. Because it must evaluate header/ footer combinations to determine file signature, and then mount and search compound files, it takes the longest of the three.

The option to mount recursively allows you to completely expand compound files that also contain compound files within them. So if you have a rar file that has been zipped, it would first mount the zip file, and then within that, mount the rar file.

Clicking Next gets you to the options for your output file (Figure 14-13). Logical evidence file is the only option, but you have the choice of the legacy .L01 format or the newer .Lx01 format. You can specify a different segment size and compression, and also choose to create an entry hash (MD5, SHA1, or both).

Finally, there is a section for handling encryption. If you haven't already, you can create your encryption keys in this section and also change where EnCase Portable gets the keys from. You can see in Figure 14-13 that EnCase already populates this with the existing key we created in Chapter 3. Clicking on the New Key button displays the Create Key dialog (Figure 14-14).

Your organization may choose to have a specific key designated to the Portable instances in use. You can easily create a new key, but be sure to store the password somewhere it can be accessed—Guidance Software does not maintain these for you, and it cannot be recovered if lost.

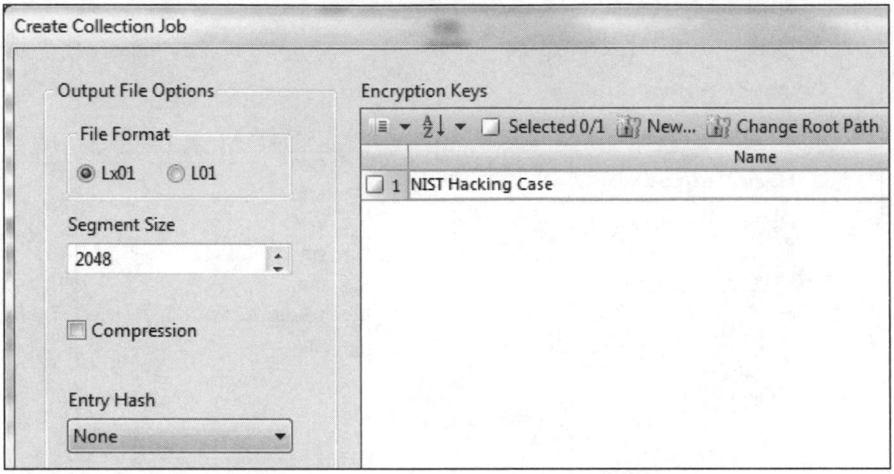

Figure 14-13 *Output file options*

If you do choose to create a key here, clicking OK creates the key and returns you to the same dialog. Either way, click Finish to complete the job creation. Back in Portable Management, you can see your new job at the bottom of the list. It is blue checked by default.

The job is now configured for use and selected. However, before you can use it, it must be pushed to your EnCase Portable device. The Jobs tab of Portable Management has a Selected Devices section, and your EnCase Portable Device should be listed there. To push a job to it, blue check the device and choose Add Jobs. The Adding Jobs Copy Status window opens and you see the progress as the job is copied over. When it completes, click on the Finished button to return to Portable Management.

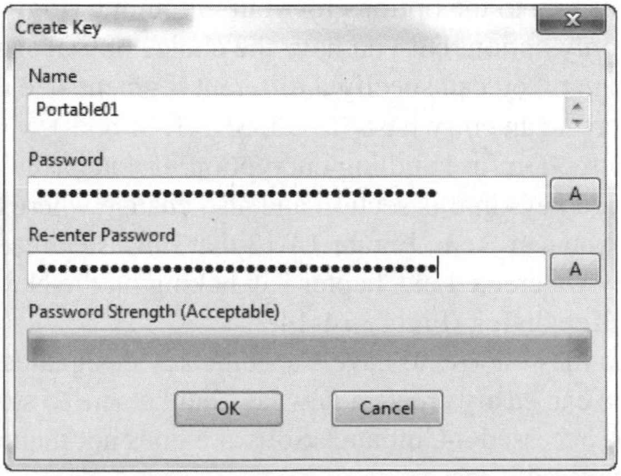

Figure 14-14 *Create new encryption key*

Duplicating a Job   You can duplicate a job prior to editing, which is a good practice, particularly if you are using the default included jobs. Since they will be overwritten with the new versions (unless you are making a separate directory tree for each version), it makes sense to always make a copy of the default jobs and work from the copy so that your changes will not be lost on upgrade. To duplicate a job, just blue check it and click the Duplicate button. You will be prompted for a name, and it will appear at the bottom of the list of jobs in the Select Jobs section.

Editing an Existing Job   As with duplicating, editing a job starts with blue checking the job you want to edit, and clicking the Edit button. This brings up the Edit: <Job Name> dialog. From here, the steps are identical to those in the "Creating a New Job" section above, and you can pick and choose the options you need.

The Evidence Tab

The Evidence tab is used to manage the evidence that has been collected using Portable. You can use this interface to bring evidence into your case and also to perform analysis. We will cover this a little later when we talk about what happens when you return to the lab from collecting evidence.

The Storage Tab

The Storage tab is used to prepare additional storage devices for use with EnCase Portable.

File Types in EnCase Portable

There are two types of files found in EnCase Portable—the actual collected evidence files, which are stored in .L01 or .E01 format, and the files that contain the summary data, which are used for analysis. These latter files are stored in .L01 format, but you cannot view them if you bring them into EnCase Forensic. They are for internal use only.

The collected evidence files are stored in \EnCase Portable Evidence\Portable Management\FileEvidence. The summary data files are stored in \EnCase Portable Evidence\Portable Management\ModuleEvidence.

Running Jobs in the Field

Now that you have EnCase Portable Device ready for use, and you have additional storage drive(s) prepared, you are ready to start collecting. You could just send people out to handle collections with the default jobs included with EnCase Portable.

TIP

In addition to training your field workers on how to use EnCase portable, you should also ensure that they know how to approach and document the scene prior to making any changes or collections. If you simply focus on having them be able to use the tool, you will find that they are missing important steps in the process of a forensically sound collection.

The EnCase Portable interface allows for running jobs as well as editing and configuring them. With this flexibility, the field user should be able to handle whatever they are faced with in the field. The forensic examiner who configures this interface does have the option of disabling the edit ability as they may want to strongly restrict the field user's ability to make changes. This is a choice that your organization is going to have to make in the best interests of the goals of the case. It may also be that some of your field users are more technically savvy than others, and you may change this based on their ability and training.

Collecting from a Powered-On Computer

If you only do collections after powering down a machine, you lose potentially valuable information. The state of a running machine provides a wealth of information—many of today's malware programs run entirely in RAM, so the collection of RAM, open ports or files, and network connections to name a few will be invaluable in an incident response situation. Also consider that sometimes if you have a running machine that may be your only chance to collect from filesystems that would be encrypted on power-down.

The act of collecting this data introduces changes to the system—this is unavoidable. However, consider that if you power down a running machine, you aren't collecting the volatile artifacts, and you know you have destroyed evidence that could have been collected and might have been extremely important. By collecting all of the evidence that you can collect, you may be able to recover data that is worth the changes that must be made to collect them. Plugging in the CodeMeter dongle installs and then removes the license drivers, for example. The important thing is that all actions are documented.

EnCase Portable can only collect the volatile data from a PC—because it needs to be in the Windows environment to function. If you are faced with a non-Windows machine, you will have to either use a different tool for collection (a non-EnCase product), or follow the procedure for collecting from a powered-off computer. EnCase Portable cannot accommodate the collection of volatile data from a non-Windows computer at this time.

NOTE

Non-EnCase products for data collection include the Volatility Framework as an open source option, Linux Memory Extractor (aka LiME) for Linux, and Mac Memory Reader from Mac Marshall for Macs.

To begin, you need to plug in the EnCase Portable USB device. You may also want to plug in additional prepared storage in case the data is larger than the 2.5 GB the device provides. Plug in the Portable device before you attach any additional storage. The drivers need to be installed and the device recognized by the operating system first. This will ensure that when you run EnCase Portable, it will have recognized the additional storage and excluded it from the list of collectible devices.

Once the operating system has recognized the device, you should get the Autoplay dialog asking what you want to do with this newly plugged in device. The dongle, as before, displays the EP_WIN label—take note of the drive letter assigned to it. Also note that the Windows Registry will show that this device has been plugged in, so simply make a note of that in your records to account for that entry. If the Autoplay dialog does not come up, you will have to do some troubleshooting to find out what is going on. That is typically done by right-clicking on the Computer icon and choosing Manage, and then Disk Management.

In the Autoplay dialog, click on the "Open folder to view files" link. This will put you into Windows Explorer, showing you the contents of the EnCase portable USB device. Double-click on the Run Portable.exe file to launch Portable.

There is an optional quiet mode that this can be run in if you don't want to interact with Windows Explorer. It will install the drivers and launch EnCase Portable without further interaction. The idea here is to minimize your interaction with the operating system on the target computer so you have less to document. You can run it from the Start menu search bar as shown in Figure 14-15. The drive letter should be replaced with the letter that was assigned to the volume when the operating system recognized it.

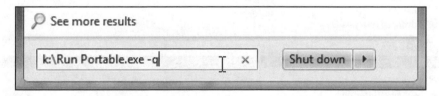

Figure 14-15   *Running Portable in quiet mode*

Either method brings up the EnCase Portable dialog, which is what the field user will be working with to perform collections. When Portable first launches, your field user will briefly see the EnCase Forensic Home screen. In a few moments, the EnCase Portable Home screen, running inside of EnCase Forensic, is displayed as a separate Portable tab, as you can see in Figure 14-16.

The job we created is listed at the top of the Available Jobs section. You can run this (or any job) by clicking on the link. Clicking on the All Jobs link expands the list of jobs you can run. Run the # Create Copy Of Drive Or Memory job by clicking on that link. You are now dropped into a status screen that will give you an indication of where in the process each job stands—this is really helpful on jobs where there are

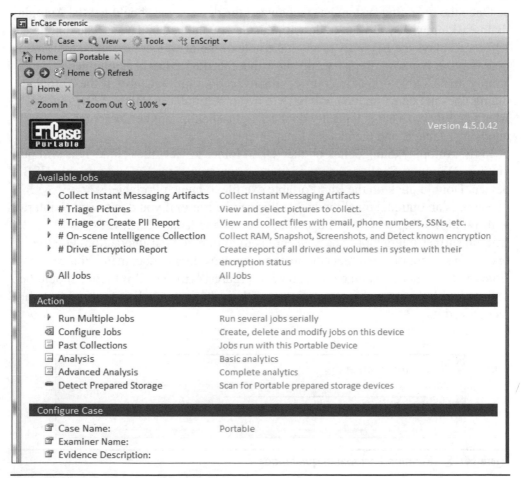

Figure 14-16   *EnCase Portable Home screen*

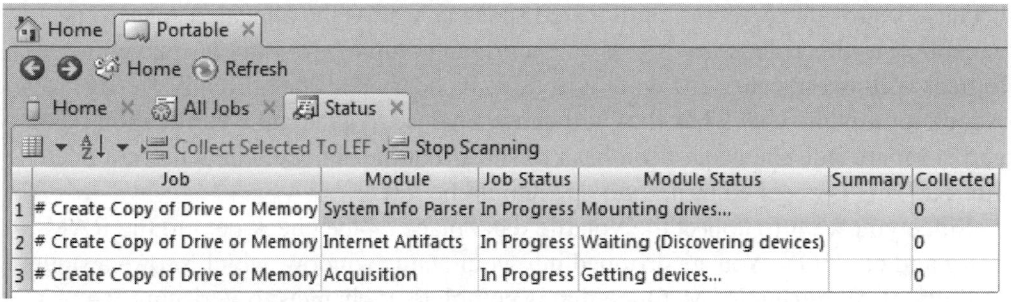
Home
Portable
Home
Refresh
Home
All Jobs
Status
Collect Selected To LEF
Stop Scanning
Job
Module
Job Status
Module Status
Summary
Collected
1 # Create Copy of Drive or Memory System Info Parser In Progress Mounting drives... 0
2 # Create Copy of Drive or Memory Internet Artifacts In Progress Waiting (Discovering devices) 0
3 # Create Copy of Drive or Memory Acquisition In Progress Getting devices... 0

Figure 14-17 *Status screen*

multiple components for EnCase to run (Figure 14-17). Our job, which can collect a drive image and/or RAM from a running machine, shows the three separate tasks the job is broken into.

The job begins with the status of initializing, where EnCase Portable scans the target computer and finds all the attached devices. Since this job covers both memory and hard drive collection, it needs to scan for potential targets. If for some reason you need to stop the job, you can click on the Stop Scanning button at the top.

When the scan completes, the Acquisition dialog is displayed with a list of targets to choose from. In this dialog, the Name column displays either the volume letter that has been assigned to that particular device (which means it is a logical device) or the numeric name (which means this is the physical device). Finally at the bottom, you see RAM, which is the memory on this target machine. Notice the logical volume of the EnCase Portable device was automatically excluded. Also note that any mounted encrypted containers may be displayed as a logical volume.

The Label column displays the name of the logical volume. If it's a physical device it may include the manufacturer or model number. In the Type column, the word "Fixed" typically means that this is installed in the computer and not removable, whereas a USB device will show up as "Detachable" because it can easily be unplugged from the system. Finally, the RAM shows up as memory device in the Type column and also gives you the size. If you use compression, the actual size required is going to be smaller than what appears here, but determining the exact size of the final collection can be tricky. You may want to ensure that you have enough storage to handle it regardless. You can insert an additional storage drive that has been prepared at this point and have EnCase recognize and be able to use it before the collection begins.

The Is Physical column gives you an indication whether this is the physical device or a logical volume. In most instances you want to image the physical device, because you want to get the unallocated space as well is the allocated space. The exception to this rule is that if it is an encrypted volume, you want to image the logical volume, because you want it to be in its decrypted state. Finally, Verify Acquisition is the check box that will cause EnCase to generate a verification hash and compare it to the acquisition hash to show that the collected data has not been altered. This is checked by default and should be left as-is.

Since you want to collect the volatile data, place a blue check next to the RAM entry and click OK. You are dropped into your status window, which shows a status initially of Acquiring RAM. Once that is complete, it changes to Verifying RAM. All of the data will be run again through the hash process and the results compared with the acquisition hash. Keep in mind that volatile data is always changing, so if you ran this collection again on the same target computer, the hash value would not be the same as your acquisition hash value. RAM collection is simply a point-in-time collection.

Finally, when your job completes, the status will read Acquired: RAM; Complete. You will note there is now a Summary Available link active under the Summary column as well. Clicking on that link takes you to the summary information for this job. You can see the evidence path, the acquisition and verification MD5 checksums, and the fact that they match.

While we are here, let's add the Summary Data to our report for later. It is a best practice to document the steps you are taking in an investigation, and I'm a big fan of doing it immediately rather than as an afterthought. To document this, blue check the RAM item and click the Add Selected To Report button at the top. This will add the item to the report, and we can move on to our next task. The Report Builder will be covered later in this chapter.

When you add this to your report, the Set Table Title dialog appears, and you can give your table entry a different title if you like. For this example, you don't need to make any changes, so just click OK.

This concludes collecting the RAM portion of collecting from a powered-on machine. You can close any open windows until you get back to the EnCase Portable interface. From there, you can choose other jobs to run or exit if this is the only task you had for this target.

Collecting from a Powered-Off Computer

When the computer is already powered off, collecting volatile data is not an option. You no longer have the constraint of only working on Windows-based computers as well—Intel-based Mac computers and Linux computers are also supported. Check with the product documentation to get the most up-to-date list of supported hardware/software.

To get started, boot the computer using EnCase Portable—either with the Portable dongle directly (if USB booting is supported) or using the Boot Disk CD provided with the product. In the laminated Quick Reference Field Guide, there is a nice table listing the interrupt key sequences required to stop the boot sequence and drop you into the BIOS where you can change the boot sequence. The system BIOS must be configured to direct the computer to boot from either the USB device or the CD boot media. You control this by interrupting the boot sequence with a specific key combination. If you don't find it on the list in the Quick Reference Field Guide, it may take some research on the part of the field user to determine the correct sequence. This is important to do ahead of time, because if a mistake is made, you could find that the field user is accidentally booting the host operating system instead of EnCase Portable. Your procedures should also cover what the field user should do if this happens, so that it is handled according to your organization's policies.

NOTE

If you do find that you must boot from the CD, you will still need to be able to insert the EnCase Portable USB device into a USB port on the target machine for license and collection purposes. Also note that if you are planning on booting from the USB device, don't plug it into a USB hub, as many systems may fail to recognize this as a bootable device.

In our example, I will be booting a Dell Inspiron laptop, which the Quick Reference Field Guide indicates uses the F12 key as the boot interrupt. So, with the EnCase Portable USB device plugged in, I power the device on and begin pressing the F12 key until it recognizes the interrupt sequence and drops me into the BIOS screen. Here I change the settings to have the system boot to the USB device, and save the changes. BIOS screens are menu driven, so pay attention to the text menus—they will typically instruct you on how to make and save changes. Incidentally, this is the type of troubleshooting that your field user may already be quite comfortable with, if they have been supporting systems for some time.

NOTE

Once you complete your collections, remember to set the BIOS back to its prior values—so be certain to make a note of what you changed. This is especially true of cases where you don't want the subject to know that the collection has been performed.

Before you exit the BIOS, since you are here anyway, it makes sense and is good practice to document the system clock settings. Once you have set the system to boot from the appropriate device, save the changes and exit. This should restart the boot—this time from the device you selected. You should see activity on the boot device (the dongle has a light, and many DVD/CD ROM drives do as well). Once the boot is complete, you will see the familiar EnCase Portable interface and can put in the case/examiner data and choose jobs to run from there. This interface displays the same regardless of the operating system on the device you are working with.

If you are collecting from a system that uses encryption, keep in mind that credentials will be required to decrypt the data. You can collect from an encrypted, powered-off machine, but unless you can obtain credentials (and the encryption used is supported by EnCase), it may not prove of much use. Refer to the product documentation to see the most up-to-date list of encryption products supported. If you are working in a corporate environment, many organizations will have credentials that can be used or the ability to provide the user's credentials. You will be prompted to provide credentials if the encryption is detected. Without valid credentials, the data cannot be collected in a decrypted state.

Once the collection is completed, you will want to verify the collection and consider encrypting the collected data prior to transport. You do this by reacquiring the data into the .EX01 format, which was covered in Chapter 3. This must be done using EnCase Forensic version 7 or higher. Keeping with best practices to refrain from working as much as possible on the target machine, this activity is best done on your forensic laptop.

The Report Builder

Once you have used the Add Selected To Report button to add data to a report, the Report Builder button becomes available. Clicking on that button gets you into the Report Builder, where you can configure the items you have added.

In the Report Builder, you select to include/exclude items you have added with the use of the blue check. Select at least one item and click the View Report button to see your report. The Set Report Name dialog appears for you to give your report a name. Name yours Volatile Data Collection Example and click OK. The data appears in a series of columns (sometimes rather jammed together columns to fit on the page depending on screen size).

Typically, these reports are exported and manipulated in another tool, such as Microsoft Word. To export your report, right-click on the report page and choose Save As from the context menu. The dialog is displayed to allow you to choose the format you want to export the data into; RTF (Rich Text Format, which is readable by most word processors) is the default. You can also choose the path where you want to save the data—and remember, if you are working on a target collection machine, you want to check that path and make sure you are saving data to your storage devices and not to the target system. Finally, you have the option to have the report open once the export is complete, but again, you want to minimize the interaction with the target machine, so that value is left unchecked by default.

Once saved, you can close out of the Report Viewer, the Report Builder, and the Acquisition Summary Information windows to get back to the EnCase Portable interface.

Typically, you won't want to do an export of the report until you have completed your jobs and added all relevant data to the report.

On-Scene Analysis

Having run your collection job(s), you can now also show the option that the field examiner has to perform on-scene analysis of the data collected. They do this by clicking on the Analyze button from the EnCase Portable interface. This brings up a dialog with the list of jobs that have been run.

You use a blue check in the Tree pane to indicate which jobs you want to run analysis against, and then click on the Analyze button. For this example, do this with the # Create Copy of Drive or Memory job that we ran earlier. The Job Summary data is provided, with both the Acquisition and Target List links. Click on the Acquisition link to show the information on the job we ran. This provides a list of machines acquired as part of this job. The name of the system is listed as a link that you can click to drill into the data. This is the way that the field user can see the contents of the collection.

Each different job will provide views into the data that are relevant to that type of collection. This is extremely useful for on-scene triage as well, so that additional actions can be taken based on the items collected and the information they provide.

After the Collection—Back at the Forensic Lab

Once you receive the EnCase Portable device and any associated storage devices after a collection, you will want to work with the data collected. To begin, plug in the devices to your forensic workstation. You can browse in Windows Explorer on the EnCase Portable device to the EnCase Portable Evidence folder where the evidence collected is stored to see what was collected. You will see the evidence files collected here (as .E01 files) plus any reports you exported if this is the directory where you chose to save them (it is the default). Finally, you will see one or more .L01 files that contain summary information about the targets collected.

If the collected evidence was also stored on the additional storage device, it will be stored under /EnCase Portable Evidence/Source Processor/*<Job Name>* with a folder for each job you ran that stored data on this device.

To start working with the data collected, you need to go into EnCase Portable Management. Again, you start EnCase Forensic and create a case, and then run the EnCase Portable Management EnScript. You will need to import the data into Portable Management to begin working with it in EnCase Forensic—it isn't just a matter of copy/pasting in Windows Explorer. Call the case Import Data and choose your paths to store the case data, clicking OK to create the case. Next, run the Portable Management EnScript as you did before (EnScript menu, choose Portable Management).

For this example, you'll be working in the Evidence tab of the Portable Management interface. You need to select the drive from the drop-down menu—if you didn't take note of the drive letter when you plugged in your Portable device, just check it in Windows Explorer. In my example, the device registered as the J:/ volume. Next, select Copy Evidence To Path at the bottom of the window. This lets you browse to where you want the evidence files imported onto your forensic workstation. By default, you are placed into the folder structure defined in the case you created. Click on the Make New Folder to create a folder for our evidence files called Evidence. It is a best practice to keep the evidence files segregated from the rest of the case files. Once the file is created, make sure it is highlighted and click OK. This brings you back into Portable Management's Evidence tab and the new path has been updated.

In the Collected Evidence Tree pane, place a Set Include (home plate) next to the top-level Evidence object. This will show all of the collected items in the Table pane. You can now see details on the collected jobs, including the names, sizes, and collection dates/times. In the Size column, note that the items below the job don't necessarily add up to the total collected listed for the job—this is because only the .E01/.L01 file is listed here, and the other .E0#/.L0# files make up the difference in the amount collected.

To import the data you want, select it with a blue check either at the job level in the Tree pane, or if you want more granularity, at the individual evidence file level in the Table pane. Note, while only the .E01/.L01 file is selected, it will copy all the associated evidence files that make up that image. For our example, blue check the job in the Tree pane.

Finally, you need to specify the Copy Options. Do you want to delete the evidence after the copy, and do you want to add the evidence to the case? The default selected is only the Add Evidence To Case box—I would be extremely wary of automatically deleting evidence collected before I was 100 percent sure that there wasn't a problem with the evidence copy. For our example, take the default and do not delete the evidence automatically. Once you have your selections complete, click on the Copy button on the top button bar to import your data.

The Importing Files From EnCase Portable Devices dialog appears and displays a progress bar. As each file is copied, it is listed in the Copy Status window. Once it completes, click Finished to return to the Portable Management window. Since you chose to add the data to the case, the evidence files will be added to your case when you click Close. You can now work with the evidence as usual in EnCase.

EnCase App Central

Guidance Software launched EnCase App Central (www.guidancesoftware.com/appcentral/Pages/default.aspx) to provide a location where people could upload the EnScripts they had developed for others to use. The developers have the option of making their work free of charge or to require licensing. If you haven't already done so, I highly recommend registering for access and at least browsing the list of available EnScripts. You may find that people have developed specific scripts that solve a problem you are experiencing or dramatically shorten the time to do common tasks.

The EnScripts from Chapter 15 will be available for download there as well, so you can see the code and bring it into EnCase without having to type it all out yourself (with the inherent fun of typos).

Summary

We've covered the major highlights of the EnCase Portable product, from installation and configuring new jobs to collecting both volatile and nonvolatile data from computers in the field. You can prepare your device for use once the current data has been wiped, and configure new devices for use with EnCase Portable. You can see how having this would help you automate collections in the field when you cannot send trained forensic personnel to the location, or even when you just want to ensure that collections are performed in a standard manner.

Finally, you can register with EnCase App Central to get access to the EnScripts that others have created to see if they can be used for your own organization's needs. In our next chapter, we will introduce EnCase's programming language—EnScript.

An EnScript Primer

The EnCase suite of products has a built-in programming language called EnScript where investigators can automate repetitive tasks. Full-blown applications can be built in EnScript. There is even a packaging facility to allow you to share your work with other users, and Guidance Software has launched their App Central Developer Network program to give programmers a market for trading and sharing EnScripts. In fact, EnScript is what their eDiscovery product is built upon, and why it requires EnCase Enterprise to run—it needs the scripting environment support from the core product.

The Basics of EnScript

For those with development experience, EnScript is similar to Java and C++ in that it is an object-oriented language. In fact, many of the constructs in EnScript work similarly to those of C++, but the language does not have all of the C++ functionality. For instance, there is no equivalent of C++ structs (data structures) in EnScript. The language also takes elements of Java that will help you if you have expertise in that language. Further, EnScript provides support for the COM and DCOM libraries from other applications, which gives it the ability to automate many of the common processing tasks associated with casework.

If this is your first experience with scripting, it can be a bit daunting—but fear not, we will break this down step by step and give you the tools to get going and expand your expertise. The subject of EnScript could fill an entire book on its own, so we will focus on just enough to get you going, and give you information on how you can learn more as your skill set grows. It should also be mentioned that EnScript is constantly evolving as a language. Each new version of the software has the potential to bring significant changes to the language as well. We have certainly seen that going just from EnCase version 6 to the current version. So while the language is evolving (and major version revisions may require you to test your scripts to verify they are still performing as planned), the potential benefits of being able to automate work within the environment remains strong enough to be worth the investment of your time and resources to learn the language.

It is important to note that this language is case sensitive, so pay close attention to your capitalization when working with EnScript. You should also know that this language is object oriented. What does that mean? It means that there is a hierarchy built into the language, with top-level classes already defined. Below them, you have classes that inherit the characteristics from those higher-level classes. We will go into this more later.

The EnScript Environment

EnCase provides a development environment for you to code, compile, and run EnScripts. From the EnScript menu, choose New Script to bring up the development environment. Alternatively, if you already have scripts you want to look at, EnScript | Edit will give you a dialog to browse to the script you want to open. You do not need to have a case open before you can create EnScripts.

When you create a new EnScript, you see that the EnCase development environment comes up (Figure 15-1), and a shell of a script is provided. This shell or template EnScript contains the lines of code shown in Figure 15-2.

Note that these words are not all the same color in the interface. The words that appear in the rectangular boxes are words that are reserved by the EnScript language to perform specific functions (and in fact they are functions as we will discuss further on) and cannot be used as names or for any other purpose in EnScript other than those

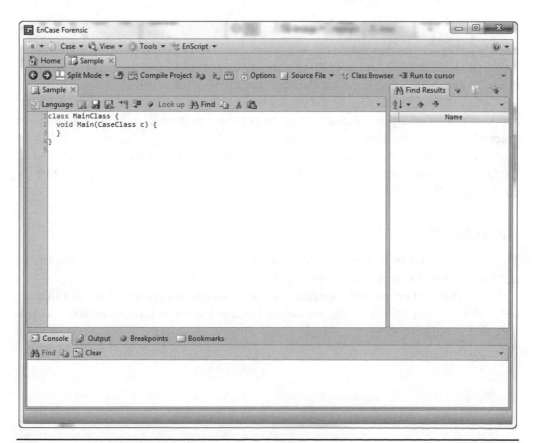

Figure 15-1 *The EnScript development environment*

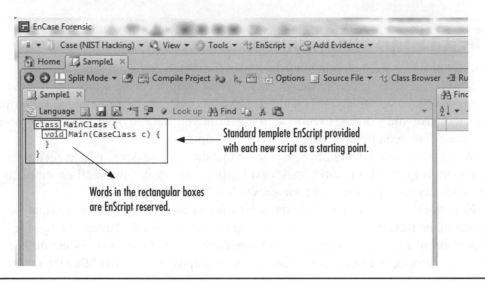

Figure 15-2   *Template EnScript*

already defined in the language. These are called reserved words, and all programming languages have them. Remember that EnScript is an object-oriented language. In order to run as a standalone script, each EnScript must have what is called a MainClass. These four lines are what get you started. I will explain them later as we start our first script. It brings up a point, though—how to get more information on the classes and other elements of the EnScript language.

EnCase has a number of resources for you to look up data about the elements of the language you are trying to use. The most useful are the EnScript Help function, the EnScript Types tab, and the Class Browser.

The EnScript Help Function

The Help function in EnScript is accessed through the menu drop-down on the far right of the session window as shown in Figure 15-3.

This will bring up the Help specifically for EnScript, as opposed to the F1 EnCase help. The window will show the version of EnCase you are running and have specific data that is only for that version in it.

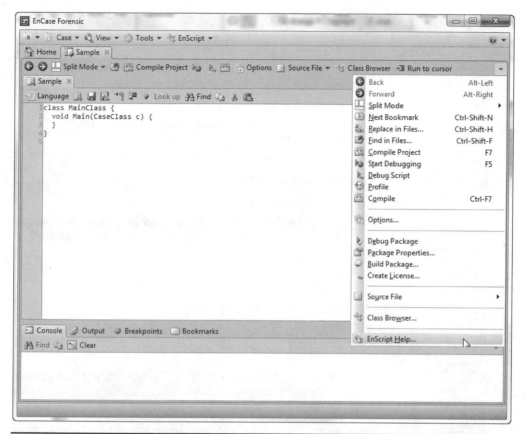

Figure 15-3 *EnScript-specific Help*

As you can see in Figure 15-4, the example I selected was the KeywordClass, and the Help file has data about the options and properties, as well as some sample code in many of the entries. Figure 15-5 shows the example code from the KeywordClass entry.

These example code sections are an excellent resource for learning how the various parts of the language work and getting sample code that shows how they are applied.

The EnScript Types Tab and the Class Browser

To get to the EnScripts Types tab, click on the Class Browser button from the button bar. This brings up the Class Browser and from there you can click on the EnScript Types tab to bring it forward. The EnScript Types tab's contents are built

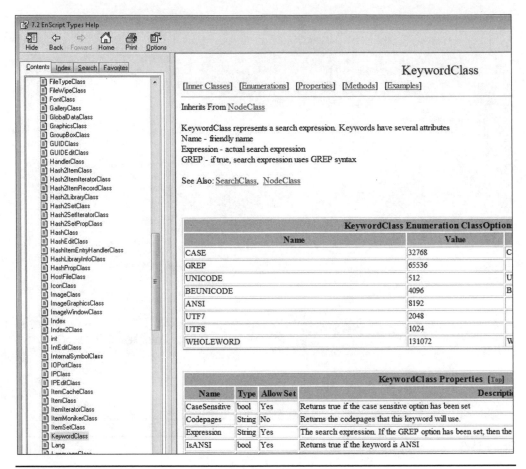

Figure 15-4   *EnScript Types Help*

dynamically for that version of the product, so that it will have the most up-to-date information on the language you are running. Thus if you have version 6 of EnCase running alongside version 7, you will see differences that were introduced in the new version reflected in this tab.

For prior users of EnCase, the view shown in Figure 15-6 should seem familiar—it looks quite a lot like the Tree/Table/View pane structure from older EnCase versions. If you click on an element in the left pane, you will see details reflected in the right pane. The same relationship holds for the right pane and the bottom pane. The Report

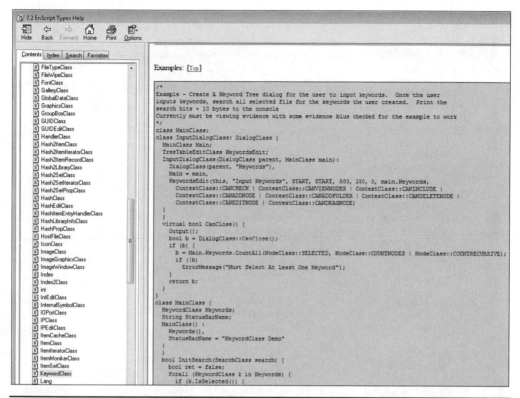

Figure 15-5 *EnScript Help example code*

tabs for both the right hand and bottom panes contain very useful information for determining how to use these elements (Figure 15-7). They also provide details on the inheritance structure of the classes.

Appendix D contains the hierarchy of the classes and is derived from the information in the EnScripts Types tab. Therefore, since this is version-dependent, you should always verify details with the current version you are working with to make sure nothing has changed.

Reading the documentation can be a bit challenging. The sections that follow provide a quick breakdown of the elements of these documents and how to interpret them.

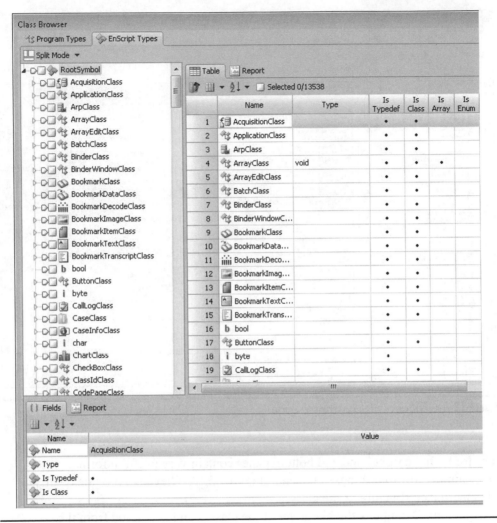

Figure 15-6 *Class Browser*

Anatomy of an EnScript

Remember when I said that EnScript is object oriented? That means that we work with objects in the language and that they have predefined properties and characteristics. The way you interact with a specific element has been defined by Guidance Software. The basic building block of this language is called a class. What is a class? You can think of a class for our purposes as a way of describing something—for example, a cell phone. What characteristics or properties would you expect a cell phone to have? How about brand and model? So for the cell phone

Figure 15-7   *Class Browser Report tabs*

class, you would define the properties like brand, model, and even potentially other objects like owners who have properties of their own.

The MainClass

The script template that is created with a new EnScript contains a class called the MainClass. This is required for the code to be recognized by the development environment as an executable EnScript. Without the MainClass statement, the script will not stand alone—it would have to be included and called from another script that had a MainClass. The class definition of the MainClass is shown here and is the first and last lines only:

```
class MainClass {
  void Main(CaseClass c) {
  }
}
```

When you tell the compiler to compile or run your EnScript, the first thing it will look for is the definition of a class with that MainClass name. It then uses the code it finds inside of those curly braces to finish constructing the script and to run it. So you can think of the MainClass section of your code as the portion that controls the running of the script. This is where you put the logic you want it to follow and call the functions you want it to perform. It is the roadmap the compiler uses to figure out what you are telling it to do.

The Main() Function

If the MainClass is the roadmap of your script, the Main() function is the step-by-step driving directions. Just having a MainClass is not sufficient for an EnScript to function. The compiler will also be looking for the Main() function. What is a function? A function is a chunk of code that performs a particular task. For example, you could have a function that looks up a zip code for a specific city in the United States and returns the zip code as a numeric value. This is the only thing this function does, and you can call it time and again when you need it. You know what it takes as an input (the city name), and you know what to expect it to return (the zip code). Functions can be as simple or complex as you make them and can take as many parameters as input as you define.

The Main() function is how you control the workings of your script—it is where you are calling the other functions that do the heavy lifting in your program. That is why I say it provides the driving directions to the MainClass—it is where you set up the logical flow of your work and it is used as the main place for controlling your EnScript.

In the template, there is another section besides just the MainClass statement. There is the Main() function that instantiates the MainClass:

```
class MainClass {
  void Main(CaseClass c) {
  }
}
```

What is this doing? Well, in the first statement, you defined the MainClass as a class. This second statement tells the compiler, "I want to use this class, so create an instance of it for me to work with." In this case, the default is to call it "c", but as CaseClass is actually referring to the case within EnCase, we could have done this:

```
class MainClass {
  void Main(CaseClass Case101) {
  }
}
```

The Main() function statement starts with the "void" reserved word. This lets the compiler know that this function won't be returning a value—we're not expecting it to give us an answer to anything. This is followed by the name of the function we're calling (Main) and, within the parentheses, the parameter we're planning to use. In this case, we're defining the CaseClass object and giving it the name Case101.

Now, it should be noted that just because we refer to this CaseClass value, it doesn't mean it will be a valid reference. We could have a different case open entirely, in which case we should be careful what we're executing against. The statement in the Main() function by default does not create a case for us. EnScripts work on the case from which you run them. This name is a placeholder.

Finally, within the function's curly braces is the place where we put all of our code. These can be thought of as the function's boundaries. Anything you create within them exists only there. If you want a variable or some other construct to exist outside of them, you must define it outside of them.

Since the template script has the bare minimum to be considered a functioning executable EnScript, it will compile and run. It will not actually do anything you can discern, however, since we have no code in the Main() function.

Our First EnScript

Now that you know how to get around and get more information about the language as you need it, let's get started on our first EnScript. For those of you who are used to learning new programming languages, you will recognize the first script is typically one that displays a line of text—most commonly "Hello World". This is so common as to be cliché.

NOTE

The sample EnScripts can be downloaded both from the McGraw-Hill Professional Computing download page (www.mhprofessional.com/templates/computing) or from EnCase App Central.

If you haven't already created a new script during the above section, then from the EnScript drop-down menu on the Home tab, choose New Enscript (Figure 15-8).

You should now be in the EnScript development environment with a dialog asking you what to name your new script. Note the default location where EnCase will store

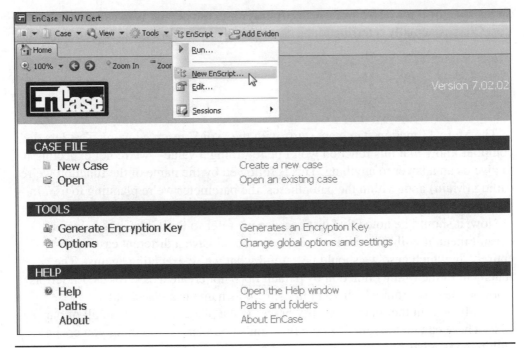

Figure 15-8   *Creating a new EnScript*

the scripts unless you change it. By default, this is under the profile of the user who launched EnCase. If this is a multiuser environment, you should designate a central location for scripts to be kept while in development, while being tested, and once they are moved into the production environment for regular use by all investigators. This will keep scripts that are still in progress or have not been completely verified from accidentally being used in casework before they are ready.

Give your script the name MyFirstEnScript and place it where you want to store your scripts going forward. EnCase will remember this location while you are in this session, but once you exit, will use the defined default until it is changed.

Commenting Your Code

Before we start programming, I want to let you know how to put comments in your code. The nature of coding is that you write something and get it working, and then time passes before you come back to it—it works, why fix it, right? The problem is that later you will go back to your code and wonder what it is doing if you didn't put the explanation in the code itself. I learned this lesson early in my development experience and now am an avid commenter. It only takes one time of going back to a complex program with a deadline to change it and realizing that you have to relearn what your mindset was at the time you wrote the original program to make you value the comments. Think of them as breadcrumbs leading you back into your code's functionality, and also consider the possibility that it won't be you doing the modification of your code. As a professional courtesy, make your code readable and sufficiently commented to allow another person to follow it.

There are two types of comments in EnScript—single-line and multiline comments. Single-line comments start with a double forward slash. Here is an example:

```
// Here is a comment
```

They are very useful, as they can be put on the same line as your code, although be careful of the placement—they should not be put in the middle of statements if the syntax does not allow it.

The second type of comment is the multiline comment. They work with a start and stop character sequence, and everything contained within them is ignored by the compiler:

```
/*  The forward slash asterisk begins the comment block
and we can continue typing text until we put in the end
comment sequence of:
*/
```

Try out both types of comments in your script. Put some blank lines after the first curly brace past the Main() function statement to give yourself some space to work in (click after the curly brace and press the ENTER key several times). Then add some comments in the blank space you created. When you enter the // or /* characters, the text turns green. This lets you know the compiler will treat them as a single comment.

Why would you want to have two different types of commenting methods? Sometimes a single line of comment will be sufficient for your purposes, but other times you want to explain more about the structure of your code and need more than the current line. Another good use is in debugging—if you have a section of code that is causing an error, it is often useful to comment the whole section, verify that is in fact the problem, and then start selectively uncommenting lines and testing. This can help narrow the problem down more quickly.

Formatting Your Code

You will see that the code samples are formatted with the text indented. This is not by default, but is done for readability. The convention I use is to indent the code for each section within the curly braces. I prefer to align the curly braces for looping constructs, which is not the default. I do this so that I can make sure at a glance that I have beginning and ending braces for each section. I find that if I line them up this way, it is easier to tell if I've missed one. This is a common coding convention, and I would recommend you adopt some type of consistent indentation that you are comfortable with. In some cases when there are multiple levels of indentation, substituting two spaces for a tab will help keep the text in line without wrapping as well.

Another feature of the development environment is that when adding structures like loops or if/else statements, it often happens that you need to change the indentation of whole blocks of code. To do this, you can select the lines you want to change and then use the TAB or SHIFT-TAB keys to indent the code right or left. This is common in development environments, and the EnCase environment indents one character per key combination used.

Displaying Text to the Console

If you don't have any more blank space, put in some more blank lines again. Now we want to add a Console.WriteLine() statement. This is a function that displays the contents we give it on the Console tab. We can put text in there inside a pair of double quotes. We can also use placeholders to pass parameters. For now, let's just give it some text. Add the following line after your comments:

```
Console.WriteLine("Hello World");
```

Remember that EnScript is case sensitive and you will need to capitalize the reserved words exactly as I show them here. The text inside the double quotes can be anything you want it to be, but the Console.WriteLine must have exactly the appearance it does here. Note the semicolon at the end of the statement. This is the statement terminator character for EnScript.

Your script should look similar to mine, as shown in Figure 15-9 (although I have added more comments and text than you may have).

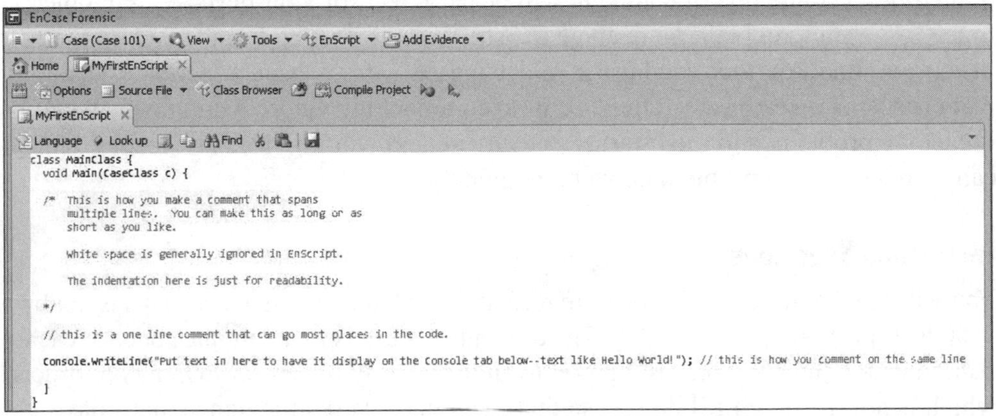

Figure 15-9 *Our script so far*

Line Numbers

When the program is compiled, the debugger will give you errors with line numbers in them. These errors won't always have the correct line numbers where the actual error is, but it is indicative of where something occurred that caused the compiler to notice there was a problem. For instance, in the template that comes up when creating a new EnScript, if we were to forget one of those curly braces, but had white space or other code in there, it would say that the error was at the very last point where it expected the curly brace, which may have not been anywhere near where it should have been in your code to function as you intended. This is a challenge in any language and is one of those things you get used to when programming.

Given that the compiler will give us errors with line numbers, it is useful to have them showing so we don't have to count down each time we get an error. To turn line numbering on, use the drop-down arrow on your session window for your script as shown in Figure 15-10 and choose Line Numbers.

Now your script should have line numbers as shown in Figure 15-11.

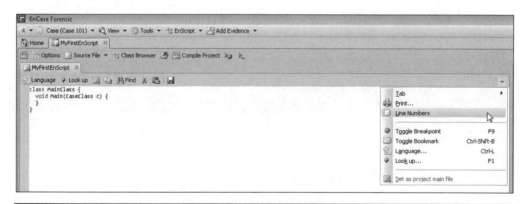

Figure 15-10   *Turning on line numbers*

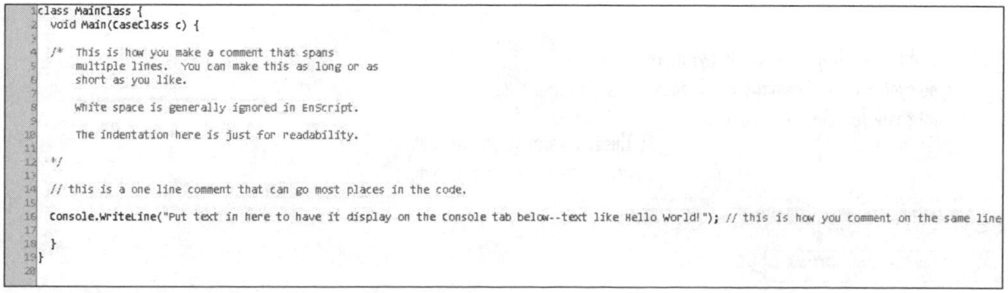

Figure 15-11   *Our EnScript with line numbers*

Compiling Our First Script

Now we are ready to compile our first script. Click the Compile button on the tab's far left, next to the Options button as shown in Figure 15-12.

You should see the Output tab on the bottom pane come forward with messages similar to those shown in the figure. If you got an error, make sure your comment blocks are properly defined and make sure you haven't accidentally deleted a curly brace or parentheses in there somewhere. If all else fails, you can start with a new script and try again, but it will help you if you can actually debug what error messages mean. For every curly brace, verify there is an opening and closing pair. For every parentheses, likewise make sure they are in open and closing pairs. When coding, I typically put this type of structure in, and then go back and fill in the contents inside the braces or parentheses. It is a good practice to do that with anything that needs to be in pairs for the syntax to work. Even with the various types of quotation marks, it is a good practice to put the whole pair in, and then go back and put the contents between them.

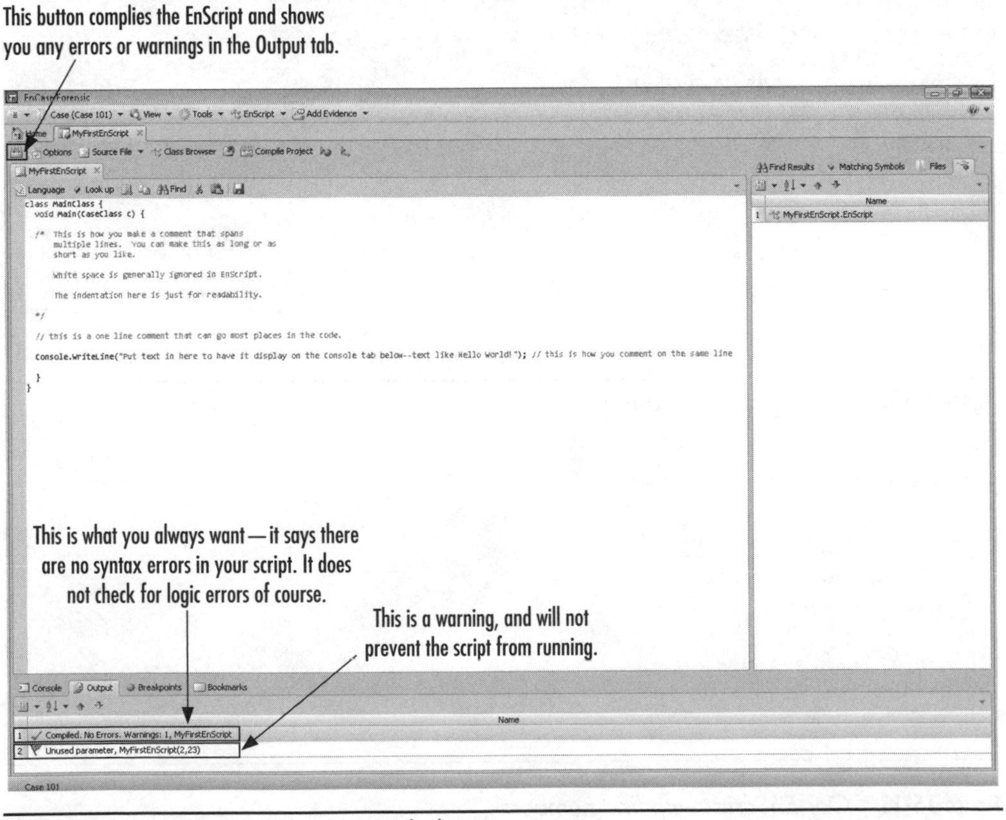
This button complies the EnScript and shows you any errors or warnings in the Output tab.
This is what you always want—it says there are no syntax errors in your script. It does not check for logic errors of course.
This is a warning, and will not prevent the script from running.
Compiled. No Errors. Warnings: 1, MyFirstEnScript
Unused parameter, MyFirstEnScript(2,23)

Figure 15-12 *MyFirstEnScript compiled*

Also verify the capitalization on all the elements of the script. For instance, if you typed Console.Writeline() instead of Console.WriteLine(), you'd get the error "Writeline is not a member of class "FileClass". Would you automatically look at this and see the capitalization error? Probably not. If you left off the ending semicolon, you would see an error "Unexpected ')'" because it is expecting the semicolon at the end of this line.

You can see that a small change will give you an error. We know the change that caused these errors. You can always experiment and see what the message is if you leave out a closing curly brace or parenthesis. You will also see how the line number given may not correspond to where you would have put the ending brace, as I mentioned earlier.

One way that comments can be useful is to comment out any lines of code that you think might be causing the error messages you are getting, and then uncommenting sections to isolate the problem slowly. This way, you can narrow down where the problem is. It is also a good way to turn off functionality in your scripts if you don't need the code at the time but don't want to lose it for future reference.

Running Our Script

Once you have your script compiling without errors (warnings can be ignored, although if you get some warning that is different from "Unused parameter, MyFirstEnscript(2,23)" you may want to investigate), you should be ready to run it. You run scripts in this environment by clicking on the button next to Compile Project that looks like a right arrow with a red dot. This is the Run button and has a keyboard shortcut of F5. You could also have used the Compile Project button, which has the keyboard shortcut of F7. You should get in the habit of compiling your script frequently as you are writing it. This will allow you to catch errors early before the changes you've made have been so significant as to make it difficult to pinpoint the error. When EnCase compiles the script, it also saves it, so you don't have to do that each time you make a change. Figure 15-13 shows what happened when I ran my script.

NOTE

We are working from within the EnScript development environment for the whole of this chapter. The process for running a script on actual case data is different. In that instance, you would be in the case itself, and choose Run from the EnScript menu to bring up the Browse dialog and choose the EnScript you want to run.

The Console tab should be presented with your text inside of it. The Clear button is useful between runs in this pane, as it will let you clear the past results of prior runs and see what the script is doing with each new run. You can also put this in your script.

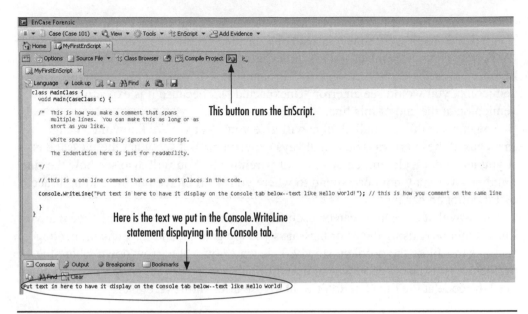

Figure 15-13 *MyFirstEnScript after running*

The Find button next to the Clear button will allow you to find specific text within the Console screen's contents. The Copy button on the far left will copy the entire contents of the Console output to the Windows clipboard so that you can include it in reports or paste it and work with it in an external application.

More About WriteLine()

Our example wrote to the Console tab—hence the reserved word Console before the WriteLine() statement. We can write to other locations with this function. In fact, anything that is a FileClass object or a type of file can be written to with this; it is very useful. First, let's look closer at that statement we used and be more specific about its components.

```
Console.WriteLine("Hello World.");
```

Console is the object we want to output our text to. The dot between Console and WriteLine() is how we tell the compiler we are talking about this object's properties or methods. So if we were talking about a cell phone's model, we would refer to it as CellPhone.Model if we'd defined the class that way.

What do I mean by object, property, and method? These are terms used in object-oriented languages. They may be new to you, so let's take a moment here and give you some definitions. Object-oriented programming languages such as EnScript refer to *objects*. These are data structures that have properties and methods. In our first EnScript, the Console is the object. A *property* is a characteristic of an object. The example above of a cell phone's model would be a property of that cell phone. A *method*, in contrast, is a function that is part of the object's class. In our example, WriteLine() is a function that can be used with the Console object to perform the task of sending the output to the screen (or Console). It is a type of FileClass object that is defined in the language and we can put to use. A *function* is simply a chunk of code that can be called by name and passed data as parameters on which to act.

Following the WriteLine, we see the pair of parentheses and the double-quoted text we want to display within. As I mentioned earlier, we can either display a group of characters (referred to as a string, which is synonymous for a variable length group of characters) or we can use placeholders in this function to display the contents of variables we have used in our program.

Finally, we have the terminating character, which lets the compiler know we're done with that line of code and it does not continue on a subsequent line.

Variables

No language would be complete without the ability to use variables. These are used to store data, control program flow, and return values as parameters. In EnScript, you must declare your variables before you use them. Variable names must not be EnScript reserved words, they cannot start with a number, and they cannot contain characters that are used as logical operators in EnScript. For example, you cannot use the ampersand (&) or pipe (|) because these have meaning within the EnScript language. EnScript also does not support pointers like C++ uses to directly access the variable's memory location.

The two main types of variables are fundamental and object. Fundamental variables are those that are natively supported in the language, while object variables are defined by a class. We will be covering only fundamental variables here.

The variable types are listed in Table 15-1, along with how many bytes each takes in memory.

In EnScript, when you declare a variable, it is given a default value. For numeric variable types, the default value is zero. The default value for the char and string variable types is the null character. The default for the bool variable type is zero. You don't

Type	Bytes	Minimum Value	Maximum Value
Numeric Types:			
byte	1	0	255
short	2	–32,768	32,768
ushort	2	0	65,535
int	4	–2,147,483,648	2,147,483,647
uint	4	0	4,294,967,295
long	8	–9,223,372,032,559,808,513	9,223,372,032,559,808,512
ulong	8	0	18,446,744,065,119,617,025
double	8	1.7E – 308	1.7E + 308
Non-numeric Types:			
char	2	Stored in Unicode	
String	(# *characters*)*2 (# *chars*)*2 + 2	Stored as array of char	
bool	1		

Table 15-1   *EnScript Variable Types*

need to set the value unless you need it to be different from the default; it won't get random contents of memory like you would in C++. Conversion between different variable types is handled automatically by the compiler in EnScript. If you provided a string variable a numeric value in passing it to a function, the compiler would handle the conversion before it got to the function for processing.

The numeric variables are fairly self-explanatory, and you would choose to use one or another of them based on how large a value you need to store. You should keep in mind any operations you plan to perform on these variables and the potential size of their results when making your selection. You can probably envision a case where multiplying two int values will give you a result that needs to be stored in a long variable type. The char, or character variable, type stores each character in Unicode, so it consumes two bytes of memory. EnCase stores all character-based data in Unicode. The string variable type is an array of char variable types with an extra null as a terminator. This means that if you store a five-character string, it will occupy (5*2) + 2 = 12 bytes of memory, since each char takes two bytes, plus the null terminator which is also of type char, so it also takes two bytes.

For string variables, you can join or concatenate two strings using the + or += operators. There is memory overhead involved that will slow down your scripts, so it isn't recommended to use it on a regular basis, but for those operations that need this, it is an option.

Boolean, or bool, variable types are assigned a value of false or true. This is stored as 0 for false and 1 for true. However, it should be noted that if you are converting a numeric value to a Boolean value, 0 will convert as false, and any other value will convert as true—even negative values.

Variables and Their Scope

Variables only exist within the code block where they are declared. So if you declare a variable within the Main() function, it has a larger scope than if you declare it within a specific function. Code blocks are bound by curly braces. You can think of them as fences for variable scope. Since the Main() function is the area where the "driving directions" are given to the program—the main program logic—variables declared here will function until the end of the program is reached. If you declare a function, it has its own set of curly braces that define the start and end of that function. Variables that are declared within this set of "fences" will only have an existence during the execution of that code. This also means that you cannot refer to a variable that exists only in one small function anywhere outside of that function, because it doesn't exist outside of that function.

It should be noted that while the variable's scope is limited, the value can be passed from the discrete functions via the function's return statement after it has been called.

Operators

You assign values to variables and perform other activities using operators. They are listed in Table 15-2.

There is an order of precedence in combining these operators. The use of parenthesis to ensure that you're getting the assignment or value you want is recommended. This is particularly true of the mathematical operators.

In addition to operators, you may encounter the need to put in some escape sequences that represent special characters in your scripts. For instance, when formatting output in the console, you may want to separate blocks of text with new lines. Table 15-3 shows a listing of escape sequences and how they are represented in your code.

The new line and tab characters are used frequently to control how a script's output displays. The \ character is used to protect the character following it from being interpreted by the compiler. For instance, if you want to have the character double-quote display and not have the compiler interpret it as the beginning or ending of a text block, you would need to use the \ character to protect or "escape" it.

Operator	Use
Mathematical Operators:	
+	Addition
-	Subtraction
*	Multiplication
/	Division
%	Remainder or modulus
Relational Operators:	
<	Less than
>	Greater than
<=	Less than or equal to
>=	Greater than or equal to
==	Equal to
!=	Not equal to
Logical Operators:	
&&	Logical AND
||	Logical OR
Bitwise Operators:	
>>	Shift bits right
<<	Shift bits left
&	Bitwise AND
^	Bitwise exclusive OR
|	Bitwise inclusive OR
Increment/Decrement Operators:	
++	Increment; can be before or after variable
--	Decrement, can be before or after variable

Table 15-2 *EnScript Operators*

Escape Sequence	Represents
\n	New line
\t	Tab
\	Escape character, used to keep the compiler from interpreting the next character

Table 15-3 *EnScript Escape Sequences*

\" would give you the literal " in your display. Consider the following WriteLine() statement:

```
Console.WriteLine("You would need to use the \\ character to protect
or \n\"escape\" it.");
```

This illustrates how to escape or protect these characters if you want them to appear literally in your code and not be interpreted by the compiler. It also shows how to use the new line character. Note there does not have to be any space between the new line character and the next character—even if it is another escaped sequence.

Now that we know how to define variables, let's add some to our script. Add the code shown in Figure 15-14 to your script.

The first line (line 16 in my example) defines an integer variable called counter. Line 17 defines an integer named ScoopsDesired and sets it equal to 5. The Console. WriteLine() statement is a bit different from what you have seen before. This is an example of using a placeholder. The {0} is a positional placeholder for a variable you name after the end of the text portion. You separate the portions inside the parenthesis of the WriteLine() statement using commas. So the {0} is replaced with the value of the ScoopsDesired variable at the time this code runs. You will see later how valuable this is when you are using looping constructs to control your code. Line 21 shows how to increment the value of the ScoopsDesired variable. In this I am incrementing as a prefix to the variable. You could also use ScoopsDesired++ to have the increment afterwards. This style of incrementing can be tricky in other

```
Language  ✔ Look up  ☐  ⬚  🔍 Find  ✂  📋  💾
 1 class MainClass {
 2   void Main(CaseClass c) {
 3
 4   /* This is how you make a comment that spans
 5      multiple lines.  You can make this as long or as
 6      short as you like.
 7
 8      White space is generally ignored in EnScript.
 9
10      This indentation here is just for readability.
11
12   */
13
14   // This is a one line comment that can go most places in the code.
15
16   int counter;
17   int ScoopsDesired = 5;
18
19   Console.WriteLine("I want {0} scoops of ice cream!", ScoopsDesired);
20
21   ++ScoopsDesired;
22
23   Console.WriteLine("I want {0} scoops of ice cream!", ScoopsDesired);
24   }
25 }
26
```

Figure 15-14 *Variables code example*

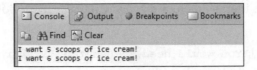

Figure 15-15   *Variables output*

contexts, but for our purposes in this script it makes no significant difference in the running of the script. Also, you could have just as easily used `ScoopsDesired = ScoopsDesired + 1;` in place of the code on line 21.

Compile and run your script. You should get some warnings, which you can ignore at this point, and you should see the code shown in Figure 15-15 as your output.

I commented out our original ConsoleWriteLine() statement with the "Hello World" sample text for readability so it isn't showing in my output.

Looping Constructs—Controlling the Flow of an EnScript

Looping constructs are logic operators that control the program flow in a language. EnScript has the common flow control statements you'd expect such as the `if`, `else if`, and `else` statements, the for loop, and the `while` and `do while` statements. There is a `switch`, `case`, `default` statement to let you choose among known and unknown choices, and `foreach`, `forall`, and `forroot` to allow parsing of certain list types. It also has `break` and `continue` for when those are needed. Finally, EnScript has an operator that acts like an if statement called the ternary operator.

The If, Else If, and Else Statements

These statements are common to most modern languages, and without them we'd be hard pressed to solve a majority of programming problems. Here is the basic syntax:

```
if(This > That)
{
  Console.WriteLine("This is greater than That.");
}
else if (This == That)
{
  Console.WriteLine("This and That are equal.");
}
```

```
else
{
    Console.WriteLine("That is greater than This.");
}
```

The beginning curly brace can be written after the closing parenthesis if you like, but I like to keep them lined up to make it easier to spot errors. Be extra careful inside of the () when using equal signs. If you use a single equal sign, you are not checking for equivalence—you are assigning a value to a variable. This is a logic error that is easy to make and can be maddening to diagnose. Note the `else if` statement where I use two equal signs. That is how you check for equivalence between two variables. Now obviously I don't have the declarations of the two variables I'm comparing in the syntax example, but you can see how this would be used.

Let's modify our script to use an `if` statement to check if the counter is equal to the number of ice cream scoops we want. Figure 15-16 shows the code for your script.

You can see I left the variable declarations alone on lines 16 and 17. I added the `if` statement on line 21, with the opening curly brace on line 22 and the closing curly

```
 1 class MainClass {
 2   void Main(CaseClass c) {
 3
 4     /* This is how you make a comment that spans
 5        multiple lines. You can make this as long or as
 6        short as you like.
 7
 8        White space is generally ignored in EnScript.
 9
10        The indentation here is just for readability.
11
12     */
13
14     // this is a one line comment that can go most places in the code.
15
16     int counter;
17     int ScoopsDesired = 5;
18
19
20
21     if (counter == ScoopsDesired)
22     {
23
24       // do nothing
25
26     }
27
28     else
29
30     {
31
32       Console.WriteLine("I want {0} scoops of ice cream, but I only have {1}!", ScoopsDesired, counter);
33
34     }
35
36     // Console.WriteLine("Put text in here to have it display on the Console tab below--text like Hello World!"); // this is
37
38
39     }
40 }
41
```

Figure 15-16   *if statement code*

brace on line 26. I have also added an `else` statement, which has its own curly braces at lines 30 and 34.

Between the parentheses of the if statement I check to see if the value of counter is equal to the value of ScoopsDesired. Notice the double equal—we want to make sure to avoid assigning the value of ScoopsDesired into counter, as we discussed before. A single equal sign here would accomplish that, so we must be sure to use double equal signs.

I have not defined any actions to take if the counter value is equal to the ScoopsDesired value, so I put a comment in there for readability. The `else` statement will fire when these two variables do not equal—which they will not since we are not incrementing the counter at any point.

Did you notice the use of two positional placeholders in the Console.WriteLine() statement? This shows you how to use one statement to display multiple variable values.

Compile and run your script. You should get output similar to mine, shown in Figure 15-17.

Since the condition resolved as not equal, the `else` clause was executed and we have our output to the console showing the value of both the ScoopsDesired and the counter variables.

The For Statement

Let's change our example to allow for using a counter inside a new looping construct—the `for` loop. The `for` loop is very common, and using a counter to control it is the usual approach people use. Here is the anatomy of a `for` loop:

```
for (statement1; condition; statement2)
{
        Code to execute until condition is met;
}
```

Statement1 is usually the declaration of the counter variable. The condition is what you want to have met to break out of the loop. Finally, statement2 is used to increment or decrement the counter.

Figure 15-18 shows more code to add to your script. Notice the indentation I am using to keep the script readable.

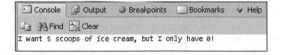

Figure 15-17   *Output from the* `if` *statement*

```
1 class MainClass {
2   void Main(CaseClass c) {
3
4   /* This is how you make a comment that spans
5      multiple lines. You can make this as long or as
6      short as you like.
7
8      White space is generally ignored in EnScript.
9
10     The indentation here is just for readability.
11
12  */
13
14  // this is a one line comment that can go most places in the code.
15
16
17  int ScoopsDesired = 5;
18
19
20  for (int counter = 1; counter <= ScoopsDesired; ++counter) //Initialize the counter, compare to see if we have enough scoops, increment counter
21  {
22    if (counter == ScoopsDesired)
23    {
24
25      Console.WriteLine("I wanted {0} scoops of ice cream, and I have {1}.  Time to eat!", ScoopsDesired, counter);
26
27    }
28
29    else
30    {
31
32      Console.WriteLine("I want {0} scoops of ice cream, but I only have {1}!", ScoopsDesired, counter);
33
34    }
35
36  }
37
38  // Console.WriteLine("Put text in here to have it display on the Console tab below--text like Hello World!"); // this is how you comment on the same line
39
40
41  }
42
43 }
44
```

Figure 15-18 *Ice cream scoops* `for` *loop*

I moved our counter declaration into the `for` loop as statement1 and gave it a value different from the default value of zero it would otherwise have. I then compared the value of counter against the value of ScoopsDesired so that we'd break out of this logic loop when they were equal. Finally, I increment the counter. The counter is initialized the first time this `for` loop is executed, but that statement is never executed again in this loop. Instead, it bounces between checking the condition (and executing the code in the curly braces) and incrementing the counter. Once the condition is met, it breaks out of the for loop and continues down the Main() function.

Once you've made your changes to your script, compile and run it. Figure 15-19 shows the output from the above code.

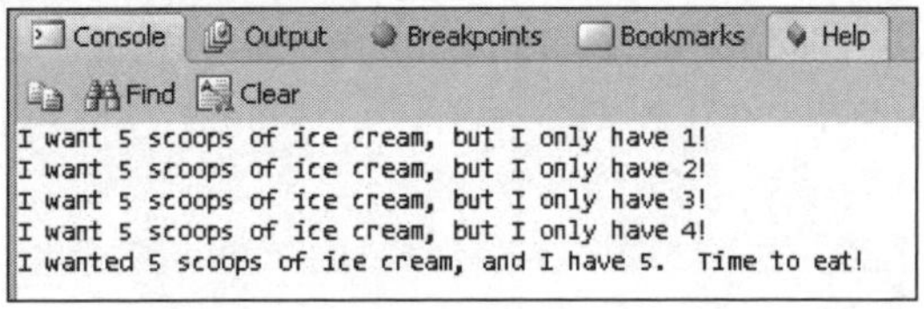

```
Console   Output   Breakpoints   Bookmarks   Help
Find   Clear
I want 5 scoops of ice cream, but I only have 1!
I want 5 scoops of ice cream, but I only have 2!
I want 5 scoops of ice cream, but I only have 3!
I want 5 scoops of ice cream, but I only have 4!
I wanted 5 scoops of ice cream, and I have 5.  Time to eat!
```

Figure 15-19 *Ice cream scoops* `for` *loop output*

Before we go any further into other looping constructs, I want to mention something else about the console tab. I have been clicking on the Clear button prior to each run so that you only see the output from one run of the script. It is cleaner that way, but wouldn't it be better to just have a line in our code that does this for us at the start? I also want to delete some of the comments I had in there so we don't run out of screen real estate so quickly. The code we need to clear the console is this:

```
SystemClass::ClearConsole();
```

In this statement, we call the function from the SystemClass called ClearConsole(). This means that we're calling the function that belongs to the SystemClass class template. We'll discuss this topic more later when we get further into classes, but it is such a useful line of code, we can include it now. I've added it up at the top of my script before the variables are declared. You'll see it in subsequent code examples as well.

The While and Do While Statements

The while statement is another way to create a logical loop. It functions in a more simple form than the for loop, in that we will have to declare our variable outside of the statement and the while loop uses just a simple condition check to function. Here is the basic syntax of a while statement:

```
while(condition)
{
    Code to execute;
}
```

We can rewrite the same code as a while loop to show how that works. Don't forget to include a statement at the outside of the if statement that increments the counter, or you'll be stuck in an infinite loop.

Your code should look something like Figure 15-20—also note I've added the ClearConsole() function on line 4. Compile your script and run it once all errors are cleared. Figure 15-21 shows the output from my script—which looks exactly like the output from the for loop we coded before.

We also have the option of using a do while loop, which is similar to the while loop, except that it will execute the code inside the curly braces at least once. The syntax for a do while loop is:

```
do
{
    Code to execute;
}
while (condition);
```

```
1 class MainClass {
2     void Main(CaseClass c) {
3
4     SystemClass::ClearConsole(); //good practice at start of all scripts
5
6     int  counter = 1;
7     int  ScoopsDesired = 5;
8
9
10    while (counter <= ScoopsDesired) //compare to see if we have enough scoops
11    {
12        if (counter == ScoopsDesired)
13        {
14
15            Console.WriteLine("I wanted {0} scoops of ice cream, and I have {1}.  Time to eat!", ScoopsDesired, counter);
16
17        }
18
19        else
20
21        {
22
23            Console.WriteLine("I want {0} scoops of ice cream, but I only have {1}!", ScoopsDesired, counter);
24
25        }
26
27        ++counter;
28    }
29
30    // Console.WriteLine("Put text in here to have it display on the Console tab below--text like Hello World!"); // this is how you
31
32
33    }
34 }
35
```

Figure 15-20   *Ice cream scoops* while *loop*

The reason it must execute at least once is that it doesn't check for the condition match until the end of the loop. This means that even if the condition is false, it will have gone through the code in the curly braces the first time.

The Break and Continue Statements

As with other languages, the break statement will allow you to force an exit from a logical loop. The continue statement will stop this iteration of the loop that is executing and continue on with the next. These are frequently used as boundary statements where minimum and maximum values are enforced, but there are other uses.

```
[>] Console   [⊞] Output   [◡] Breakpoints   [□] Bookmarks   [◡] Help
[⬚] [🔍] Find [🔲] Clear
I want 5 scoops of ice cream, but I only have 1!
I want 5 scoops of ice cream, but I only have 2!
I want 5 scoops of ice cream, but I only have 3!
I want 5 scoops of ice cream, but I only have 4!
I wanted 5 scoops of ice cream, and I have 5.  Time to eat!
```

Figure 15-21   *Ice cream scoops* while *loop output*

Here is the syntax inside of an if statement:

```
if (true)
{
    continue;
/* This is met, so it stops this loop's execution and moves back up to
   the if statement to test the condition again.*/
}
else
{
    break;   //this breaks us out of the loop entirely.
}
```

For this example, I set the condition to true, which effectively makes it a constant. You would see a warning if you compiled it this way of "Condition is constant". EnScript's compiler is letting you know that you are testing a condition that by definition won't change.

CAUTION

This would result in an infinite loop given the `continue` *statement here, so be sure not to use this code as-is.*

Using a constant in a logic statement is a trick for debugging when you need to eliminate the condition as the source of the problem.

The Switch, Case, Default Statement

Many programming languages have a case statement that lets you define specific conditions you want to test for, and a default value that catches anything that doesn't fit in the cases you've defined. In EnScript this statement is called the `switch`, `case`, `default` statement. Here is the syntax:

```
switch (condition)
{
    case "result1":
        code to execute;
    break;
    case "result2":
        code to execute;
    break;
    default:   //doesn't match either of the above results
        code to execute;
}
```

A good example use for this type of statement is if you are looking for specific compound file types like .zip or .pst, and you want to only grab those. You could set up the `switch`, `case`, `default` statement to test the file extension (or signature if you prefer) and have only those that match defined. The default code would merely discard the files that aren't of interest and move on.

Note the `break` keyword in each defined case block. This keyword lets the compiler know this is the end of the code block for this specific case definition. The advantage of this type of logic construct is that it is faster than an `if` statement that does the same thing would be. The drawback is that you can only compare against a list of defined cases.

The Foreach, Forall and Forroot Statements

These are used most frequently to address arrays, such as a string array of chars. The syntax is:

```
String Path = "c:\\Data\\Myfiles";
foreach (char element in Path)
{
        Console.WriteLine("{0}", element);
}
```

The above is creating a char variable called element and using it to walk through our Path array of characters. I have used the \ to escape the back slashes in the path so they will print. It prints one character per line. Note that String has an initial cap—it is the exception to the reserved words for variable types. If you tried to use a lowercase first letter on this, you would get an error saying "string is an unknown identifier". Figure 15-22 shows the output from running the script. Note how it puts each character on a separate line.

The Ternary Operator

The ternary operator acts like a looping construct, although it is defined as an operator. Specifically, it acts like an `if` statement and is referred to sometimes as an "inline `if` statement." It consists of three parts: a statement and two values. Here is an example:

```
bool HasIceCream;
Console.WriteLine(HasIceCream ? 1 : 0);
```

What will the above display on the console? Well, if you recall, when a bool variable is declared, it has a default value of zero or false. So this will display a zero in the Console tab.

Figure 15-22 *Foreach example output*

The Debugger

By now you have potentially run into some errors and needed to troubleshoot your code. EnScript does have a debugger, and certain types of errors will automatically drop you into it. It should be noted that, technically, every time we run our script within this development environment, we are actually running it in debug mode. However, unless there is an issue, it won't drop us into where we are forced to start stepping manually through the code.

Functions

As we've discussed before, functions are blocks of code that do a specific job. There are built-in functions to EnScript, and you can also create your own functions. In fact, you can create a library of functions and call them from your scripts.

Why write functions instead of keeping all your code in the Main()? Well, part of it is that breaking jobs into small manageable chunks makes it easier to deal with, like most problems. Another benefit it that if you have small jobs that need to be done in multiple scenarios, you only have to write the code once, and then you can call it again and again. Also, if you did put the same code in multiple places and needed to make a change, you'd have to change the code in each place you had it rather than just once in your function. Finally, if you have multiple people on your team who are interested in learning EnScript—or who are already proficient in the language—you can delegate coding a specific function to them to complete and then just call their function in your EnScript. It doesn't even have to be in the same script file—you can include other files and then call them from within your script.

Create a new EnScript and enter the code shown in Figure 15-23. This will give you a start on handling functions. Now let's walk through the code. You can see the Main() function between lines 2 and 13. Once past that ending curly brace, you see the ComputeFactorial function. What we're doing here is declaring a function definition for a new function within MainClass::Main(). Our function does one basic job and returns an integer value when it is done.

```
int ComputeFactorial (int FactNum)
```

To break down what this initial line of code is doing, we can go word by word. The first word int indicates that the function will return an integer value back to the calling function. The second word `ComputeFactorial` is the name of the

```
1  class MainClass {
2    void Main(CaseClass c) {
3
4      SystemClass::ClearConsole(); //good practice at start of all scripts
5
6      int ReturnVal,
7          FactNumber = 8;
8
9      ReturnVal = ComputeFactorial(FactNumber);
10     Console.WriteLine("The factorial of {0} is: {1}", FactNumber, ReturnVal);
11
12
13   }
14
15     int ComputeFactorial (int FactNum)
16     {
17
18     int FactVal = 1;
19
20       for (int counter = 1; counter <= FactNum; ++counter)
21       {
22
23           FactVal = FactVal * counter;
24
25
26       }
27
28     return FactVal;
29
30     }
31
32
33
34
35
36 }
37
```

Figure 15-23 *ComputeFactorial function*

function we are defining. Every function must have its open and closed parentheses, and inside of them is what we are expecting to have passed to us as a parameter. In our case, we're expecting to have an integer passed to us, and it should be the number for which we want the factorial computed. I set this in the Main() function in a variable, but we could also have asked the user for this value.

Between lines 16 and 30 are the boundaries for this function. Remember, the braces are effectively the fences of a function or looping construct. The code on line 18 declares an integer variable and initializes it to 1. Then we have our for loop between lines 20 and 26. In that, we do the actual work of computing the factorial of the given number. Once we break out of the loop when counter becomes equal to FacNum, we return our computed value in the variable FactVal.

That takes care of our function. Going back to the Main() function, I first clear the console. You can see that I then define ReturnVal and then set it equal to the return value that our function will return on line 9. This assignment calls the function to compute the return value. I then write out the text that lets us check what the return value was set to. Figure 15-24 shows the output of this script.

If you have a function that is not going to return a value, the int should be changed to void. For example:

```
void ComputeFactorial (int FactNum)
```

The return line from our function on line 28 would no longer be valid since we are not returning anything according to our definition. If you left it in the script after changing the first line of the function, you'd get an error "Cannot convert void to int". I mentioned before that conversions of variables from one type to another are automatically handled by the compiler—this is an example of that behavior being unsuccessful.

This function is also one where you should be thinking of whether the int type is a good fit for the return value you may want to provide. Factorial values can get very large very quickly—perhaps another numeric type would be better.

Your function can return only one value, but it can accept multiple parameters as arguments when called. They should be a comma-separated list between the parentheses on the definition line of the function. Your function can, however, write multiple variables' contents into global variables if you have them defined. This is a way to get around the one return value rule in functions.

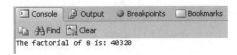

Figure 15-24   *ComputeFactorial function output*

Passing by Reference or Value

Most languages allow you to pass a variable by either reference or value, and EnScript is no exception. Passing by value is what we have been doing up to now—the compiler will make a copy of the variable's value in memory and use that to perform the calculations requested. So passing by value is like being in Vegas—what happens in the function stays in the function. The changes to the variable's value will occur on the copy, and do not affect the actual value of the variable of the same name outside of the function while it executes. To change this behavior, we can pass the variable by reference—meaning that we are actually passing the variable itself and not a copy of it when we call a function. We do this by putting an ampersand (&) in front of the name to tell the compiler that we want to pass by reference.

Here is a quick example; note the ampersand in the function statement:

```
int HowManyRecords;

Console.WriteLine("I have {0} records",HowManyRecords, CountMyRecords
(HowManyRecords));  //calling the function, with the variable

int CountMyRecords(int &counter)  //telling EnScript to pass by
reference not value
{
     Code to execute;
}
```

Classes

One of the common features most object-oriented languages share is the concept of classes. Certainly this is true for C++ and Java, where much of EnScript gets its programming parentage. Do you absolutely have to know how to write classes to program in EnScript? No, but it is much more useful if you at least have an understanding of how they work. Everything you create in EnScript is created inside a class—whether it is the MainClass() or some other class, you are using them when you program in this language. Certainly, if you are going to be processing records in cases, you'll need to know how to use classes to manipulate your case data.

What Is a Class?

A class is basically the blueprint or specification that you use to instantiate (create a specific instance of) individual objects. Classes include variables, sometimes referred to as attributes (or properties), and methods, which are defined as functions within the class. Just like an architect would use a blueprint to describe how to build a 50-story skyscraper, we use classes to describe the properties and methods of the objects we create.

Let's use an example of an aircraft class. While there have been many different types of airplanes built since they were first invented, we want to create a very specific type of aircraft with the attributes that we define and the capabilities that we need. The individual plane is called an instance of the AircraftClass(). You can have multiple instances of the same class with different properties assigned to them, such as size of engines, wingspan, passenger capacity, manufacturer, and so on. Their capabilities such as how fast or far they can fly are represented as methods. By defining these common properties and methods into a class, you can keep them grouped together instead of having to keep track of numerous variables and values.

The Aircraft Class

To get started creating our first class, we need to create a new EnScript. We can then put the class definition for our AircraftClass() class above the MainClass() code as shown in Figure 15-25. Generally, like a variable, before you can use a class, you must declare it. This means that before you can use a class in the MainClass() code, you need to declare it above, which is why we're putting this code above the MainClass(). Remember, we need the MainClass() to control the overall flow of the program.

Once we've declared it, we will want to start defining the associated properties. Figure 15-26 shows an example of some of the attributes we might want to store

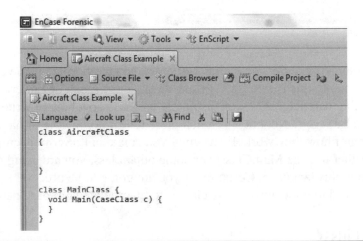

Figure 15-25 *AircraftClass example (new EnScript)*

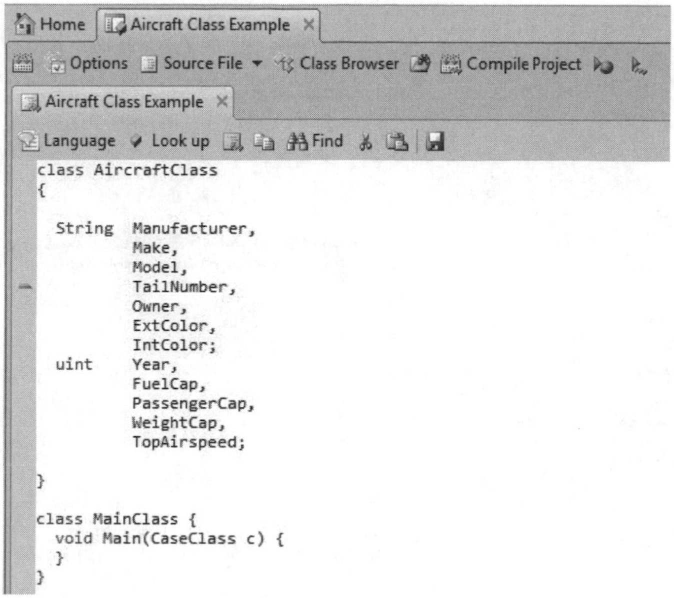

Figure 15-26 *AircraftClass example properties*

about our individual aircrafts. This is similar to building a database table—you have to define the fields that you will track and what data type they will have before you can start putting information into them.

The Constructor

Once you define a class, you must use a special function called the constructor to instantiate it (call it into existence with memory allocated to it). You will see constructors in predefined classes as you use them in EnScript. If you select the class name in the EnScript development window and press the F1 key, you will see some helpful information in the Matching Symbols tab as shown in Figure 15-27.

Not every class requires a constructor function, but the quick way to tell if a predefined class does require it is in this Matching Symbols tab. If you see an entry prefaced with the C, that means that the constructor must be used. In the example shown in Figure 15-27, you can see that EntryFileClass, which I highlighted and pressed F1 to bring up the context information, has a constructor, so it must be used with one. Later, we will see where a constructor is not required, so you will see the difference.

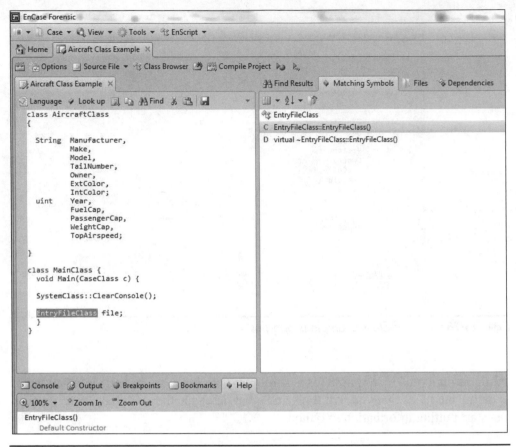

Figure 15-27 *Constructor help example*

Looking at the same data for the SystemClass (Figure 15-28), you can see there is no constructor listed, so you can just call its methods as we do with the ClearConsole() function.

Constructors can also be used to accept parameters, depending on how you have set up the class. If you didn't define a constructor, the EnScript compiler will use the default constructor, which doesn't take any parameters. This is something you should definitely keep in mind when creating your class definitions.

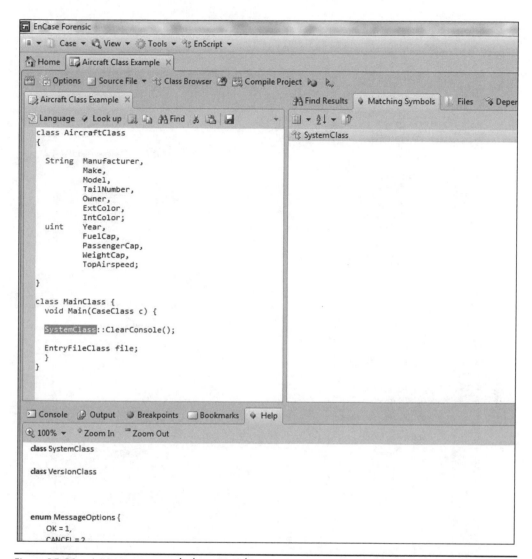

Figure 15-28 *No constructor help example*

Figure 15-29 shows an example with our AircraftClass() on how to instantiate the object and assign and display the values.

As you can see, I've assigned values to several of our properties, and included a WriteLine() to display who owns this particular instance of the object. You can also just set the properties to values when you instantiate the object by passing

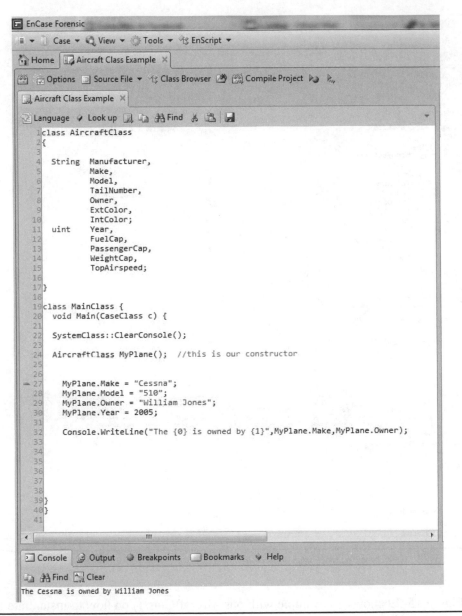

Figure 15-29 *MyPlane instantiated*

parameters in the constructor. This is a bit more complex, so let's break it down into sections. First we need to make some changes to the constructor (Figure 15-30).

We pass in the parameters we want this constructor to accept, naming them similar to but not quite the same as our defined properties in the class statement above. I do

```
 1  class AircraftClass
 2  {
 3
 4    String Manufacturer,
 5           Make,
 6           Model,
 7           TailNumber,
 8           Owner,
 9           ExtColor,
10           IntColor;
11
12
13    uint Year,
14         WingSpan,
15         PassengerCap,
16         WeightCap,
17         TopAirSpeed;
18
19
20    AircraftClass(const String &manufacturer,
21                  const String &make,
22                  const String &model,
23                  const String &tailnum,
24                  const String &owner,
25                  const String &extcolor,
26                  const String &intcolor,
27                  uint year,
28                  uint wingspan,
29                  uint passcap,
30                  uint weightcap,
31                  uint topairspeed)   //our constructor
32    {
```

Figure 15-30   *AircraftClass constructor changes*

this primarily for readability so that when I come back to this script after a period of time, I don't have to work so hard to puzzle out what I'm passing or assigning and where. Next we need to assign the values of the parameters in the constructor to the global properties in the class (Figure 15-31). This is still part of our constructor, and it goes inside the constructor's curly braces. Note the ampersand (&) in front of the const Strings. This is an indication that I am passing these parameters by reference, not by value, as discussed previously.

Finally, we can instantiate the AircraftClass() with the values we choose as shown in Figure 15-32. You can see that we're assigning the values as positional parameters to the variables in the constructor. By this I mean that the first value will go in the first field in the constructor, and the rest of them will follow the same order.

To verify that the parameters are correctly populating, I used a series of WriteLine() statements to display the values. Figure 15-33 shows the results.

Using all these WriteLine() statements is functional, but not very elegant. This is particularly true if we had multiple instances of AircraftClass() that we were trying to work with. Instead, we can create a method to handle this type of display of data.

```
18
19
20   AircraftClass(const String &manufacturer,
21                 const String &make,
22                 const String &model,
23                 const String &tailnum,
24                 const String &owner,
25                 const String &extcolor,
26                 const String &intcolor,
27                 uint year,
28                 uint wingspan,
29                 uint passcap,
30                 uint weightcap,
31                 uint topairspeed)  //our constructor
32   {
33
34   // assign the values from the constructor to the global values of the class
35
36   Manufacturer = manufacturer;
37   Make = make;
38   Model = model;
39   TailNumber = tailnum;
40   Owner = owner;
41   ExtColor = extcolor;
42   IntColor = intcolor;
43   Year = year;
44   WingSpan = wingspan;
45   PassengerCap = passcap;
46   WeightCap = weightcap;
47   TopAirSpeed = topairspeed;
48
49   }
50
51
52 } // end of AircraftClass section
53
```

Figure 15-31   *AircraftClass assigning values*

We need to define a new method just after our constructor, called GetValue(). This will use the built-in string handling function String::Format to put our WriteLine() statement together and return it in the returnValue variable (Figure 15-34).

```
52 } // end of AircraftClass section
53
54
55 class MainClass {
56   void Main(CaseClass c) {
57
58   SystemClass::ClearConsole();
59
60   AircraftClass MyPlane("Bombardier Aerospace","Learjet","60XR","423D-5","Jane Smith","Blue","Grey",2005,59,10,23500,522);
61
62   // Verify the values are correctly getting into the properties we've defined by printing them out real quick.
63
64     Console.WriteLine(MyPlane.Manufacturer);
65     Console.WriteLine(MyPlane.Make);
66     Console.WriteLine(MyPlane.Model);
67     Console.WriteLine(MyPlane.TailNumber);
68     Console.WriteLine(MyPlane.Owner);
69     Console.WriteLine(MyPlane.ExtColor);
70     Console.WriteLine(MyPlane.IntColor);
71     Console.WriteLine(MyPlane.Year);
72     Console.WriteLine(MyPlane.WingSpan);
73     Console.WriteLine(MyPlane.PassengerCap);
74     Console.WriteLine(MyPlane.WeightCap);
75     Console.WriteLine(MyPlane.TopAirSpeed);
76
77
78
79 } // end of Main section
80 } // end of MainClass section
81
```

Figure 15-32   *AircraftClass instantiating with values*

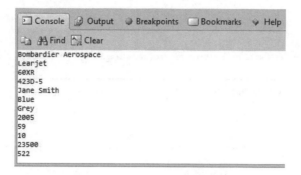

Figure 15-33   *AircraftClass values displaying output*

```
42   IntColor = intcolor;
43   Year = year;
44   WingSpan = wingspan;
45   PassengerCap = passcap;
46   WeightCap = weightcap;
47   TopAirSpeed = topairspeed;
48
49   } //end of our constructor
50
51   String GetValue()
52   {
53
54     String returnValue;
55
56     returnValue += String::Format("The plane belonging to {0} can hold {1} passengers and fly as fast as {2} mph.",
57                         Owner,PassengerCap,TopAirSpeed);
58
59     return returnValue;
60
61   } //end of GetValue
62
63
64 } // end of AircraftClass section
65
```

Figure 15-34   *AircraftClass Get Value() method*

This will format the string nicely for us with all the parameters we've specified and put it into returnValue. Now that we have it there, we need to use it in our Main() section to have the data displayed (Figure 15-35).

Now the ConsoleWriteLine() statement is very concise, and if we had multiple instances, it would be much easier to keep track of which one will display. Finally, after running the script, Figure 15-36 shows the output.

```
66
67 class MainClass {
68   void Main(CaseClass c) {
69
70     SystemClass::ClearConsole();
71
72     AircraftClass MyPlane("Bombardier Aerospace","Learjet","60XR","423D-5","Jane Smith","Blue","Grey",2005,59,10,23500,522);
73
74     Console.WriteLine(MyPlane.GetValue());
75
76   } // end of Main section
77 } // end of MainClass section
78
```

Figure 15-35   *AircraftClass using the return value*

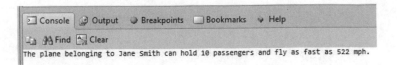

Figure 15-36   *AircraftClass method output*

Summary

This section was intended to give you an introduction to using classes and how they work on a basic level. The material to treat this thoroughly would fill a book on its own, and the resources I discussed at the start of this chapter should give you a place to look for further study. Remember that you can get the code examples from this chapter from the McGraw-Hill Professional Computing download page and from EnCase App Central.

Will you need to be proficient in EnScript to perform investigations with EnCase? No, but in learning the language, you can automate some of the tasks that are performed regularly to ensure they are handled consistently and efficiently each time. The benefit of being able to launch an EnScript to perform a repetitive, tedious, and otherwise time-consuming manual task is that the investigator is now freed up to handle the work that requires human expertise.

Appendixes

Rosetta Stone for Windows Operating Systems

During my time as a Unix system administrator, supporting a large variety of different operating systems, I found a website that was particularly helpful—it was the Rosetta Stone for Unix (http://bhami.com/rosetta.html), and it listed in a table layout how to do common system administrator tasks across some of the various flavors of Unix. I've often wished for something similar for the different versions of Windows. So here is a quick table that shows where common artifacts can be found among the various end-user flavors of Windows.

Artifact	XP Location	Vista Location	Windows 7 Location
User profile	c:\Documents and Settings\<userid>	c:\Users\<userid>	c:\Users\<userid>
User's Ntuser.dat	c:\Documents and Settings\<userid>	c:\Users\<userid>	c:\Users\<userid>
Registry hives (SAM, Security, Software, System)	c:\Windows\system32\config	c:\Windows\system32\config	c:\Windows\system32\config
Link (.LNK) files for a user's profile	c:\Documents and Settings\<userid>\Recent	c:\Documents and Settings\<userid>\Recent	c:\Documents and Settings\<userid>\AppData\Roaming\Microsoft\Windows\Recent
Windows Prefetch	\Windows\Prefetch\B00DFAAD.PF (boot trace); others will have .pf extension	\Windows\Prefetch\B00DFAAD.PF (boot trace); others will have .pf extension	\Windows\Prefetch\B00DFAAD.PF (boot trace); others will have .pf extension
Time Zone	HKEY_LOCAL_MACHINE\System\CurrentControlSet\Control\TimeZoneInformation, HKEY_LOCAL_MACHINE\Software\Microsoft\Windows NT\CurrentVersion\Time Zones	HKEY_LOCAL_MACHINE\System\CurrentControlSet\Control\TimeZoneInformation, HKEY_LOCAL_MACHINE\Software\Microsoft\Windows\Windows NT\CurrentVersion\Time Zones	HKEY_LOCAL_MACHINE\System\CurrentControlSet\Control\TimeZoneInformation, HKEY_LOCAL_MACHINE\Software\Microsoft\Windows\Windows NT\CurrentVersion\Time Zones

EnCase Version 7
Keyboard Shortcuts

This is a brief list of the most commonly used keyboard shortcuts in EnCase version 7 and above. The keyboard shortcuts may change, depending on where in the EnCase interface you are at the time. This is not an exhaustive list, and the shortcuts may change as the software evolves as well.

EnCase Keyboard Shortcuts Quick Reference

Action	Key Combo
Open a file (i.e., an existing case file)	CTRL-O
Print	CTRL-P
Exit	ALT-F4
Case save	CTRL-S
Global save	CTRL-SHIFT-S
**Table Pane	Table View**	
Hide column	CTRL-H
Sort ascending	CTRL-Q
Sort descending	CTRL-SHIFT-Q
Add sort	CTRL-A
Add reverse sort	CTRL-SHIFT-A
Exclude highlighted entry	CTRL-E
Go to leftmost entry	HOME
Go to rightmost entry	END
Delete all selected	CTRL-DELETE
Column Keyboard Shortcuts	
Unicode column	CTRL-SHIFT-U
Case sensitive	CTRL-SHIFT-A
Excluded	CTRL-SHIFT-E

Action	Key Combo
Table Pane | Report View	
Zoom in	+
Zoom out	-
Table Pane | Gallery View	
Select item	SPACE BAR
Go to parent	BACKSPACE
Fewer columns	CTRL -
More columns	CTRL +
Fewer rows	SHIFT -
More rows	SHIFT +
Table Pane | Timeline View	
Higher resolution	+
Table Pane | Disk View	
Go to	CTRL-G
Bookmark data	CTRL-B
Close tab	CTRL-F4
Previous tab	CTRL-SHIFT-TAB
Next tab	CTRL-TAB
Index case	CTRL-I
Launch Case Processor	ALT-P
Send to responder	ALT-R
Help	F1
Refresh	F5

Sample Run Books

s promised, these are the step-by-step Run Books that correspond with the exercises we went through in each chapter. I have indicated the chapter where you can find the descriptive text as a cross-reference. While many of these may be ready for use as-is, you should always look at them first and make sure that they are in line with the practices and procedures of your organization. These are included as templates and should form the basis for your own customizations.

Creating a New Case (Chapter 2)

1. Launch EnCase.
2. Click New Case on the Home screen.
3. Choose case template type.
4. Fill in information on file paths, examiner, etc.
5. Save the case.
6. Copy additional files/folders from your organization's template folder in Windows Explorer.

Relocating Evidence Manually (Chapter 2)

1. Create a hash of the file(s) you need to relocate.
2. Copy the file(s) to their destination.
3. Create a hash of the same file(s) on the destination location.
4. Compare the hash(es) to verify nothing has changed.
5. If the hash(es) do not match, go back to step 1 and repeat until they do.
6. Document what you did, including preserving both hash sets.

Backing Up the Current Case (Chapter 3)

1. With your case open, choose Case Backup from your Case menu, and choose Use Current Case from the options.

2. Click the Create Scheduled button on the menu bar to create an immediate backup of the case file to use the parameters you chose when you created the case, or click the Create Custom if you want to change the parameters.

3. Verify that your new backup is listed in the appropriate section.

Reacquiring .E01/.Ex01 Evidence (Chapter 3)

1. With the evidence file open in the Evidence Browser, Entries view, blue check the device you want to reacquire in the Tree pane.

2. Right-click on the device name in the Tree pane and choose Acquire | Acquire from the context menu.

3. Provide the output path for the new evidence file you are creating on the Location tab.

4. Choose your compression and hash options, and add encryption if desired on the Format tab.

5. Adjust block size, stop/start sectors, error granularity, and reader threads on the Advanced tab as desired.

6. Click OK to reacquire this into the .Ex01 format.

Reacquiring .L01/.Lx01 Evidence (Chapter 3)

1. With the evidence file open in the Evidence Browser, Entries view, blue check the device you want to reacquire in the Tree pane.

2. Right-click on the device name in the Tree pane and choose Acquire | Create Logical Evidence File from the context menu.

3. Provide the output path for the new evidence file you are creating on the Location tab. Also provide a name, evidence number, case number, and other details that can be specified in the Location tab.

4. The Logical tab will have the source already populated from the Evidence Browser. If you want to specify a target folder within the evidence file, you can list it here, and examine the other choices on this tab.

5. On the Format tab, choose Current (Lx01) from the Evidence File Format drop-down. Also choose your hash, compression, file segment size, and encryption options.

6. Click OK to reacquire this evidence file into the .Lx01 format.

Encrypting an Evidence File (See Reacquiring Evidence)

Adding/Acquiring a Local Device (Chapter 4)

1. Follow your organization's practices on write blocking and attaching devices to be imaged/previewed. Once the device has been recognized by the operating system, note the drive letter assigned and the volume name of the device you want to add.

2. From the EnCase Home screen, with your case open, click the Add Evidence link.

3. Choose Add Local Device from the Add Evidence screen.

4. In the Add Local Device dialog, make your selections and click Next to have EnCase scan your system for devices.

5. Blue check the device you want to acquire in the list, and make any changes to the default checked columns.

6. Click Finish and you will be dropped into the Evidence tab with the newly added device as the last item in the list.

7. Click the link for the newly added device. In the Tree pane, blue check the top level of the device and right-click.

8. Choose Acquire from the context menu, and then Acquire or Create Logical Evidence File as appropriate.

9. Fill in the details in the dialog and click OK to acquire the device.

Adding an EnCase Evidence File (Logical or Physical) (Chapter 4)

1. From the EnCase Home screen, click the Add Evidence link.

2. From the Add Evidence screen, click the Add Evidence File link.

3. Browse to where you have stored your EnCase evidence file. Select the top-level file (.E01/.L01/.Ex01/.Lx01) and click Open.

4. The evidence is opened in the Evidence tab.

Adding a Raw Image (Chapter 4)

1. From the EnCase Home screen, click the Add Evidence link.

2. From the Add Evidence screen, click the Add Raw Image link.

3. In the Add Raw Image dialog, specify the image type and other details.

4. In the Component Files window, click the New button (or right-click and choose New from the context menu, or press the INSERT key).

5. Browse to where you stored the image file(s). Select all image files associated with this image and click Open.

6. Verify that you have all of the files showing in the Component Files window and that they are in ascending order.

7. Click OK.

8. The evidence is opened in the Evidence tab.

Acquiring a Smartphone (Chapter 4)

1. Follow your organization's procedure for connecting the smartphone to the forensic workstation, and ensure it has been recognized by the operating system. It will also need to be unlocked.

2. From the EnCase Home screen, click the Add Evidence link.

3. From the Add Evidence screen, click the Acquire Smartphone link.

4. In the Acquire Smartphone dialog, verify that your device has been detected. Select your device.

5. Make any changes to the categories to be acquired.

6. Specify an output path for the logical evidence file that will be created when the smartphone is acquired.

7. Click Finish. You will see a status bar progress as EnCase acquires the smartphone.

8. The evidence is opened in the Evidence tab.

Creating a New Case (Chapter 5)

1. Launch EnCase.

2. Click New Case on the Home screen.

3. Choose case template type.

4. Fill in information on file paths, examiner, etc.

5. Save the case.

6. Copy additional files/folders from template folder in Windows Explorer.

Verifying an Evidence File without Opening a Case (Chapter 5)

1. Choose Verify Evidence Files from the Tools menu.

2. Choose the file you want to verify from the dialog.

3. Click Open. The verification process will launch, and the progress bar will show at the bottom right corner of the interface.

Setting the Time Zone (Chapter 5)

1. With the evidence file open in your case, navigate to the System registry hive under C:\Windows\System32\config.

2. Mount the system hive (see directions for mounting compound files) and view the file once it is mounted.

3. Determine which ControlSet was active when the system was imaged by looking at the value of the HKEY_LOCAL_MACHINE\System\Select key.

4. Navigate into that ControlSet and determine the value of the HKEY_LOCAL_ MACHINE\System\<Active ControlSet>\Control\TimeZoneInformation, paying attention to the bias and whether daylight saving time is in play.

5. Set EnCase's time zone to match by right-clicking on the drive letter of the evidence file and choosing Modify Time Zone Settings from the Device submenu.

6. You can set your time zone in the Time Properties window that displays.

7. Save the case.

Processing and Preparation of Initial Case Evidence (Chapter 5)

1. Add your evidence.

2. Once the automatic evidence verification has completed, compare acquisition and verification hashes and note that you have verified they match.

3. Determine the time zone of the acquired evidence and set EnCase to match.

4. Start Evidence Processor and choose what processes you want to run.

5. Save the case once Evidence Processor completes.

Mounting Files with Internal Structure (Compound Files) Individually (Chapter 6)

1. With the compound file in the Table pane, right-click on the name of the file.

2. Choose Entries from the context menu and then View File Structure from the menu that opens to the right.

3. When EnCase finishes processing that file, it will appear with a green plus sign next to the name, and the name will now be a hyperlink. Click the name to view the file.

Manually Verifying Evidence (Chapter 6)

1. With your case open, choose Evidence from the Browse section of the case Home page. This opens the Evidence Browser.

2. Select your evidence item and click on the Report tab in the View pane.

3. Scroll down to find the acquisition and verification hashes and note that they match.

4. Make a Note bookmark for your report that you verified this by inspection.

Regenerating the Case.sqlite Database (Chapter 8)

1. Close EnCase (if open).

2. Remove the Case.sqlite file from under the EnScript folder in your case directory.

3. Start EnCase.

4. Click on Case Analyzer from the Home screen.

5. Click Case. EnCase will regenerate the contents of the database and you will have a Case.sqlite in your EnScript folder again.

Searching in the Evidence Browser (Chapter 9)

1. In the top level of the Evidence Browser where just your evidence is listed in the Table pane, blue check the evidence you would like to run your search against.

2. Click the Raw Search All button from the top button bar. (This is a drop-down menu; you can choose to rerun an existing search or choose New Raw Search All.)

3. Create your keywords or import a keyword list. Set the options for each keyword.

4. Make your selections for undelete and entry slack, etc.

5. Verify the contents of the Name field.

6. Click OK. Watch the progress bar at the bottom right.

7. Your keyword search results can be viewed by opening the Search tab (choose Search from the View menu) and clicking on the Keyword tab.

Running an Existing Condition (Chapter 10)

1. Choose Run from the Condition drop-down menu in the Evidence Browser.

2. Browse to where the condition is stored, select it, and click OK.

Running an Existing Filter (Chapter 10)

1. Choose the filter you want to run from the Filter menu in the Evidence Browser if it has been run before. If it doesn't appear, choose Run from the Filter menu.

2. Browse to where the filter is stored, select it, and click OK.

3. Select the scope you want to run the filter against.

Creating a Hash Library (Chapter 11)

1. Choose Manage Hash Library from the Tools menu.

2. Choose New Hash Library from the toolbar.

3. Browse to where you want the hash library stored and give it a name.

Creating a New Hash Set Inside the Library (Chapter 11)

1. Choose New Hash Set from the button bar.

2. In the Create Hash Set dialog, give your hash set a name, category, and tags.

3. Click OK.

Adding Results to Your Hash Library from a Case (Chapter 11)

1. In the Table pane (Evidence Browser), select the files you want to add.

2. Right-click and choose Add To Hash Library from the Entries option.

NOTE

Hashes must have already been generated in the Evidence Processor for this to be meaningful.

Importing the NSRL Hash Library (Chapter 11)

1. Download the version from the Guidance Software email that has been converted to EnCase format.

2. Decompress the file once downloaded.

3. Choose Manage Hash Library from the Tools menu. This opens the Hash Library Manager.

4. Open the NSRL library by clicking the Open Hash Library button on the button bar and navigating to the location where you stored it.

5. To make this your secondary hash library path (for easy access), click the Hash Libraries link in the Case section of the Home tab and set the path to where you put the files.

Generating a Report (Chapter 12)

1. From the Home screen in EnCase, click the Reports hyperlink. This opens the Reports tab.

Creating a New Report Template (Chapter 12)

1. From the Reports tab, click on the Go To Template button at the top left. This opens the Report Templates tab.

2. Click the New button on the Table tab to create a new template. You can also press the INSERT key. Either one brings up the New Report Template dialog.

3. Enter a unique descriptive name and indicate if you want this is be a new report template or a section of an existing report.

4. Make any adjustments to the Format section (Paper, Margins, Header, and Footer).

5. Click OK.

Preparing a Case Package for Archiving (Chapter 13)

1. With your case open in EnCase, choose Create Package from the Case menu.

2. Under Purpose For Packaging, choose Archive.

3. Choose the items you want to have packaged by blue checking them.

4. Provide a folder destination for your package.

5. Click Create.

Wiping a Drive with EnCase (Chapter 13)

1. Have the device to be wiped inserted and recognized by the operating system. Take note of the volume name and letter the operating system assigns.

CAUTION

It is recommended that this is the only drive you have attached, for safety.

2. With no case open in EnCase, choose Wipe Drive from the Tools menu.

3. In the Wipe Drive dialog, click Next to have EnCase scan your forensic workstation for attached devices.

4. Blue check the physical device (numeric value in the Name column, not a letter) you want wiped. Click Next.

5. In the Drives dialog, specify if you want the wiped sectors to be verified as wiped, and change the wipe character if you wish. Click Finish.

6. Verify the information in the dialog, and type "Yes" in the text box if you are satisfied with the accuracy.

7. Click OK to begin the wiping process.

8. Update logs for the device per your organization's policies.

Restoring the EnCase Portable USB Device (Chapter 14)

Using EnCase Forensics — Requires Forensic Dongle

1. Save off any license or cert files to a separate device.

2. Insert the EnCase Portable device into the forensic workstation.

3. Launch EnCase Forensic.

4. Create a case (temporary).

5. Add the Portable Evidence file to the case (click the Add Evidence link, then browse to your EnCase installation folder/Portable directory and select the EnCase Portable.E01 file).

6. Click on the link for the evidence file to open it in the Entries tab.

7. Choose Restore from the Device menu drop-down.

8. Click Next to start the device scan.

9. Highlight the EnCase Portable device (WIBU- device, EP_WIN volume label) and click Next.

10. Choose to wipe and verify. Click Finish.

11. Type "Yes" in the dialog that asks if you are sure you want to do this once you have verified the drive selection is correct.

12. Exit EnCase Forensics without saving the case.

Using the DVD — No Forensic Dongle Required

1. Save off any license or cert files to a separate device.

2. Insert the EnCase Portable device into the forensic workstation.

3. Insert the DVD into your forensic workstation. Run Setup.exe if needed.

   Choose Restore Boot Drive from the DVD menu. EnCase Forensic is opened in Acquisition mode with a case already opened and the EnCase Portable evidence file already added.

4. Choose Restore from the Device menu drop-down.

5. Click Next to start the device scan.

6. Highlight the EnCase Portable device (WIBU- device, EP_WIN volume label) and click Next.

7. Choose to wipe and verify. Click Finish.

8. Type "Yes" in the dialog that asks if you are sure you want to do this once you have verified the drive selection is correct.

Using the File Update — No Forensic Dongle Required

1. Save off any license or cert files to a separate device

2. Insert the EnCase Portable device into the forensic workstation.

3. Double-click on the file you downloaded from the Guidance Software email link (ef_restore_portable_<*version*>_<*language*>.exe) to launch. EnCase Forensic is opened in Acquisition mode with a case already opened and the EnCase Portable evidence file already added.

4. Choose Restore from the Device menu drop-down.

5. Click Next to start the device scan.

6. Highlight the EnCase Portable device (WIBU- device, EP_WIN volume label) and click Next.

7. Choose to wipe and verify. Click Finish.

8. Type "Yes" in the dialog that asks if you are sure you want to do this once you have verified the drive selection is correct.

Preparing Additional Storage Devices for Use with EnCase Portable (Chapter 14)

1. Wipe and verify the additional storage device.

2. Create a filesystem on the additional storage device.

3. On the forensic workstation, plug in the new storage device, noting the drive letter assigned.

4. Plug in the EnCase Portable device.

5. Navigate in Windows Explorer to the Utilities folder on the EnCase Portable device.

6. Double-click on Prepare Storage.vbs to launch.

7. Enter the drive letter for the additional storage device in the dialog (not case sensitive) and click OK.

Launching EnCase Portable Management (Chapter 14)

1. Launch EnCase Forensics with the security dongle plugged in.

2. Create a new case (temporary).

3. Choose EnCase Portable Management from the EnScript menu, if it appears (which means you have run it before). If it doesn't appear, choose Run and browse to choose the script. You are dropped into the default location for EnScript storage, and there is a Portable directory there. Navigate into the Portable directory and run Portable Management.EnPack.

Collecting from a Powered-On Computer (Chapter 14)

1. Plug in the EnCase Portable USB device plus any additional storage devices you may need.

2. Note the drive letter assigned as the operating system recognizes the device(s).

3. From the Autoplay dialog, choose "Open folders to view files".

4. Double-click Run Portable.exe to launch EnCase Portable.

5. Choose jobs to run by blue checking them and clicking the Run Job button.

6. Follow any prompts and provide choices as needed.

Collecting from a Powered-Off Computer (Chapter 14)

1. Refer to the Quick Reference Guide for the boot interrupt key sequence for the make/model of the system you are going to collect from.

2. Insert the EnCase Portable device (and CD if needed) and power on the computer. Begin hitting the key sequence immediately until the system drops you into the BIOS.

3. Take note of the BIOS settings before you make any changes. Then change the settings to boot from the USB device, or if that is not supported, the CD drive. Save your changes and exit the BIOS screen. The system will now boot using the device you configured. The EnCase Portable interface will be displayed.

4. Choose jobs to run by blue checking them and clicking the Run Job button.

5. Follow any prompts and provide choices as needed.

Importing Evidence from EnCase Portable into EnCase Forensic (Chapter 14)

1. Launch EnCase Forensics with the security dongle plugged in and recognized.

2. Insert the EnCase Portable device and any additional storage you used in the collection. Note the device letters assigned.

3. Create a case.

4. Launch EnCase Portable Management and click on the Evidence tab.

5. Select the device letter that corresponds to your EnCase Portable device.

6. Select and appropriate Copy Evidence to Path location (this will default to within your case directory).

7. Blue check the evidence you want to import.

8. Specify the copy options.

9. Click the Copy button on the top button bar.

10. Click Finished when the copy is complete.

11. Exit Portable Management. The evidence is now available for use in EnCase Forensic.

EnScript Class Hierarchy

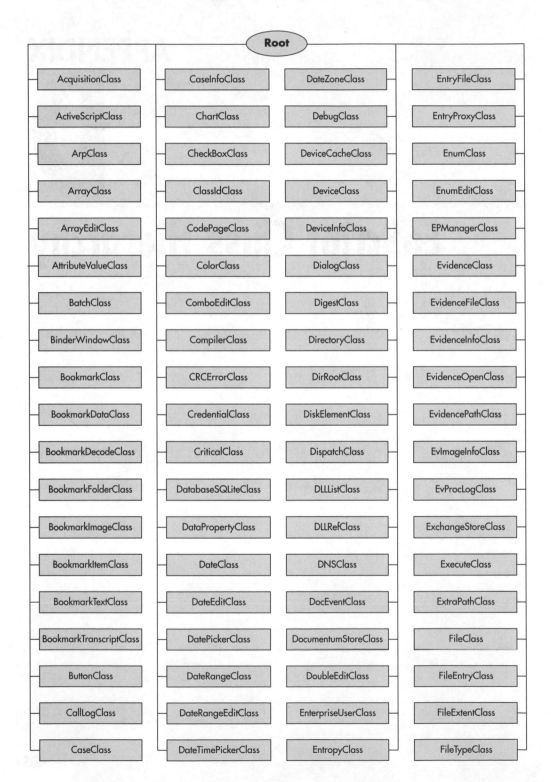

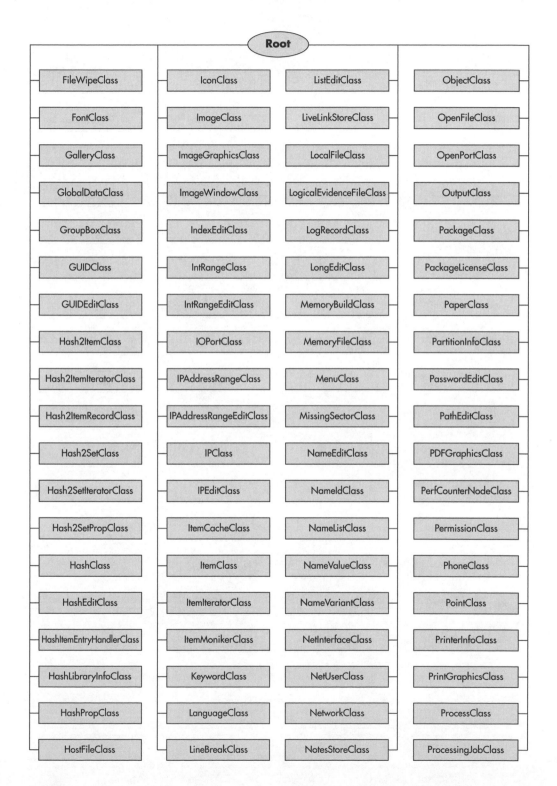

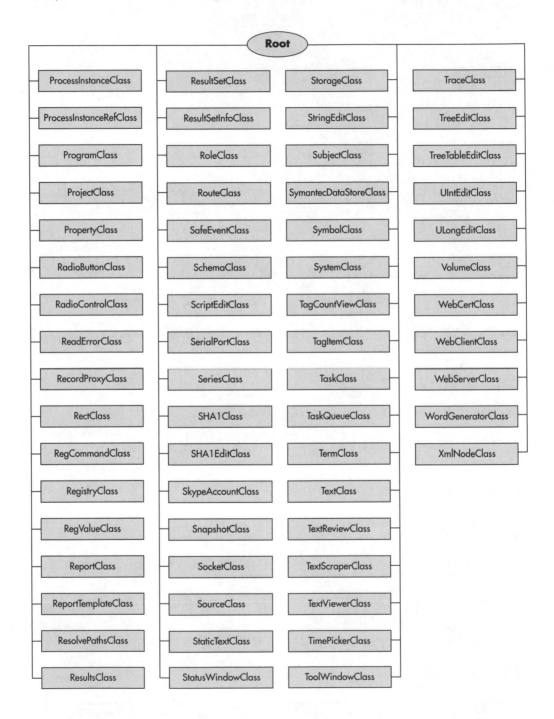

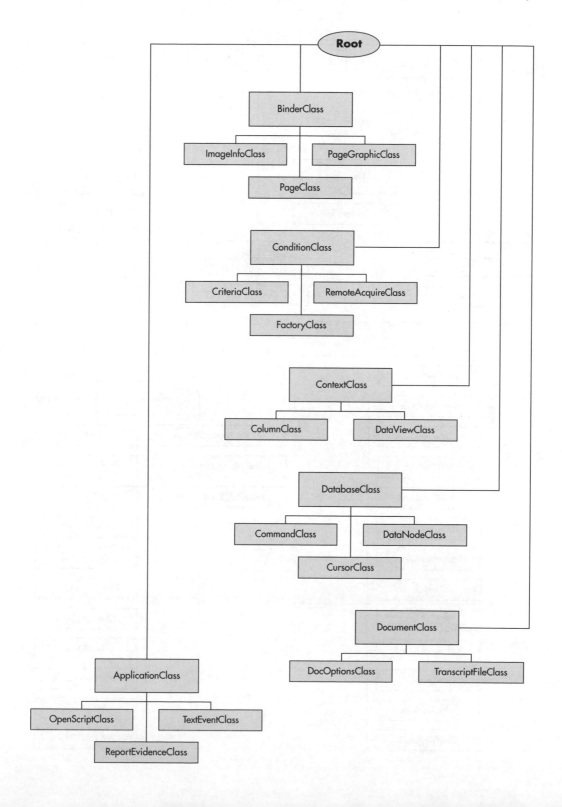

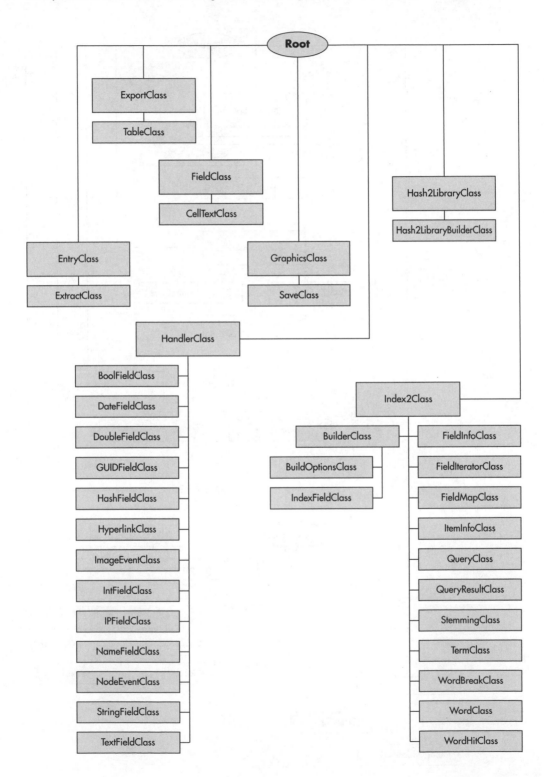

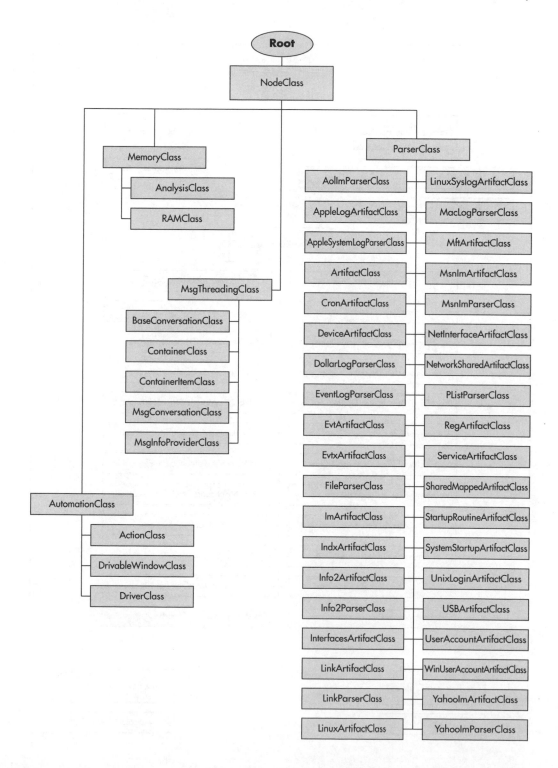

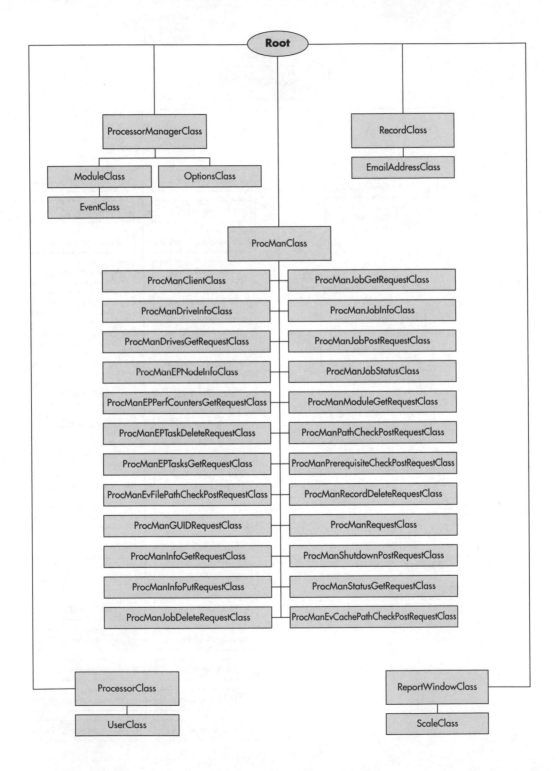

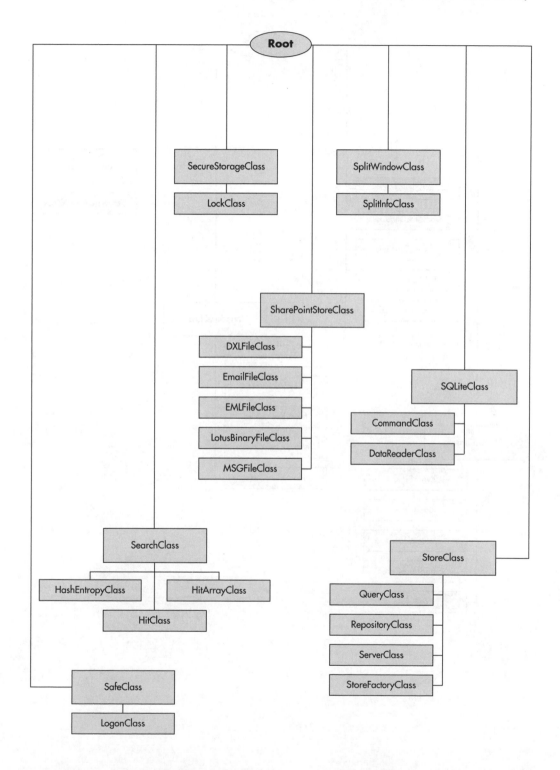

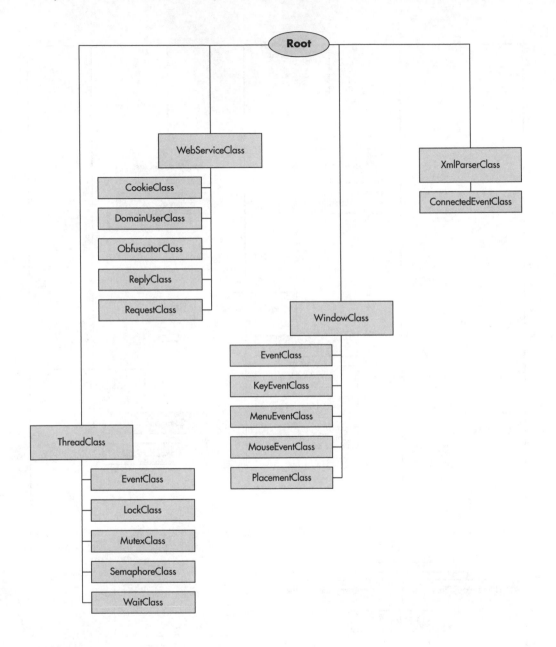

Index